AN AUDIT APPROACH TO COMPUTERS

A New Practice Manual

AN AUDIT APPROACH TO COMPUTERS

A New Practice Manual

BRIAN JENKINS MA FCA
&
ANTHONY PINKNEY FCA

(Coopers & Lybrand)

The Institute of Chartered Accountants
in England and Wales,
Chartered Accountants' Hall,
Moorgate Place,
London, EC2P 2BJ.
1983

The views expressed in this publication are the authors' own and are not necessarily those of the Council of The Institute.

No responsibility for loss occasioned to any person acting or refraining from action as a result of any material in this publication can be accepted by the authors or publisher.

This book is set in V.I.P. Times Roman 10 pt. on 12
Printed in Great Britain by
Redwood Burn Ltd, Trowbridge, Wiltshire
Designed by Malcolm Young MSIA MSTD

The authors wish to thank the many people who have assisted them in writing and illustrating this book. In this connection they are grateful to many of the partners and staff of their firm, in particular Mr. Greville C. B. Gidley-Kitchin, FCA, Mr. David Clark, ACA, Mr. Michael Fleming, MBCS, and the staff of their London drawing office. In addition they wish to thank their colleagues overseas, in particular, Mr. Donald A. Brown, CA (Canada), Mr. Jan C. van Dijk, RA (The Netherlands), Mr. Stanley D. Halper, CPA (USA), Mr. Kenneth P. Johnson, CPA (USA) and Mr. Robert S. Lynn, FCA (Australia).

Preface

Scope and Relevance of the Book

The principal purpose of this book, which is intended to take the place of a book with the same title published in 1966, is to describe a practical approach to the expression of an audit opinion on the financial statements of companies where the processing and storage of accounting data is by computer. This approach is summarised in Chapter 1 and dealt with in greater detail, together with the related audit techniques and documentation, in Chapters 2 to 10. The book will thus be of particular relevance to the **practising accountant** involved in audits of this nature.

The approach suggested in this book has also formed a suitable practical basis of work for an **internal audit department**. The methods and documentation outlined here can be amended to suit their particular objectives. These objectives often include computer security and efficiency reviews. Accordingly Chapter 12 deals with computer security and, in the discussions of computer systems and controls in Chapters 2, 4, 5 and 6, the desirable features for increasing the efficiency of computer processing have been mentioned, where appropriate.

As practising accountants become increasingly involved with clients using computers, the organisation and training of their staff to carry out computer audit work becomes more important. Some practical suggestions on this subject are contained in Chapter 13. These suggestions have also proved helpful to internal audit departments.

Computer processing, when carried out at a service bureau rather than an in-house computer, also has an effect on internal control requirements and thus on audit procedures. This effect is considered in Chapter 11. A suggested method by which a user might select a bureau, and the considerations in working with a bureau, are also contained in Chapter 11, since the auditor is often asked to comment on these matters. The procedures to be followed by a user in selecting and installing an in-house computer are more detailed and complex and fall outside the scope of this book.

It is hoped that this book will also be of interest to **management**. Management has the responsibility of establishing satisfactory controls for computer systems. This is not always easy when computers are first used for accounting applications and it is hoped that the information regarding computer systems and controls outlined in Chapters 2, 4, 5 and 6, which are based on wide practical experience, will be of assistance.

Finally, it is hoped that the contents of this book will be of assistance both to **tutors** concerned with the teaching of either computer or audit personnel and to **students**. There will be an increasing demand for those competent in the methods and techniques mentioned in this book, much of which has formed the basis of the computer audit courses run by The Institute of Chartered Accountants in England and Wales.

Terminology Used

Definitions

Where it is considered helpful, definitions of the words and phrases used have been given. The definition is normally provided on the first occasion when the word or phrase is used and reference can be made thereto from the index.

Computer user

The computer user is referred to throughout as either the **company** or the **client.** The reader is asked to substitute an alternative term if more appropriate.

The auditor

Throughout the discussion of the audit approach in Chapters 2 to 10 the general term **auditor** is used and no attempt is made to indicate what type (general auditor or computer audit specialist) or level (senior, manager or partner) of auditor is involved at each stage. However, practical suggestions regarding the type and level of staff that would be suitable for the various aspects of the work are made in Chapter 13.

Brian Jenkins

Anthony Pinkney

Contents

Chapter 2, Appendix A. Examples of Computer Systems

Chapter 3. Evaluation of Internal Control: The Audit Approach

Chapter 3, Appendix A. Control Objectives

Chapter 4. Evaluation of Controls:
User Controls and Programmed Procedures

Chapter 5. Evaluation of Controls: Integrity Controls (1)

Chapter 6. Evaluation of Controls: Integrity Controls (2)

Chapter 7. Functional Tests

Chapter 9. Validation Procedures

Chapter 9, Appendix A. Example of a Programme of Validation Procedures

Chapter 9, Appendix B. Examples of the Use of Computer Audit Programs

Example I – Accounts receivable ledger
Example II – Inventories ledger

Chapter 10. The Use of Computer Programs   *Paragraphs*

Chapter 10, Appendix A. Examples of the Use of Questionnaires

Chapter 10, Appendix B. Examples of the Use of Coding Sheets

Chapter 10, Appendix C. Example of a Print-out

Chapter 11. Service Bureaux

Chapter 12. Computer Security

Chapter 13. Organisation and Training   *Paragraphs*

List of Figures

1

An Audit Approach
to Computers

Introduction

1.01   This book is based on the principles and documentation of an audit
        approach which has been developed for application to accounting sys-
        tems whatever the method adopted for the processing of data. In this
        chapter this audit approach is summarised and the main features of
        applying it to computer systems outlined.

The Audit Approach

1.02   The audit approach is designed to enable the auditor to achieve in the
        most efficient manner the principal objective of the audit, which is to
        ascertain whether, in his opinion, the financial statements on which he is
        reporting show a true and fair view of the state of affairs at a given date
        and of the results for the period ended on that date.

Principal features

1.03   Before outlining the steps in the overall audit approach it may be helpful
        to mention certain of its principal features. First, each task undertaken by
        the auditor is a necessary part of the total work leading up to his report on
        the financial statements. Thus the audit procedures and documentation
        are designed to enable the auditor to concentrate his effort in identifying
        those items and activities which are likely to affect the overall truth and
        fairness of the financial statements. He would then pay less attention to
        other matters which are not relevant for this purpose or are immaterial.
        Items would not be relevant if they related solely to efficiency of proces-
        sing and would be immaterial if an error of such size as to distort the truth
        and fairness of the financial statements could not arise. The auditor may
        choose to concern himself with these matters, but they are not essential to
        arriving at his audit opinion.

1.04   The second principal feature is that all stages in the audit are related to
        each other. In this way the results of each step can be assessed and the
        various strengths and weaknesses disclosed can be taken into account in
        planning and executing the next stage. The most important example of
        this is in the relationship between the audit work on evaluation of controls
        and the validation (or verification) of items in the financial statements.
        The third principal feature, which is related to the second, is the oppor-

1

tunity that is provided to adopt alternative audit procedures so as to enable the most efficient audit to be carried out in the particular circumstances. The most obvious example is the option of placing reliance for audit purposes on the system of internal control and carrying out audit work thereon, or deciding it is more efficient to place no reliance on the controls and to proceed instead, as regards, in particular, the validity and accuracy of data, to extended audit work on the financial statements themselves.

1.05 The fourth major feature is that the approach is designed so that managers and partners are involved at each important stage of the audit. While it has always been the practice for managers and partners to review the work done, they have in the past often been insufficiently involved at the planning stage. As a result, required work may not have been carried out and time may have been spent on unnecessary procedures. Using the approach suggested in this book, managers and partners are required to decide on, for example, the audit approach to be adopted, the levels of test to be carried out and the audit response where weaknesses are found. The role of the manager and partner is further considered in Chapter 13.

1.06 The last important feature is that the approach and documentation were developed internationally. As a result, a few of the phrases and definitions may seem strange to the English reader. No attempt has been made to adapt these phrases and definitions as it is not thought that they will lead to difficulty. Indeed, it is considered noteworthy that the approach and documentation outlined in this book are in daily use on a world-wide basis. However, in so far as they depend on statutory requirements, the detailed practices described in this book are based on UK law and may need amendments to suit the requirements of countries where the statutory obligations of the auditor are different.

1.07 The steps in carrying out the work are divided as follows:

- Understanding and recording the system.
- Evaluation of internal control.
- Functional tests.
- Audit response to internal control weaknesses.
- Validation procedures.

In the following paragraphs each step is briefly described, together with a reference to the main features of its adoption in the audit of computer systems. The steps are illustrated in chart form in Figure 1.

Understanding and recording the system

General approach

1.08 In order to decide on his audit approach, the auditor will first need to understand and record the procedures and controls comprising a company's accounting system. The auditor normally obtains his understanding by reading systems descriptions and by discussions with company staff. He usually records his understanding of the system by use of flowcharts or, in those cases where their preparation may be more efficient, by narrative notes.

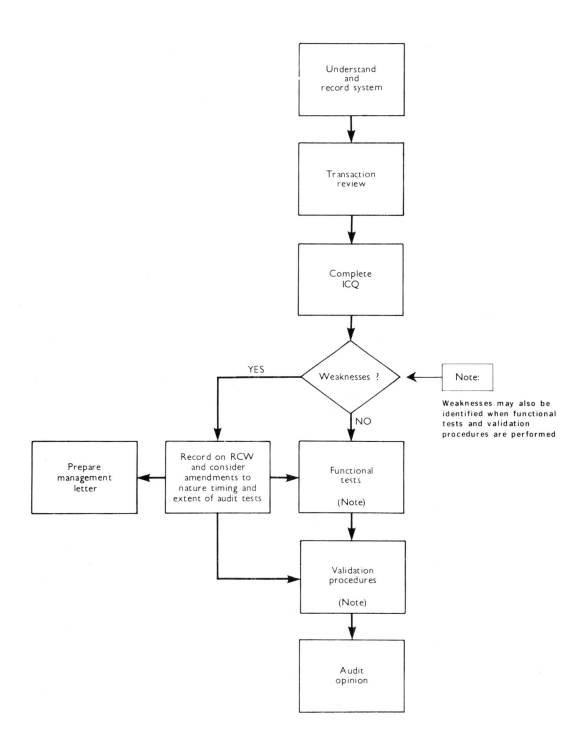

FIG. 1. Steps in the audit approach (1.07)

3

1.09   After the flowcharts or narrative notes have been prepared, or updated, and before doing any other audit work, it is common for the auditor to trace one or more transactions through each part of the system. This process is referred to as a **transaction review** in this book. Its purpose is to enhance subsequent audit efficiency by ensuring, so far as is possible, that the auditor's understanding of the system is correct and that it has been accurately recorded. It also assists staff to familiarise themselves with the system in subsequent years.

Computer systems

1.10   There are particular features in understanding computer systems because of the distinctive nature of computer processing. These features are discussed in the first part of Chapter 2 and examples of typical computer systems are described in the appendix to that chapter. Particular points in recording computer systems and carrying out transaction reviews are dealt with in the second part of Chapter 2.

Evaluation of internal control

General approach

1.11   The auditor is concerned with a company's system of internal control because he will normally wish, where possible, to place reliance thereon in order to limit, and phase the timing of, his subsequent audit work on the financial statements. A further important purpose is to report to management weaknesses that come to his notice, so as to assist management in carrying out its obligations to establish and maintain controls that will ensure, as far as possible, the reliability of the company's accounting records and the safeguarding of its assets.

1.12   In assessing the degree of reliance that he can place on the internal controls, the auditor will need to distinguish between what are referred to in this book as "basic controls" and "disciplines over basic controls". **Basic controls** are those controls designed to ensure that valid transactions, and only valid transactions, are processed and recorded completely and accurately. **Disciplines over basic controls** are those features of the system which are designed to ensure that the basic controls continue to operate properly and that the assets are safeguarded. They comprise segregation of duties, supervision of the results of one person's work by another, separation of the custody of assets from the accounting responsibility for them and physical arrangements that prevent unauthorised access to assets or accounting records. Disciplines over basic controls are referred to hereafter for convenience as **disciplines.**

1.13   The importance of the distinction between basic controls and disciplines lies in the extent to which the auditor uses them as a means of gaining the audit satisfaction that is necessary to place reliance on the continued and proper operation of the basic controls. Where the disciplines are limited or non-existent, which is often the case in companies where there is a limited number of staff in the accounting function, there is little or no assurance that the basic controls will continue to operate properly and the auditor must accordingly extend his work.

Computer systems

1.14 The nature of basic controls and disciplines in computer systems is considered in Chapter 3. In addition to the manual controls carried out on the data being processed, referred to herein as **user controls**, the auditor will be concerned with the other types of procedures and controls which are unique to computer systems, termed **programmed procedures** and **integrity controls**. Programmed procedures include steps in the computer programs that may assist in the control of the data being processed, while integrity controls are the controls, mainly in the computer department, over, inter alia, the implementation, security and use of programs and security of files.

1.15 The method of evaluating internal controls in a computer system is considered in Chapter 3 and a suitable **internal control questionnaire** ("ICQ") is described. The **ICQ** is referred to as "integrated" which means it can be used to evaluate controls in both computer and non-computer systems. Extracts of those parts of the ICQ which are needed to evaluate computer systems are contained in the appendix to Chapter 3 for illustration purposes.

1.16 A more detailed consideration of the control requirements and techniques in computer systems, and how they can be evaluated using the ICQ, is contained in Chapter 4, as regards user controls and programmed procedures, and in Chapters 5 and 6, as regards integrity controls.

Functional tests

General approach

1.17 The auditor must carry out suitable tests to provide evidence that the controls on which he wishes to place reliance have continued to operate properly throughout the period under review. These tests, which are also called compliance tests or procedural tests, are referred to as **functional tests** in this book.

1.18 In general the auditor will wish to carry out functional tests on all those controls which he identified and expected to rely on when he was completing the ICQ. However he may decide that, rather than rely on the controls and carry out functional tests, it would be more efficient to extend his validation tests of the related items in the financial statements.

1.19 The auditor will normally carry out his functional tests on the disciplines before those on the basic controls. This is because, unless the disciplines have operated satisfactorily, the auditor is unlikely to be able to place reliance on the basic controls. The approach he adopts to the basic controls is thus largely dependent on the results of his tests on the disciplines.

1.20 Functional testing will for the most part comprise what are termed in this book "examination of evidence" and "reperformance". **Examination of evidence** consists of the inspection of records, documents, reconciliation reports and the like for evidence that a specific control appears to have been properly carried out. An example is the inspection of signatures or initials on a supplier's invoice evidencing that the invoice has been matched with a goods received note. **Reperformance** consists of the repeating, either in whole or in part, of the same work processes as those performed by the company's employees, for example the actual matching by the auditor of a supplier's invoice with the corresponding goods received note, in order to obtain assurance that the signature or initials seen on the supplier's invoice really do mean that the matching process has been carried out. There are some controls that cannot be tested by examination or reperformance, for example the counting and examination of incoming goods or the physical security of stores. In these circumstances the control procedure may need to be tested by **observation** and **enquiry,** for example at the relevant location, in order to ascertain whether a specific control appears to be operating. When testing by observation, the auditor should bear in mind the possibility that the observed control may not operate when he is not present.

Computer systems

1.21 The techniques for functional testing in computer systems are considered in Chapter 7 and specimen tests for use when testing the more common controls and procedures are contained in appendix A to that chapter.

1.22 A feature in computer systems is the frequent inability to carry out conventional audit tests because visible evidence is not available as a routine. The alternative techniques include audit test data, program code analysis and the use of software. These techniques, which are unique to computer systems, are described in Chapter 7 and appendices B and C (audit test data) and appendix D (program code analysis).

1.23 There are particular factors to be taken into account in deciding on the levels of functional test to be adopted in computer systems and these are discussed in Chapter 7.

1.24 Before commencing functional tests the auditor should bear in mind that audit efficiency can sometimes be improved by choosing instead one of two other approaches which are practicable in computer systems. The first alternative is for the auditor to use computer programs to examine large volumes of processed data, thus adopting extended validation procedures to supplement any reliance he places on the controls. The other possibility is to increase the work he carries out on the programmed procedures, thus reducing his reliance on the integrity controls.

The audit response to control weaknesses

General approach

1.25 Where the auditor wishes to place reliance on the system of internal control, he will need to identify all weaknesses and consider the effect which they may have on his subsequent audit procedures. Weaknesses may arise from the absence of a required control or the failure to exercise a control.

1.26 It is an important feature of the audit approach outlined in this book that, as regards each weakness, the auditor must decide, taking all the relevant factors into account, whether the weakness could lead to a material error or irregularity appearing in the financial statements.

1.27 If, in his opinion, material error could not arise, the auditor will not normally make any change to the audit procedures to take account of the weakness. This is because he is not required to take account of the possibility that an immaterial error exists in the financial statements on which he is reporting.

1.28 If the auditor decides that, arising from the effects of a weakness, material error could occur, he must take the necessary steps to satisfy himself whether or not error has arisen and, if it has, he must determine its extent. In order to obtain this satisfaction, he will need to alter or add to the audit procedures which he would otherwise carry out. In those exceptional cases where the effect of a control weakness cannot be ascertained by changes in audit procedures, the auditor will need to consider whether it may be necessary to qualify his audit report.

Computer systems

1.29 The factors to be taken into account in deciding whether material error could arise, and the resulting effect on audit procedures where it is decided that material error could arise, are considered in Chapter 8, with particular reference to computer systems. A suitable document to use in this work, called a **record of control weaknesses** (''RCW''), is described.

1.30 The reporting of weaknesses to clients, examples of common weaknesses and breakdowns in computer systems and computer fraud are also considered in Chapter 8.

Validation procedures

General approach

1.31 **Validation procedures,** which are also called verification procedures or substantive tests, represent the final stage of the audit leading to the expression of an audit opinion. They have as their main objective the substantiation of account balances and other information contained in the financial statements. In addition, validation procedures complement functional tests since they provide further evidence as to whether the internal controls have continued to operate.

1.32 Normally, the most important factors governing the nature, timing and extent of validation procedures are the materiality of the account balances and the degree of reliance that can be placed on the company's internal controls. By timing is meant the extent of the opportunity to carry out some or all of the work at a time other than after the year end, if this is of assistance to the client or the auditor. Where the internal controls are satisfactory, the validation procedures can be limited and carried out, to an appropriate extent, before the year end. If the controls are unsatisfactory, the validation procedures must be extended and the opportunity for carrying out much of the work before the year end decreases. As has already been seen, the auditor may also prefer to extend his validation procedures rather than to place reliance on the controls.

1.33 Where the auditor performs what are termed in this book **extended validation procedures**, his procedures will be modified in either or both of the following ways:

(a) He may alter the procedures, and either go to a greater depth in the procedures already contemplated by, for example, seeking more complete documentary evidence in support of payments made. Alternatively he may perform additional procedures not otherwise contemplated by, for example, confirming accounts payable with suppliers in cases where this would not otherwise be done.

(b) He may perform more tests of the nature already contemplated by, for example, verifying a greater proportion of the items making up an account balance or, in verifying completeness of recording, by checking a greater number of items or for a longer period of time.

Computer systems

1.34 Where records supporting balance sheet and income and expenditure accounts are maintained by computer, the objectives of the validation procedures and the relationship between the system of internal control and the validation procedures remain the same. However, because of, first, the opportunity to make use of computer programs to examine the data held on computer files and, secondly, the distinctive control features in computer systems, there are often changes in the validation procedures. In Chapter 9 general matters relating to the nature, timing and extent of validation procedures are discussed, together with the impact that computers may have on them.

1.35 The audit use of computer programs represents the principal change and advance in technique in the audit of computer systems. The two most significant features in using computer programs are that, first, all relevant items are normally examined, whereas when manual tests are used only a sample is normally examined, and, secondly, additional information of assistance to the auditor can often be produced. The combination of these two factors usually enables the auditor to carry out more effective or more efficient extended validation procedures than are practicable by manual means.

1.36 Examples of the wide uses of computer programs for validation purposes and the procedures for incorporating them into the other validation procedures are outlined in Chapter 9. Two illustrations of the use of computer programs to assist in the validation of accounts receivable and inventories are included in appendix B to that chapter.

1.37 Increasing use has been made by auditors of general purpose computer programs which can carry out similar tasks on a variety of files and installations. Programs of this type are termed **computer audit packages** in this book. It is not intended to review and analyse the various computer audit packages. However, in Chapter 10 the more important facilities, based on practical experience, that should be available in a computer audit package are indicated.

1.38 It is advisable to establish formal procedures to control the use of computer programs. This will help ensure that programs are only used in cases where the cost can be justified, that the contemplated objectives are appropriate, and that the costs are controlled. Examples of suitable procedures are outlined in Chapter 10.

Summary

1.39 The audit approach in a computer system is similar to that in a non-computer system. The auditor should understand and record the accounting system, evaluate the system of internal control and carry out functional tests to satisfy himself that the controls are working in practice. In so doing, the auditor will have to evaluate and test new forms of control and he will need to use new techniques.

1.40 The auditor's object in placing reliance on the system of internal control is to limit, and phase the timing of his subsequent audit work on the financial statements. He must thus carefully assess the effect of all control weaknesses on the nature, timing and extent of his procedures. The use by the auditor of computer programs to assist in validation procedures represents a major advance in audit techniques. The auditor may find that a computer program to examine data can, in certain circumstances, be more efficient than relying on the system of internal control.

2

Understanding and Recording the System

General Approach

2.01 In order to decide on his audit approach, the auditor will first need to **understand** and **record** the procedures and controls comprising a company's accounting system. The auditor normally obtains his understanding by reading systems descriptions and by discussions with company staff. He usually records his understanding of the system by use of **flowcharts** or, in those cases where their preparation may be more efficient, narrative notes.

2.02 After the flowcharts or narrative notes have been prepared, or updated, and before doing any other audit work, it is common for the auditor to trace one or more transactions of each type through the system to confirm that the system has been properly understood and recorded. This process is termed a **transaction review** in this book. Its purpose is to enhance subsequent audit efficiency by ensuring so far as possible that the auditor's understanding of the system is correct and that it has been accurately recorded.

2.03 There are particular features in understanding computer systems because of the distinctive nature of computer processing. These features are discussed in the first part of this chapter and examples of typical computer systems are described in the appendix to this chapter. Particular points in recording computer systems and carrying out transaction reviews are dealt with in the second part of the chapter.

Understanding Computer Systems

Technical computer knowledge required

2.04 In order to understand and record computer systems effectively, the auditor must have a basic understanding of the principles of computers and computer processing and it is assumed that the reader of this book will have such an understanding. This would include a knowledge of the basic units of a computer configuration, their inter-relationship, the nature of computer processing from input to output, the concepts of programming and the functions of the operating system. If the reader does not have this basic knowledge, it is readily available from existing literature and courses. Any further detailed knowledge required will vary from system to system and depend primarily on the complexity of computer processing in any particular system and the resulting impact on the controls.

Computer processing features of audit relevance

2.05 It is not a purpose of this book to describe in detail the methods of computer processing. However, it may be helpful to outline those features that are of primary concern to the auditor in obtaining an understanding of computer systems and to define certain terms that will be used in subsequent chapters. It is convenient to consider these features under the headings:

- **Input** – the initial recording of a transaction and subsequent activity until it is written to a magnetic file in the computer.
- **Processing** – all the work carried on within the computer.
- **Output** – the provision of information by the computer normally to a file or in the form of a print-out.

2.06 In dealing with input, processing and output some common features relating to all types of system are first described, by reference to batch systems. The characteristics of batch systems are illustrated in Figure 2. Next particular features relating to input and output in on-line systems and processing in real-time systems are described. A description of the particular features of systems where data is organised as a database is then given. Finally, mention is made of the principal features of systems using distributed processing.

Input

2.07 The work of input can be divided into three stages – recording transactions, converting the data into input media and writing the input to a magnetic file. In most cases, the methods of recording transactions are the same as in non-computer systems and are not considered here. On occasions, the computer may be programmed to initiate data. This happens, for example, where the computer is programmed to produce purchase orders when the balance of stock on hand falls below a minimum level. This type of activity is more conveniently considered under processing.

2.08 There are a number of methods of converting data into input media. Those which are in general use include the traditional punched cards and paper tape, and devices for recording data directly onto magnetic tape or disc. The latter are often arranged as a number of operator key stations using teletype terminals linked to a small computer, which can be programmed to check the data comprehensively before submission to the main computer. This can be of great advantage in detecting errors and identifying queries at an early stage.

2.09 The methods described above involve the conversion of data into machine readable form prior to entry into the computer. Other methods

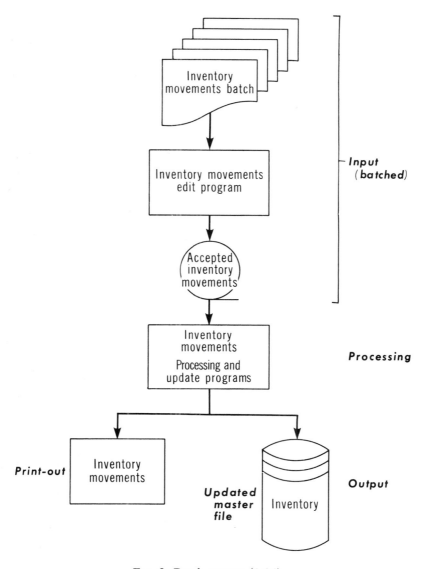

FIG. 2. Batch system (2.06)

in which the computer reads in data in a form similar to a conventional alphabet without the need for prior conversion include magnetic ink character recognition (MICR) and optical character recognition (OCR). In these cases the data is encoded, usually mechanically, onto the source document using a special type fount and is fed into the computer through a special reader using magnetic or optical reading techniques. Optical mark recognition (OMR) is a simpler form of OCR enabling hand written marks to be used. The recognition of hand written characters is not yet in widespread use. A variety of other data entry devices exist, many of them special purpose, to enable the computer input data to be captured as a by-product of the transaction being recorded. Examples of these devices are outlined below under "On-line input and output".

13

2.10 The input data may be read into the main computer locally or transmitted through a private network or the public switched telecommunications network to a central computer. At the central location, the data may be accumulated "off-line" on a separate terminal device, or read directly into the main computer ("on-line"), depending on the circumstances.

Processing

2.11 Processing may be defined as all the work carried on in the computer. Although by no means exhaustive, the following is a useful summary of the processing work that will normally be of significance to the auditor:

- Editing.
- Calculating, summarising and categorising.
- Initiating transactions.
- Updating master or pipeline files.

These functions are described in the following paragraphs.

Editing

2.12 **Editing** is the programmed checking of data normally carried out during the first computer run when the input is written to a magnetic file. It usually consists of a mixture of validity and reasonableness checks. It can also include the matching of input with data already held on files.

Calculating, summarising and categorising

2.13 **Calculating** is defined as matching two sets of data and generating a third set, for example multiplying hours by rate to produce pay, or multiplying quantity shipped by a sales price to produce the sales value. The process typically consists of matching standing data, for example the price, which is held permanently on a master file, with transaction data, for example quantity, which is input and processed once only. **Summarising** means the accumulating of all transactions, often after calculating as explained above, and the generating of a total, for example total value of sales for the day. **Categorising** consists of analysing a summarised total, for example sales analysed by area. Categorising is normally carried out by reference to a code included in the data input for each transaction.

Initiating transactions

2.14 The computer can be programmed to **initiate** transactions in two ways:

(a) The processing of a transaction may create the condition. For example, the processing of a stock issue reduces stock below minimum level and a purchase order is produced. In these cases the condition is normally recognised by a comparison with standing data, for example the minimum stock level. This form of generation of data is likely to be particularly common where the files are organised as a database.

(b) A signal to initiate transactions may be input. For example, the input of a date will lead to the production of cheques for all suppliers' invoices dated prior to a certain date; the input of a stage of production reached will generate the appropriate charges to work in progress; the input of a requisition code will generate a listing of the components to be issued.

Updating master or pipeline files

2.15 **Master files** are similar to ledgers in a non-computer system and may be defined as those files holding financial and reference data of importance to more than one processing run, for example accounts receivable and inventory ledgers, and price files. **Pipeline files** are temporary files similar to suspense accounts in a non-computer system and normally only hold transaction data, for example outstanding orders or records of goods received. **Updating** may be defined as the process of writing transactions to or from master or pipeline files, for example, in the case of accounts receivable, writing invoices and cash receipts to the file or deleting dormant customer accounts from the file. The method of updating depends on the file organisation in use. Tape files are updated by reading sequentially the old master file and the current transaction file and writing a new master file. Discs may also be processed in this manner but it is an advantage of disc processing that it can access directly and alter the records that require to be changed by current transactions, rather than having to read and rewrite the whole file. Direct access is used to update files organised as databases, which introduce distinctive features in relation to updating, as described in paragraphs 2.24 to 2.32.

Output

2.16 **Output** is defined to include both the updated master files and any related printed reports in the form of listings, analyses, exception reports or accounting documents, for example invoices. Information for third parties is sometimes transferred directly on magnetic file, for example credit transfer details from the bank to its customer and sales statistics from branches to head office for consolidation. Output may also take the form of punched cards or paper tape or be converted to microfiche or film.

On-line input and output

2.17   An **on-line** system involves one or more input devices which can continuously and immediately access the computer in order to input data or ask for information held on master files to be displayed or printed, commonly called an enquiry facility. An outline flowchart of an on-line system is shown in Figure 3, and may be contrasted with that of a batch system in Figure 2.

2.18   The main impact of on-line systems is on input and output; processing normally remains the same as in batch systems. The most important change relates to output, as the enquiry facility brings the master files into immediate contact with users.

2.19   There are, in addition, two significant changes relating to input:

    (a) Input is normally by individual transaction rather than by batch and often a variety of transactions can follow one another. Transactions are "batched" on magnetic file at the computer.

    (b) The opportunity for continuous and random access to the computer from a number of terminals introduces the need for complex software to organise the input and enquiry activity.

2.20   Developments in direct reading techniques include the use of light pens and point of sale devices. Light pens are sensory devices used to read and transmit information. They may be used to read information on coded labels or to mark and thus input items displayed on a VDU screen. They are useful, for example, for the input of cash receipts which match with invoices held in the system and displayed on the screen, or for recording stock by passing the pen over the coded labels attached to each item in a store.

2.21   Point of sale devices are terminals which are used in retail organisations to input accounting data at the time that a transaction is concluded. It is possible to record all the information relevant to the sale, for example stock number, quantity, selling price and date of sale. Data may be recorded by keying a cash register terminal or by a direct reading device such as a light pen which is used to read magnetically encoded stock labels. Data captured may be used to update stock and accounts receivable records, produce stock and sales information and initiate stock re-ordering processes. It is common for the data captured to be written to magnetic cassettes or discs "off-line" prior to final processing.

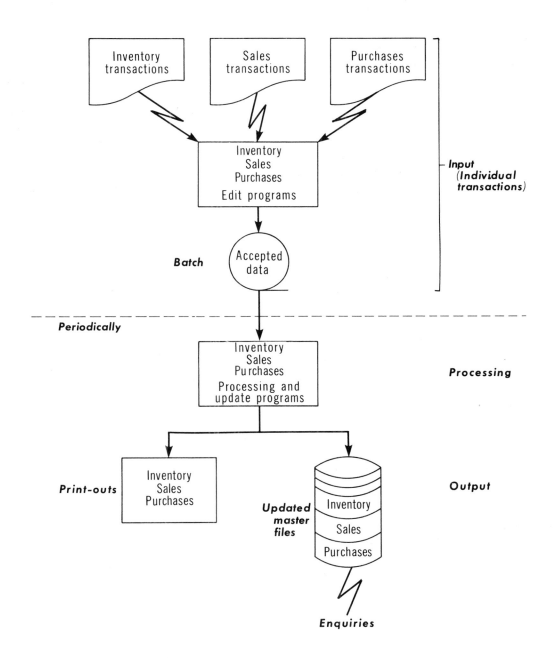

FIG. 3. On-line system (2.17)

Real-time processing

2.22 **Real-time** processing is defined as the processing and output of transactions as and when they are input.

2.23 An outline flowchart of a real-time system is shown at Figure 4, and may
be contrasted with those of a batch system (Figure 2) and an on-line
system (Figure 3). The main impact of real-time systems is on processing
and the operations of input and processing become less distinct. Unlike
batch and on-line systems, processing must be carried out for the individual transactions. In other than real-time systems the relevant processing programs are initiated by the operator and the complete batch is
input and processed. In real-time systems all relevant programs must be
available at all times and the transaction must be capable of calling in the
processing programs. This is done by coding on the transactions. It is for
this reason that real-time systems can be spoken of as "transaction
driven" rather than "program driven".

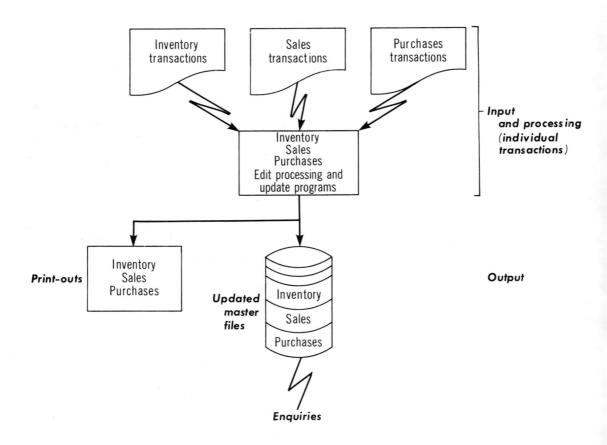

FIG. 4. Real-time system (2.23)

2.24 **Database** is a form of data organisation which attempts to store data in a manner suitable for use for more than one application. Data which would in a conventional system be held on several logical files is commonly stored within a single database. In addition, a database provides for the recording of logical relationships between individual data items. The main advantages of a database are that repetitive recording of the same data for different applications is reduced and the ability to relate data from different applications is improved. For example, a database might record, inter alia, details of customers, orders and shipments and indicate the items relating to each other by means of indices or pointers. Databases may be used in conjunction with real-time or on-line or batch processing.

2.25 Database systems affect the manner in which data is read from the database (for processing or output) and updated to the database. The procedures for reading and updating a database differ from those used in non-database systems because of the different method of data organisation in database systems and the different method that application programs use in database systems to obtain the data required for processing.

2.26 In non-database systems specific files are related to specific application programs. Each file will have a unique layout and each application program will contain a description of the records on the file or files that the program processes. In COBOL programming this is called the File Description (FD).

2.27 In database systems, the descriptions of the data on the database are held independently of the application programs, on the database library. Two types of data description are required. First, it is necessary to describe the physical nature of all the data on the database, including its location, nature, and the relationships between the various data elements. Secondly, because any single application program is likely to need to access only a small part of the data held on the database, it is necessary to describe the data available to, and used by, each application program.

2.28 The Conference on Data Systems Languages (CODASYL) has produced standard terms for these two descriptions, namely **schema** (for the description of all the data on the database) and **sub-schema** (for the data available to a particular program). Other terms are used for schema and sub-schema and the IBM terminology **data base description** or **DBD** (for schema) and **program specification block** or **PSB** (for sub-schema) is frequently encountered.

19

2.29   Each application program contains the information necessary to identify the sub-schema relating to that program. It is then necessary to identify the sub-schema on the database library and relate it to the data held on the database through the schema. The desired data can then be read from or written to the database. The work of relating the application programs, sub-schema and schema, and reading and updating the database is controlled by software termed the **database management system** (DBMS) which uses a special **data management language** (DML) to carry out these functions. The process of reading and updating a database is illustrated in Figure 5.

2.30   It has already been stated that the major characteristic of database systems is the sharing of data by more than one application. Even in non-database environments, systems are commonly encountered where data is used by more than one program although this is likely to be confined to sharing within specific applications. This gave rise to the establishment of **data dictionary directory** systems, either manual or programmed, the purpose of which was to establish a record of all data items in the system, their characteristics and how they were used by the application programs.

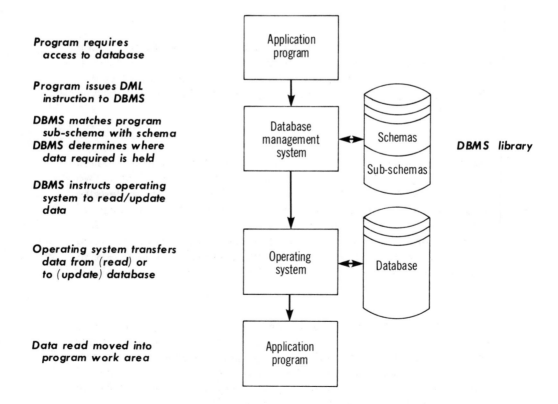

20   FIG. 5. Database – reading and updating (2.29)

2.31   With the advent of databases, and the possibility of sharing data between applications on a wider and more complex scale than before, the establishment of a data dictionary directory became an important aid to the efficient design and maintenance of a database. Most dictionaries for database systems are programmed rather than manual. Programmed dictionaries can be integrated with the DBMS.

2.32   The information about each data item typically maintained by the data dictionary system includes:

   (a) Descriptions (names used for data item; description of content).

   (b) Relationships with other data items.

   (c) Departments and source documents using the data item.

   (d) Programs and transactions accessing the data item and for what reason (insert; amend; delete; read only).

   (e) Output containing the data item.

   (f) Edit tests applied to the data item (format; reasonability; compatibility).

   (g) Picture statement (numeric; alphanumeric).

   (h) How held on database (compacted; encrypted).

   (i) Logical address and physical location.

Distributed processing

2.33   A further development in the design of computer-based systems is the introduction of distributed processing techniques. As the name implies, the main feature of these techniques is that, instead of all processing being carried out on one large central computer, processing which is relevant only to individual locations is carried out on small computers installed at each location. These small computers may, in their turn, have terminals attached to them. Information as required, normally in summary form, may then be transmitted either to the central computer or to another local computer with a more powerful configuration for further processing, probably using a data transmission network, although other methods may be used depending on the volumes, distances and costs involved. This technique is particularly appropriate, for example, for a company operating a number of department stores, where credit control and inventory control may be carried out locally using a small computer linked to point of sale terminals.

2.34   Clearly, because of the range of equipment available, the potential for variety in distributed systems is large, and it is important that the timing and content of information transferred between computers is understood. The processing on each individual computer will, however, fall into one of the categories already discussed.

Examples of computer systems

2.35 Having described in general terms those features of computer processing that may be of significance to the auditor, their application to specific accounting systems can be reviewed. This is done by describing typical computer systems using, where applicable, the definitions already given in this chapter. Although the details of computer systems differ, depending on the systems' requirements and the precise method of design, their main outlines are often similar. The typical systems are described in the appendix to this chapter and comprise:

- Sales accounting.
- Purchase accounting.
- Inventory control.
- Payroll.
- Fixed assets.

It is likely that most computer systems processing these activities will be similar to those described.

Recording the System

The advantages of flowcharting

2.36 When an accounting system, whether computer-based or not, has been understood by the auditor, it should be recorded as a basis for evaluating the controls. Flowcharting is used more frequently than narrative because greater discipline can be applied to the preparation and contents of flowcharts and they are easier to understand and review. Flowcharting enables the recording to be standardised so that new staff can work with flowcharts prepared by other staff in earlier years. This is particularly important in recording computer systems which are normally more complex than non-computer systems. As a result, it is preferable to record computer systems principally in flowchart form.

2.37 It is not a purpose of this book to elaborate in detail on any particular method of flowcharting. There are several well-proven methods in use. Most general flowcharting techniques are easily applied to recording computer systems. However, there are certain points of particular relevance in flowcharting such systems. In the following paragraphs a particular flowcharting technique is outlined, so as to provide a framework within which to describe and illustrate these particular points.

A flowcharting technique

2.38 This particular flowcharting technique has been specifically designed to record a company's system in a convenient manner to enable the auditor to determine the controls that are significant for his purposes and to provide the basis for transaction reviews. Separate flowcharts are prepared for each transaction processing system or major part thereof. The principal feature of the technique is a main "flowline" which records the flow of processing and the documents involved. The flowline runs from the beginning to the end of each system, starting with the inception of transactions and ending with their entry in the accounting records and passing into and out of the departments where the transactions are processed. The concept of the flowline is illustrated in Figure 6 in relation to a sales system.

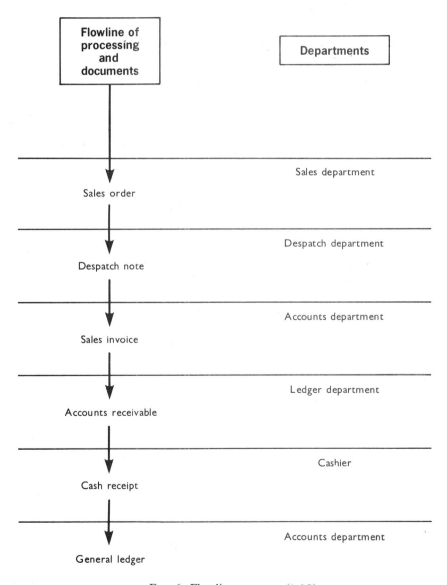

Fig. 6. Flowline concept (2.38)

2.39 Within this framework the following important conventions are applied:

(a) Standard symbols are used which are, so far as possible, self-explanatory.

(b) Procedures are flowcharted in operational sequence.

(c) All copies of documents are explained and accounted for insofar as they have accounting significance.

(d) The title or position and, where practicable, the name of the persons performing the procedures are shown.

(e) Narrative is kept to a minimum. Where detailed descriptions are needed, they are attached as appendices.

The flowcharts for part of the sales processing in a non-computer system are shown in Figure 7.

FLOWCHART DESCRIPTION ..... **SALES SYSTEM - NON-COMPUTER** ....

Warehouse

Stores clerk – D. Wilde

Sequentially numbered despatch note set prepared. Signed as evidence of despatch. One copy filed in numerical sequence in warehouse.

Despatch note

N

To customer

Accounts dept

Invoice clerk – B. Lord

Numerical sequence of despatch notes checked manually, missing numbers investigated.

Despatch note priced and extended.

Authorised price list

Invoice prepared from evaluated despatch note.

Invoice

A

Fig. 7. Detailed flowcharts for a non-computer system (2.39)

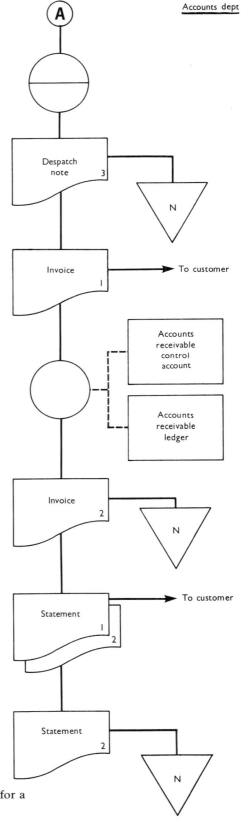

Accounts dept

Accounts clerk – R. Pearson

Pricing and extension of invoices checked independently and evidenced.

Despatch notes filed in numerical order.

Despatch note 3

N

Accounts clerk – R. Pearson

Invoice sent to customer.

Invoice 1 → To customer

Machine operator – L. Clarke

Invoice details posted to accounts receivable ledger and totals posted to control account.

Accounts receivable control account

Accounts receivable ledger

Invoices filed in numerical order.

Invoice 2

N

Invoice clerk – B. Lord

Customer statements prepared manually, one copy sent to customer. (monthly)

Statement 1 2 → To customer

Statements filed in numerical order.

Statement 2

N

FIG. 7 (continued). Detailed flowcharts for a non-computer system (2.39)

Flowcharting computer systems

2.40   An important aim when flowcharting computer systems is to integrate into a single flowchart the computer and non-computer parts of the system. This is achieved easily with the flowcharting method described above. The flowline moves on the flowchart into and out of the computer department at the appropriate stages and, as far as possible, the same flowcharting conventions and symbols (as for non-computer systems) are used to illustrate the processing in that department. Additional symbols are, of course, required for devices unique to computer systems, such as tape and disc files, but these are readily understandable. Flowcharts for part of the sales processing in a computer system are shown in Figure 8. A comparison of these flowcharts with those in Figure 7 illustrates the similarity of the flowcharts prepared for computer and non-computer systems.

FLOWCHART DESCRIPTION .... SALES SYSTEM - COMPUTER ....

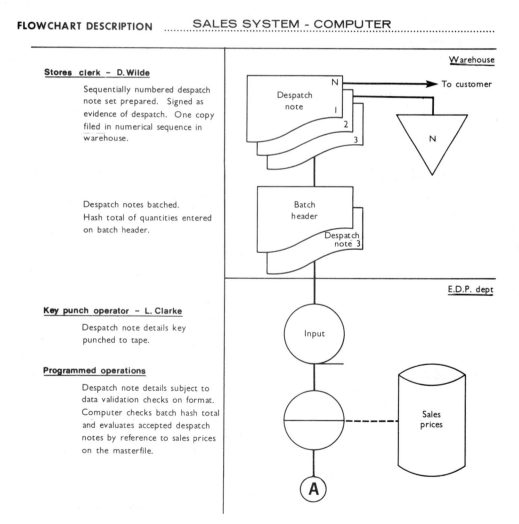

Stores clerk – D. Wilde

Sequentially numbered despatch note set prepared. Signed as evidence of despatch. One copy filed in numerical sequence in warehouse.

Despatch notes batched. Hash total of quantities entered on batch header.

Key punch operator – L. Clarke

Despatch note details key punched to tape.

Programmed operations

Despatch note details subject to data validation checks on format. Computer checks batch hash total and evaluates accepted despatch notes by reference to sales prices on the masterfile.

FIG. 8. Detailed flowcharts for a computer system (2.40)

Narrative	Document flow

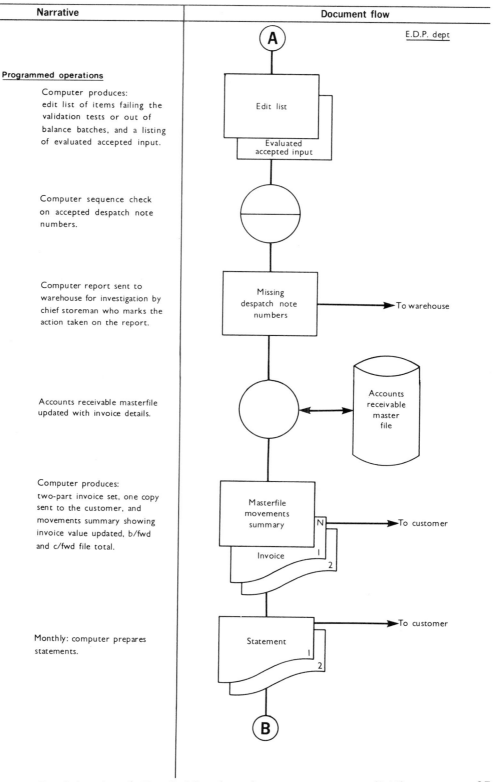

Narrative

Programmed operations

Computer produces:
edit list of items failing the
validation tests or out of
balance batches, and a listing
of evaluated accepted input.

Computer sequence check
on accepted despatch note
numbers.

Computer report sent to
warehouse for investigation by
chief storeman who marks the
action taken on the report.

Accounts receivable masterfile
updated with invoice details.

Computer produces:
two-part invoice set, one copy
sent to the customer, and
movements summary showing
invoice value updated, b/fwd
and c/fwd file total.

Monthly: computer prepares
statements.

Document flow

E.D.P. dept

A

Edit list

Evaluated
accepted input

Missing
despatch note
numbers → To warehouse

Accounts
receivable
master
file

Masterfile
movements
summary   N → To customer

Invoice   1
          2

Statement → To customer
          1
          2

B

Fig. 8 (continued). Detailed flowcharts for a computer system (2.40)   27

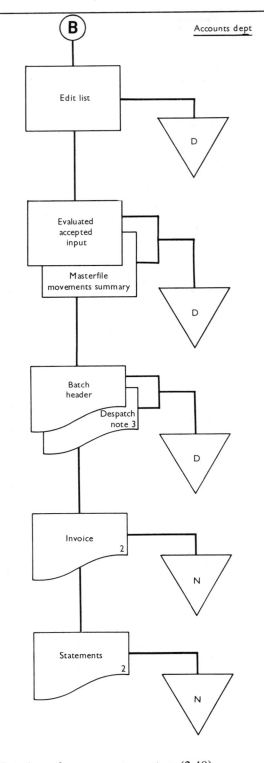

Accounts clerk – R. Pearson

Rejected despatch notes on edit listing investigated, corrected and resubmitted by accounts clerk who notes the action taken on the edit listing. This list and the action taken is reviewed by the assistant accountant, who signs the edit listing as evidence of his review.

Asst. accountant – R. Gadd

Total on the list of evaluated accepted input is agreed to the total invoice value on the masterfile movements summary by assistant accountant.

Accounts clerk – R. Pearson

Batches of despatch notes filed in date order.

Invoices filed in numerical sequence.

Statements filed in account number order.

Fig. 8 (continued). Detailed flowcharts for a computer system (2.40)

2.41   Another important aim when recording the computer parts of a system is to keep the flowcharts and narrative as simple as possible. This facilitates understanding by non-technical audit staff and highlights the operations of importance to the auditor. Various aids to simplification are discussed in the following paragraphs.

Overview flowcharts

2.42   In computer systems it is desirable to prepare an overview flowchart for each important computer application. These charts would normally be prepared prior to detailed flowcharting and would convey the scope of computer processing. They provide a convenient means for assessing, at an early stage, the impact that computer processing may have on the audit approach.

2.43   The overview flowchart will normally indicate significant input, master files and output, both in terms of routine and exception reports. Illustrations of typical overview flowcharts are given with the examples of computer systems in the appendix to this chapter. It may also be useful in more complex systems to show the flow of data through the separate sub-systems within the overall processing cycle, indicating the points in the processing at which the various reports and files are produced.

Programmed operations

2.44   When preparing the flowcharts, the recording of programmed operations can usually be limited to those of significance to the auditor. These operations would include all programmed procedures, as defined in paragraph 3.12, and the other operations that are necessary to understand the overall flow of processing.

2.45   Programmed operations are conveniently recorded with the same symbols as for manual operations and controls. There will often need to be a description of the method used in a program to perform a particular operation or control, for example the way in which a sales order is tested for credit status. This can be done by inserting a cross reference on the flowchart to the client's detailed program documentation or to a narrative description following the flowchart.

Standing data amendments

2.46   The procedures relating to the amendments of standing data are usually difficult to incorporate in the flowcharts dealing with the processing of the master files concerned. It is preferable to prepare separate flowcharts or narrative records for these procedures.

Rejection procedures

2.47   Rejections normally arise at the edit and updating stages of processing. The company usually has standard procedures to investigate, correct and resubmit rejections. Accordingly, these procedures, when standard, are normally only flowcharted or described in narrative form once. Thereafter, when rejections arise, a reference to the rejection flowchart or narrative should be made on the main flowchart.

Periodic controls

2.48 Control procedures that are only carried out periodically and separately from the normal processing of data, such as control account reconciliations, are often recorded separately and in narrative form. A cross reference can be entered at the most suitable point on the flowcharts.

Integrity controls

2.49 Integrity controls, while relevant to the consistency of processing, generally operate separately from the flow of data through the accounting system. Accordingly, it is not practicable to incorporate them in the main flowcharts of the accounting applications. As the procedures will usually be relevant to all accounting applications processed, they should be separately flowcharted or, more commonly, recorded in narrative form.

Company documentation

2.50 Company documentation is usually of considerable use to the auditor in understanding and recording computer systems. This is because it often needs to be more detailed and precise than that prepared for non-computer systems. Two distinct groups of documentation will be of importance to the auditor – the documentation prepared for particular accounting systems and the documentation prepared for the general work of design, implementation and operation of systems as a whole. These may be termed **systems documentation** and **standards documentation** respectively and are discussed in the following paragraphs.

Systems documentation

2.51 Systems documentation consists of a general description of the system and more detailed descriptions and related documentation of the manual and programmed procedures. The general description is normally called an outline systems description and provides a helpful overall description in terms that are easily understandable. It will outline the complete system, comprising both manual and programmed procedures, and will show the inter-relationship of the various parts.

2.52 For the clerical procedures, manuals are normally prepared for staff in user departments and control sections in computer departments detailing the procedures to be followed in respect of data collection and input, and the action to be taken on rejections and printed output. These manuals are a useful source of information for understanding and recording manual procedures.

2.53 For the programmed procedures, there will be various levels of detailed documentation, including systems descriptions, containing details of the individual programs within each application, and a description of the contents of each program. Both of these descriptions provide the auditor, particularly in more complex systems, with a convenient source of information regarding the programmed procedures. At a more detailed level, there will be block diagrams and listings of the instructions in the programs.

Standards documentation

2.54 It is common for the procedures that are followed in the design, implementation and operation of computer systems to be standardised and explained in manuals. The design and implementation manuals will also often include details as to the procedures to be followed when systems and programs are amended. There will usually be operations manuals setting out the duties of operating staff and librarians. The operating instructions for particular systems will also normally be based on the standard procedures included in the manuals. These manuals are a useful source of information for understanding and recording those aspects of the integrity controls with which the auditor is concerned.

Use of company documentation

2.55 When recording computer systems, there may be scope for making use of flowcharts prepared by the company, either as a substitute for the separate preparation of flowcharts or as a more detailed record of programmed procedures to which the auditor's flowcharts can be referenced. The auditor's flowcharts can also often be referenced to clerical procedure manuals. Likewise the narrative records of integrity controls may be kept to a minimum by referencing to the company's standards documentation.

Transaction Reviews

General

2.56 Having completed his flowcharts or narrative record of the system, the auditor will normally trace one or more transactions through each part of the company's accounting system in order to confirm his understanding of the system, as recorded in his flowcharts or narrative records.

2.57 The transaction review should cover each operation shown on the flowcharts and should include examination of evidence that the operation

31

has been performed, enquiry of the company's personnel as to procedures followed and reperformance, to the extent practicable, of the company's procedures. When carrying out the transaction review, the auditor should be alert to the possibility that operations with audit significance may have been omitted from the flowcharts.

2.58 If the transaction reviews confirm the auditor's understanding of the company's system, and that understanding has been correctly recorded in the auditor's flowcharts or narrative records, no further work with regard to transaction reviews is necessary. If the transaction reviews indicate that the auditor's initial understanding of the system was not correct, he should make further enquiries in order to ascertain the procedures in force and revise his documentation of the system accordingly.

Computer systems

2.59 When carrying out a transaction review in a computer system, two features will need to be borne in mind:

(a) It will often not be possible to trace an individual transaction into computer-produced summaries or analyses such as, for example, a payroll total or a monthly expenditure analysis. In these cases it will usually be sufficient to trace items to batches or computer-produced reports and to trace the totals, via any subsequent summaries, through the subsequent operations.

(b) It will often not be practicable to identify and select transactions which will confirm the proper functioning of programmed operations. For example, it will be difficult to select exceptional transactions in order to confirm that they appear on exception reports. In these cases it will usually be sufficient to examine evidence that, *prima facie,* the operation has functioned properly, for example by a review of exception reports.

If further confirmation is required as regards the operations described in (a) and (b) above, at the time of carrying out the transaction review, it will be necessary to use one of the techniques for testing programmed procedures described in Chapter 7.

2.60 Where the auditor has confirmed that the detailed systems documentation properly reflects the programmed procedures that exist in operational programs, he may decide that examination of program documentation is adequate to confirm his understanding of the programmed operations instead of tracing transactions through the system.

2.61 It is not practicable to carry out a transaction review in respect of integrity controls because, as stated earlier, they generally operate separately from the flow of data through the accounting system. Instead the auditor can confirm his understanding of these procedures by the examination of evidence and observation of the procedures while evaluating the controls.

Summary

2.62   In order to understand and record computer systems effectively the auditor must have a basic understanding of the principles of computers and computer processing. The processing features of significance to the auditor can be divided between input, processing and output. Processing may include editing, calculating, summarising and categorising, initiating transactions and updating master or pipeline files. There are special considerations for on-line input and output, real-time processing and database organisation.

2.63   There are advantages in recording computer systems by means of flowcharts. The computer and non-computer parts of the system should be integrated in a single flowchart. Thus the same conventions and symbols, as are used in non-computer systems, should be used as far as possible in flowcharting computer systems. It is desirable to keep the flowcharts as simple as possible and various aids to simplification can be employed. These include the preparation of overview flowcharts and the suggested methods of recording programmed operations, standing data amendments and rejection procedures. Use can often be made of company documentation.

2.64   The auditor should usually carry out a transaction review to confirm his understanding and recording of the system by tracing selected transactions through the system. Alternative techniques may be necessary where this is not practicable, such as tracing to computer-produced summaries. Where the auditor is satisfied that the detailed systems documentation properly represents the system in force, he may decide that he can rely on the examination of such documentation to confirm his understanding and recording of the system.

2: Appendix A
Examples of Computer Systems

Introduction

1   In this appendix typical examples of the following computer systems are described:

   - Sales accounting.
   - Purchase accounting.
   - Inventory control.
   - Payroll.
   - Fixed assets.

   As stated in paragraph 2.35, it is likely that most computer systems processing these activities will be similar to those described.

2   In practice, particularly as regards sales accounting, purchase accounting and inventory control, systems of differing complexity will be encountered depending upon the extent to which computer processing is used. In order to distinguish between systems of varying complexity it is convenient to break these systems down into their component parts and describe the features of computer processing in each component. After describing the components in this way, it can be seen how the components, whether computer or non-computer, are linked together to provide the total system. In practice computer systems are often designed and implemented in just this manner, beginning with a simple system having only one computer-based component, and then gradually adding further computer-based components until finally a complex computer system exists.

Sales Accounting

The components

3   Most sales accounting systems comprise three components, **order processing**, the processing of orders resulting in the despatch of goods, **invoicing**, the processing of despatch details to produce invoices, and **accounts receivable processing**, the recording of transactions in the accounts receivable ledger. The computer may be involved in each of these activities, as described in the following paragraphs.

35

Order processing

4   Order processing is illustrated in Figure 9. The initial input in this component will be *sales orders*. Two important checks may be carried out during *editing*. First, and most likely, the *finished goods inventory file* may be referred to, in order to establish that there is sufficient stock to satisfy the order. Secondly, and less frequently, the *accounts receivable file* may be referred to, in order to assess the credit status of the customer. This latter test usually involves calculation. The order is evaluated, using prices held on a master file, shown in Figure 9 as the *finished goods inventory file,* added to the customer's outstanding balance and the resulting notional balance is compared with the credit limit. The credit limit would be held as standing data in the customer's record on the accounts receivable file. Orders failing one of these tests are either *rejected* or, frequently, held in suspense on an *open orders file* until the stock is sufficient or the customer's balance outstanding reduced. Accepted orders are written to an *accepted orders file,* usually both in quantity and value, and *despatch notes* are produced together with a *summary* for control purposes.

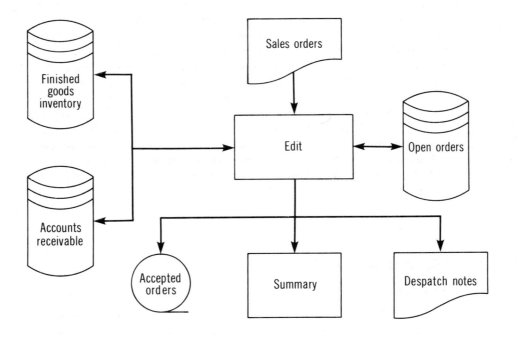

FIG. 9(1). Sales accounting – order processing (para. 4)

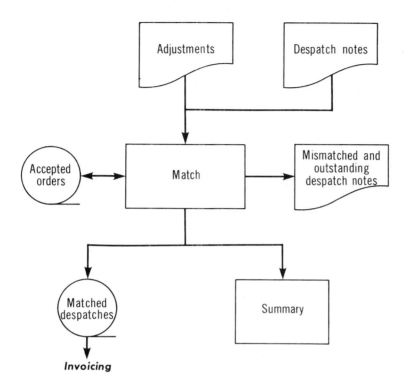

FIG. 9(2). Sales accounting – order processing (para. 5)

5   When the goods have been shipped, the *despatch notes* are re-input as illustrated in the second part of Figure 9. They are *matched* with the *accepted orders file.* Matched items are deleted from the accepted orders file and written to a *matched despatches file.* A *summary* is usually accumulated for control purposes. The file of matched despatches will be input for invoicing as described in paragraph 6. *Mismatched items* will be reported or rejected. The *accepted orders file* at any time thus contains details of despatch notes produced but not yet re-input. This file, which is a pipeline file, will be read periodically and records remaining unmatched for a given period printed out. The print-out thus provides details of *outstanding despatch notes.* A facility is usually necessary to process adjustments to the pipeline file so that entries on the file can be amended, for example where the goods actually despatched differ from those ordered, or can be eliminated, for example in respect of cancelled orders.   37

Invoicing

6   Invoicing is illustrated in Figure 10. The input to the invoicing component
will be *despatch details.* These will either be *files of matched despatches,*
if order processing is by computer, or *documents,* if order processing is
carried out manually. Often there will be both a file and documents, for
example a file for home sales and documents for export sales. The
computer will *calculate* the value of each transaction, if this has not
already been carried out during order processing, by matching quantities
despatched with the relevant *price* held as standing data on a master file,
usually the inventory file or a separate prices file. *Quantity discounts* can
be calculated and applied in a similar manner. The computer will produce
invoices and a *file of evaluated despatches* which will be input to accounts
receivable processing, as described in paragraph 7. A *summary* is often
produced for control purposes. *Exception reports* may be produced as a
result of the calculation (for example, high value invoices or discount).

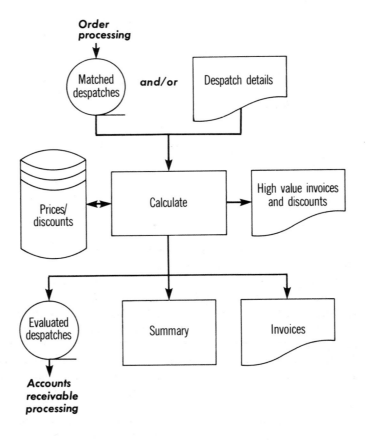

FIG. 10. Sales accounting – invoicing (para. 6)

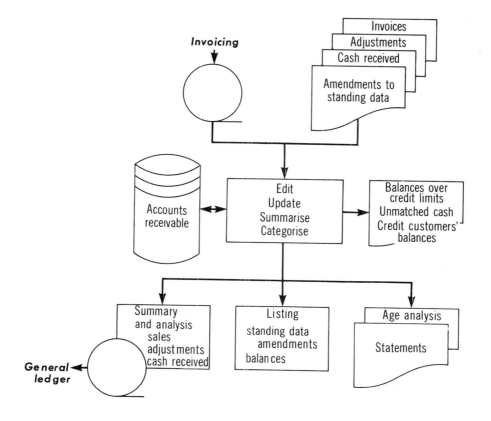

FIG. 11. Sales accounting – accounts receivable processing (para. 7)

Accounts receivable processing

7   Accounts receivable processing is illustrated in Figure 11. The *accounts receivable file* will be updated by both transaction data and standing data. The main types of transaction data will be charges to customers, adjustments and cash received from customers. Charges to customers will be input in the form of a *file of evaluated despatches,* if invoicing is by computer, or in the form of *documents* if invoices are manually prepared.

8   The computer will *update* the customers' accounts on the accounts receivable file with the evaluated despatches or invoices and "simultaneously" *summarise* the total of sales transactions for posting to the general ledger. This total may then be *categorised* by reference to an input code for financial reasons, for example as a basis for the payment of commission, or for operational reasons, for example geographically. The summaries of sales transactions may be printed out or written to a file for direct input into a *general ledger* computer application. Where the processing of the general ledger is integrated with accounts receivable processing, the updating may be simultaneous. An *exception report* may be

39

produced of balances over credit limits as a result of updating charges to customers.

9 Procedures will always be necessary to input corrections in respect of mispostings arising from incorrect input coding or to write off a small balance where a customer has not paid an invoice in full and it is not intended to press for payment. The input documents required are referred to as *adjustments*.

10 Where a single document is used for a variety of purposes, the particular purpose will be indicated by an input code. In more advanced systems, certain of the adjustments, for which the input of documents is needed in simpler systems, may be initiated by the computer. For example, the computer may be programmed to write off small balances outstanding for longer than a specified time. In addition to updating the accounts receivable file, the computer may *summarise* and *categorise* the total of adjustments for posting to the general and cost ledgers in the same way as for invoices.

11 The method of updating details of *cash received* will depend on the manner in which transaction data is stored on the accounts receivable file. Where all transactions, including paid invoices and cash receipts, are held on the file, the details of cash receipts are written to and stored on the customers' records. In this simple case, only the account number need be matched. Where, however, only unpaid invoices, usually referred to as open items, are held on the file, cash receipts are processed by indicating, and subsequently deleting, the related invoices which are paid from the file. In these cases it is necessary to match cash receipts against the related invoices. This can be done in one of four ways:

(a) Manual allocation prior to processing.

(b) Programming the computer to allocate the cash to the relevant items. This is normally practicable when only one periodic debit arises, as in the case of utilities or insurance companies, or where one specific sale is paid off over several instalments, as in the case of hire purchase companies.

(c) Programming the computer to allocate the cash against the earliest part of the balance. This method will not identify specific invoices remaining unpaid when later invoices are paid, for example in respect of disputed items.

(d) Programming the computer to allocate the cash and make allowances for certain differences, for example discount. Further small differences up to a certain amount may also be written off.

Cash received which cannot be matched (*unmatched cash*) will normally be reported for investigation.

12 *Amendments to standing data* will be processed to alter the standing data held on the accounts receivable file. They will be needed to open new customers' accounts and close old accounts. Their further use will depend

largely on the extent of reference and financial standing data that is held on the file. A typical file layout is shown in Figure 12 illustrating the wide variety of data that may be stored and for which amendment routines may be necessary. In some systems the computer may calculate changes to standing data on the basis of input, for example rental based on the input of house characteristics. In advanced systems the computer may initiate amendments to standing data, for example increments to discounts based on records of sales. A *listing of standing data amendments* made will normally be produced.

13   It would be normal for the accounts receivable file to be read periodically to:

(a) produce *statements;* and

(b) *categorise* open items or balances by age and *summarise* these categories to provide an *age analysis.*

During updating of the accounts receivable file, and these periodic readings of the file, the computer would normally *summarise* the items or balances and produce information for control purposes. *Lists of balances* and *exception reports,* such as a list of credit balances, may be produced.

Utilities

14   Where a permanent or long-term service is provided rather than goods shipped, there may not be an input to start the billing cycle. In these cases, such as electricity and gas billing, the date on which a meter reading sheet should be initiated will be held as standing data. Current dates will be input as parameters and the computer will produce the relevant meter reading sheets, or renewal notices. Details of documents produced will be written to a pipeline file which will be processed as described in paragraph 5. Sometimes billing will combine transaction data, such as meter readings, and standing data, such as the rental.

Accounts Receivable Ledger: File Layout	
Description	Number of Characters
Customer details	
1 Closed account indicator	1
2 Account number	8
3 Previous account number if applicable	8
4 Depot number	4
5 Traveller number	4
6 Call day	4
7 Early closing day	2
8 Area number	4
9 Sales statistics code	4
10 Agent code	4
11 Agent commission	4

FIG. 12. Accounts receivable ledger – file layout (para. 12)

12	VAT code	1
13	Payment type indicator	1
14	Statement suppress indicator	1
15	Weekly statement indicator	1
16	Statement date	2
17	Date of last order	6
18	Overdue account indicator	1
19	Credit limit	8
20	Date last paid late	6
21	Bad debt indicator	1
22	Quantity discount rate code	3
23	Wholesale discount %	3
24	Wholesale discount indicator	1
25	Settlement date discount – 10 days %	3
26	Settlement date discount – 30 days %	3
27	Settlement date discount – 60 days %	3
28	Settlement date discount – 90 days %	3
29	Settlement date discount indicator	1
30	Special prices indicator – Group 1	1
31	Special prices indicator – Group 2	1
32	Special prices indicator – Group 3	1
33	Special prices indicator – Group 4	1
34	Special prices indicator – Group 5	1
35	Balance outstanding	8
36	Sales – this month	8
37	Sales – last 6 months	8
38	Sales – previous 6 months	8
39	Sales – budget for year	8
40	Sales for year – Group 1	8
41	Sales for year – Group 2	8
42	Sales for year – Group 3	8
43	Sales for year – Group 4	8
44	Sales for year – Group 5	8
45	Delivery name	34
46	Delivery address line 1	34
47	Delivery address line 2	34
48	Delivery address line 3	34
49	Delivery telephone number	12
50	Statement address indicator	1
51	Statement name	34
52	Statement address line 1	34
53	Statement address line 2	34
54	Statement address line 3	34
55	Statement telephone number	12
		477

Transaction details—may be repeated 25 times

56	Item type (invoice, credit note, cash, adjustment, discount)	1
57	Item reference number	6
58	Date	6
59	Net value	8
60	VAT value	8
61	Matched indicator	1
		30

Fig. 12 (continued). Accounts receivable ledger – file layout (para. 12)

The systems

15 The components described in paragraphs 3 to 13 may be combined to form any of the following sales accounting systems:

- Accounts receivable.
- Invoicing.
- Order processing.

The scope of each system is described in paragraphs 16 to 18.

Accounts receivable systems

16 The computer processes the accounts receivable ledger, and order processing and invoicing are non-computer operations. This type of system is illustrated in the overview flowchart in Figure 13.

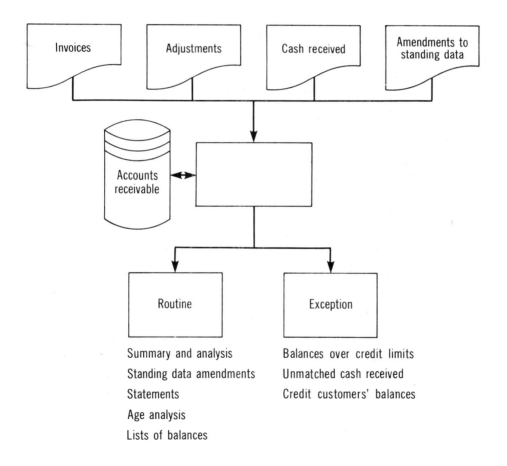

FIG. 13. Accounts receivable system – overview flowchart (para. 16)

43

Invoicing systems

17 The computer is involved in invoicing and processing the accounts receivable ledger, but order processing remains a manual operation. It is common for such systems to be integrated with the processing of inventory records for finished goods. The despatch details are used not only to process sales but also to update the inventory file at the same time or in a subsequent run. This type of system, including finished goods inventory, is illustrated in Figure 14.

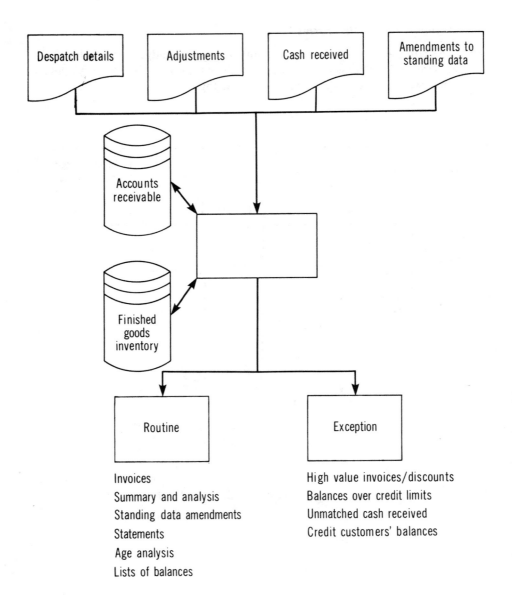

FIG. 14. Invoicing system – overview flowchart (para. 17)

Order processing systems

18 The computer is involved in the processing of all components of sales accounting. This type of system is illustrated in Figure 15. In some systems of this nature, sales orders are not only processed to produce despatch notes but also at the same time to produce invoices, update the accounts receivable ledger and provide sales totals. The subsequent despatch details are not re-input. These systems are often called "pre-debiting" systems. They can only be effective where it can be safely assumed that stocks are available for despatch, for example in mail order companies, and are usually combined with computer inventory systems.

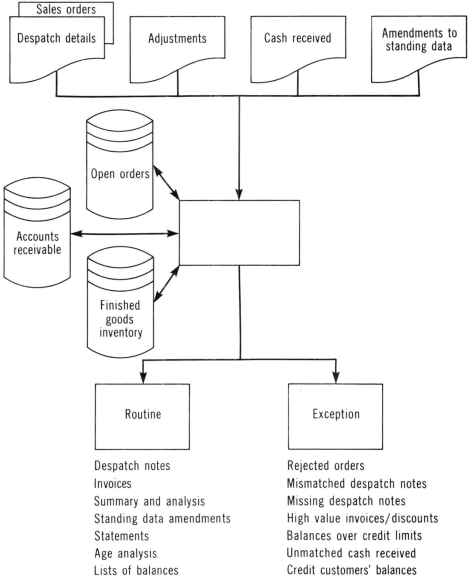

Routine	Exception
Despatch notes	Rejected orders
Invoices	Mismatched despatch notes
Summary and analysis	Missing despatch notes
Standing data amendments	High value invoices/discounts
Statements	Balances over credit limits
Age analysis	Unmatched cash received
Lists of balances	Credit customers' balances

FIG. 15. Sales order processing system – overview flowchart (para. 18)

45

Purchase Accounting

The components

19 In a similar manner to sales, purchase accounting systems can be conveniently divided into three components, **order processing, goods received processing** and **accounts payable processing**. The computer may be involved in each of these activities as described in the following paragraphs.

Order processing

20 Order processing is illustrated in Figure 16. Purchase orders are either *input* or *initiated* by the computer. A typical method for the computer to initiate orders is by comparing the stock balance with a minimum stock level held as standing data on the *inventory file*. Orders input, or initiated and printed by the computer, will be written to a pipeline record and a

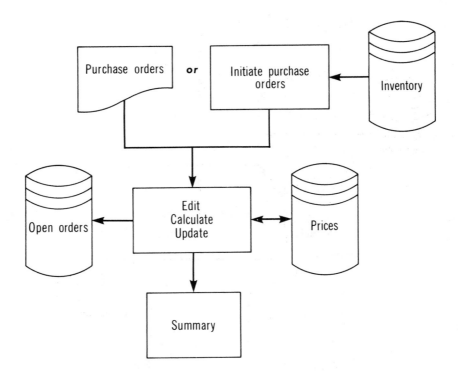

FIG. 16(1). Purchase accounting – order processing (para. 20)

summary produced for control purposes. This may be on a separate file or on a master file, for example the accounts payable file. (For consistency, the file is referred to throughout this description as a *pipeline file*.) Sometimes the computer will *calculate* the value of orders input, or initiated, by reference to *prices* input or held as standing data on a master file.

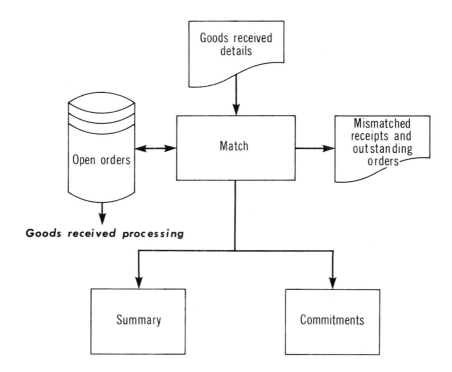

FIG. 16(2). Purchase accounting – order processing (para. 21)

21 *Open orders* will remain on the pipeline file until *matched* with the *details of goods received*. The pipeline file will be read periodically and orders for which goods have not been received for a given period will be printed out. Where the orders records are held in value, the value of *outstanding purchase commitments* can be summarised and printed out.

Goods received processing

22 Goods received processing is illustrated in Figure 17. *Goods received details* will be input and, if order processing is also by computer, *matched* with the order record on the *pipeline file*. When matched, it is usual for an indicator to be set on the record indicating that the goods have been received. Where order processing is not by computer, the goods received details will be written to the *pipeline file,* and a *summary* is normally produced for control purposes. It is common for the computer to calculate the value of goods received, if not already done in respect of orders. The computer will normally carry out this calculation by reference to *standard prices* held as standing data on a master file.

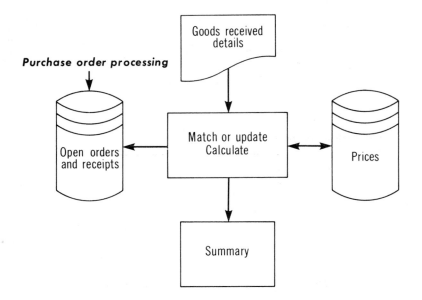

FIG. 17(1). Purchase accounting – goods received processing (para. 22)

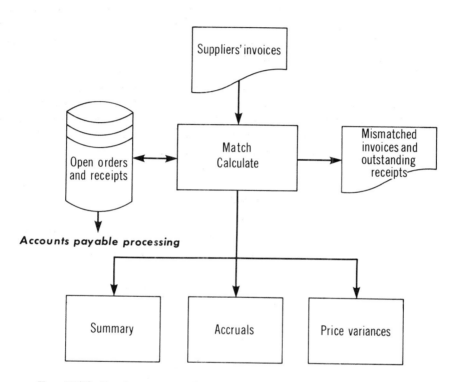

FIG. 17(2). Purchase accounting – goods received processing (para. 23)

23   Goods received details will remain on the pipeline file until *matched* with the *suppliers' invoice details.* At the time of matching, provided the goods received details are held at standard cost value, the computer may *calculate* the *price variance.* The pipeline file will be read periodically and goods received not matched with suppliers' invoices *(outstanding receipts)* for a given period will be printed out. Where the goods received records are held in value, the total *accrued liability* in respect of goods received can be summarised and printed out.

49

Accounts payable processing

24 Accounts payable processing is illustrated in Figure 18. The accounts payable file will be updated by both transaction data and standing data. The main types of transaction data will be suppliers' invoices, adjustments and details of cash paid. Where goods received processing is by computer and *suppliers' invoices* are *matched* with goods received records, a facility must be incorporated in the system so that invoices relating to items other than inventory can be accepted. This is usually achieved by the input of dummy goods received details, or by including an indicator on the relevant invoices which the computer recognises as an instruction to by-pass the pipeline file for those items.

25 *Adjustments* will, as in sales systems, always be necessary to correct mispostings. They may also be needed for other purposes, for example to facilitate quick payment of suppliers' invoices when the payer is entitled to a cash discount. An adjustment will then have to be made to the accounts payable file to record the discount taken.

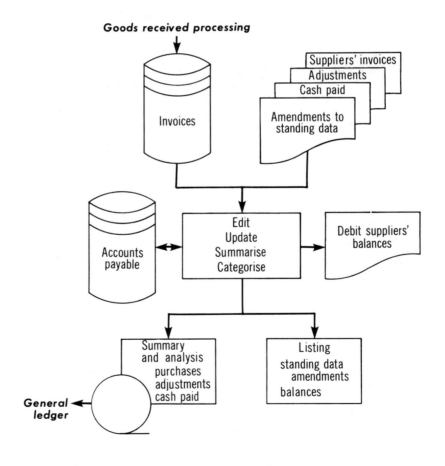

FIG. 18. Purchase accounting – accounts payable processing (para. 24)

26 The method by which *details of cash paid* are updated will depend on whether items are selected for payment manually or by the computer. Where items are selected manually, the details of items paid will require to be input and updated in the same manner as suppliers' invoices. The computer will match on either the account number alone or the account number, invoice number and value. Where the computer selects items for payment, the details will normally be updated at the time of selection. The methods of selection are dealt with later under the heading "Payment of creditors". Any manual changes to items selected will be input and updated as adjustments.

27 Suppliers' invoices and adjustments will be *summarised* and *categorised* for posting to the general and cost ledgers. These summaries may be printed out or written to a file for direct input into a *general ledger* computer application. Where the processing of the general and cost ledgers is integrated with accounts payable processing, updating may be simultaneous.

28 As in sales systems, *amendments to standing data* will be needed to open and close suppliers' accounts, and alter the various standing data fields. A file layout is shown in Figure 19 illustrating the wide variety of data that may be held and for which amendment routines may be necessary. A *listing of standing data amendments* made will normally be produced.

29 During updating of the accounts payable file the computer would normally *summarise* the items or balances and produce information for control purposes. *Lists of balances* and *exception reports,* for example debit balances, may also be produced.

Accounts Payable Ledger: File Layout

Description	Number of Characters
Supplier details	
1 Supplier number	6
2 Supplier name	15
3 Date opened	6
4 Date last amended	6
5 Address line 1	20
6 Address line 2	20
7 Address line 3	20
8 Cheque limit	4
9 Terms	4
10 Value outstanding – credit	6
11 Value outstanding – debit	6
12 Payment due week 1	6
13 Payment due week 2	6
14 Payment due week 3	6
15 Payment due week 4	6

FIG. 19. Accounts payable ledger – file layout (para. 28)

16	Cheque name	20
17	Rebate code	1
18	National giro number	8
19	Bank code	10
20	Total value invoices year to date	8
21	Total value invoices previous years	8
		192

Transaction details — may be repeated 30 times

22	Transaction type	2
23	Date of transaction	6
24	Transaction number	6
25	Order number	6
26	Value (including VAT)	8
27	VAT	8
28	Discount on invoice	4
29	Nominal ledger code	6
30	Stock reference number	8
31	Payment date	6
32	Payment indicator	1
		61

FIG. 19 (continued). Accounts payable ledger – file layout (para. 28)

Payment of creditors

30 Any purchase accounting system may include computer involvement in the payment of creditors. Within this definition of computer processing are included all cases where the computer selects items for payment. As a result of the selection the computer may produce:

(a) details from which cheques are manually or mechanically prepared;

(b) cheques for manual or mechanical signature; or

(c) pre-signed cheques.

The computer will also normally print out remittance advices showing the make-up of the payments. The normal selection criteria are date and, less frequently, discount indicator. The computer compares the dates on invoices with a date input as a constant and selects, for example, all items more than four weeks old. The computer may be programmed to recognise an indicator on invoices which means that discount is available if payment is prompt. The computer may also be programmed to calculate discount by reference to discount terms held as standing data. However, the processing of invoices by computer for early payment can be complex and invoices of this nature are often diverted on receipt for separate manual payments. Manually produced cheques may also be required for other purposes. Details of such payments would be input as adjustments.

The systems

31 The components described in paragraphs 20 to 29 may be combined to form any of the following purchase accounting computer systems:

- Accounts payable.
- Goods received processing.
- Order processing.

The scope of each system is described in paragraphs 32 to 34.

Accounts payable systems

32 The computer processes the accounts payable ledger, and order processing and goods received processing are non-computer operations. This type of system is illustrated in Figure 20.

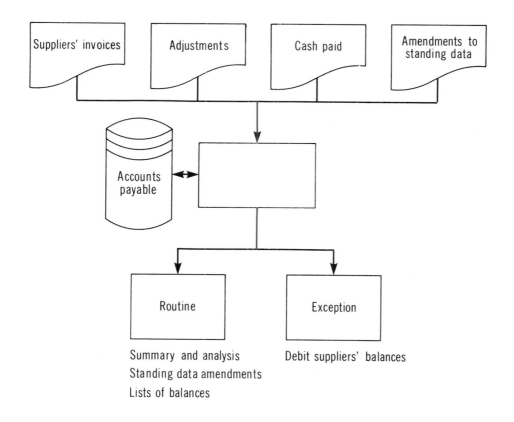

FIG. 20. Accounts payable system – overview flowchart (para. 32)

Goods received processing systems

33 The computer is involved in goods received processing and processing the accounts payable ledger, but order processing remains a manual operation. It is common for such systems to be integrated with the processing of raw materials inventory records. The goods received details are used not only to process purchases, but also to update the inventory file for raw materials in the same run or in a subsequent run. This type of system, including raw materials inventory, is illustrated in Figure 21.

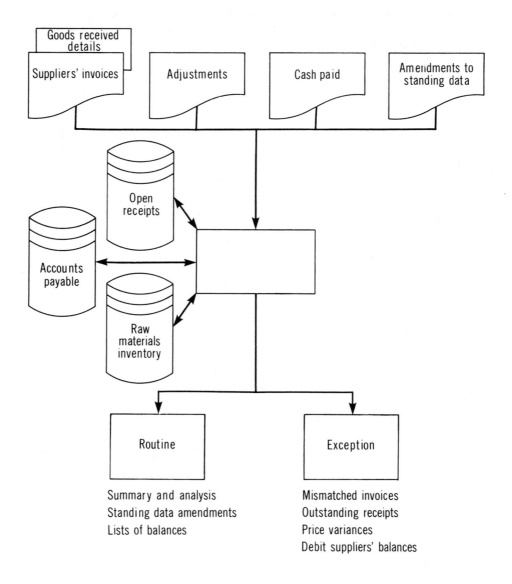

FIG. 21. Goods received processing system – overview flowchart (para. 33)

34 The computer is involved in the processing of all components of purchase accounting. This type of system is illustrated in Figure 22.

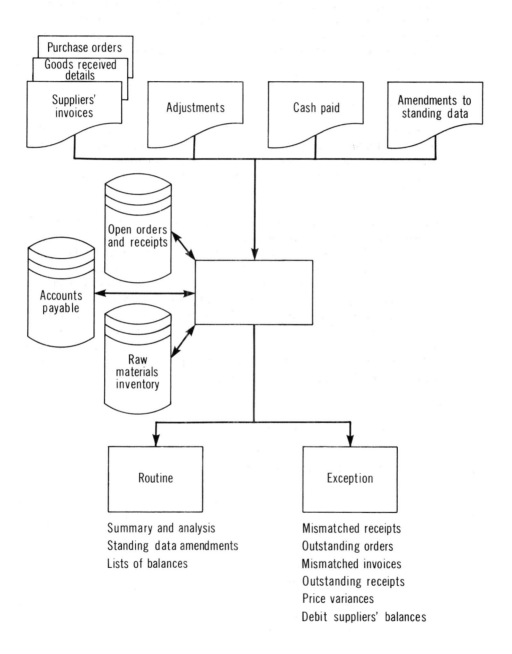

FIG. 22. Purchase order processing system – overview flowchart (para. 34)

Inventory Control

The components

35 Inventory control is a term commonly used for a wide variety of computer systems that process movements in inventories. Inventory control can be conveniently divided into three main components, **inventory recording, inventory values** and **inventory counting**. Although inventory recording can also be broken down into the three components of raw materials, work in progress and finished goods, it is considered easier to discuss them together.

Inventory recording

36 The records will be held on master files. Where raw materials, work in progress and finished goods inventory recording is integrated, it is normal for separate files to be maintained for each category. However, the maintenance of integrated inventory records is a typical use for database organisation.

37 The raw materials, work in progress and finished goods inventory files will be updated by both transaction data and standing data. The main types of transaction data will be *inventory movements*. There will also be a need for *adjustments* to correct mispostings. Adjustments may also be necessary to input differences between book and actual stock revealed by inventory counting. This is described further in paragraph 44. *Summaries* and *analyses* of movements and adjustments will be produced. *Amendments to standing data* will be needed to open and close records of stock items and to alter the various standing data fields. A *listing of standing data amendments* made will normally be produced. An example of an inventory file layout is shown in Figure 23.

Inventory Ledger: File Layout

Description	Number of Characters
Part number details	
1 Part number	14
2 Product group	6
3 Stock description	30
4 Unit of measure code	1
5 Made in/Bought out indicator	2
6 Stores location	5
7 Latest purchase price	9

FIG. 23. Inventory ledger – file layout (para. 37)

8	Reorder level		7
9	Reorder quantity		7
10	Safety stock		7
11	Maximum stock		7
12	Production reserve		7
13	Leadtime		3
14	Average weekly demand		7
15	Standard cost		9
16	Current selling price		11
17	Price effective date		6
18	New price increase percentage		5
19	New selling price		11
20	Bin stock		7
21	Allocated stock		7
22	Despatch stock		7
23	Outstanding sales orders		7
24	Outstanding purchase orders		7
25	Issues		7
26	Receipts	Current	7
27	Demand	Week	7
28	Despatches	Details	7
29	Adjustments		7
30	Issues		7
31	Receipts	Current	7
32	Demand	Month	7
33	Despatches	Details	7
34	Adjustments		7
35	Issues		7
36	Receipts	Weekly	7
37	Demand	Averages	7
38	Despatches		7
39	Adjustments		7
40	Last year's standard cost		9
41	Physical stock check count		3
42	Physical stock check frequency in weeks		2
43	Date of last physical count		6
44	Opening stock this year		7
45	Outstanding purchase requisition indicator		1
46	Outstanding purchase requisition quantity		7
47	Latest purchase quantity		7
48	Last issue date		6
49	Date of last purchase		6
50	Forecast total demand		7
51	Forecast spares demand		7
			362

FIG. 23 (continued). Inventory ledger – file layout (para. 37)

38 Particular features relating to raw materials, work in progress and finished goods inventory recording are outlined in the following paragraphs.

Raw materials

39 Raw materials recording is illustrated in Figure 24. *Receipts of inventory* will be input from goods received records which, if the systems are integrated, will also be processed for *purchase accounting.* Issues to production will usually be made prior to computer processing, details being input from *production schedules* or requisitions. However, in more advanced systems the computer may be programmed to initiate the issues required on the basis of the input of a *production number.* Information as to the materials necessary for the relevant job are held as standing data and the computer prints out the issue documentation, including *production schedules,* and updates the *raw materials file.* In these cases the file is updated in respect of issues prior to the actual issue from the stores. *Stock items below minimum levels* may be reported to assist in ordering.

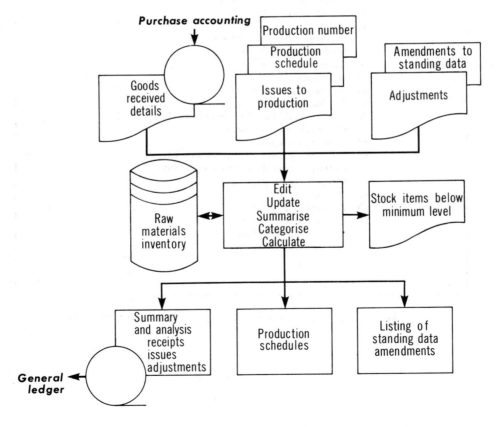

FIG. 24. Inventory control – raw materials recording (para. 39)

Work in progress

40   Work in progress recording is illustrated in Figure 25. Details of *issues to production* will, as described above, be input from production schedules or requisitions or be initiated by the computer. The updating of the *work in progress file* is often carried out simultaneously with the updating of the raw materials file. *Labour charges* are usually input from manually prepared input documents or from a file produced during payroll production. Actual gross pay would be *categorised* by the computer by reference to an input code. In some cases standard labour charges are held as standing data and the computer may be programmed to calculate *variances*. Overhead rates are normally held as standing data on the work in progress inventory file and the computer calculates the appropriate amount. Details of *transfers to finished goods* will usually be input from manually prepared documentation. In advanced systems the computer may be programmed to initiate the details of the transfer on the basis of the input of a *completion request*. The transfer details are held on the work in progress inventory file as standing data. The computer may be programmed to calculate *variances* between actual and standard quantities produced.

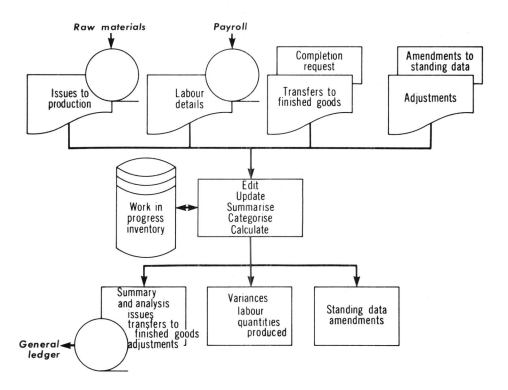

FIG. 25. Inventory control – work in progress recording (para. 40)

Finished goods

41 Finished goods recording is illustrated in Figure 26. *Completed work* will, as described above, be input from manual documentation or initiated by ·the computer. The updating of the *finished goods file* is often carried out simultaneously with the updating of the work in progress file. When the finished goods are sold, *details of despatches* are input. Often the updating of the finished goods file will be integrated, as described earlier, with *sales accounting.* If the cost of finished goods is held on file, the cost of sales will be *summarised* by the computer. The unit cost of sales will normally be held as standing data.

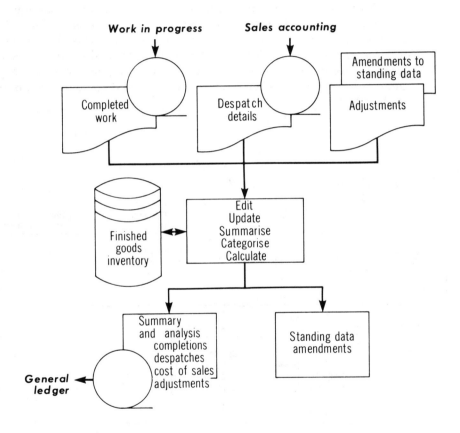

FIG. 26. Inventory control – finished goods recording (para. 41)

Inventory values

42   Although it is normal for the inventory balances and movements to be
held in quantities only, prices are also often held in the form of standing
data. In this way the *value of inventory* can be regularly *calculated.* In the
case of raw materials, the relevant cost may be the actual cost price, which
will be updated every time a purchase is made, or an average cost price,
which will be calculated after each purchase, or a standard cost price. If
standard cost is used, the computer will be programmed to calculate
variances. If average cost is used, the computer will often be programmed
to calculate changes to average cost arising from each new purchase and
report *changes over a certain norm.* These procedures are illustrated in
the first part of Figure 27.

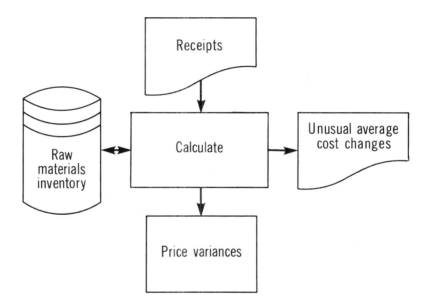

Fɪɢ. 27(1). Inventory control – inventory values (para. 42)

43   The computer may be programmed to *calculate* and report periodically information relevant to the value of inventory. Depending on the system this may include details as to excess stock, obsolete stock and slow-moving stock. *Excess stock* is usually calculated by comparing inventory on hand with past usage or future requirements. *Obsolete stock* is calculated by reference to past usage or by the setting of an indicator, for example in respect of a component for a finished product which is no longer in production. *Slow-moving stock* is calculated by reference to the date of the last movement. The scope of reports of this nature is governed mainly by the range of information held on the file. These procedures are illustrated in the second part of Figure 27.

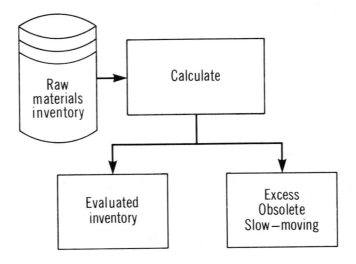

FIG. 27(2). Inventory control – inventory values (para. 43)

Inventory counting

44   The need for adjustments to input differences between book and actual stock has already been noted. These may result from a periodical count of all the stock. However, when inventory records are processed by computer, it is easier to ensure their reliability and thus continuous stock-taking becomes more likely. If continuous stocktaking is carried out, one of the following three methods will normally be followed:

   (a) The stock is counted and compared with the most recent print-out of the balance on the file adjusted for outstanding issues and receipts. These adjustments can be made manually or by the computer. Differences are processed by the input of an *adjustment*. A manual record is kept of items to be counted.

   (b) Stock is counted, compared and adjustments processed as in (a). At the same time as the adjustments are processed, the *date of the stock count* is input. The computer records the date and produces a regular report of *items which have not been counted* for a specified period.

(c) Stock is counted and the *details of the physical balances* are input. The computer calculates any differences between the physical and book inventory balance. The differences are often automatically processed and reported. In some cases, only *differences over a specified amount* are reported.

Provision will also often be made for *negative stock balances* to be reported. An example of inventory counting is illustrated in Figure 28.

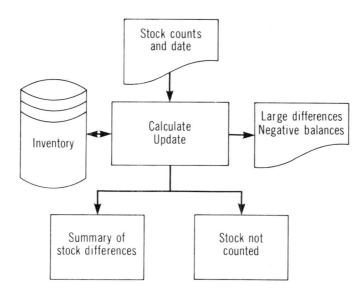

FIG. 28. Inventory control – inventory counting (para. 44)

The systems

45   The components described in paragraphs 35 to 44 can be combined to form a wide variety of computer systems that process inventory movements. They may vary from the simple recording of raw materials or finished goods to integrated recording, valuation and counting of materials, work in progress and finished goods and computer-controlled production planning. It has already been seen how inventory recording systems may be integrated with purchases and sales accounting and how replenishment of raw materials may be initiated by the computer. As a result it is not realistic to show a series of groupings of components. An example of an integrated inventory control system, combining most of the features discussed, is illustrated in Figure 29.

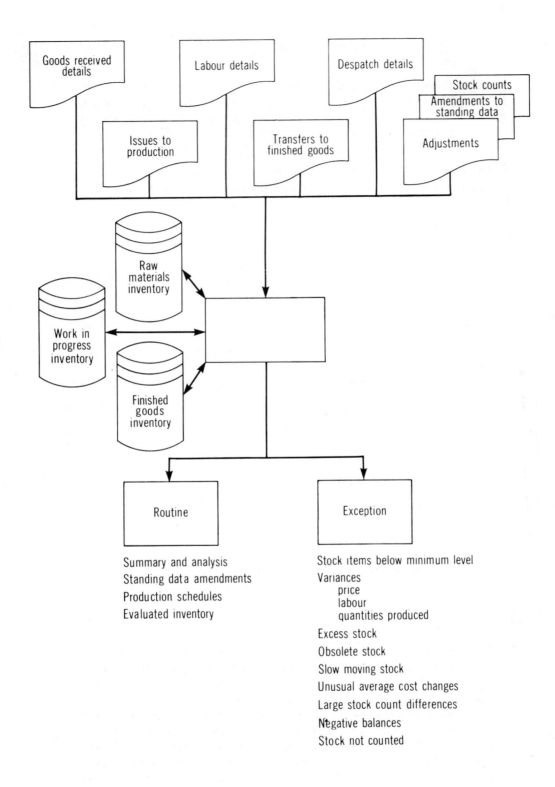

Goods received details

Labour details

Despatch details

Stock counts

Amendments to standing data

Issues to production

Transfers to finished goods

Adjustments

Raw materials inventory

Work in progress inventory

Finished goods inventory

Routine

Exception

Summary and analysis
Standing data amendments
Production schedules
Evaluated inventory

Stock items below minimum level
Variances
    price
    labour
    quantities produced
Excess stock
Obsolete stock
Slow moving stock
Unusual average cost changes
Large stock count differences
Negative balances
Stock not counted

FIG. 29. Integrated inventory control system – overview flowchart (para. 45)

Payroll

46   In wages and salaries systems, which are illustrated in Figure 30, the most important output is usually the printed payroll with its various accounting totals of gross pay and deductions. Thus the principal concern is with the standing data held on the master files, for example rates of pay, and the input and processing of the transaction data, for example hours worked or work done. When considering wages and salaries systems, it is convenient to deal with standing data before payroll production.

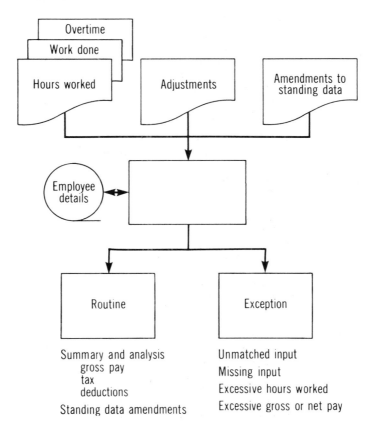

FIG. 30. Payroll – overview flowchart (para. 46)

Standing data

47   *Amendments to standing data* will be processed to record starters and leavers on the employee master file and to alter rates of pay, details of allowances and deductions. A typical employee details master file layout, illustrating the wide variety of data that may be held, and for which amendment routines may be necessary, is shown in Figure 31. In some systems the computer may be programmed to calculate changes to standing data on the basis of input, for example increments to rates of pay as a

65

result of changes to personal details such as age or the passing of examinations. In advanced systems the computer may be programmed to initiate amendments to standing data, for example increments to rates of pay on anniversary of starting date.

Payroll: File Layout

Description	Number of Characters
Employee details	
1 Employee's reference number	6
2 Sex	1
3 Starter/leaver indicator	1
4 Employee's title indicator	1
5 Employee's initials	5
6 Employee's surname	15
7 Employee's date of birth	6
8 National insurance number	9
9 Income tax code	5
10 Company number where employee works	4
11 Section number	2
12 Bank and branch sorting code	6
13 Bank account indicator	1
14 Date started	6
15 Date left	6
16 Staff coding	2
17 Basic annual salary	7
18 Previous salary prior to last increase/decrease	7
19 Date of last salary increase/decrease	6
20 Annual allowance – No 1	6
21 Annual allowance – No 2	6
22 Annual allowance – No 3	6
23 Total gross monthly standard salary	6
24 Pension fund indicator	1
25 Pension fund monthly contribution	5
26 Date of entry into pension fund	6
27 Pension fund accumulator for $\frac{1}{2}$ year	6
28 Pension fund accumulator for 1 year	6
29 Pension fund accumulator for whole of service	7
30 National insurance code	3
31 Employer's national insurance contributions	4
32 Employee's national insurance contributions	4
33 Monthly loan repayments	5
34 Number of loan repayments outstanding	2
35 Number of monthly repayments at start	2
36 Accumulated gross pay to date	7
37 Accumulated gross pay to date from previous employment	7
38 Accumulated tax paid to date	6

FIG. 31. Payroll – file layout (para. 47)

39	Accumulated tax paid to date from previous employment	6
40	Tax free pay for one month	5
41	Tax month number	2
42	Tax district	15
43	Tax district reference number	11
44	Bank account number	8
45	Bank name	30
46	Bank address 1st line	30
47	Bank address 2nd line	30
48	Bank address 3rd line	30
		358

FIG. 31 (continued). Payroll – file layout (para. 47)

Payroll production

48 In wages systems it is usually necessary to input details of *hours worked* or *work done*. The input may be of all hours worked or variances from standard hours held as standing data. Variances would include *overtime, holidays* and *absences*. The computer is often programmed to report cases where *hours input exceed a defined norm*.

49 The transaction data will be *matched* with the relevant employee details on the master file. Unmatched input or employee details should be rejected, when there is duplicate input, or reported when there is no input. The computer will then *calculate* the pay details for each employee, *update* the transaction data on the master file and *summarise* the accounting totals for posting to the general ledger. The totals are often *categorised* as a basis for further processing, for example posting to cost accounts. The summaries may be produced for non-computer processing or subsequent input to the *nominal* and *cost ledger* computer applications. This input may be by document or the file created during payroll production. The computer is often programmed to report cases where *gross* or *net pay* exceeds a defined norm.

50 In salaries systems it is normal for the monthly or annual salary to be held as standing data. The only input will be any *adjustments* or *overtime details*. The computer will be programmed to select or calculate the salary and take account of any input.

Fixed Assets

51 It is becoming common to maintain records of fixed assets on computer. The cost of the fixed assets, depreciation rates and accumulated depreciation to date are normally held on the master file. The file layout for a

67

typical fixed assets file is shown in Figure 32. *Purchases* will be input from manually prepared documents or, as is often the case, from a categorised file from the purchase accounting application. Capitalised *wages* and *materials* will be dealt with in a similar manner. Input documents will be prepared for *disposals* and *adjustments*. It is normal for the fixed asset movements to be *summarised, categorised* and printed out for control purposes.

52 Depreciation rates will be held as standing data and may require to be amended from time to time. The computer will *calculate* and *summarise* depreciation for posting to the general ledger either by input documents or file. Information may be provided of *fully depreciated assets* and *profits and losses* on disposals may be calculated. Details of *assets inspected* may be input and the computer can report *assets not inspected*.

53 A fixed assets system is illustrated in Figure 33.

Fixed Assets Ledger: File Layout

Description	Number of Characters
Asset details	
1 Asset category	2
2 Asset reference number	10
3 Purchase date	6
4 Input document reference	6
5 Taxation code	3
6 Location code	3
7 Purchase method	1
8 Gross cost	8
9 Valuation method	1
10 Valuation	8
11 Valuation date	6
12 Standard life (months)	4
13 Depreciation method	1
14 All time cumulative depreciation	8
15 Residual life months	4
16 Rental method	1
17 All time cumulative rental	8
18 Rental suspension	1
19 Cumulative depreciation	8
20 Cumulative rental	8
21 Depreciation this month	8
22 Rental this month	8
23 Depreciation roundings	2
24 Rental roundings	2
25 Date of last physical inspection	6
	123

FIG. 32. Fixed assets ledger – file layout (para. 51)

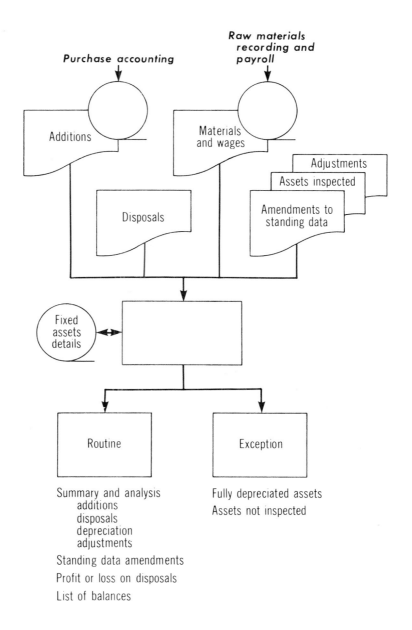

FIG. 33. Fixed assets – overview flowchart (para. 53)

3

Evaluation of Internal Control: The Audit Approach

General Approach

The scope of evaluation

3.01 The auditor is concerned with a company's system of internal control because he will normally wish, where possible, to place reliance thereon in order to limit, and phase the timing of, his subsequent audit work on the financial statements. A further important purpose is to report to management weaknesses that come to his notice, so as to assist management in carrying out its obligations to establish and maintain controls that will assure, as far as possible, the reliability of the company's accounting records and the safeguarding of its assets.

3.02 In some countries, the phrase "internal control" is often taken to cover the methods, procedures and organisational arrangements adopted not only for the safeguarding of assets and ensuring the reliability of the accounting records, but also for the promotion of operational efficiency and adherence to management policies. Those internal controls which are relevant to the expression of an audit opinion on financial statements are classified as **internal accounting controls** and the others are classified as **operational controls**. In practice, some internal accounting controls will also have operational aspects. For the purpose of this book, the phrase internal controls is used for internal accounting controls.

3.03 The approach and documentation outlined in this book are directed primarily to the evaluation of internal controls. This is because the operational controls are not relevant to the expression of an audit opinion on financial statements. However, the evaluation of operational controls, particularly by the internal auditor, is often an important aid to management. The approach outlined in this book can also be applied to the evaluation of operational controls; additional material would then need to be included in the documentation for this purpose.

Basic controls and disciplines

3.04　In assessing the degree of reliance that he can place on the internal controls, the auditor will need to distinguish between what are termed "basic controls" and "disciplines". As already mentioned, **basic controls** are those controls designed to ensure that valid transactions, and only valid transactions, are processed and recorded completely and accurately. **Disciplines** are those features of the system which are designed to ensure that the basic controls continue to operate properly.

3.05　The importance of the distinction between basic controls and disciplines lies in the extent to which the auditor can place reliance on the continued and proper operation of the basic controls. Where the disciplines are limited or non-existent, which is often the case in companies where there is a limited number of staff in the accounting function, there is little or no assurance that the basic controls will continue to operate properly and the auditor will need to extend his work on the items in the financial statements or, where appropriate, carry out further tests on the operation of the basic controls.

The Approach in Computer Systems

The nature of controls in a computer system

3.06　As in non-computer systems, the object of controls is to ensure that authorised data is completely and accurately processed. Some controls in computer systems carried out manually, mainly in user departments, remain similar to those found in non-computer systems. Controls of this nature are termed **user controls** in this book. However, the nature of computer processing imposes, and provides the opportunities for, significant changes in the methods of controlling and processing data. The extent of change will depend on the scope of computer processing in each system. The principal changes are:

(a) Many accounting and control procedures, which were previously carried out manually, will be replaced by steps in the computer programs. The procedures that will be of concern to the auditor are referred to in this book as **programmed procedures**.

(b) The continued and proper operation of programmed procedures can be controlled by effective integrity controls. **Integrity controls** is the term given in this book to those controls, mainly in the computer department, over, *inter alia,* the implementation, security and use of computer programs. As a result, whereas in a non-computer system the effective operation of the equivalent procedures is normally based on checking the results of processing, in a computer system it is rare to check fully by manual means the results of processing because reliance can be placed on the integrity controls for the consistent operation of programmed procedures.

(c) The reduced checking of the output from processing means that extra care is necessary to ensure that the data used in processing is valid. This is particularly true of standing data, such as rates of pay or inventory prices, which is held permanently on the master files. Controls are needed to ensure that the data remains properly held. These controls will normally comprise a combination of checking the data on files and preventing unauthorised access to the files. These latter controls are termed data file security controls in this book and form part of the integrity controls referred to above.

3.07 Thus, in the audit of a computer system, the auditor will be concerned with the user controls and the procedures and controls which are unique to computer systems and which have been briefly mentioned above – programmed procedures and integrity controls. These different types of procedures and controls are considered further in the following paragraphs.

User controls

3.08 User controls are defined as manual controls carried out on the data being processed. Users, for this purpose, may include all those who are not involved in computer operations. They thus include user departments and, in some cases, control sections within computer departments.

3.09 Some user controls will be unrelated to computer processing. These would include such controls as checking the quality and condition of goods received or ensuring that all transactions are initially recorded. Other user controls will be related to computer processing and will only be effective if the related programmed procedure operates properly. For example, the investigation of items reported by the computer as missing or exceptional will only be effective if the missing or exceptional items are properly reported. In certain cases, there will be other user controls which have as their purpose the checking of programmed procedures, for example the detailed checking to source data of a print-out of standing data amendments.

3.10 User control techniques will be broadly similar to those in non-computer systems. The main difference will be that many of the controls will be carried out on computer output rather than manually-produced reports. A further difference is that certain procedures become more formalised, for example the correction of errors. User controls include such techniques as checking computer output to source data or pre-determined totals, checking computer reconciliations and investigating computer-produced rejections and exception reports.

3.11 The three types of user control are illustrated in Figure 34 which shows part of a sales accounting system. The checking of quantities shipped is unrelated to computer processing. The investigation of missing documents is related to computer processing and will only be effective if the related programmed procedure, in this case the checking of the sequence of despatched documents, operates properly. The review of invoices has as its purpose the checking of a programmed procedure – the calculation of invoices.

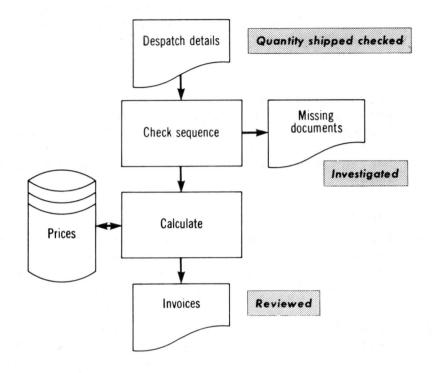

FIG. 34. User controls (3.11)

Programmed procedures

3.12 Programmed procedures can be divided into two types:

- Certain programmed procedures replace *control functions previously carried out manually.* They may test the completeness, accuracy and validity of the data being processed. They include edit tests, the accumulation of the data being processed and agreement with control totals, the accumulation of items on master files and reconciliation with file totals and the identification and reporting of incorrect, exceptional and missing data.

- Other programmed procedures replace *manual operations of an accounting rather than control nature,* for example the calculation and production of sales invoices and payrolls, the updating of master files and the generation of data within the computer.

3.13　The extract of a sales accounting system previously used to illustrate user controls is shown again in Figure 35 to illustrate examples of the two types of programmed procedures, the checking of the sequence of despatch documents, which replaces a manual control, and the calculation of invoices, which replaces a manual accounting function.

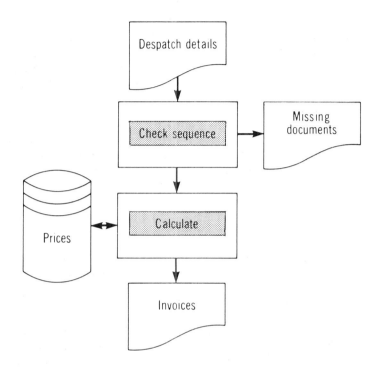

FIG. 35. Programmed procedures (3.13)

Integrity controls

3.14　Integrity controls are those general controls, mainly in the computer department, that are concerned with the computer programs and data files. It is convenient for audit purposes to divide the integrity controls according to their purpose, using the terms by which they will be referred to in this book, as follows:

> **Implementation controls**, designed to ensure that appropriate programmed procedures are effectively included in the program, both when the system originally becomes operational and when changes are subsequently made. They include the controls over the design, testing and taking into operational use of new systems and program changes and the related documentation.

D

Program security controls, designed to ensure that unauthorised changes cannot be made to programmed procedures. They include the controls over the security of programs both while in use (i.e. on the computer) and when not in use (in a physical library).

Computer operations controls, designed to ensure that programmed procedures are consistently applied. They include the controls that programs and data files are properly set up and run in accordance with authorised instructions.

Data file security controls, designed to ensure that unauthorised changes cannot be made to data files. They include the controls over the security of data files both while in use, particularly from unauthorised access through remote terminals, and when not in use (in a physical library).

3.15　The integrity controls will be a combination of manual controls and procedures included in what is termed in this book the system software. **System software** may be defined as those programs, such as the operating system, on whose functioning the auditor may wish to place reliance, although they do not process accounting data. The extent of reliance on system software will vary. For example, when programs are not being used for processing, they may be held under manual control in a physical library or under software control on the computer.

3.16　In general, the same integrity controls are applied to all systems being developed or processed at a computer installation.

3.17　The extract of a sales accounting system previously used to illustrate user controls and programmed procedures is shown again in Figure 36 to illustrate the scope of integrity controls. The implementation, program security and computer operations controls relate to the programmed procedures (sequence check and calculation of invoices) while the data file security controls protect the prices file.

Disciplines

3.18　The disciplines over basic controls in computer systems are similar to those in non-computer systems and can conveniently be divided into the same three types – supervisory controls, segregation of duties and custodial controls. These disciplines, which are all manual in nature, operate in both the user and computer departments and are discussed further in the following paragraphs.

Supervisory controls

3.19　Supervisory controls consist of the supervision of the operation of a basic control to ensure that it continues to operate. For example, in a user department, there would need to be a regular check by a responsible official that the investigation of data rejected by the computer is being carried out regularly. Likewise, in the computer department, the adequacy of the testing procedures for program changes would require to be reviewed and approved by a suitable computer department manager.

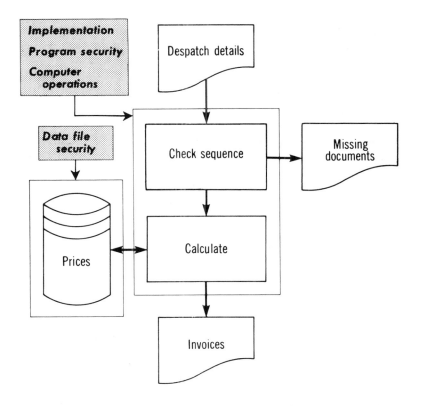

FIG. 36. Integrity controls (3.17)

Segregation of duties

3.20　Segregation of duties involves the work of one person providing a check over the operation of another. In relation to user controls an obvious example is that the persons carrying out controls on data should be independent of computer operations. In relation to integrity controls it is important, for example, that those responsible for testing and implementing new systems should not also be responsible for operating those systems.

Custodial controls

3.21　Custodial controls are concerned with the custody of assets and can involve:

- Separation of responsibility for the custody of assets from the records which account for them; for example, the user controls relating to a computer inventory file should be performed or checked by persons other than those involved in maintaining physical custody of the inventory.

- Physical arrangements which prevent unauthorised access to assets or their related records – for example the security arrangements applied to the cash office or terminals.

77

3.22 The extract of a sales accounting system previously used to illustrate user controls, programmed procedures and integrity controls is shown again in Figure 37 to illustrate examples of disciplines. The disciplines shown relate to the user controls. Those persons checking quantities shipped should not also have custody of inventories, the work of investigating missing documents should be supervised and those persons responsible for reviewing sales invoices should be independent of computer operations. In practice, further disciplines would be required both as regards the user controls illustrated and the integrity controls.

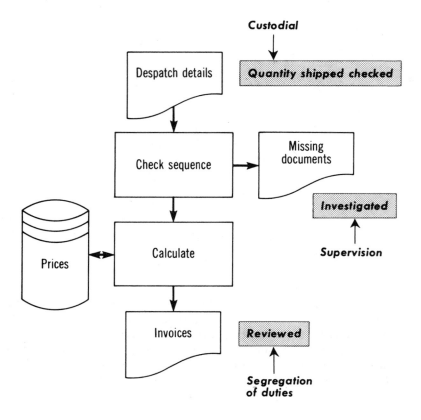

FIG. 37. Disciplines (3.22)

Determining the controls on which to place reliance

3.23 In any system, determining the controls on which to place reliance is usually a question of identifying the controls which the company has established to ensure the completeness and accuracy of the relevant accounting records. This will normally involve an evaluation of user controls, programmed procedures and integrity controls. However, there are occasions when the auditor will need to make a choice as to the way in which he will proceed and the alternatives are outlined in the following paragraphs.

3.24   There is still a tendency for companies to establish more controls than either the management or the auditor may need to rely on. This usually results from a duplication of user controls and programmed procedures. The auditor will normally wish to choose only the controls on which to place reliance. His choice will be dictated by the relative audit efficiencies involved.

3.25   In some simple computer systems, the auditor may not need to rely on integrity controls because the effective operation of programmed procedures is ensured by the user controls. For example, if a computer listing of missing prenumbered documents included the numbers of all documents that should have been processed, with an identification of those documents that were missing, and the user controls included, in addition to an investigation of missing numbers, a review to determine that all documents sent for processing appeared on the listing, the auditor would not need to place reliance on the integrity controls. Situations of this nature are becoming less common and, in any event, the auditor will wish to decide whether it is more efficient to place reliance on the integrity controls.

3.26   In certain circumstances, the auditor may decide that it is more efficient to reduce his reliance on the integrity controls by increasing the level of reperformance which he carries out on the programmed procedures. In this way he may be able to satisfy himself that they continued to function properly throughout the period under audit.

3.27   When new computer systems are introduced, the auditor may often decide it is more efficient to reduce his reliance on implementation controls by testing the programmed procedures as at the date the system first went operational. In this way he avoids the need to rely on the implementation controls as regards the introduction of that system.

Timing of evaluation

3.28   It is highly desirable to evaluate the controls in a computer system before it becomes operational. This is more important than in a non-computer system for the following reasons:

(a) It is difficult to make changes to a computer system once it is operational. The auditor should therefore make any suggestions or recommendations at the relevant stage of development so that they can be incorporated without problem. Indeed, clients often encourage or specifically require the auditor's evaluation and comments prior to implementation.

(b) The auditor will need to know the nature and extent of programmed procedures in order to decide whether to rely on and test the implementation controls. Without adequate lead time before implementation he may be unable to plan and perform the tests.

(c) The auditor may be able to arrange for additional features to be included in the system that will assist his subsequent audit tests. For example, facilities may be arranged to obtain print-outs on request or for additional fields to be included on master files for subsequent examination by a computer audit program.

3.29 It should be added that, whilst for the above reasons it will be highly desirable for the auditor to review systems prior to their going live, this will not in all cases be possible. Where he is required to evaluate systems which have been in operation for some time, the auditor should bear in mind the possible difficulty of making program changes, which he may nevertheless deem desirable. In these cases he should consider, where practicable, making alternative recommendations to strengthen the user controls.

Additional services

3.30 The scope of the auditor's evaluation of control has already been outlined in paragraphs 3.01 to 3.03. In addition, in computer systems, there are two further services which the auditor is well suited to carry out on behalf of his client. Although these may enhance subsequent audit efficiency, it should be remembered that they are not of direct relevance to the forming of an audit opinion on financial statements.

3.31 First, it may be helpful for the auditor to provide advice on the general approach to controls in a computer system. Frequently companies will be relatively unfamiliar with the design and control of computer systems and will welcome general advice from the auditor. The auditor is often well-qualified to provide this advice as he is likely to have wide experience of the controls applicable to computer systems.

3.32 Secondly, it may be helpful for the auditor to review and test the implementation controls, as applied to specific systems, during each important stage of development, although he does not himself propose to rely on the implementation controls. In this way he can bring any deficiencies that come to his notice to the client's attention in time for remedial action to be taken. Serious faults in operational systems, which, as indicated, can be difficult to correct, can be avoided by these means.

The Internal Control Questionnaire

Design of the ICQ

3.33 The ICQ described in this book has been designed with three features which it may be helpful to outline initially:

- It is designed to evaluate controls, and not to record the details of the system. The recording process will have already taken place, by way of flowcharts or narrative notes, before the ICQ is used. This has already been discussed in Chapter 2.

- It is integrated, that is to say designed to enable the auditor to evaluate basic controls and disciplines in relation to wholly computer systems, wholly non-computer systems and mixed non-computer and computer systems of any kind. How this is achieved is described in later paragraphs.

- It is application-orientated, that is to say separate questions are asked about sales, purchase and other systems rather than common questions for computer systems in general.

Control objectives

3.34   The ICQ is based on the principle of the **control objective**. Any business involves a number of major accounting activities which require to be adequately controlled, and for each of which there must be several significant control objectives. For example, a common activity of importance to the majority of business concerns will be control of accounts payable. In particular, it will be necessary to ensure that all proper creditors, but only those creditors, are entered in the accounts payable records. This requirement can be summarised in the control objective *"All valid accounts payable transactions, and only those transactions, should be accurately recorded as accounts payable"*.

3.35   If the controls relevant to a control objective are not achieved, doubt is cast on the reliability of the accounting activity concerned, which in turn brings into question the accuracy of the related item or items in the financial statements. If, for example, there is inadequate control over the identification of goods received but not invoiced, the amount shown for creditors in the financial statements is susceptible to error. The use of control objectives facilitates the relating of control weaknesses to their accounting significance and enables weaknesses to be more readily assessed in relation to their possible impact on the financial statements.

3.36   The ICQ referred to in this book consists of thirty-three standard control objectives designed to apply to the common activities of most industrial and commercial undertakings. These control objectives are listed in appendix A to this chapter. The auditor evaluates the controls relevant to the achievement of each control objective by reference to a series of questions. Questions for the relevant basic controls and disciplines are therefore provided for each of the control objectives.

3.37   It may be necessary to design supplementary control objectives for less common activities that may be sufficiently important in a particular business to warrant separate systems of processing and control, for example returnable containers delivered. In addition, other specialised listings of control objectives and questions will be useful for evaluating the activities of specialised undertakings such as insurance companies, banks and building societies.

3.38   To assist in using the ICQ, the standard control objectives (each with its related questions) have been grouped into three cycles, one for each of the main activities of a manufacturing company; these are called the payments, production and revenue cycles. The remaining control objectives, which do not fall naturally into any of these cycles, are included in a separate section of the ICQ. The listing of control objectives in appendix A to this chapter is divided into these groups.

Computer and manual questions

3.39   Although the control objectives remain the same however transactions are processed, alternative sets of questions are available for applicable control objectives so as to recognise the difference in processing and control techniques between computer and non-computer systems. There are some control objectives that only have one common set of questions to be used whether processing is manual or by computer. This is because either there are insufficient differences in control techniques to warrant separate sets of questions or the procedures relating to the control objectives are unlikely to be processed by computer.

3.40   For each relevant control objective, the auditor will select either the manual or computer set of questions, as appropriate. In this way the need to correlate a general purpose ICQ with a separate appendix for computer processing is avoided.

3.41   Computer questions for a selection of control objectives are included in appendix B to this chapter. These are included for illustration purposes and do not comprise a complete set of those questions required in practice. Reference will be made to the questions in subsequent chapters. The manual sets of questions have not been included as it is not a purpose of this book to consider the appropriate questions to ask where non-computer processing is employed. However, a review of the computer questions will indicate that they can be integrated with the types of question normally used to evaluate the controls in non-computer systems.

3.42   In appendix B the questions that relate to the disciplines, as defined in paragraphs 3.18 to 3.22, have been marked off as follows:

    C – Custodial controls.
    D – Segregation of duties.
    S – Supervisory controls.

Questions that are not marked with a letter relate to basic controls.

3.43   The purpose of marking the questions in this manner is to assist the auditor whose response to weaknesses relating to basic controls will usually be different from his response to weaknesses relating to disciplines.

Controls over standing data

3.44   There is a separate section of the ICQ **(Standing Data Controls)** for evaluating controls over the amendment and maintenance of standing data on master files. Under each control objective to which these controls apply, there is a question with respect to the overall adequacy of the relevant controls.

Integrity controls

3.45   There is a separate section of the ICQ **(Integrity Controls)** for evaluating integrity controls. Under each control objective there is a question with respect to the overall adequacy of implementation, program security and computer operations controls. Under each control objective where controls over data file maintenance are relevant, and in the standing data controls section, there is a question with respect to the overall adequacy of data file security controls.

Selecting the questions

3.46   Computer questions will be used when any of the processing relating to a control objective is performed by computer. The ICQ is so designed that any combination of manual and computer questions can be assembled to form the ICQ. These combinations can be illustrated by showing how the control objectives with computer and manual questions will be selected for evaluating the various examples of sales and purchase accounting computer systems described in the appendix to Chapter 2.

Sales accounting

3.47   As can be seen in appendix A, there are six control objectives in the revenue cycle which are relevant to sales accounting computer systems. These are numbers 30, 31, 33, 34, 35 and 38. One of these control objectives (number 33 which deals with returns by customers) has common questions, thus leaving five control objectives for which it must be decided whether to use manual or computer questions. In addition, control objective 55, which deals with the adequacy of the provision for doubtful debts, will be relevant to sales accounting.

3.48   Three types of sales accounting systems were described in paragraph 15 of appendix A to Chapter 2 – accounts receivable systems, invoicing systems and order processing systems. The number of control objectives with manual and computer questions required for each of these systems is described in the following paragraphs.

D*

3.49   **Accounts receivable systems,** where the computer maintains the accounts receivable ledger, and order processing and invoicing are non-computer operations, require the following three control objectives with computer questions:

> Control objective 35
> *"All valid accounts receivable transactions, and only those transactions, should be accurately recorded as accounts receivable".*

> Control objective 38
> *"General ledger entries arising from the revenue cycle should be accurately determined".*

> Control objective 55
> *"All doubtful accounts receivable should be identified (either individually or by categories) as a basis for determining any provisions required for such accounts".*

In accounts receivable systems, manual questions would be used for the other control objectives, 30, 31 and 34, since the computer is not involved in the processing relevant to these objectives.

3.50   **Invoicing systems,** where the computer is involved in invoicing and maintaining the accounts receivable ledger, but order processing remains a manual operation, require five control objectives with computer questions. These five control objectives are the three noted in paragraph 3.49 for accounts receivable systems to which are added the following two control objectives:

> Control objective 31
> *"Control should be established over goods shipped and services performed as a basis for:*
> > *(a) making charges to customers for all such sales;*
> > *(b) determining the amount of the related revenues which have not been entered as accounts receivable;*
> > *(c) where required, making the related entries in the detailed inventory records".*

> Control objective 34
> *"All charges and credits should be appropriately checked as being valid before being entered in the accounts receivable records".*

In invoicing systems manual questions would be used only for control objective 30.

3.51   **Order processing systems,** where the computer is involved in the processing of all components of sales accounting, require six control objectives with computer questions. These six control objectives are the five noted in paragraph 3.50 for invoicing systems to which is added:

> Control objective 30
> *"Records should be maintained of unfulfilled sales commitments as a basis for determining any provision required for losses arising therefrom".*

Thus in order processing systems computer questions would be used for all control objectives.

Sales accounting and finished goods inventory

3.52 It is common for invoicing and order processing systems to be integrated with the maintenance of inventory records for finished goods. Where this is so, computer questions will be used for control objective 37 (finished goods records) and, depending on the scope of the inventory control system, computer questions may also be used for control objectives 52 (inventory costs) and 53 (provisions against inventory). Thus, sales accounting systems may require from three to nine control objectives with computer questions, as can be seen in Figure 38 which summarises the combinations.

Type of System

Control Objective	Sales Accounting			Sales Accounting and Finished Goods Inventory	
	Accounts receivable	Invoicing	Order processing	Invoicing and stock	Order processing and stock
30	M	M	C	M	C
31	M	C	C	C	C
34	M	C	C	C	C
35	C	C	C	C	C
37	M	M	M	C	C
38	C	C	C	C	C
52	M	M	M	C	C
53	M	M	M	C	C
55	C	C	C	C	C

C = Computer questions
M = Manual questions

Fig. 38. Use of computer and manual ICQ questions – sales accounting and finished goods inventory systems (3.52)

Purchase accounting

3.53 There are six control objectives in the payments cycle relevant to purchase accounting systems. These are numbers 1 to 5 and 13. One of these control objectives (number 3 dealing with returns to suppliers) has common questions, thus leaving five control objectives for which it must be decided whether to use manual or computer questions.

3.54 Three types of purchase accounting systems were described in paragraph 31 of appendix A to Chapter 2 – accounts payable systems, goods received processing systems and order processing systems. The number of control objectives with computer questions required for each of these systems is given in the following paragraphs.

3.55 **Accounts payable systems**, where the computer maintains the accounts payable ledger, and order processing and goods received processing are non-computer operations, require two control objectives with computer questions:

> Control objective 5
> *"All valid accounts payable transactions, and only those transactions, should be accurately recorded as accounts payable".*

> Control objective 13
> *"General ledger entries arising from the payments cycle should be accurately determined".*

In accounts payable systems, manual questions would be used for the other control objectives, 1, 2 and 4, since the computer is not involved in the processing relevant to these objectives.

3.56 **Goods received processing systems**, where the computer is involved in goods received processing and maintaining the accounts payable ledger, but order processing remains a manual operation, require four control objectives with computer questions. These four control objectives are the two in paragraph 3.55 for accounts payable systems to which are added:

> Control objective 2
> *"Control should be established over goods and services received as a basis for:*
> *(a) determining and recording the liability for goods and services received but not entered as accounts payable;*
> *(b) where required, posting items to detailed inventory records."*

> Control objective 4
> *"Invoices and related documentation should be properly checked and approved as being valid before being entered as accounts payable".*

In goods received processing systems manual questions would be used only for control objective 1.

3.57 **Order processing systems**, where the computer is involved in the processing of all components of purchase accounting, require five control objectives with computer questions. These five control objectives are the four noted in paragraph 3.56 for goods received processing systems to which is added:

> Control objective 1
> *"Purchases should be initiated only on the basis of appropriate authorisations and records of commitments should be maintained as a basis for:*
> *(a) determining that transactions are executed in accordance with authorisations;*
> *(b) establishing the amount of any provision required for losses arising from unfulfilled commitments."*

Thus in order processing systems computer questions would be used for all control objectives.

3.58 It is common for any of the purchase accounting systems described to include computer involvement in the payment of creditors. In these cases computer questions would be used for control objective 9 (disbursements).

Purchase accounting and raw materials inventory

3.59 It is also common for goods received processing and order processing systems to be integrated with the maintenance of inventory records for raw materials. Where this is so, computer questions will be used for control objective 10 (raw material records) and, as explained in paragraph 3.52, computer questions may also be used for control objectives 52 and 53. Thus purchase accounting systems may require from two to nine control objectives with computer questions, as can be seen in Figure 39 which summarises the combinations.

Other systems

3.60 Simple systems require few control objectives with computer questions. For example, payroll requires control objectives 6 and 13 with computer questions and fixed assets also require only two control objectives with

Type of System

Control Objective	Purchase Accounting			Purchase Accounting and Raw Materials Inventory	
	Accounts payable	Goods received	Order processing	Goods received and stock	Order processing and stock
1	M	M	C	M	C
2	M	C	C	C	C
4	M	C	C	C	C
5	C	C	C	C	C
9	C	C	C	C	C
10	M	M	M	C	C
13	C	C	C	C	C
52	M	M	M	C	C
53	M	M	M	C	C

C = Computer questions
M = Manual questions

Fig. 39. Use of computer and manual ICQ questions – purchase accounting and raw material inventory systems (3.59)

computer questions, numbers 12 and 13. At the other extreme, highly integrated computer systems will require many control objectives with computer questions. The examples have illustrated how, when stocks are integrated with sales or purchase accounting, there may be up to nine control objectives with computer questions. In the most complex systems where payments, production and revenue are integrated, up to twenty-three control objectives with computer questions may be required.

Completion of the ICQ

Identifying the control objectives

3.61 The first step in the completion of the ICQ is to identify the control objectives relevant to the business and on which the auditor wishes to place reliance. In some cases the auditor may decide not to evaluate the control procedures because either:

(a) the activity to which a control objective relates will be insignificant from an audit viewpoint on the grounds that, in total, the transactions and related assets or liabilities are not material to the financial statements; or

(b) although the subject matter of a control objective is material, it is more efficient to employ extended validation procedures of account activities and balances rather than rely on the related control procedures, for example, as regards control objective 12, where fixed asset records can be examined and depreciation calculated using a computer audit program.

In addition, the auditor will need to consider whether there are any significant business activities that are not covered by the standard objectives and for which supplementary control objectives and detailed questions should be devised.

Answering the questions

3.62 Once the relevant control objectives have been identified, it will be necessary to select the manual or computer sets of questions, as indicated in paragraphs 3.46 to 3.60. Each set of questions has the same column for answers as those illustrated in the extract from the ICQ in Figure 40. The procedure for completing the answers is as follows:

(a) Each question has been phrased so that it is answered "yes" or "no" and thereby indicates, respectively, by a tick in the appropriate column, the presence or absence of a control procedure.

(b) The questions are answered, as far as possible using the information contained in the flowcharts or other record of the system, and the appropriate reference is entered in the ICQ.

(c) Where a "yes" answer is recorded, the operation of the control will normally be subsequently tested. A reference to the appropriate functional test is included.

Control Objective

6. *Payments in respect of wages and salaries should be:*

    (a) made only to company employees at authorised rates of pay;

    (b) where required, in accordance with records of work performed;

    (c) accurately calculated.

Questions	Flow-chart Ref.	Yes	No	'Yes' Answers Functional test Ref.	'No' Answers CC	RCW
Standing Payroll Data List below the standing data fields used in the preparation of payrolls (e.g. rate of pay, deductions, employee number, commission rates) and state on which file these fields are recorded Employee number (EMPNUM) Rate of pay (EMPPAY) Tax code (EMPTAX) N.I. deduction (EMPNIC) Loan deductions (EMPLOAN) Bonus rate (EMPBON) } Employee master file (EMPMASTER)						
6.1 In respect of each field listed above, review the answers to the standing data controls section. Are there adequate controls over: (a) where applicable, file creation; (b) the authorisation of amendments; (c) the completeness of writing amendments to the file; (d) the accuracy of writing amendments to the file; (e) the maintenance of the data on the file?	7/5-11 2/17 2/24 2/26 3/08	✓ ✓ ✓	 ✓ ✓	M/13 M/14 M/15	 ✓	✓

Fig. 40. ICQ – specimen layout (3.62)

3.63 Where one or more "no" answers arise, the following steps should be taken:

(a) The first step is to determine whether there are compensating controls. For example, a weakness in the input controls to a raw materials file might be compensated for by regular physical checking of the inventory, or a weakness in the maintenance controls over an accounts payable file might be compensated for by regular checking of the accounts payable with statements from suppliers. Where compensating controls are identified, they are recorded in the ICQ under the heading "compensating controls" and are referenced to the questions to which they relate.

(b) Where there are no compensating controls, a control weakness is assumed to exist which may affect audit procedures and which should be reported to the client. These assumed weaknesses are entered on the Record of Control Weaknesses ("RCW") and are dealt with as outlined in Chapter 8 "The Audit Response to Internal Control Weaknesses".

3.64 The following procedures are required for recording weaknesses relating to controls over standing data and integrity controls:

(a) where the assessment to the overall question in a control objective is "no", it will normally be appropriate to record the overall weakness and the detailed weaknesses together;

(b) where the assessment to the overall question is "yes" in spite of "no" answers to the supporting questions, the auditor should state why the weaknesses do not have a material effect on the overall adequacy of the related controls;

(c) where a weakness relates to the overall adequacy of standing data or data file security controls, the data thereby at risk, such as rates of pay or sales prices, should be recorded;

(d) where a weakness relates to the overall adequacy of implementation, program security or computer operations controls, the programmed procedures thereby at risk should be recorded.

3.65 The disposal of each "no" answer is recorded by placing a tick in either the column of the ICQ headed "CC" (compensating control) or in the column headed "RCW" as appropriate.

Summary

3.66 In order to carry out an effective evaluation it is first necessary to understand the nature of controls in a computer system. In addition to the manual controls carried out on the data being processed, referred to as "user controls", the auditor will be concerned with the further types of procedures and control which are unique to computer systems, termed "programmed procedures" and "integrity controls". Programmed procedures include steps in the program that may assist in the control of the data being processed. Integrity controls are the controls over the programs and files and comprise implementation, program security, computer operations and data file security controls. These different types of controls comprise both basic controls and disciplines. The disciplines are similar to those in non-computer systems and can conveniently be divided into the same three types, supervisory controls, segregation of duties and custodial controls. These disciplines, which are all manual in nature, operate in both the user and computer departments.

3.67   When he comes to his evaluation of the controls in a computer system, the auditor may often find more controls than he needs to rely on, and will make a choice, dictated by audit efficiency, as to those on which to place reliance. For practical reasons he will wish to carry out his evaluation before the system becomes operational. In so doing, there may be additional services, for example general advice on controls, which the auditor can provide to his client.

3.68   As a means to evaluate controls, an integrated ICQ based on control objectives and related questions is suggested. While the control objectives remain the same however transactions are processed, alternative questions are available to recognise the differences in processing and control techniques between computer and non-computer systems. In this way a single integrated ICQ for the whole system (both computer and non-computer) can be assembled and the need to correlate a general purpose ICQ with a separate appendix for computer processing is avoided.

3: Appendix A
Control Objectives

This appendix includes the thirty-three standard control objectives contained in the ICQ considered herein. They are designed to apply to the common activities of most industrial and commercial undertakings. To assist in using the ICQ, the standard control objectives have been grouped into three cycles, one for each of the main activities of a manufacturing company; these are called the payments, production and revenue cycles. The remaining control objectives, which do not fall naturally into any of these cycles, are grouped together under the heading "Other Control Objectives".

Payments cycle

1   Purchases should be initiated only on the basis of appropriate authorisations and records of commitments should be maintained as a basis for:

   (a) determining that transactions are executed in accordance with authorisations;

   (b) establishing the amount of any provision required for losses arising from unfulfilled commitments.

2   Control should be established over goods and services received as a basis for:

   (a) determining and recording the liability for goods and services received but not entered as accounts payable;

   (b) where required, posting the items to detailed inventory records.

3   Control should be established over goods returned to and claims on suppliers as a basis for:

   (a) obtaining credit for all such items;

   (b) where required, posting the items to detailed inventory records.

4   Invoices and related documentation should be properly checked and approved as being valid before being entered as accounts payable.

5   All valid accounts payable transactions, and only those transactions, should be accurately recorded as accounts payable.

6   Payments in respect of wages and salaries should be:

   (a) made only to company employees at authorised rates of pay;

   (b) where required, in accordance with records of work performed;

   (c) accurately calculated.

93

7   Payroll deductions should be correctly accounted for and paid to the third parties to whom they are due.

8   Reimbursements of imprest and similar funds (e.g. postage and other franking meters, payroll deduction stamps) should be made only for valid transactions.

9   Disbursements from bank accounts should be made only in respect of valid transactions.

10   Accurate detailed records should be maintained of materials and supplies inventories.

11   Additions to and disposals of property, plant and equipment should be properly authorised.

12   Accurate records should be maintained of the cost and accumulated depreciation of property, plant and equipment.

13   General ledger entries arising from the payments cycle should be accurately determined.

Production cycle

20   Control should be established over:

    (a) issues from inventories of materials and supplies to production, and returns;

    (b) charges to production for labour and overheads;

    (c) transfers from production to inventories of parts and finished products;

as a basis, where required, for making the entries in the inventory records.

21   Accurate inventory records should be maintained of work in progress.

22   General ledger entries arising from the production cycle should be accurately determined.

30 Records should be maintained of unfulfilled sales commitments as a basis for determining any provision required for losses arising therefrom.

31 Control should be established over goods shipped and services performed as a basis for:

(a) making charges to customers for all such sales;

(b) determining the amount of the related revenues which have not been entered as accounts receivable;

(c) where required, making the related entries in the detailed inventory records.

32 Control should be established over cash sales of goods and services as a basis for:

(a) accounting for all such sales;

(b) where required, making the related entries in the detailed inventory records.

33 Control should be established over goods returned and claims received from customers as a basis for:

(a) determining and recording the liability for goods returned and claims received but not entered in the accounts receivable records;

(b) where required, making the related entries in the detailed inventory records.

34 All charges and credits should be appropriately checked as being valid before being entered in the accounts receivable records.

35 All valid accounts receivable transactions, and only those transactions, should be accurately recorded as accounts receivable.

36 Control should be established over all cash and cheques received and they should be deposited promptly in the company's bank accounts.

37 Accurate detailed records should be maintained of finished products.

38 General ledger entries arising from the revenue cycle should be accurately determined.

95

Other control objectives

50   All valid general ledger entries, and only those entries, should be accurately recorded in the general ledger.

51   Adequate procedures should be followed to confirm the physical existence of inventories recorded in the general ledger.

52   Costs attributable to inventories should be accurately determined.

53   Adequate steps should be taken to identify all inventories for which provisions may be required.

54   Adequate steps should be taken to confirm the physical existence of, and, if appropriate, the title to, property, plant and equipment.

55   All doubtful accounts receivable should be identified (either individually or by categories) as a basis for determining any provisions required for such accounts.

56   Adequate steps should be taken to confirm the accuracy of the bank balances shown in the general ledger.

57   Investments should be adequately safeguarded and accurately accounted for.

3: Appendix B
Computer Questions

1   This appendix includes the computer questions for control objectives 2, 4, 5, 6, 9, 10, 12, 13 and 34. These are included for illustration purposes and do not comprise a full set of the computer questions required in practice. However, they are representative and include examples of all the principal types of question used in the ICQ described herein. These questions are explained in Chapter 4.

2   A review of the questions will show that in all control objectives reference is made to the integrity controls section. The integrity controls section is also included in this appendix and the questions are explained in Chapters 5 and 6. Chapter 5 also contains an explanation of how the integrity controls section is used.

3   In many control objectives reference is made to the standing data controls section. This section is included in this appendix and its use is explained in paragraph 4.94.

4   Several comments relating to the detailed structure of the ICQ are made in paragraphs 4.92 to 4.98.

Control objective

2.   *Control should be established over goods and services received as a basis for:*

  (a)   determining and recording the liability for goods and services received but not entered as accounts payable;
  (b)   where required, posting items to detailed inventory records.

Initial recording of receipt of goods and services

2.1   Are the following checked by suitable methods (e.g. by counting or weighing and inspecting goods received) and the results recorded at the time of their receipt for subsequent checking with the related invoices:

  (a)   nature, quantity and condition of goods received (including property, plant and equipment and major supplies, e.g. fuel, stationery);
  (b)   major services received (to the extent practicable)?

Completeness of input and updating

2.2 Is the principal control that all details of goods and, where applicable, services received are input to the computer and updated
one of the following (specify which):

(a) computer matching with a file of purchase commitments placed;
If yes, answer 2.3 to 2.6

(b) computer sequence check of serially numbered input documents;
If yes, answer 2.7 to 2.12

(c) agreement of manually established batch totals (specify totals
used)?
If yes, answer 2.13 to 2.17

Computer matching

2.3 Review the answers to control objective 1. Are the matching
procedures adequate to confirm that details of goods and, where
applicable, services received are input completely?

2.4 Is a total (specify total used) of accepted items accumulated by the
computer during the matching run and either:

(a) agreed to the total of items written to the receipts file; or
(b) carried through intermediate processing (including summarisation
of totals or changes in the totals used) so that it is established that
all accepted input items are updated to the receipts file?

2.5 Is the reconciliation of totals in 2.4 carried out:

(a) manually; or
(b) by the computer and, if so, is adequate evidence of this check
printed out?

2.6 Are there adequate procedures for the:

(a) investigation and correction of differences disclosed by the
matching process; (2.3)
(b) investigation and correction of differences disclosed by the update
reconciliations? (2.5)

Computer sequence check

2.7 Are there adequate procedures to ensure that all transactions are
recorded on a serially numbered document?

2.8 Is the method used in the program for the checking of numerical
sequence appropriate (e.g. does it cater for changes in sequence
and more than one sequence running at a time)?

2.9 Is a print-out of missing documents produced at regular intervals (e.g. weekly)?

2.10 Is a total (specify total used) of accepted items accumulated by the computer during the sequence check run and either:

(a) agreed to the total of items written to the receipts file; or
(b) carried through intermediate processing (including summarisation of totals or changes in the totals used) so that it is established that all accepted input items are updated to the receipts file?

2.11 Is the reconciliation of totals in 2.10 carried out:

(a) manually; or
(b) by the computer and, if so, is adequate evidence of this check printed out?

2.12 Are there adequate procedures for:

(a) investigation of missing documents; (2.9)
(b) investigation and correction of differences disclosed by the update reconciliations? (2.11)

Batch totals

2.13 Are there adequate controls that:

(a) a document is raised for all goods and services received;
(b) all documents are included in a batch;
(c) all batches are submitted for processing?

2.14 Are pre-determined control totals either:

(a) input and agreed by the computer with the accumulation of individual items accepted and, if so, is adequate evidence of this check printed out; or
(b) agreed manually with the total of accepted items accumulated and printed out by the computer?

2.15 Are the totals in 2.14 either:

(a) agreed to the total of items written to the receipts file; or
(b) carried through intermediate processing (including summarisation of totals or changes in the totals used) so that it is established that all accepted input items are updated to the receipts file?

2.16 Is the reconciliation of totals in 2.15 carried out:

(a) manually; or
(b) by the computer and, if so, is adequate evidence of this check printed out?

99

2.17 Are there adequate procedures for:

(a) investigation and correction of differences disclosed by the input reconciliations; (2.14)
(b) resubmission of all rejections;
(c) investigation and correction of differences disclosed by the update reconciliations? (2.16)

Disciplines over completeness controls

2.18 Are the following procedures either performed or checked by persons other than those involved in computer operations:

(a) investigation and correction of differences disclosed by the matching process; (2.6a) (D)
(b) investigation of missing documents; (2.12a) (D)
(c) manual agreement of input totals; (2.14b) (D)
(d) investigation and correction of differences disclosed by the input reconciliations; (2.17a) (D)
(e) resubmission of all rejections; (2.17b) (D)
(f) manual agreement of update totals; (2.5a, 2.11a, 2.16a) (D)
(g) investigation and correction of differences disclosed by the update reconciliations? (2.6b, 2.12b, 2.17c) (D)

2.19 Are the results of the following procedures reviewed and approved by a responsible official:

(a) investigation and correction of differences disclosed by the matching process; (2.6a) (S)
(b) investigation of missing documents; (2.12a) (S)
(c) manual agreement of input totals; (2.14b) (S)
(d) investigation and correction of differences disclosed by the input reconciliations; (2.17a) (S)
(e) resubmission of all rejections; (2.17b) (S)
(f) manual agreement of update totals; (2.5a, 2.11a, 2.16a) (S)
(g) investigation and correction of differences disclosed by the update reconciliations? (2.6b, 2.12b, 2.17c) (S)

Accuracy of input and updating

2.20 Are there adequate controls that the following fields are accurately input and updated (e.g. batch totals, edit checks in programs, reporting of non-matched items):

(a) quantity/value;
(b) inventory/vendor reference fields;
(c) price;
(d) date?

2.21 Are there adequate procedures for:

(a) the agreement of totals, where applicable;
(b) investigation and correction of differences or exceptions?

2.22 Are the following procedures either performed or checked by persons other than those involved in computer operations:

(a) agreement of totals, where applicable; (2.21a) (D)
(b) investigation and correction of differences or exceptions? (2.21b) (D)

2.23 Are the results of the following procedures reviewed and approved by a responsible official:

(a) agreement of totals, where applicable; (2.21a) (S)
(b) investigation and correction of differences or exceptions? (2.21b) (S)

Liability for unprocessed invoices

2.24 If the computer evaluates details of goods and services received, review the answers to the standing data controls section as regards prices and vendors. Are there adequate controls over:

(a) where applicable, file creation;
(b) the authorisation of amendments;
(c) the completeness of writing amendments to the file;
(d) the accuracy of writing amendments to the file;
(e) the maintenance of the data on file?

2.25 Is the method used in the program for the calculation of value appropriate?

2.26 Are there adequate controls over the file holding details of outstanding goods and, where applicable, services received so that such details are completely and accurately maintained and subject only to authorised adjustments (e.g. manual control account)?

2.27 Is the method used in the program to match invoices to goods and, where applicable, services received appropriate (e.g. to flag or delete matched items)?

2.28 Is a print-out of items outstanding for an unreasonable length of time (e.g. all over one month) produced at regular intervals?

2.29 Are unmatched records of goods and, where applicable, services (2.28) reviewed on a regular basis (e.g. monthly) to determine the reasons for any such receipts which have not been matched within a reasonable period of time?

2.30 Are there systematic procedures for determining on a regular basis the liabilities for major services received and payments to be made other than any checked by the procedures in 2.26 to 2.29 (e.g. telephone services, municipal taxes or rates, liabilities under leases, royalties, commissions)?

2.31 Are the following procedures either performed or checked by persons other than those involved in computer operations:

(a) maintenance control over the outstanding goods and services received file; (2.26) (D)

(b) review of unmatched records of goods and, where applicable, services received; (2.29) (D)

(c) determination of liability for services not covered in 2.26 to 2.29? (2.30) (D)

2.32 Are the results of the following procedures reviewed and approved by a responsible official:

(a) maintenance control over the outstanding goods and services received file; (2.26) (S)

(b) review of unmatched records of goods and, where applicable, services received; (2.29) (S)

(c) determination of liability for services not covered in 2.26 to 2.29? (2.30) (S)

Entries in inventory records

2.33 Where required, are the records of goods received (2.1) used to post quantities to detailed inventory records?

Integrity controls

2.34 List below the programmed procedures relied upon for the purposes of this control objective.

In respect of the programmed procedures listed above, review the answers to the integrity controls section. Are there adequate controls to ensure that:

(a) appropriate programmed procedures are implemented in respect of:
   (i) where applicable, new systems;
   (ii) program changes;

(b) unauthorised changes cannot be made to programmed procedures;

(c) programmed procedures are consistently used?

Compensating controls

If any "no" answers are compensated by alternative controls, identify such controls below.

Control objective

4. *Invoices and related documentation should be properly checked and approved as being valid before being entered as accounts payable.*

Detailed checking of documentation

4.1   Are invoices for goods and, where applicable, services received checked manually or by the computer (specify which) as to:

(a) quantities and condition of goods received and services rendered;
(b) nature and quantities of goods ordered;
(c) prices and other terms?

Computer checking

Quantities

4.2   As regards the computer checking of invoices with quantities of goods and services received, review the answers to control objective 2:

(a) are there adequate controls that:
   (i) quantities of goods and services received have been accurately recorded and maintained on the file; (2.2 to 2.32)
   (ii) unauthorised records are not added; (2.26)
(b) is the method used in the program to match quantities on invoices with goods and services received records appropriate; (2.27)
(c) are differences disclosed by the matching process adequately investigated and suitable action taken? (2.29)

4.3   If the control that the nature and quantity of goods and services invoiced agrees with that ordered is achieved by the comparison of purchase invoices with receiving records which previously (control objective 2) have been compared to records of goods and services ordered, review the answer to 1.32. Is the method used in the program to match goods and services received to purchase commitments appropriate?

Prices

4.4   If purchase invoices are checked by computer with a record of goods and services ordered and/or received for prices and other terms, review the answers to questions 2.26 to 2.32:

(a) is the method used in the program to match invoices to goods and services received and goods and services received to purchase orders appropriate;
(b) are there adequate controls that unauthorised records are not added to the relevant files?

103

4.5　If invoice/credit memoranda prices are checked by computer with a standard price file:

(a) review the answers to the standing data controls section as regards prices. Are there adequate controls over:
(i) where applicable, file creation;
(ii) the authorisation of amendments;
(iii) the completeness of writing amendments to the file;
(iv) the accuracy of writing amendments to the file;
(v) the maintenance of the data on the files;
(b) is the method used in the program for matching appropriate;
(c) is suitable action taken on variances (e.g. items exceeding a predetermined tolerance are reported and investigated)?

4.6　If extensions and additions of invoices/credit memoranda are checked by the computer:

(a) is the method used in the program appropriate;
(b) is suitable action taken on differences?

4.7　Are the procedures in 4.5(c) and 4.6(b) performed or checked by persons other than those involved in computer operations? (D)

4.8　Are the results of the procedures in 4.5(c) and 4.6(b) reviewed and approved by a responsible official? (S)

Manual checking

4.9　Where invoices for goods received are manually checked, are they checked with respect to:

(a) quantities and conditions of goods received (to receiving records);
(b) nature and quantities of goods ordered (to purchase orders);
(c) prices and other terms (to purchase orders or suppliers' price lists)?

4.10　Are invoices for services received, other than those checked in 4.2 to 4.8, compared with the underlying documentation (e.g. completion reports, leases, records of meter readings) or, if such documentation is not available, approved by a responsible official?

4.11　Are credit (or debit) memoranda checked to confirm that:

(a) they agree with the original records of the goods returned or claims made;
(b) where applicable, the prices agree with the original invoice?

4.12　Are the extensions and additions of invoices and credit (or debit) memoranda checked to an adequate extent?

4.13　Do the invoices and credit (or debit) memoranda bear adequate evidence that the manual checking (4.9 to 4.12) has been carried out?

4.14   Are the following functions performed by separate individuals:

(a) preparation of purchase commitments; (D)
(b) preparation of receiving records; (D)
(c) checking of purchase invoices; (4.9 to 4.13) (D)
(d) computer operations? (D)

4.15   If invoices and credit (or debit) memoranda are checked manually, are they subject to final written approval by a responsible official prior to entry as accounts payable? (S)

4.16   Are adjustments to suppliers' accounts properly documented?

4.17   Are the adjustments and related documentation (4.16) reviewed and approved by a responsible official prior to entry in the accounts payable records? (S)

Integrity controls

4.18   List below the programmed procedures relied upon for the purposes of this control objective.

In respect of the programmed procedures listed above, review the answers to the integrity controls section. Are there adequate controls to ensure that:

(a) appropriate programmed procedures are implemented in respect of:
(i) where applicable, new systems;
(ii) program changes;
(b) unauthorised changes cannot be made to programmed procedures;
(c) programmed procedures are consistently used?

Compensating controls

If any "no" answers are compensated by alternative controls, identify such controls below.

105

Control objective

5. *All valid accounts payable transactions, and only those transactions, should be accurately recorded as accounts payable.*

Accounting for and control over processing of all transactions

Indicate below which of the following are input to update the accounts payable file:

(a) purchase invoices;
(b) credit (or debit) memoranda;
(c) adjustments to suppliers' accounts;
(d) details of cash payments;
(e) other (specify).

Completeness of input and updating

5.1 Is the principal control that all documents in (a) to (e) above are input to the computer and updated one of the following (specify which for each type of input):

(a) computer matching with a file of goods received;
If yes, answer 5.2 to 5.5

(b) agreement of manually established batch totals (specify totals used);
If yes, answer 5.6 to 5.10

(c) computer sequence check of serially numbered input documents;
If yes, answer 5.11 to 5.16

(d) checking of print-outs of items written to the accounts payable file?
If yes, answer 5.17 to 5.20

Computer matching

5.2 Review the answers to control objective 2. Are the matching procedures adequate to confirm that invoices are input completely?

5.3 Is a total (specify total used) of accepted items accumulated by the computer during the matching run and either:

(a) agreed to the total of items written to the accounts payable file; or
(b) carried through intermediate processing (including summarisation of totals or changes in the totals used) so that it is established that all accepted input items are updated to the accounts payable file?

5.4   Is the reconciliation of totals in 5.3 carried out:

   (a) manually; or

   (b) by the computer and, if so, is adequate evidence of this check printed out?

5.5   Are there adequate procedures for:

   (a) investigation and correction of differences disclosed by the matching process; (5.2)

   (b) investigation and correction of differences disclosed by the update reconciliations? (5.4)

Batch totals

5.6   Are there adequate controls that:

   (a) a document is raised for each transaction;

   (b) all documents are included in a batch;

   (c) all batches are submitted for processing?

5.7   Are pre-determined control totals either:

   (a) input and agreed by the computer with the accumulation of individual items accepted and, if so, is adequate evidence of this check printed out; or

   (b) agreed manually with the total of accepted items accumulated and printed out by the computer?

5.8   Are the totals in 5.7 either:

   (a) agreed to the total of items written to the accounts payable file; or

   (b) carried through intermediate processing (including summarisation of totals or changes in the totals used) so that it is established that all accepted input items are updated to the accounts payable file?

5.9   Is the reconciliation of totals in 5.8 carried out:

   (a) manually; or

   (b) by the computer and, if so, is adequate evidence of this check printed out?

5.10   Are there adequate procedures for:

   (a) investigation and correction of differences disclosed by the input reconciliations; (5.7)

   (b) resubmission of all rejections;

   (c) investigation and correction of differences disclosed by the update reconciliations? (5.9)

Computer sequence check

5.11 Are there adequate procedures to ensure that all transactions are recorded on a serially numbered document?

5.12 Is the method used in the program for the checking of numerical sequence appropriate (e.g. does it cater for changes in sequence and more than one sequence running at a time)?

5.13 Is a print-out of missing documents produced at regular intervals (e.g. weekly)?

5.14 Is a total (specify total used) of accepted items accumulated by the computer during the sequence check run and either:

(a) agreed to the total of items written to the accounts payable file; or
(b) carried through intermediate processing (including summarisation of totals or changes in the totals used) so that it is established that all accepted input items are updated to the accounts payable file?

5.15 Is the reconciliation of totals in 5.14 carried out:

(a) manually; or
(b) by the computer and, if so, is adequate evidence of this check printed out?

5.16 Are there adequate procedures for:

(a) investigation of missing documents; (5.13)
(b) investigation and correction of differences disclosed by the update reconciliations? (5.15)

Checking of print-outs

5.17 Are there adequate controls that all documents are submitted for processing (e.g. by checking against retained copy, by manual sequence check)?

5.18 Is there a regular (e.g. monthly) review of source documents for unprocessed items?

5.19 Is the method used in the program for the production of the print-out appropriate (e.g. does it contain details of items that have been written to the accounts payable file)?

5.20 Are there adequate procedures for investigation and correction of differences disclosed by the checking?

5.21 Are the following procedures either performed or checked by persons other than those involved in computer operations and in maintaining a manual accounts payable control account:

(a) investigation and correction of differences disclosed by the matching process; (5.5a) (D)
(b) manual agreement of input totals; (5.7b) (D)
(c) investigation and correction of differences disclosed by the input reconciliations; (5.10a) (D)
(d) resubmission of all rejections; (5.10b) (D)
(e) investigation of missing documents; (5.16a) (D)
(f) regular (e.g. monthly) review of source documents for unprocessed items; (5.18) (D)
(g) investigation and correction of differences disclosed by the checking of print-outs; (5.20) (D)
(h) manual agreement of update totals; (5.4a, 5.9a, 5.15a) (D)
(i) investigation and correction of differences disclosed by the update reconciliations? (5.5b, 5.10c, 5.16b) (D)

5.22 Are the results of the following procedures reviewed and approved by a responsible official:

(a) investigation and correction of differences disclosed by the matching process; (5.5a) (S)
(b) manual agreement of input totals; (5.7b) (S)
(c) investigation and correction of differences disclosed by the input reconciliations; (5.10a) (S)
(d) resubmission of all rejections; (5.10b) (S)
(e) investigation of missing documents; (5.16a) (S)
(f) regular (e.g. monthly) review of source documents for unprocessed items; (5.18) (S)
(g) investigation and correction of differences disclosed by the checking of print-outs; (5.20) (S)
(h) manual agreement of update totals; (5.4a, 5.9a, 5.15a) (S)
(i) investigation and correction of differences disclosed by the update reconciliations? (5.5b, 5.10c, 5.16b) (S)

Accuracy of input and updating

5.23 Are there adequate controls that the following fields are accurately input and updated (e.g. batch totals, edit checks in program, reporting of non-matched items):

(a) value;
(b) vendor reference?

5.24 Are there adequate procedures for:

(a) the agreement of totals, where applicable;
(b) investigation and correction of differences or exceptions?

5.25 Is the method used in the program for the updating of individual accounts appropriate?

5.26 Are the following procedures either performed or checked by persons other than those involved in computer operations and in maintaining a manual accounts payable control account:

(a) agreement of totals, where applicable; (5.24a) (D)
(b) investigation and correction of differences or exceptions? (5.24b) (D)

5.27 Are the results of the following procedures reviewed and approved by a responsible official:

(a) agreement of totals, where applicable; (5.24a) (S)
(b) investigation and correction of differences or exceptions? (5.24b) (S)

Authorisation

5.28 If data is authorised prior to the establishment of the controls for completeness and accuracy of input (e.g. prior to establishment of batch control totals or recording on a sequentially numbered document), are there adequate controls (e.g. checking authorisation after batch control totals established or sequentially numbered document raised) that:

(a) no unauthorised alterations are made to authorised data during subsequent processing;
(b) unauthorised data is not added;
(c) authorised items are not omitted from subsequent processing?

Computer-generated data – payment details

5.29 Where the computer is programmed to generate cheques on the basis of information held on file, review the answers to control objective 9. Are there adequate controls that only valid items are selected for payment and the amount is accurately calculated (e.g. calculation of discount)?

5.30 Is a total (specify total used) of generated items accumulated by the computer and agreed with a total of items written off the accounts payable file:

(a) manually; or
(b) by the computer and, if so, is adequate evidence of this check printed out?

5.31 Are there adequate procedures for the investigation and correction of differences disclosed by the update reconciliations?

5.32 Are the following procedures either performed or checked by persons other than those involved in computer operations and in maintaining a manual accounts payable control account:

(a) manual agreement of update totals; (5.30a) (D)
(b) investigation and correction of differences disclosed by the update reconciliations? (5.31) (D)

5.33 Are the results of the following procedures reviewed and approved by a responsible official:

(a) manual agreement of update totals; (5.30a) (S)
(b) investigation and correction of differences disclosed by the update reconciliations? (5.31) (S)

Maintenance of the accounts payable file

5.34 Is an accumulation of the items on the file regularly reconciled with either:

(a) a manual control account maintained by a user department; or
(b) a control record on file and, if so, is adequate evidence of the reconciliation printed out?

5.35 Where the reconciliation is carried out by the computer: (5.34b)

(a) is the brought forward total checked; or
(b) if not, are there adequate controls (review the answers to the integrity controls section) to ensure that unauthorised changes cannot be made to data files?

5.36 Are there adequate procedures for investigating differences disclosed by the reconciliations (5.34, 5.35a) before any adjustments are made?

5.37 Are the following procedures either performed or checked by persons other than those involved in computer operations and in maintaining a manual accounts payable control account:

(a) manual agreement of totals; (5.34a) (D)
(b) checking of brought forward total; (5.35a) (D)
(c) investigation and correction of differences disclosed by the reconciliations? (5.36) (D)

5.38 Are the results of the following procedures reviewed and approved by a responsible official:

(a) manual agreement of totals; (5.34a) (S)
(b) checking of brought forward total; (5.35a) (S)
(c) investigation and correction of differences disclosed by the reconciliations? (5.36) (S)

111

Agreement with suppliers' records

5.39   Are the accounts payable subsidiary records periodically reconciled to suppliers' records (e.g. by comparison with suppliers'
statements)?

5.40   Is the procedure in 5.39 either performed or checked by persons
other than those who are involved in:

(a) maintenance of a manual accounts payable control account; (D)
(b) computer operations? (D)

5.41   Are the results of the reconciliation in 5.39 reviewed and
approved by a responsible official? (S)

Integrity controls

5.42   List below the programmed procedures relied upon for the purposes of this control objective.

In respect of the programmed procedures listed above, review the
answers to the integrity controls section. Are there adequate controls to ensure that:

(a) appropriate programmed procedures are implemented in respect
of:
  (i) where applicable, new systems;
  (ii) program changes;
(b) unauthorised changes cannot be made to programmed procedures;
(c) programmed procedures are consistently used?

Compensating controls

If any "no" answers are compensated by alternative controls, identify
such controls below.

Control objective

6. *Payments in respect of wages and salaries should be:*

(a) made only to company employees at authorised rates of pay;
(b) where required, in accordance with records of work performed;
(c) accurately calculated.

Standing payroll data

List below the standing data fields used in the preparation of payrolls (e.g. rate of pay, deductions, employee number, commission rates) and state on which file these fields are recorded.

6.1   In respect of each field listed above, review the answers to the standing data controls section. Are there adequate controls over:

(a) where applicable, file creation;
(b) the authorisation of amendments;
(c) the completeness of writing amendments to the file;
(d) the accuracy of writing amendments to the file;
(e) the maintenance of the data on the file?

Transaction payroll data

6.2   If employees are paid on the basis of time worked:

(a) is the payroll based on adequate time records;
(b) where applicable, are time records checked to supporting records of time spent, manually or by the computer (specify which);
(c) are time records (6.2a) approved;
(d) do the time records (6.2a) or payroll indicate that overtime has been properly authorised (e.g. reference to clock card or a computer-produced exception report of abnormal time)?

6.3   If employees are paid on the basis of output, are the payments based on output records that are:

(a) reconciled to production records that are under accounting control either manually or by computer (specify which);
(b) properly approved (e.g. by reference to production records or a computer-produced exception report of abnormal output)?

6.4   If salaried or other employees not included in 6.2 and 6.3 above are paid for overtime, is the payroll based on time records which indicate that the overtime has been properly authorised (e.g. by reference to overtime records or a computer-produced exception report of abnormal overtime)?

113

6.5 Where the authorisation in 6.2d, 6.3b and 6.4 above is based on computer-produced exception reports, are the methods used in the program to determine abnormal items appropriate?

6.6 If employees receive commissions on sales, are the commissions based on sales records that are reconciled with sales (less, where applicable, returns) recorded in the books?

6.7 Are the following procedures either performed or checked by persons other than those involved in computer operations:

(a) checking of time records to supporting records of time spent; (6.2b) (D)
(b) approval of time records; (6.2c) (D)
(c) checking of payments to output records; (6.3a) (D)
(d) approval of output records; (6.3b) (D)
(e) approval of overtime for salaried or other employees not included in 6.2 and 6.3; (6.4) (D)
(f) reconciliation of commissions with sales? (6.6) (D)

Payroll preparation

Completeness of input

6.8 Is the principal control that all transaction payroll data is input to the computer one of the following (specify which):

(a) computer matching with the employee record on the file;
If yes, answer 6.9 to 6.11

(b) agreement of manually established batch totals (specify totals used)?
If yes, answer 6.12 to 6.14

Computer matching

6.9 Review the answers to 6.1. Are there adequate controls that only authorised employees are held on the files?

6.10 Is the method used in the program to match the transaction payroll data with the employee record appropriate (e.g. to reject duplicate or unmatched input)?

6.11 Are there adequate procedures for the investigation and correction of differences disclosed by the matching process? (6.10)

Batch totals

6.12 Are there adequate controls that:

(a) all documents are included in a batch;
(b) all batches are submitted for processing?

6.13 Are pre-determined control totals either:

(a) input and agreed by the computer with the accumulation of individual items accepted and, if so, is adequate evidence of this check printed out; or

(b) agreed manually with the total of accepted items accumulated and printed out by the computer?

6.14 Are there adequate procedures for:

(a) investigation and correction of differences disclosed by the input reconciliations; (6.13a)
(b) resubmission of all rejections?

Disciplines over completeness controls

6.15 Are the following procedures either performed or checked by persons other than those involved in computer operations:

(a) investigation and correction of differences disclosed by the matching process; (6.11) (D)
(b) manual agreement of input totals; (6.13b) (D)
(c) investigation and correction of differences disclosed by the input reconciliations; (6.14a) (D)
(d) resubmission of all rejections? (6.14b) (D)

6.16 Are the results of the following procedures reviewed and approved by a responsible official:

(a) investigation and correction of differences disclosed by the matching process; (6.11) (S)
(b) manual agreement of input totals; (6.13b) (S)
(c) investigation and correction of differences disclosed by the input reconciliations; (6.14a) (S)
(d) resubmission of all rejections? (6.14b) (S)

Accuracy of input

6.17 Are there adequate controls that the following fields are accurately input (e.g. batch totals, edit checks in program, reporting of non-matched items):

(a) hours;
(b) employee numbers;
(c) allowances;
(d) inventory reference, where applicable?

6.18 Are there adequate procedures for:

(a) agreement of totals, where applicable;
(b) investigation and correction of differences or exceptions?

6.19 Are the following procedures either performed or checked by persons other than those involved in computer operations:

(a) agreement of totals, where applicable; (6.18a) (D)
(b) investigation and correction of differences or exceptions? (6.18b) (D)

6.20 Are the results of the following procedures reviewed and approved by a responsible official:

(a) agreement of totals, where applicable; (6.18a) (S)
(b) investigation and correction of differences or exceptions? (6.18b) (S)

Completeness and accuracy of payroll processing

6.21 As regards the computer calculations of gross amounts due, deductions and net amounts due:

(a) is the method used in the program for the calculation appropriate;
(b) are there adequate controls over the accuracy of the calculation (e.g. an exception report of abnormal pay)?

6.22 Where input to the payroll is a cumulative file of transactions, is a total of accepted items accumulated during the input run?

6.23 Is the total of accepted items (6.22) either:

(a) agreed to the payroll; or
(b) carried through intermediate processing (including summarisation of totals or changes in the totals used) so that it can be established that all accepted input items are included in the payroll?

6.24 Is the reconciliation of totals in 6.23 carried out:

(a) manually; or
(b) by the computer and, if so, is adequate evidence of this check printed out?

6.25 Are there adequate procedures for the investigation and correction of differences disclosed by the payroll reconciliation?

6.26 Are the following procedures either performed or checked by persons other than those involved in computer operations:

(a) manual agreement to payroll totals; (6.24a) (D)
(b) investigation and correction of differences disclosed by the payroll reconciliations? (6.25) (D)

6.27 Are the following procedures reviewed and approved by a responsible official:

(a) manual agreement to payroll totals; (6.24a) (S)
(b) investigation and correction of differences disclosed by the payroll reconciliations? (6.25) (S)

Authorisation

6.28 If data is authorised prior to the establishment of the controls for completeness and accuracy of input (e.g. prior to establishment of batch control totals or recording on a sequentially numbered document), are there adequate controls (e.g. checking author-isation after batch control totals are established or sequentially numbered documents raised) that:

(a) no unauthorised alterations are made to authorised data during subsequent processing;
(b) unauthorised data is not added;
(c) authorised items are not omitted from subsequent processing?

6.29 Are payrolls subject to the final written approval of a responsible official before they are paid?

Payments to employees

6.30 Do persons other than those involved in computer operations compare payroll cheques, either individually or in the aggregate, with payrolls? (D)

6.31 Are the results of the procedures in 6.30 reviewed and approved by a responsible official? (S)

6.32 If employees are paid in cash:

(a) is cash withdrawn only for the net amount of the payroll; (C)
(b) do persons, other than those involved in the control and processing of payroll data, physically control cash until it is distributed to employees; (C)
(c) are unclaimed wages promptly recorded and controlled by persons other than those involved in the control and processing of payroll data? (C)

Integrity controls

6.33 List below the programmed procedures relied upon for the purposes of this control objective.

In respect of the programmed procedures listed above, review the answers to the integrity controls section. Are there adequate controls to ensure that:

(a) appropriate programmed procedures are implemented in respect of:
 (i) where applicable, new systems;
 (ii) program changes;
(b) unauthorised changes cannot be made to programmed procedures;
(c) programmed procedures are consistently used?

Compensating controls

If any "no" answers are compensated by alternative controls, identify such controls below.

117

Control objective

9. *Disbursements from bank accounts should be made only in respect of valid transactions.*

___

Control of issue and usage of cheques

9.1   Are supplies of unissued cheques properly safeguarded? (C)

9.2   Is the system such that:

   (a) the usage of cheques is accounted for by persons other than those who have custody of unissued cheques; (9.1) (C)
   (b) spoiled cheques are under adequate control? (C)

9.3   Are the results of the procedures in 9.2 reviewed and approved by a responsible official? (S)

Selection of items for payment

9.4   Review the answers to control objectives 5 and 6. Are there adequate controls that only authorised items are held on the accounts payable and payroll files?

9.5   Is the method used in the program:

   (a) for selecting items for payment appropriate (e.g. to produce cheques on desired date, to take advantage of cash discount, to prevent selection twice);
   (b) to carry out calculation appropriate (e.g. discount, summarisation)?

9.6   Are the amendments to the computer-selected items for payment (e.g. to delay or accelerate payments) reviewed and approved by a responsible official? (S)

9.7   Is a total of items selected accumulated by the computer and either:

   (a) agreed to the total of cheques issued or the bank transfer directly; or
   (b) agreed to the total of cheques issued or the bank transfer after approval and resubmission of the listing of selected items?

9.8   Where cheques or supporting documents are produced by the computer, as regards the names, addresses and bank details of payees and discount terms, review the answers to the standing data controls section. Are there adequate controls over:

   (a) where applicable, file creation;
   (b) the authorisation of amendments;
   (c) the completeness of writing amendments to the file;
   (d) the accuracy of writing amendments to the file;
   (e) the maintenance of the data on the file?

9.9   Is the authorisation and maintenance in 9.8 carried out by persons other than those involved in dealing with:

(a) payroll transaction data; (C)
(b) accounts payable transaction data; (C)
(c) imprest and similar funds? (C)

Signing of cheques

9.10   Where cheques are prepared on pre-signed forms:

(a) are cheques over a reasonable amount countersigned by officials other than those who approve transactions for payment;
(b) where appropriate (e.g. payrolls), is a limit as to the amount payable stated on the cheques?

9.11   Where the cheques are manually signed or countersigned, are the cheques signed by officials, other than those involved in computer operations and who approve transactions for payment, in respect of:

(a) accounts payable (control objective 5); (C)
(b) payrolls and payroll deductions (control objectives 6 and 7); (C)
(c) reimbursement of imprest and similar funds (control objective 8); (C)
(d) other payments? (C)

9.12   Where cheques are manually signed, does the signatory review supporting documentation for large value items?

9.13   If a mechanical cheque signer is in use, is there adequate control over the custody and use of the signer and the signature plate? (C)

General

9.14   Are the supporting documents effectively cancelled by, or under the control of, the signatories to prevent subsequent re-use? (C)

9.15   Are cheques and bank transfers for transactions which, because of special circumstances, do not pass through the normal approval procedures referred to in 9.4 to 9.13, initiated only on the basis of proper documentation of the validity of the transactions?

9.16   Is the documentation in 9.15 reviewed and approved by a responsible official before cheques and bank transfers are initiated? (S)

Control of cheques and bank transfers after signing

9.17   After signing, are cheques and bank transfers forwarded directly to the payees (or to the bank with the bank transfer lists) without being returned to the originators or others who are in a position to introduce documents into the cash disbursement system? (C)

119

Comparison of disbursement records

9.18 Are all cheques and individual bank transfers as listed in the disbursement records compared manually or by computer (specify which) as to name or number, dates and amounts with transactions passed through the company's bank accounts (e.g. as part of the bank reconciliation procedures – control objective 56)?

9.19 When done manually, is the comparison in 9.18 carried out by persons other than those:

(a) involved in preparation of cheques and bank transfers or who can introduce documents into the disbursements system; (D)
(b) involved in computer operations? (D)

9.20 Are the results of the procedures in 9.19 reviewed and approved by a responsible official? (S)

Integrity controls

9.21 List below the programmed procedures relied upon for the purposes of this control objective.

In respect of the programmed procedures listed above, review the answers to the integrity controls section. Are there adequate controls to ensure that:

(a) appropriate programmed procedures are implemented in respect of:
  (i) where applicable, new systems;
  (ii) program changes;
(b) unauthorised changes cannot be made to programmed procedures;
(c) programmed procedures are consistently used?

Compensating controls

If any "no" answers are compensated by alternative controls, identify such controls below.

Control objective

10. *Accurate detailed records should be maintained of materials and supplies inventories.*

NOTE: The answers to the following questions should normally cover the following (whether on the client's premises or in the hands of third parties):

(a) all purchased inventories (including items purchased for resale);
(b) manufactured parts and sub-assemblies in store, where they are accounted for by the client as part of purchased inventories rather than as finished products (control objective 37).

State below the client's inventory categories covered by the answers.

Validity of entries in inventory records

10.1 Are all entries input to the materials and supplies records:

(a) supported by adequate documentation;
(b) priced by reference to an appropriate source (control objective 52);
(c) checked to an appropriate extent, e.g. relative to value (where appropriate);
(d) properly approved, where applicable?

Accounting for and control over processing of all transactions

Indicate below which of the following are input to update the materials and supplies inventories file (specify whether in quantity and/or value):

(a) file/documents of goods received;
(b) file/documents of transfers to work in progress or finished products;
(c) file/documents of goods shipped;
(d) adjustments;
(e) returns;
(f) other (specify).

121

Completeness of input and updating

10.2 Is the principal control that all files and documents in (a) to (f) above are input to the computer and updated one of the following (specify which for each type of input):

(a) agreement of manually established batch totals (specify totals used);
If yes, answer 10.3 to 10.7

(b) computer sequence check of serially numbered input documents;
If yes, answer 10.8 to 10.13

(c) reliance on controls over the purchases application;
If yes, answer 10.14 to 10.18

(d) reliance on controls over the work in progress application;
If yes, answer 10.14 to 10.18

(e) reliance on controls over the sales application?
If yes, answer 10.14 to 10.18

Batch totals

10.3 Are there adequate controls that:
(a) a document is raised for each transaction;
(b) all documents are included in a batch;
(c) all batches are submitted for processing?

10.4 Are pre-determined control totals either:
(a) input and agreed by the computer with an accumulation of individual items accepted and, if so, is adequate evidence of this check printed out; or
(b) agreed manually with the total of accepted items accumulated and printed out by the computer?

10.5 Are the totals in 10.4 either:
(a) agreed to the total of items written to the material and supplies inventories file; or
(b) carried through intermediate processing (including summarisation of totals or changes in the totals used) so that it is established that all accepted input items are updated to the materials and supplies inventories file?

10.6 Is the reconciliation of totals in 10.5 carried out:
(a) manually; or
(b) by the computer and, if so, is adequate evidence of this check printed out?

10.7 Are there adequate procedures for:
(a) investigation and correction of differences disclosed by the input reconciliations; (10.4)
(b) resubmission of all rejections;
(c) investigation and correction of differences disclosed by the update reconciliations? (10.6)

10.8 Are there adequate procedures to ensure that all transactions are recorded on a serially numbered document?

10.9 Is the method used in the program for the checking of numerical sequence appropriate (e.g. does it cater for changes in sequence and more than one sequence running at a time)?

10.10 Is a print-out of missing documents produced at regular intervals (e.g. weekly)?

10.11 Is a total (specify total used) of accepted items accumulated by the computer during the sequence check run and either:
   (a) agreed to the total of items written to the materials and supplies inventories file; or
   (b) carried through intermediate processing (including summarisation of totals or changes in the totals used) so that it is established that all accepted input items are updated to the materials and supplies inventories file?

10.12 Is the reconciliation of totals in 10.11 carried out:

   (a) manually; or
   (b) by the computer and, if so, is adequate evidence of this check printed out?

10.13 Are there adequate procedures for:

   (a) investigation of missing documents; (10.10)
   (b) investigation and correction of differences disclosed by the update reconciliations? (10.12)

Reliance on controls over the purchases/work in progress/sales applications

10.14 Review the answers under control objectives 2, 5, 21 and 31, as applicable. Are there adequate controls that all items are accurately input to the purchases/work in progress/sales applications?

10.15 Is the method used in the program to select and accumulate items relevant to the materials and supplies inventories application appropriate?

10.16 Is a total (specify total used) of selected items accumulated by the computer during the selection run and either:

   (a) agreed to the total of items written to/off the materials and supplies inventories file; or
   (b) carried through intermediate processing (including summarisation of totals or changes in totals used) so that it can be established that all selected items are updated to the materials and supplies inventories file?

123

10.17 Is the reconciliation of totals in 10.16 carried out:

(a) manually; or
(b) by the computer and, if so, is adequate evidence of this check printed out?

10.18 Are there adequate procedures for investigation and correction of differences disclosed by the reconciliation? (10.17)

Disciplines over completeness controls

10.19 Are the following procedures either performed or checked by persons other than those involved in computer operations and in maintaining a manual materials and supplies control account:

(a) manual agreement of input totals; (10.4b) (D)
(b) investigation and correction of differences disclosed by the input reconciliations; (10.7a) (D)
(c) resubmission of all rejections; (10.7b) (D)
(d) investigation of missing documents; (10.13a) (D)
(e) manual agreement of update totals; (10.6a, 10.12a, 10.17a) (D)
(f) investigation and correction of differences disclosed by the update reconciliations? (10.7c, 10.13b, 10.18) (D)

10.20 Are the results of the following procedures reviewed and approved by a responsible official:

(a) manual agreement of input totals; (10.4b) (S)
(b) investigation and correction of differences disclosed by the input reconciliations; (10.7a) (S)
(c) resubmission of all rejections; (10.7b) (S)
(d) investigation of missing documents; (10.13a) (S)
(e) manual agreement of update totals; (10.6a, 10.12a, 10.17a) (S)
(f) investigation and correction of differences disclosed by the update reconciliations? (10.7c, 10.13b, 10.18) (S)

Accuracy of input and updating

10.21 Are there adequate controls that the following fields are accurately input and updated (e.g. batch totals, edit checks in program, reporting of non-matched items):

(a) quantity;
(b) value;
(c) inventory reference?

10.22 Are there adequate procedures for:

(a) agreement of totals, where applicable;
(b) investigation and correction of differences or exceptions?

10.23 Is the method used in the program for the updating of individual accounts appropriate?

10.24 Are the following procedures either performed or checked by persons other than those involved in computer operations and in maintaining a manual materials and supplies control account:

(a) agreement of totals, where applicable; (10.22a) (D)
(b) investigation and correction of differences or exceptions? (10.22b) (D)

10.25 Are the results of the following procedures reviewed and approved by a responsible official:

(a) agreement of totals, where applicable; (10.22a) (S)
(b) investigation and correction of differences or exceptions? (10.22b) (S)

Computer-generated data

10.26 Are the methods used in the program to generate the data and related control record appropriate (e.g. minor physical count adjustments)?

10.27 Is there a control over the accuracy of the data generated (e.g. reasonableness check, manual review of generated data)?

10.28 Are all entries in the materials and supplies inventories file generated by the computer reviewed and approved by a responsible official? (S)

10.29 Is a total (specify total used) of generated items accumulated by the computer and agreed with a total of items written to/off the materials and supplies inventories file:

(a) manually; or
(b) by the computer and, if so, is adequate evidence of this check printed out?

10.30 Are there adequate procedures for investigation and correction of differences disclosed by the update reconciliations?

10.31 Are the following procedures either performed or checked by persons other than those involved in computer operations and in maintaining a manual materials and supplies control account:

(a) manual agreement of update totals; (10.29a) (D)
(b) investigation and correction of differences disclosed by the update reconciliations? (10.30) (D)

10.32 Are the results of the following procedures reviewed and approved by a responsible official:

(a) manual agreement of update totals; (10.29a) (S)
(b) investigation and correction of differences disclosed by the update reconciliations? (10.30) (S)

125

Authorisation of adjustments

10.33 If data is authorised prior to the establishment of the controls for completeness and accuracy of input (e.g. prior to establishment of batch control totals or recording on a sequentially numbered document), are there adequate controls (e.g. checking authorisation after batch control totals are established or sequentially numbered documents raised) that:

(a) no unauthorised alterations are made to authorised data during subsequent processing;
(b) unauthorised data is not added;
(c) authorised items are not omitted from subsequent processing?

Maintenance of the materials and supplies inventories file

10.34 Is an accumulation of the items on the file regularly reconciled with either:

(a) a manual control account maintained by a user department; or
(b) a control record on file and, if so, is adequate evidence of this reconciliation printed out?

10.35 Where the reconciliation is carried out by the computer: (10.34b)

(a) is the brought forward total checked; or
(b) if not, are there adequate controls (review the answers to the integrity controls section) to ensure that unauthorised changes cannot be made to data files?

10.36 Are there adequate procedures for investigating differences disclosed by the reconciliations (10.34, 10.35a) before any adjustments are made?

10.37 Are the following procedures either performed or checked by persons other than those involved in computer operations (D), in maintaining a manual materials and supplies control account (D) and in maintaining physical custody of inventory (C):

(a) manual agreement of totals; (10.34a)
(b) checking of brought forward total; (10.35a)
(c) investigation and correction of differences disclosed by the reconciliations? (10.36)

10.38 Are the results of the following procedures reviewed and approved by a responsible official:

(a) manual agreement of totals; (10.34a) (S)
(b) checking of brought forward total; (10.35a) (S)
(c) investigation and correction of differences disclosed by the reconciliations? (10.36) (S)

10.39 In the cases where adjustments to the detailed records are required and amounts are not easily quantified (e.g. losses due to evaporation), do the methods used to determine such adjustments appear reasonable?

10.40 Are separate general or subsidiary ledger accounts maintained for all adjustments to inventory valuation (e.g. for provisions, variances, adjustments arising on physical verification)?

Physical control

10.41 Are areas where materials and supplies are held protected against access by unauthorised personnel? (C)

10.42 Are all materials and supplies inventories physically verified at least annually, either by cycle or periodic counts (control objective 51)?

10.43 Are the procedures in 10.42 either performed or checked by persons other than those involved in computer operations? (D)

Integrity controls

10.44 List below the programmed procedures relied upon for the purposes of this control objective.

In respect of the programmed procedures listed above, review the answers to the integrity controls section. Are there adequate controls to ensure that:

(a) appropriate programmed procedures are implemented in respect of:
   (i) where applicable, new systems;
   (ii) program changes;
(b) unauthorised changes cannot be made to programmed procedures;
(c) programmed procedures are consistently used?

Compensating controls

If any "no" answers are compensated by alternative controls, identify such controls below.

Control objective

12.   *Accurate records should be maintained of the cost and accumulated depreciation of property, plant and equipment.*

Detailed records

12.1   Are property, plant and equipment subsidiary ledgers maintained manually or on the computer for the following classifications (specify which for each type and complete manual questions for items not processed by computer):

(a) land and buildings;
(b) leasehold improvements;
(c) plant and machinery;
(d) furniture, fixtures and fittings;
(e) office equipment;
(f) motor vehicles;
(g) property, plant and equipment leased or loaned to third parties;
(h) other property, plant and equipment (specify below)?

12.2   Do the computer subsidiary ledgers provide the following details for each item:

(a) adequate identification;
(b) the cost;
(c) the accumulated depreciation;
(d) the date of purchase?

12.3   Are the computer subsidiary ledgers regularly updated (e.g. monthly) in respect of:

(a) cost of additions and disposals;
(b) depreciation for the period?

Accounting for and control over processing of all transactions

Indicate below which of the following are input to update the computer subsidiary ledgers:

(a) file of additions from other applications;
(b) manually prepared documents of additions;
(c) manually prepared documents of disposals;
(d) adjustments.

12.4   Is the principal control that all property, plant and equipment transactions above are input to the computer and updated one of the following (specify which for each type of input):

(a) agreement of manually established batch totals (specify totals used);
     If yes, answer 12.5 to 12.9

(b) computer sequence check of serially numbered input documents;
     If yes, answer 12.10 to 12.15

(c) reliance on controls over the purchases application;
     If yes, answer 12.16 to 12.20

(d) reliance on controls over the payroll application;
     If yes, answer 12.16 to 12.20

(e) reliance on controls over the work in progress application?
     If yes, answer 12.16 to 12.20

Batch totals

12.5   Are there adequate controls that:

(a) a document is raised for each transaction;
(b) all documents are included in a batch;
(c) all batches are submitted for processing?

12.6   Are the pre-determined control totals either:

(a) input and agreed by the computer with the accumulation of individual items accepted and, if so, is adequate evidence of this check printed out; or
(b) agreed manually with the total of accepted items accumulated and printed out by the computer?

12.7   Are the totals in 12.6 either:

(a) agreed to the total of items written to the property, plant and equipment file; or
(b) carried through intermediate processing (including summarisation of totals or changes in the totals used) so that it is established that all accepted input items are updated to the property, plant and equipment file?

12.8   Is the reconciliation of totals in 12.7 carried out:

(a) manually; or
(b) by the computer and, if so, is adequate evidence of this check printed out?

129

12.9 Are there adequate procedures for:

(a) investigation and correction of differences disclosed by the input reconciliations; (12.6)
(b) resubmission of all rejections;
(c) investigation and correction of differences disclosed by the update reconciliations? (12.8)

Computer sequence check

12.10 Are there adequate procedures to ensure that all transactions are recorded on a serially numbered document?

12.11 Is the method used in the program for the checking of numerical sequence appropriate (e.g. does it cater for changes in sequence and more than one sequence running at a time)?

12.12 Is a print-out of missing documents produced at regular intervals (e.g. weekly)?

12.13 Is a total (specify total used) of accepted items accumulated by the computer during the sequence check run and either:

(a) agreed to the total of items written to the property, plant and equipment file; or
(b) carried through intermediate processing (including summarisation of totals or changes in the totals used) so that it is established that all accepted input items are updated to the property, plant and equipment file?

12.14 Is the reconciliation of totals in 12.13 carried out:

(a) manually; or
(b) by the computer and, if so, is adequate evidence of this check printed out?

12.15 Are there adequate procedures for:

(a) investigation of missing documents; (12.12)
(b) investigation and correction of differences disclosed by the update reconciliations? (12.14)

Reliance on controls over the purchases/payroll/work in progress applications

12.16 Review the answers under control objectives 2, 5, 6 and 21, as applicable. Are there adequate controls that all items are accurately input to the purchases/payroll/work in progress applications?

12.17 Is the method used in the program to select and accumulate items relevant to the property, plant and equipment application appropriate?

12.18 Is a total (specify total used) of selected items accumulated by the computer during the selection run and either:

  (a) agreed to the total of items written to/off the property, plant and equipment file; or

  (b) carried through intermediate processing (including summarisation of totals or changes in the totals used) so that it is established that all selected input items are updated to the property, plant and equipment file?

12.19 Is the reconciliation of totals in 12.18 carried out:

  (a) manually; or

  (b) by the computer and, if so, is adequate evidence of this check printed out?

12.20 Are there adequate procedures for investigation and correction of differences disclosed by the update reconciliations? (12.19)

Disciplines over completeness controls

12.21 Are the following procedures either performed or checked by persons other than those involved in computer operations and in maintaining a manual property, plant and equipment control account:

  (a) manual agreement of input totals; (12.6b) (D)

  (b) investigation and correction of differences disclosed by the input reconciliations; (12.9a) (D)

  (c) resubmission of all rejections; (12.9b) (D)

  (d) investigation of missing documents; (12.15a) (D)

  (e) manual agreement of update totals; (12.8a, 12.14a, 12.19a) (D)

  (f) investigation and correction of differences disclosed by the update reconciliations? (12.9c, 12.15b, 12.20) (D)

12.22 Are the results of the following procedures reviewed and approved by a responsible official:

  (a) manual agreement of input totals; (12.6b) (S)

  (b) investigation and correction of differences disclosed by the input reconciliations; (12.9a) (S)

  (c) resubmission of all rejections; (12.9b) (S)

  (d) investigation of missing documents; (12.15a) (S)

  (e) manual agreement of update totals; (12.8a, 12.14a, 12.19a) (S)

  (f) investigation and correction of differences disclosed by the update reconciliations? (12.9c, 12.15b, 12.20) (S)

Accuracy of input and updating

12.23 Are there adequate controls that the following fields are accurately input and updated (e.g. batch totals, edit checks in program, reporting of non-matched items):

(a) cost;
(b) depreciation rate;
(c) identification and/or description;
(d) date of purchase?

12.24 Are there adequate procedures for:

(a) the agreement of totals, where applicable;
(b) investigation and correction of differences or exceptions?

12.25 Is the method used in the program for the updating of individual accounts appropriate?

12.26 Are the following procedures either performed or checked by persons other than those involved in computer operations and maintaining a manual plant, property and equipment control account:

(a) agreement of totals, where applicable; (12.24a) (D)
(b) investigation and correction of differences or exceptions? (12.24b) (D)

12.27 Are the results of the following procedures reviewed and approved by a responsible official:

(a) agreement of totals, where applicable; (12.24a) (S)
(b) investigation and correction of differences or exceptions? (12.24b) (S)

Depreciation

12.28 In respect of depreciation rates, review the answers to the standing data controls section. Are there adequate controls over:

(a) where applicable, file creation;
(b) the authorisation of amendments;
(c) the completeness of writing amendments to the file;
(d) the accuracy of writing amendments to the file;
(e) the maintenance of the data on the file?

12.29 Are the methods used in the program for the calculation of depreciation appropriate?

12.30 Is a total of generated depreciation charges accumulated by the computer and agreed with a total of items written to the property, plant and equipment file:

(a) manually; or
(b) by the computer and, if so, is adequate evidence of this check printed out?

12.31 Are there adequate procedures for the investigation and correction of differences disclosed by the update reconciliations?

12.32 Is the method used in the program for updating of individual accounts appropriate?

12.33 Are the following procedures either performed or checked by persons other than those involved in computer operations:

(a) manual agreement of update totals; (12.30a) (S)
(b) investigation and correction of differences disclosed by the update reconciliations? (12.31) (D)

12.34 Are the results of the following procedures reviewed and approved by a responsible official:

(a) manual agreement of update totals; (12.30a) (D)
(b) investigation and correction of differences disclosed by the update reconciliations? (12.31) (S)

Maintenance of the property, plant and equipment file

12.35 Is an accumulation of the items (e.g. cost, accumulated depreciation) on the file regularly reconciled with either:

(a) a manual control account maintained by a user department; or
(b) a control record on file and, if so, is adequate evidence of the reconciliation printed out?

12.36 Where the reconciliation is carried out by computer: (12.35b)

(a) is the brought forward total checked; or
(b) if not, are there adequate controls (review the answers to the integrity controls section) to ensure that unauthorised changes cannot be made to data files?

12.37 Are there adequate procedures for investigating differences disclosed by the reconciliations (12.35, 12.36a) before any adjustments are made?

12.38 Are the following procedures either performed or checked by persons other than those involved in computer operations and in maintaining a manual property, plant and equipment control account:

(a) manual agreement of totals; (12.35a) (D)
(b) checking of brought forward total; (12.36a) (D)
(c) investigation and correction of differences disclosed by the reconciliations? (12.37) (D)

133

12.39 Are the results of the following procedures reviewed and approved by a responsible official:

(a) manual agreement of totals; (12.35a) (S)

(b) checking of brought forward total; (12.36a) (S)

(c) investigation and correction of differences disclosed by the reconciliations? (12.37) (S)

Property, plant and equipment leased or loaned from third parties

12.40 Are suitable records maintained of assets leased or on loan from third parties?

Integrity controls

12.41 List below the programmed procedures relied upon for the purposes of this control objective.

In respect of the programmed procedures listed above, review the answers to the integrity controls section. Are there adequate controls to ensure that:

(a) appropriate programmed procedures are implemented in respect of:
   (i) where applicable, new systems;
   (ii) program changes;

(b) unauthorised changes cannot be made to programmed procedures;

(c) programmed procedures are consistently used?

Compensating controls

If any "no" answers are compensated by alternative controls, identify such controls below.

Control objective

13. *General ledger entries arising from the payments cycle should be accurately determined.*

Classification of expenditures

13.1   Is the coding of the following transactions for posting to general ledger accounts checked to an appropriate extent:

(a) invoices and other supporting documentation related to the payment of accounts payable;
(b) payrolls;
(c) reimbursements of imprest and similar funds;
(d) disbursements from bank accounts not covered in (a) to (c) above;
(e) depreciation of property, plant and equipment?

13.2   Is the coding (13.1) of the following transactions approved by responsible officials:

(a) invoices and other supporting documentation related to the payment of accounts payable; (S)
(b) payrolls; (S)
(c) reimbursements of imprest and similar funds; (S)
(d) disbursements from bank accounts not covered in (a) to (c) above; (S)
(e) depreciation of property, plant and equipment? (S)

13.3   Are there adequate controls that the coding of transactions is accurately input (e.g. validity checks in program) in respect of:

(a) invoices and other supporting documentation related to the payment of accounts payable;
(b) payrolls;
(c) reimbursements of imprest and similar funds;
(d) disbursements from bank accounts not covered in (a) to (c) above;
(e) depreciation of property, plant and equipment?

Summarisation of expenditures

13.4   Are there adequate controls that the following computer-produced analyses are complete and accurate (e.g. manual or programmed reconciliations):

(a) invoices and other supporting documentation related to the payment of accounts payable;
(b) payrolls;
(c) reimbursements of imprest and similar funds;
(d) disbursements from bank accounts not covered in (a) to (c) above;
(e) depreciation of property, plant and equipment?

13.5 Is the method used in the program to categorise and summarise the following computer-produced analyses appropriate:

(a) invoices and other supporting documentation related to the payment of accounts payable;
(b) payrolls;
(c) reimbursements of imprest and similar funds;
(d) disbursements from bank accounts not covered in (a) to (c) above;
(e) depreciation of property, plant and equipment?

13.6 Where the computer-produced analyses are further categorised and/or summarised manually, are there adequate controls (e.g. reconciliation of totals) that the manual summaries are complete and accurate?

13.7 Are the manual procedures in 13.4 and 13.6 either performed or checked by persons other than those involved in computer operations? (D)

13.8 Are the analyses referred to in 13.4 and 13.6 approved by a responsible official before posting to the general ledger accounts? (S)

Integrity controls

13.9 List below the programmed procedures relied upon for the purposes of this control objective.

In respect of the programmed procedures listed above, review the answers to the integrity controls section. Are there adequate controls to ensure that:

(a) appropriate programmed procedures are implemented in respect of:
  (i) where applicable, new systems;
  (ii) program changes;

(b) unauthorised changes cannot be made to programmed procedures;

(c) programmed procedures are consistently used?

Compensating controls

If any "no" answers are compensated by alternative controls, identify such controls below.

Control objective

34. *All charges and credits should be appropriately checked as being valid before being entered in the accounts receivable records.*

Standing data fields

List below the standing data fields used in the calculation of charges and credits (e.g. price, discount) and state on which file these fields are recorded.

34.1 In respect of each field listed above, review the answers to the standing data controls section. Are there adequate controls over:

(a) where applicable, file creation;
(b) the authorisation of amendments;
(c) the completeness of writing amendments to the file;
(d) the accuracy of writing amendments to the file;
(e) the maintenance of the data on the file?

Special terms and manual pricing

34.2 Are there adequate controls that special terms or manually submitted prices are:

(a) authorised by a responsible official;
(b) input completely and accurately without subsequent alteration?

Calculation of charges and credits

34.3 Where the calculation of charges or credits is carried out by the computer program:

(a) is the method used in the program for the calculation appropriate;
(b) are there adequate controls over the accuracy of the calculation (e.g. periodic check on calculation, overall calculation check)?

34.4 Are credit memoranda:

(a) prepared from the actual records of goods returned or claims made;
(b) checked with those records by persons other than the preparers of the credit memoranda and persons who record returns and claims? (D)

34.5 Are credit memoranda checked by persons other than the preparers of the credit memoranda to confirm that the prices agree with the original invoice or other appropriate documentation? (D)

137

34.6 Are the extensions and additions of credit memoranda/invoices (where applicable) checked to an adequate extent by persons other than the preparers? (D)

34.7 Is there a procedure for the persons who carry out the checking (34.5 and 34.6) to report recurring errors in the preparation of credit memoranda/invoices (where applicable) to a responsible official? (S)

34.8 Are all credit memoranda subject to final approval by a responsible official before they are issued and prior to entry in the accounts receivable records? (S)

Adjustments

34.9 Are all manually prepared adjustments to customers' accounts (including requests for credit) properly documented and authorised by a responsible official prior to entry in the accounts receivable records? (S)

Integrity controls

34.10 List below the programmed procedures relied upon for the purposes of this control objective.

In respect of the programmed procedures listed above, review the answers to the integrity controls section. Are there adequate controls to ensure that:

(a) appropriate programmed procedures are implemented in respect of:
  (i) where applicable, new systems;
  (ii) program changes;

(b) unauthorised changes cannot be made to programmed procedures;

(c) programmed procedures are consistently used?

Compensating controls

If any "no" answers are compensated by alternative controls, identify such controls below.

Standing Data Controls

Master file ....

NOTE: A separate section should be completed for each master file when indicated in the body of the questionnaire.

Obtain a copy of the file layout, mark on it all standing data fields that have accounting significance.

File creation

NOTE: This question is only relevant to the audit of the accounting period during which the file was initially created.

1   Are there adequate controls that all data fields of accounting significance are completely and accurately set up initially on the file?

Authorisation of amendments

2   Are all manually prepared amendments to standing data authorised by a responsible official?

3   If data is authorised prior to the establishment of the controls for completeness and accuracy of input (e.g. prior to establishment of batch control totals), are there adequate controls (e.g. checking authorisation after batch control totals are established) that:

(a) no unauthorised alterations are made to authorised data during subsequent processing;

(b) unauthorised data is not added;

(c) authorised items are not omitted from subsequent processing?

Completeness of writing input amendments to the file

4   Is the principal control that amendments to standing data are completely written to the file one of the following (specify which):

(a) checking of print-outs of items written to the file;
    If yes, answer 5 to 8

(b) agreement of manually established batch totals (specify totals used)?
    If yes, answer 9 to 13

Checking of print-outs

5   Are there adequate controls that all documents are submitted for processing (e.g. by checking against retained copies; by manual sequence check)?

139

6   Is there a regular (e.g. monthly) review of source documents for unprocessed items?

7   Is the method used in the program for the production of the print-out appropriate (e.g. does it contain details of items that have been written to the master file)?

8   Are there adequate procedures for the investigation and correction of differences disclosed by the checking?

Batch totals

9   Are there adequate controls that:

(a) a document is raised for each transaction;
(b) all documents are included in a batch;
(c) all batches are submitted for processing?

10   Are pre-determined control totals either:

(a) input and agreed by the computer with the accumulation of individual items accepted and, if so, is adequate evidence of this check printed out; or
(b) agreed manually with the total of accepted items accumulated and printed out by the computer?

11   Are the totals in 10 either:

(a) agreed to the total of items written to the master file; or
(b) carried through intermediate processing (including summarisation of totals or changes in the totals used) so that it is established that all accepted input items are updated to the master file?

12   Is the reconciliation of totals in 11 carried out:

(a) manually; or
(b) by the computer and, if so, is adequate evidence of this check printed out?

13   Are there adequate procedures for:

(a) investigation and correction of differences disclosed by the input reconciliations; (10)
(b) resubmission of all rejections;
(c) investigation and correction of differences disclosed by the update reconciliations? (12)

14   Are the following procedures either performed or checked by per-
     sons other than those who deal with the related transaction data or
     are involved in computer operations:

(a) regular (e.g. monthly) review of source documents for unprocessed
    items; (6) (D)
(b) investigation and correction of differences disclosed by the checking
    of print-outs; (8) (D)
(c) manual agreement of input totals; (10b) (D)
(d) investigation and correction of differences disclosed by the input
    reconciliations; (13a) (D)
(e) resubmission of all rejections; (13b) (D)
(f) manual agreement of update totals; (12a) (D)
(g) investigation and correction of differences disclosed by the update
    reconciliations? (13c) (D)

15   Are the results of the following procedures reviewed and approved
     by a responsible official:

(a) regular (e.g. monthly) review of source documents for unprocessed
    items; (6) (S)
(b) investigation and correction of differences disclosed by the checking
    of print-outs; (8) (S)
(c) manual agreement of input totals; (10b) (S)
(d) investigation and correction of differences disclosed by the input
    reconciliations; (13a) (S)
(e) resubmission of all rejections; (13b) (S)
(f) manual agreement of update totals; (12a) (S)
(g) investigation and correction of differences disclosed by the update
    reconciliations? (13c) (S)

Accuracy of input and updating of amendments to the file

16   Are there adequate controls that all data fields of accounting
     significance are accurately written to the file (e.g. detailed checking
     of print-outs of items written to the file; agreement of manually
     established batch totals; programmed reasonableness checks)?

17   Are there adequate procedures for:

(a) the agreement of totals, where applicable;
(b) investigation and correction of differences or exceptions?

18   Is the method used in the program for updating individual accounts
     appropriate?

                                                              141

19 Are the following procedures either performed or checked by persons other than those who deal with related transaction data or are involved in computer operations:

(a) agreement of totals, where applicable; (17a) (D)
(b) investigation and correction of differences or exceptions? (17b) (D)

20 Are the results of the following procedures reviewed and approved by a responsible official:

(a) agreement of totals, where applicable; (17a) (S)
(b) investigation and correction of differences or exceptions? (17b) (S)

Computer-generated amendments to the file

21 Are the methods used in the program to generate the data appropriate?

22 Is there a check over the accuracy of the data generated (e.g. reasonableness check; manual review of data)?

23 Are the results of the check (22) reviewed and approved by a responsible official? (S)

24 Is a total of the items in 22 accumulated by the computer and agreed with the total of items written to the file:

(a) manually; or
(b) by the computer and, if so, is adequate evidence of this check printed out?

25 Are there adequate procedures for the investigation and correction of differences disclosed by the update reconciliations?

26 Are the following procedures either performed or checked by persons other than those involved in computer operations:

(a) manual agreement of update totals; (24a) (D)
(b) investigation and correction of differences disclosed by the update reconciliations? (25) (D)

27 Are the following procedures reviewed and approved by a responsible official:

(a) manual agreement of update totals; (24a) (S)
(b) investigation and correction of differences disclosed by the update reconciliations? (25) (S)

28 Is the control that the standing data fields of accounting significance remain correctly stored on the file a suitable combination of the following:

(a) adequate controls over security of data files (review the answers to the integrity controls section);

(b) regular (e.g. monthly) manual agreement of an independently maintained control total with a print-out of the total of balances on the file by a user department;

(c) regular (e.g. monthly) detailed checking on a cyclical basis of print-outs of items on the file to source data by user departments?

29 Is the file regularly examined to identify standing data requiring action (e.g. the provision of exception reports of prices not changed for over twelve months)?

30 Are there adequate procedures for:

(a) investigation of differences disclosed by the checking (28) before any adjustments are made;

(b) investigation and correction of data requiring action? (29)

31 Are the following procedures either performed or checked by persons other than those who deal with related transaction data or are involved in computer operations:

(a) manual agreement of totals; (28b) (D)

(b) cyclical checking; (28c) (D)

(c) investigation and correction of differences; (30a) (D)

(d) investigation and correction of data requiring action? (30b) (D)

32 Are the results of the following procedures reviewed and approved by a responsible official:

(a) manual agreement of totals; (28b) (S)

(b) cyclical checking; (28c) (S)

(c) investigation and correction of differences; (30a) (S)

(d) investigation and correction of data requiring action? (30b) (S)

143

Integrity Controls

Implementation controls

New systems

1   Are system descriptions and changes thereto prepared as a basis for:

(a) understanding and approval of the programmed procedures by the user departments;
(b) control of system design and programming by the data processing function?

2   Are the system descriptions in 1 reviewed and approved by responsible officials: (S)

(a) in the user departments;
(b) in the data processing function?

3   Are the:

(a) methods (e.g. test data; parallel running); and
(b) scope (e.g. volumes tested)

of the testing procedures adequate to establish the proper operation of programmed procedures?

4   Are the testing procedures either performed or checked by persons other than those involved in writing the programs? (D)

Program changes

5   Are all program changes (other than immediate modifications) initiated only on the basis of appropriate written authorisations?

6   Are program changes controlled in such a way that it can subsequently be established that they have all been accounted for (e.g. by sequential prenumbering or by entry of change forms in a register)?

7   Is a regular review made of modifications not yet implemented to determine the reasons for the delay?

8   In order to provide a sound basis for the design and programming of changes:

(a) are systems and programs adequately documented;
(b) are programs written in accordance with suitable programming standards?

9   Are the:

(a) methods (e.g. test data); and
(b) scope (e.g. volumes tested)

of the testing procedures adequate to establish the proper operation of programmed procedures in:

(i) the changed program;
(ii) where applicable, other unchanged programs in the system?

10 Are the testing procedures either performed or checked by persons other than those involved in writing the program changes? (D)

Cataloguing

11 Does a responsible official in the user department review, where applicable, and approve: (S)

(a) the instructions for user procedures and controls;
(b) the results and completion of testing;
(c) the date of taking into production of tested programs?

12 Does a responsible official in the data processing function review, where applicable, and approve: (S)

(a) the system and program documentation to ensure that it is complete, up-to-date and in accordance with the company's standards;
(b) the instructions for job set-up and computer operations;
(c) the results and completion of testing;
(d) the taking into production of tested programs?

13 Are the system software procedures appropriate to ensure that:

(a) tested source programs are properly converted to executable form (e.g. by the compiler and linkage editor);
(b) the correct version of the program is taken into production (e.g. by the checking of generation numbers);
(c) unauthorised changes are not made to tested programs before they are taken into production (e.g. password protection);
(d) all forms of the program (e.g. source, object and executable) are the same?

14 Review the answers to the system software section. Are there adequate controls over the implementation and security of system software?

15 Is adequate evidence of the system software procedures printed out and reviewed by persons other than those involved in system software or computer operating functions? (D)

16 Are there adequate controls over manual procedures relating to cataloguing (e.g. the control of previous versions where programs are held off-line)?

17 Are the results of the procedures in 15 and 16 reviewed and approved by a responsible official? (S)

Immediate modifications

18 Where immediate modifications have to be made to production programs bypassing normal procedures, are there adequate procedures to ensure that changes are correctly made and approved (e.g. by retroactively applying the standard procedures)?

19 Are the results of the procedures in 18 reviewed and approved by a responsible official? (S)

Program security controls

Programs in use

20 Is the principal control that unauthorised changes cannot be made to production programs while in use:

(a) manual review of computer-produced report of jobs processed;
    If yes, answer 21 to 23

(b) manual authorisation of jobs before processing;
    If yes, answer 24 and 25

(c) regular comparison of production programs with independently controlled copies;
    If yes, answer 26 to 29

(d) password protection of production programs?
    If yes, answer 30 to 35

Manual review

21 Are the system software procedures appropriate to ensure that all production programs accessed are reported?

22 Review the answers to the system software section. Are there adequate controls over the implementation and security of system software?

23 Are there adequate procedures to review the reports of jobs processed?

Manual authorisation

24 Are jobs approved by reference to appropriate evidence (e.g. authorised processing schedules)?

25 Are there adequate controls that:

 (a) no unauthorised changes are made to authorised jobs after authorisation;

 (b) unauthorised jobs are not added?

Program comparisons

26 Are comparisons made on a surprise basis?

27 Are the system software procedures appropriate to achieve a suitable comparison?

28 Review the answers to the system software section. Are there adequate controls over the implementation and security of system software?

29 Are there adequate procedures for investigation of differences?

Password protection

30 Where production programs are password protected, are the system software procedures appropriate to identify and stop unauthorised attempts to access the programs?

31 Review the answers to the system software section. Are there adequate controls over the implementation and security of system software?

32 Are there adequate procedures for the investigation of the reports of unauthorised attempts to access programs?

33 Are there adequate controls over the:
 (a) issue;
 (b) use;
 (c) security

 of passwords?

34 Do the controls in 33 apply at all times when program libraries are on-line to terminals (e.g. during testing)?

35 Are there adequate controls over the:
 (a) issue;
 (b) use;
 (c) security

 of keys and badges that activate terminals?

147

Disciplines

36 Are the following procedures either performed or checked by persons other than those involved in computer operations, system design and programming: (D)

(a) review of jobs processed; (23)
(b) authorisation of jobs before processing; (24)
(c) investigation of differences arising from program comparisons? (29)

37 Are the following procedures either performed or checked by persons other than those involved in computer operations, system design and programming or terminal use: (D)

(a) investigation of unauthorised attempts to access programs; (32)
(b) issue, use and security of passwords; (33)
(c) issue, use and security of keys and badges? (35)

38 Are the results of the following procedures reviewed and approved by a responsible official: (S)

(a) review of jobs processed; (23)
(b) authorisation of jobs before processing; (24)
(c) investigation of differences arising from program comparisons; (29)
(d) investigation of unauthorised attempts to access programs; (32)
(e) issue, use and security of passwords; (33)
(f) issue, use and security of keys and badges? (35)

Non-production

39 Are programs adequately protected during periods of non-production (e.g. by removal to the physical library or by the presence of an operator)?

Utility programs

40 Where there are utility programs which can make changes to production programs, is access to and use of these utilities restricted to authorised personnel?

41 Is each use of these utilities identified, reported and reviewed by a responsible official in the data processing function (e.g. as part of the review of system logs)? (S)

Physical security

42 Are computer operators, job control and other operations personnel responsible for handling and processing production jobs precluded from: (C)

(a) writing or making amendments to production programs and system software;

(b) gaining access to source listings, flowcharts, file layouts and other program documentation?

43 Are system analysts and production program and system software programmers forbidden unsupervised access to the computer room? (C)

44 Do the restrictions in 42 and 43 apply during shifts outside the normal working period (e.g. weekends) and during periods of non-production work (e.g. program testing)?

Off-line programs

45 When not in use, are programs securely held by persons other than those involved in system design and programming? (C)

46 Are programs only issued in accordance with appropriate authorisation?

47 Are there adequate records so that programs issued can be accounted for?

48 Are there adequate procedures to ensure the prompt return of programs (e.g. by a regular review of the records to determine the reasons why any have not been returned)?

49 Are the procedures in 47 and 48 either performed or checked by persons other than those responsible for: (D)

(a) computer operations;

(b) system design and programming?

50 Where the records in 47 are computer-based, are the system software procedures appropriate to maintain accurate records?

51 Are the results of the procedures in 48 and 49 reviewed and approved by a responsible official? (S)

52 Review the answers to the system software section. Are there adequate controls over the implementation and security of system software?

53 Do the controls in 45 to 51 apply during shifts outside the normal working period (e.g. weekends) and during periods of non-production work (e.g. program testing)?

Computer operations controls

Job set-up

54   Are there adequate job set-up instructions (e.g. including details for JCL, parameters and sequence of operations) for:

(a) each application;
(b) system software?

55   Are all changes to the instructions initiated only on the basis of appropriate written authorisation?

56   Are there adequate controls to ensure that the instructions remain correct and up-to-date (e.g. periodic independent review of the instructions)?

57   Are there adequate controls that the job control statements and parameters used in processing are in accordance with the instructions (e.g. review of computer listing of statements and parameters used)?

58   Are the procedures in 57 either performed or checked by persons other than those responsible for job set-up and computer operating? (D)

59   Are the results of the procedures in 57 reviewed and approved by a responsible official? (S)

Operations software

60   Are the system software procedures (e.g. supervisor program) appropriate to ensure that production programs are properly processed?

61   Review the answers to the system software section. Are there adequate controls over the implementation and security of system software?

Computer operating

62   Are there adequate operating instructions for all operator actions?

63   Are all changes to the instructions initiated only on the basis of appropriate written authorisation?

64   Are there adequate controls to ensure that the instructions remain correct and up-to-date (e.g. periodic review by the operations manager)?

65   Is the control that operators comply with operating instructions and do not adversely affect the results of processing a suitable combination of:

(a) supervision in the computer room;
If yes, answer 66

(b) review of a record of processing?
If yes, answer 67 to 72

Supervision

66   Is a supervisor present in the computer room at all times, including shifts outside the normal working period?

Record of processing

67   Where the record is computer-produced:

(a) are the system software procedures appropriate to ensure that all unusual situations (e.g. hardware malfunctions, re-runs, abnormal endings) and consequent operator actions are automatically recorded;

(b) are there adequate controls over the implementation and security of system software (review the answers to the system software section)?

68   Where the record is manually-produced, are there adequate controls to ensure that all unusual situations and consequent operator actions are automatically recorded (e.g. review by the operations supervisor)?

69   Are there adequate controls to ensure that the records reviewed are complete (e.g. recorded on a pre-numbered form; recorded on the run sheet)?

70   Are all unusual situations and consequent operator actions adequately investigated?

71   Is the investigation in 70 either performed or checked by persons other than those involved in computer operations? (D)

72   Are the results of the procedures in 70 reviewed and approved by a responsible official? (S)

Use of correct data files

73   Are there adequate procedures to ensure that:

(a) correct files are used (e.g. software check on file-id, internal volume serial number, creation date and generation number);

(b) all volumes of a multivolume file are used?

151

74 Where reliance is placed on system software to ensure the use of correct files:

(a) are the system software procedures appropriate (e.g. to distinguish between different generations of a master file);

(b) are there adequate controls over the implementation and security of system software (review the answers to the system software section)?

75 Is adequate evidence of the system software procedures printed out and reviewed by persons other than those involved in computer operations or system software? (D)

76 Are the results of the procedures in 73 and 75 reviewed and approved by a responsible official? (S)

Recovery from processing failure

77 Are there appropriate back-up arrangements over the following so that, in the event of a failure, the recovery process does not introduce an erroneous change into the system:

(a) production programs;
(b) system software;
(c) data files?

78 Is the action taken during the recovery process reviewed and approved by a responsible official? (S)

Data file security controls

Data files in use

79 Is the principal control that unauthorised changes cannot be made to data files while in use:

(a) manual review of computer-produced report of jobs processed;
If yes, answer 80 to 82

(b) manual authorisation of jobs before processing;
If yes, answer 83 and 84

(c) software protection of data files?
If yes, answer 85 to 90.

80 Are the system software procedures appropriate to ensure that all data files accessed are reported?

81 Review the answers to the system software section. Are there adequate controls over the implementation and security of system software?

82 Are there adequate procedures to review the reports of jobs processed?

Manual authorisation

83 Are jobs approved by reference to appropriate evidence (e.g. authorised processing schedules)?

84 Are there adequate controls that:
  (a) no unauthorised changes are made to authorised jobs after authorisation;
  (b) unauthorised jobs are not added?

Software protection

85 Where files are software protected, are the system software procedures appropriate to identify and stop unauthorised attempts to access the files?

86 Review the answers to the system software section. Are there adequate controls over the implementation and security of system software?

87 Are there adequate procedures for the investigation of the reports of unauthorised attempts to access data files?

88 Are there adequate controls over the:
  (a) issue;
  (b) use;
  (c) security

  of passwords?

89 Do the controls in 88 apply at all times when data files are on-line to terminals (e.g. during testing)?

90 Are there adequate controls over the:
  (a) issue;
  (b) use;
  (c) security

  of keys and badges that activate terminals?

153

Disciplines

91   Are the following procedures either performed or checked by persons other than those involved in computer operations: (D)

(a) review of jobs processed; (82)
(b) authorisation of jobs before processing? (83)

92   Are the following procedures either performed or checked by persons other than those involved in computer operations and terminal use:

(a) investigation of unauthorised attempts to access data files; (87)
(b) issue, use and security of passwords; (88)
(c) issue, use and security of keys and badges? (90)

93   Are the following procedures reviewed and approved by a responsible official: (S)

(a) review of jobs processed; (82)
(b) authorisation of jobs before processing; (83)
(c) investigation of unauthorised attempts to access data files; (87)
(d) issue, use and security of passwords; (88)
(e) issue, use and security of keys and badges? (90)

Non-production

94   Are data files adequately protected during periods of non-production (e.g. by removal to the library or by the presence of an operator)?

Utility programs

95   Where there are utility programs which can make changes to data files, is access to and use of these utilities restricted to authorised personnel?

96   Is each use of these utilities identified, reported and reviewed by a responsible official in the data processing function (e.g. as part of the review of system logs)?

Physical security

97   Are computer operators, job control and other operations personnel responsible for handling and processing production jobs precluded from:

(a) writing or making amendments to production programs and system software;
(b) gaining access to source listings, flowcharts, file layouts and other program documentation?

98 Are system analysts and production program and system software programmers forbidden unsupervised access to the computer room and libraries?

99 Do the restrictions in 95 and 97 apply during shifts outside the normal working period (e.g. weekends) and during periods of non-production work (e.g. program testing)?

Off-line files

100 Are data files securely held when not in use?

101 Are data files only issued in accordance with appropriate authorisation?

102 Are there adequate records so that data files issued can be accounted for?

103 Are there adequate procedures to ensure the prompt return of data files (e.g. by a regular review of the records to determine the reasons why any have not been returned)?

104 Are the procedures in 101 and 103 either performed or checked by persons other than those responsible for: (D)

   (a) computer operations;
   (b) system design and programming?

105 Are the results of the procedures in 101 and 103 reviewed and approved by a responsible official? (S)

106 Where the records in 102 are computer-based, are the system software procedures appropriate to maintain accurate records?

107 Review the answers to the system software section. Are there adequate controls over the implementation and security of system software?

108 Do the controls in 100 to 102 apply during shifts outside the normal working period (e.g. weekends) and during periods of non-production work (e.g. program testing)?

155

System software

Implementation controls

109 Are specifications for the implementation of system software and changes thereto prepared or obtained as a basis for:

(a) understanding and approval by those who will use it;
(b) control of system programming work?

110 Are the system software specifications in 109 reviewed and approved by: (S)

(a) those responsible for the system software function (e.g. manager of system software);
(b) those responsible for using the software (e.g. operations manager; production programs programming manager)?

111 Are system software changes controlled in such a way that it can subsequently be established that they have all been accounted for (e.g. by sequential pre-numbering or by entry of change forms in a register)?

112 Is a regular review made of changes not yet implemented to determine the reasons for delay?

113 Are the:

(a) methods (e.g. review of system generated output); and
(b) scope (e.g. testing with production programs)

of the testing procedures adequate to establish:

(i) the proper operation of system software;
(ii) the inclusion of appropriate options in the case of supplied software?

114 Does a responsible official in the department which will use the system software (e.g. computer operations manager; system development manager) review, where applicable, and approve: (S)

(a) the instructions for using the system software;
(b) the results and completion of testing;
(c) the date of implementation?

115 Does a responsible official (e.g. system software manager) review, where applicable, and approve: (S)

(a) the system software documentation to ensure that it is complete, up-to-date and in accordance with the company's standards;
(b) the instructions for job set-up and computer operations;
(c) the results and completion of testing;
(d) the taking into production of tested system software?

116 Are there adequate controls to ensure that the tested system software is properly taken into production?

117 Is adequate evidence of the cataloguing procedures printed out and reviewed by persons other than those involved in system software or computer operating functions?

118 Are there adequate controls over manual procedures relating to cataloguing (e.g. the control of previous versions where system software is held off-line)?

119 Are the results of the procedures in 117 and 118 reviewed and approved by a responsible official? (S)

120 Where immediate modifications have to be made to system software bypassing normal procedures, are there adequate procedures to ensure that the changes are correctly made and approved (e.g. by retroactively applying the standard procedures)?

121 Are the results of the procedures in 120 reviewed and approved by a responsible official? (S)

Security controls

122 Are there adequate controls (specify) that unauthorised changes cannot be made to system software:

(a) during operations;
(b) at other times?

123 Is the operation of the controls in 122 reviewed and approved by a responsible official? (S)

4

Evaluation of Controls: User Controls and Programmed Procedures

Introduction

4.01 In this chapter and Chapters 5 and 6 the detailed control considerations in computer systems that are relevant to the auditor and how they can be evaluated using the ICQ described in the previous chapter are considered. User controls and programmed procedures are dealt with in this chapter and integrity controls in Chapters 5 and 6. During the discussion in this chapter reference may usefully be made to the selected computer questions included in appendix B to Chapter 3. This chapter is written from the point of view of the auditor rather than those concerned in the design of systems. As a result, it should not be viewed as a statement of either all, or the best, control techniques that should be used for any particular system. However, there are certain overall design concepts which it may be helpful to discuss, before considering the controls in detail.

Design Concepts

Control structure

4.02 The control structure adopted for each application should take account of the whole sequence of processing from the time when the transactions occur to the time when the management report or other output document is used. In particular, the system of control should extend until output documents have reached their final destination and may include work which has to be carried out as a result of the information shown in them, for example the investigation of exception reports.

4.03 In the past it has often been the practice for only a small part of each job to be processed on the computer and for the greater part of the system of control to be outside the computer department. The present trend is for the computer to process more of each application and it follows that the control techniques to be applied in the computer department become increasingly important. Furthermore, a substantial number of the control features may be incorporated within the computer programs. In these circumstances, an adequate control structure is essential for efficient and reliable processing and it should be designed as an integral part of the system of processing, rather than included as an afterthought or as a result of external pressure, for example from an auditor.

4.04 Once the requirements of the whole system of control for any application have been established, it becomes necessary to see how these can be satisfied, bearing in mind the wide range of control techniques available and the differences which exist in complexity, efficacy and expense. In particular, allowance can often be made for a control weakness at one point by the inclusion of an appropriate control at another stage in processing. The object is to ensure that the overall system of control is effective.

Controls and standards of accuracy

4.05 When designing a system of control, it is often difficult, on the one hand, to ensure that no vital control has been omitted and, on the other hand, to avoid controls for their own sake. In particular, consideration has to be given to the real purpose of each control and a balanced judgement made between the cost of operating the control and the risk of any loss that might be experienced if it were omitted.

Types of data to be controlled

4.06 The distinction between **standing data** and **transaction data** has already been made in Chapter 2. In general, an error in a single item of transaction data will have a limited effect, whereas an error in standing data, which may be used each time the file is processed, may have more far-reaching effects. It is therefore usual for higher standards of control to be appropriate for standing data than for transaction data.

4.07 The different data fields within a record may also vary in the degree to which standards of accuracy and extent of checking are important. Transactions will normally contain some data which requires to be converted into financial terms, for example the quantity of an item sold, and some which is only included for reference purposes, for example a customer order number. Although a higher standard of accuracy may usually be appropriate for the financial data than for the data included for reference purposes only, reference data can also be of major importance, as is discussed later in this chapter.

4.08 The factors set out in paragraphs 4.06 and 4.07 need to be taken into account by the auditor in his evaluation of internal control in order to ensure that any recommendations he makes to management are both desirable and practicable.

User Controls and Programmed Procedures

4.09 **User controls** and **programmed procedures** can be defined as all those controls and procedures designed to ensure that valid transactions, and only valid transactions, are processed and recorded completely and accurately. They are thus similar to what are often called "procedural controls". They can be conveniently considered under the following headings which correspond, where appropriate, to the main groupings of computer questions for the various control objectives:

- Completeness of input and updating.

- Accuracy of input and updating.

- Computer-generated data.

- Validity of data processed.

- Calculation, summarisation and categorisation procedures.

- Maintenance of data on files.

- File creation.

Except where specifically mentioned, the considerations are similar for both standing and transaction data.

Completeness of input and updating

4.10 It is important that all transactions are recorded, input and updated on the relevant master file. This requirement is referred to as the completeness of input and updating. It should not be confused with the accuracy of input and updating which is dealt with in paragraphs 4.40 to 4.53. The reason for the distinction is one of convenience in that different techniques are often used to control, on the one hand, completeness and, on the other, accuracy. Completeness means simply all the transactions, whereas accuracy is concerned with the data of each transaction. It follows from this definition that the controls that ensure the resubmission of rejected data relate to completeness.

4.11 In practice, there is a number of control techniques by which the completeness of input and updating is usually controlled. There are various input controls, any one of which may then be combined with one of several updating controls. In the following paragraphs the various control techniques – batch totals, checking of print-outs, computer sequence check and computer matching – are outlined, together with examples of the relevant questions in the ICQ.

Selecting the controls on which to place reliance

4.12   The auditor will often find that more than one technique for ensuring completeness of input is in use for particular transactions. Where possible, he will wish to place reliance on only one technique. He will normally choose the one that is the most effective and whose functioning he can confirm in the most efficient manner. In order to assist the auditor to select the principal control, before the detailed questions are asked regarding completeness of input, there is a question requiring the auditor to identify the principal control from among the alternative techniques. The techniques are listed in the likely order of selection by the auditor and their order may thus vary between different control objectives depending on the type of input. As an example, the following question is asked in control objective 5 when considering the completeness of input to the accounts payable file:

"5.1   *Is the principal control that all documents are input to the computer and updated one of the following (specify which for each type of input):*

(a) *computer matching with a file of goods received;*
   If yes, answer 5.2 to 5.5

(b) *agreement of manually established batch totals (specify totals used);*
   If yes, answer 5.6 to 5.10

(c) *computer sequence check of serially numbered input documents;*
   If yes, answer 5.11 to 5.16

(d) *checking of print-outs of items written to the accounts payable file?*
   If yes, answer 5.17 to 5.20"

Batch totals

4.13   The use of batch totals is a common control technique in batch systems but is seldom used in on-line or real-time systems. In batch systems the technique is found in two basic forms:

● A suitable total for the batch is established manually and recorded in a register. The batch is input and the computer accumulates and prints out the batch total. The total on the print-out is manually agreed with the total recorded in the register. This form of the technique is illustrated in Figure 41.

● The batch total is established manually and input with the batch. The computer accumulates the batch total and compares it with the total input. The computer prints out whether totals are agreed or disagreed. Where totals disagree, the batch is normally rejected. This form of the technique is illustrated in Figure 42.

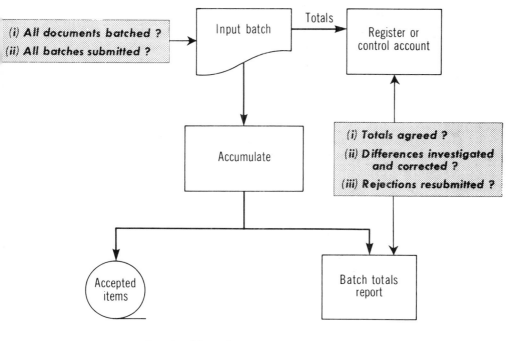

FIG. 41. Manual agreement of batch totals (4.13)

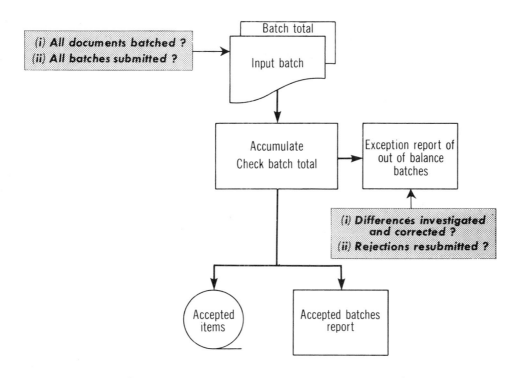

FIG. 42. Computer agreement of batch totals (4.13)

163

4.14   In order to ensure completeness of input and updating, a document count will normally suffice as the minimum level of batch total required. If more than one transaction appears on certain of the documents, a transaction count will be necessary. In practice, batch totals are often based on an important data field, such as value or quantity, and this is equally effective.

4.15   The use of batch totals is only effective as a control technique for completeness from the time that the documents are batched. For this technique to be fully effective it is therefore necessary for there to be adequate controls to ensure that:

(a) all documents are batched; and

(b) all batches are presented for processing.

These requirements will often be met by checking the sequence of numbered documents or batches.

4.16   In control objectives where the input and updating of data is relevant and the use of batch totals is a possible technique, the following questions are asked:

"1. *Are there adequate controls that:*
    (a) *a document is raised for each transaction;*
    (b) *all documents are included in a batch;*
    (c) *all batches are submitted for processing?*
2. *Are pre-determined control totals either:*
    (a) *input and agreed by the computer with the accumulation of individual items accepted and, if so, is adequate evidence of this check printed out; or*
    (b) *agreed manually with the total of accepted items accumulated and printed out by the computer?*
3. *Are there adequate procedures for:*
    (a) *investigation and correction of differences disclosed by the input reconciliations;*
    (b) *resubmission of all rejections?"*

Checking of print-outs

4.17   This technique, which is illustrated in Figure 43, consists of the checking of individual input documents with a detailed listing of items processed by the computer. When relying on this technique, it is necessary to ensure that all documents are included for processing. This is usually achieved by:

(a) retaining a copy in the originating department of all documents sent for processing (the print-out is then checked with the retained copy); or

(b) checking the sequence of input documents or using document counts.

Checking of print-outs is a particularly effective control. It is, however, time-consuming and costly. It is thus normally only used as a technique to control the input and updating of standing data amendments and important accounting adjustments such as write-offs. It is particularly appropriate in batch and on-line systems.

4.18 In control objectives where the input and updating of data is relevant, and the checking of print-outs is a possible technique, the following questions are asked:

"1. *Are there adequate controls that all documents are submitted for processing (e.g. by checking against retained copy; by manual sequence check)?*

2. *Is there a regular (e.g. monthly) review of source documents for unprocessed items?*

3. *Is the method used in the program for the production of the print-out appropriate (e.g. does it contain details of items that have been written to the file)?*

4. *Are there adequate procedures for investigation and correction of differences disclosed by the checking?*"

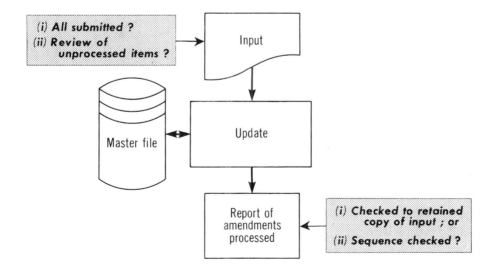

FIG. 43. Checking of print-outs (4.17)

165

Computer sequence check

4.19   This technique, which is illustrated in Figure 44, consists of the computer checking the numbers on documents input and reporting missing and duplicate numbers for manual investigation. This technique is appropriate in batch, on-line and real-time systems.

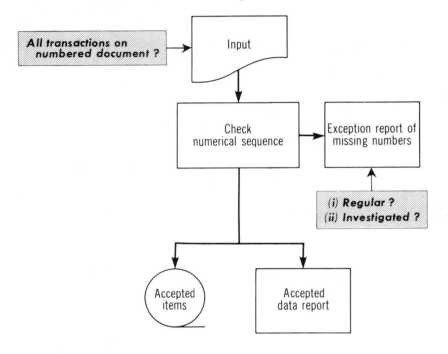

FIG. 44. Computer sequence check (4.19)

4.20   For this control technique to be effective, the following user controls and programmed procedures must be present:

(a) There must be procedures to ensure that all documents are recorded on a standard serially numbered form. Control should exist over the issue of the forms so that a limited number of series are in use at any time.

(b) The method used in the program for checking the numerical sequence must be logically sound. In considering the method, the following points should be borne in mind:

(i) Changes in sequence must be catered for. This can be achieved by the input of parameter cards (see paragraph 6.07) containing the numbers to be checked or by setting up a file containing a table of all numbers which have been issued. Alternatively, the computer may report a change in sequence when it cannot find, say, ten consecutive numbers.

(ii) More than one sequence running at the same time must be

166

catered for. The techniques will be similar to those employed for changes in sequence.

(iii) Where a parameter card is used to identify the first and last sequence numbers, there should be a check to ensure that the first number in a sequence follows on from the last number of the previous sequence.

(iv) Duplicate numbers should be identified and reported. If a table file of numbers (see (b)(i) above) is maintained, duplicates from earlier runs can easily be identified. If there is no table, duplicates can only be identified if they fall between the numbers of the parameter cards input.

(c) Reports of missing and duplicate numbers must be produced frequently to enable prompt follow-up action to correct the error. If reports are not frequently and regularly produced, an error in the sequence logic may not be identified.

(d) There must be adequate manual procedures to investigate missing and duplicate numbers. If a cumulative list of outstanding items is reported, control over investigation work is rendered easier.

4.21   In control objectives where the input and updating of data is relevant, and a computer sequence check is a possible technique, the following questions are asked:

"1. *Are there adequate procedures to ensure that all transactions are recorded on a serially numbered document?*
2. *Is the method used in the program for the checking of numerical sequence appropriate (e.g. does it cater for changes in sequence and more than one sequence running at a time)?*
3. *Is a print-out of missing documents produced at regular intervals (e.g. weekly)?*
4. *Are there adequate procedures for investigation of missing documents?*"

Computer matching

4.22   This technique, which is illustrated in Figure 45, consists of the computer matching data on documents input with information held on master or pipeline files. Outstanding items, being those that have not yet been matched, are reported for manual investigation. As examples, the computer might match clock card details input with an employees' master file and identify and report missing and duplicate clock cards, or the computer might match suppliers' invoices input with a pipeline file of goods received details and periodically report outstanding goods received records. In these examples the matching process is an effective control over the completeness of input of clock cards and suppliers' invoices. This technique is more practicable in on-line and real-time systems than batch systems because of the greater opportunity to match the input with up-to-date master or pipeline files during editing.

167

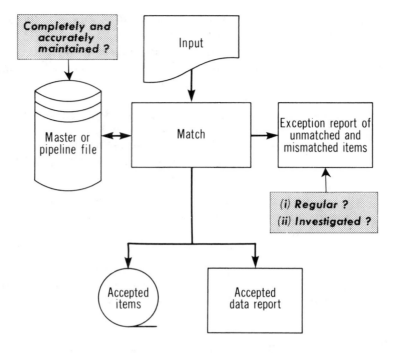

FIG. 45. Computer matching (4.22)

4.23　For this control technique to be effective, the following user controls and programmed procedures must be present:

(a) There must be adequate controls over the file holding details of items to be matched. This will usually be achieved by a regular agreement of file totals with an independent control account.

(b) All adjustments to the data on file should be properly authorised, for example cancelled orders in a sales order processing system.

(c) The method used in the program for matching must be logically sound. In general more than one field of data should be matched, for example both document number and quantities where goods received details are matched with suppliers' invoices.

(d) There must be adequate manual procedures to follow up out-standing and mismatched items. If reports contain a cumulative list of outstanding items, control over investigation work is rendered easier.

4.24　In control objectives where the input and updating of data is relevant, and computer matching is a possible technique, questions of the following type are asked (the example quoted is for the computer matching of purchase invoices with goods received notes in control objective 2):

"1. *Are there adequate controls over the file holding details of outstanding goods and, where applicable, services received so that such details are completely and accurately maintained and subject only to authorised adjustments (e.g. manual control account)?*

2. *Is the method used in the program to match invoices to goods and, where applicable, services received appropriate (e.g. to flag or delete matched items)?*

3. *Is a print-out of items outstanding for an unreasonable length of time (e.g. all over one month) produced at regular intervals?*

4. *Are unmatched records of goods and, where applicable, services reviewed on a regular basis (e.g. monthly) to determine the reasons for any such receipts which have not been matched within a reasonable period of time?"*

Updating

4.25   In certain cases, particularly in the more simple batch systems, the control over the completeness of input will also control the completeness of updating. Examples are the checking of print-outs, provided the check is carried out with a print-out produced after updating, and the manual agreement of batch totals, provided the total being checked is produced after updating. These two control techniques will usually only be possible where there is no, or little, intermediate processing and the data updating the file is identical to that input as, for example, when processing standing data amendments or details of cash receipts to an accounts receivable file. More frequently the data input will be subject to further processing before updating, for example calculation and updating of charges to customers. In these cases, specific updating controls will need to be relied on.

4.26   The specific updating controls in batch systems should normally include the following programmed procedures:

(a) A control total of accepted items should be accumulated during the run in which the computer sequence check, computer matching or other input control is carried out, and the total should be written to a control record on the file. This total should be suitable to ensure completeness of updating of the data and is usually of the most significant data field.

(b) During each subsequent processing run until the master file is updated the individual records should be accumulated as they are read and be agreed with the total in the control record.

(c) Where a calculation is carried out, such as quantity times value, a new control total for the product field will usually be accumulated as in (a) and will then be used as in (b). The accumulation of the new control total should take place in a run in which the existing control total is agreed.

(d) The same procedure as in (c) should be followed where summarisation is carried out, as, for example, where daily sales transactions are merged to form a weekly file before the master file is updated.

169

4.27 It is still considered best practice for the computer to print out the relevant totals after each processing run until the master file is updated and for these totals to be manually checked. However, it is also acceptable for the computer to carry out run-to-run reconciliations without subsequent manual checking. In these cases it is important that the computer prints out adequate evidence of the reconciliation. This would normally mean that the totals used in the reconciliation should be printed, rather than a simple narrative comment that reconciliation has been achieved. This form of updating control is illustrated in Figure 46.

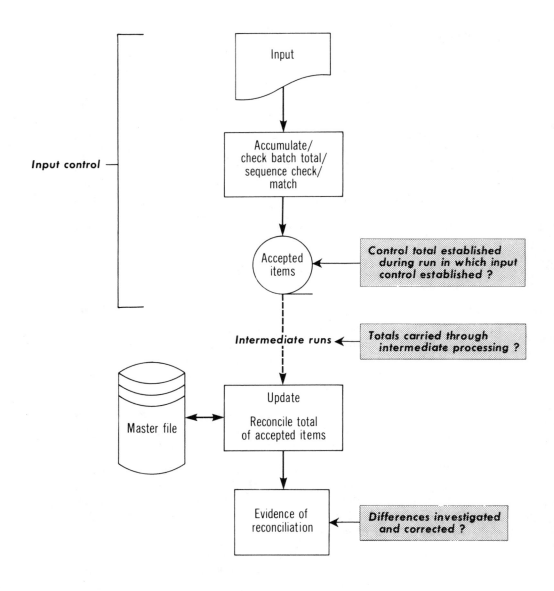

FIG. 46. Computer reconciliation of accepted item totals (4.27)

4.28 In addition to assessing the updating controls the auditor will need to ascertain the extent to which they are subject to manual checking. This is because he will generally wish to rely where possible on manual checking, since it will be easier to see evidence of the operation of the controls when carrying out his audit tests. It is for this reason that, in dealing with updating controls in the ICQ, a question is asked whether the reconciliations are carried out manually or by the computer. This form of updating is illustrated in Figure 47.

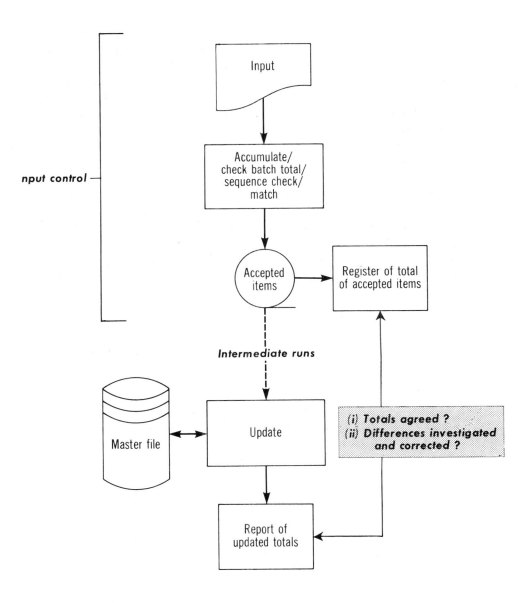

FIG. 47. Manual reconciliation of accepted item totals (4.28)

171

4.29　In real-time systems, and in those on-line systems where trans-actions are processed individually rather than in batches, the con-cept of a "run", as used in paragraphs 4.26 and 4.27 does not apply. Transactions input to such systems trigger the relevant programs required to process the particular transaction. During processing, separate totals of the different transaction types will be progressively accumulated at appropriate points in the system. Periodically, for example daily, the contents of the master file will be reorganised and during this process the movements on the file since the last reconciliation can be agreed with the totals accumulated during processing.

4.30　Where files are organised as a database, the updating control totals reconciled at the time may consist of the number of records added to, and deleted from, the database. Reliance will be placed, at the time, on the software procedures to make all required linkages set up to establish the logical relationships between individual data items. Periodically, the complete establishment of linkages will be proved by reconciling the vari-ous logical groupings, usually in value terms. For example, in respect of accounts receivable records, separate reconciliations may be made of outstanding invoices, credit notes, cash and adjustments.

4.31　In the ICQ, the questions regarding the completeness of updating follow immediately the questions relating to completeness of input. Thus, in control objectives where input and updating of data is relevant, the questions set out below follow the questions regarding both computer sequence check and computer matching (the example quoted is in respect of updating items to the accounts payable file following an input control of computer sequence check in control objective 5):

"1. *Is a total (specify total used) of accepted items accumulated by the computer during the sequence check run and either:*
　　(a) *agreed to the total of items written to the accounts payable file;*
　　　 or
　　(b) *carried through intermediate processing (including sum-marisation of totals or changes in the totals used) so that it is established that all accepted input items are updated to the accounts payable file?*

　2. *Is the reconciliation of totals in 1 carried out:*
　　(a) *manually; or*
　　(b) *by the computer and, if so, is adequate evidence of this check printed out?*

　3. *Are there adequate procedures for investigation and correction of differences disclosed by the update reconciliations?"*

4.32　Where checking of print-outs produced after updating is used as the control, no specific updating questions are asked because the checking controls both input and updating. Where batch totals form the input control, the first updating question is slightly different to that set out in paragraph 4.31 and is as follows (using the same example as in paragraph 4.31):

"*Are the totals* (i.e. input batch totals) *either:*

(a) *agreed to the total of items written to the accounts payable file; or*

(b) *carried through intermediate processing (including summarisation of totals or changes in the total used) so that it is established that all accepted input items are updated to the accounts payable file?"*

This is to recognise that the totals are used to control both input and updating.

Rejections

4.33 The data input for processing in a computer system will often contain incorrect items, but, unlike non-computer systems, it is not normally possible or practical to investigate and adjust each incorrect item as it occurs during processing. Incorrect items are most commonly identified during input, when edit checks (see paragraph 4.46) are carried out, and during updating when transactions cannot be matched with master file records. This incorrect data has to be either rejected from the processing or transferred to a suspense file within the computer system.

4.34 Detailed procedures are required for the prompt investigation, correction and resubmission of rejections and items held on suspense files. It may also be necessary to adjust previously-established control totals.

4.35 The speed of correction of rejections may be important in on-line systems where input data is matched with master files. If rejections are left uncorrected, the master files will not be up to date when the validity of subsequent input is checked. This would be of particular importance where, for example, cash requests are matched with a customer's overdraft balance. Speed of correction may also be important where database file organisation is used, since several users may depend on common input and not all may be aware of outstanding rejections.

4.36 As regards rejections at the input stage, the auditor, being concerned with the principal controls, will normally only need to rely on the rejection procedures where batch totals form the principal input control. This is because, where checking of print-outs, computer sequence check or computer matching is the control on which he has chosen to rely, rejections will usually continue to be identified as items that are unprocessed, missing or unmatched and the investigation of these items will reveal any breakdowns in rejection procedures. This is not the case where batch totals form the principal control because it is unlikely that the computer will store and continue to report details of rejected items or batches.

4.37 The nature of the monitoring of the rejection procedures will depend on whether the batch totals are checked manually or by the computer. If the totals are checked manually, there will be a register and rejections must be recorded therein when the control totals are adjusted. If the totals are checked by computer, there will be no previously-established total and no record of the adjustment. Thus, in these cases, there is less evidence of the volume of rejections and a greater reliance on the supervision of the detailed procedures for dealing with rejections.

4.38 In the ICQ the questions relating to batch totals include the question:

"Are there adequate procedures for resubmission of all rejections?"

4.39 The auditor will always be concerned with rejections arising at the update stage. Thus, whenever updating questions are asked in the ICQ, the auditor will need to consider the procedures for dealing with rejections when answering the question:

"Are there adequate procedures for investigation and correction of differences disclosed by the update reconciliations?"

Accuracy of input and updating

4.40 It is important that the data on transactions is accurately input and updated. For these purposes input includes **transcription** from source data to input documents and then the **conversion** of the data on input documents into machine-readable form, as illustrated in Figure 48. Where input is keyed direct to tape or disc, or documents are read direct into the computer, as described in paragraphs 2.08 and 2.09, transcription from source data to input documents is unlikely to occur. Accuracy of input and updating can only be achieved if all data fields of accounting significance are adequately controlled. The requirement for control is greater at the input stage than during processing, because it is unusual for data to become corrupted once it is in the computer.

Data fields to be controlled

4.41 Initially, it is necessary for the auditor to establish the data fields that require to be controlled and the degree of control that is necessary. In this context, it has to be recognised that it may not be practicable to achieve an exhaustive degree of control over all data fields. The identification of the data fields that require a high degree of control is not necessarily obvious. All "financial" data fields are important, that is to say either value fields or fields that will enter into a calculation of value such as hours or quantities. In addition, certain "reference" data fields will be important. These may include reference numbers, dates and indicators.

Reference numbers

4.42 The accuracy of reference numbers of personal accounts, inventory lines and general ledger codings will be important to ensure that correct

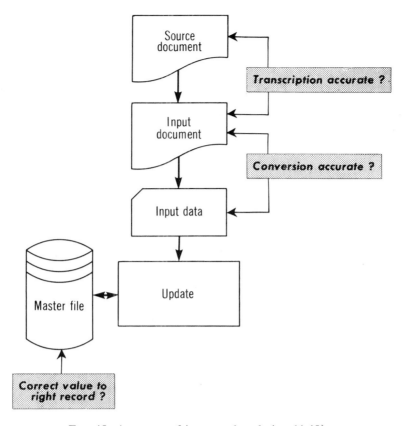

FIG. 48. Accuracy of input and updating (4.40)

accounts are updated. The accuracy of reference numbers of inventory lines will also be important to ensure that pricing is properly carried out.

Dates

4.43　The accurate input and updating of dates can be important in many circumstances. Dates held as standing data may initiate the computer accounting process. Examples of dates used in this manner include the date stock is to be reported for counting, the date of credit sale agreements and when repayment instalments are due and, in relation to utilities, the date on which a customer's meter is to be read and thus, a set time thereafter, a bill is to be raised. Failure to input and update accurately dates of this nature may lead to loss of revenue or the failure to carry out control procedures. Dates input as part of transactions may also be important, as, for example, in the case of sales or inventory transactions where computer ageing of customers and inventory balances is relied on or, in the case of suppliers' invoices, where the computer is programmed to generate cheques on specified dates.

Indicators

4.44　The accurate input and updating of indicators can also be important. An indicator is a field on a data record, the content of which determines how a transaction is to be treated by the application programs. Often the type or

175

sign (i.e. positive or negative) of a transaction is identified by means of an indicator and an error in its input and updating could lead to the opposite effect to that intended. For example, in wages and salaries systems it is common for a similar form to be used for those starting and leaving employment, the distinction being made by a different indicator for a starter and a leaver. Indicators can also be important from a control point of view as, for example, where a stock item is defined as high security stock and is input with an indicator so that the program selects it for count more frequently.

Control techniques

Use of completeness controls

4.45   Some of the techniques by which accuracy of input and updating is achieved are similar to those used for completeness of input and updating. These are checking of print-outs, directed to the accuracy of the fields examined, batch totals, directed to the accuracy of the fields totalled and agreed, and computer matching, which checks the accuracy of the fields that are matched. These techniques may be used singly to achieve both completeness and accuracy or separately to achieve accuracy with another technique being used for completeness.

Edit checks

4.46   Except for checking of print-outs, it is unusual for the techniques outlined in paragraph 4.45 to control all important data fields and use will be made of programmed procedures to check the accuracy of other data fields, usually during input. These procedures are normally called "edit checks". There are often several checks and considerable scope is available if care is taken at the program specification stage. The different types of edit checks are considered in paragraphs 4.48 and 4.49.

4.47   The opportunity for editing is usually greater in on-line and real-time systems where input data can often be comprehensively matched with master files. This process can be extended where the files are organised as a database, and more data is available for matching. For example, a sales invoice which could, in a conventional system, only be compared with a constant for size, could, in a database, be compared with the previous experience of sales to the customer concerned.

4.48   *Format checks, existence checks and check digit verification* – These can be described as follows:

- **Format checks**. These test the format of input records and ensure, for example, that all data fields are present and contain alphabetic or numeric characters, as appropriate. Checks of this nature will usually be required for operational reasons and may be helpful to the auditor to ensure that reference data such as dates and indicators are present.

- **Existence checks.** These test reference numbers with previously-established lists of valid numbers held on a file or in the program. They can be useful in ensuring that only valid general ledger codes are input.

- **Check digit verification**. Using this technique the program carries out a mathematical test on reference numbers which enables it to identify most incorrectly transcribed numbers.

It will be noted that the effect of format checks, existence checks and check digit verification is to identify errors as early as possible in the processing cycle. If the checks were not present, the errors would emerge at the updating stage when it was found that items could not match with a record on the relevant master file. In more advanced systems when master files are on-line, the validity of reference numbers can usually be more effectively checked by matching with the master file records at the input stage, thus reducing the importance of these checks.

4.49   *Reasonableness checks and dependency checks* — These can be briefly described as follows:

- **Reasonableness checks**. These are checks to test whether the data is reasonable in relation to a standard or previous input. The standard is held on a file or in the program and can be used where it is possible to define a standard against which the data input can be compared. Examples are hours worked, quantities shipped and interest rates. In cases where a standard is not appropriate, it may be practical to compare data input with previous input. Examples are units consumed in utilities and prices of goods purchased.

- **Dependency checks**. These are checks to test whether the contents of two or more data fields are logically possible on the same input document. Considerable ingenuity can be exercised in devising tests of this nature which can provide a strong control over the accuracy of the fields concerned. Examples are that requests for final bills, in utilities, must have an up-to-date meter reading present, shipments of refrigerated goods must include a charge for refrigerated transport, and hire purchase agreements must have a valid start date.

Reasonableness and dependency checks are likely to be of particular importance since they are often applied to the data fields, such as indicators, that it is difficult or impracticable to control in any other manner.

Verification of conversion and scrutiny of output

4.50   In many systems it is still common to verify conversion by carrying out the operation a second time, for example in the preparation of punched cards or paper tape. However, reliance on verification of punching is diminishing as it becomes easier and cheaper to identify conversion errors by the use of the edit checks described in paragraphs 4.48 and 4.49. Where fields cannot be subjected to these tests, verification of punching remains an important element of control. As an alternative, it may be practical to carry out a manual scrutiny of output to obtain a degree of satisfaction that data has been input and updated accurately. Reliance on a scrutiny of this nature would probably only be reasonable where the fields concerned were less important, for example those used in a geographical analysis of sales.

Selecting the controls on which to place reliance

4.51 In practice the auditor is likely to be confronted with a combination of the controls outlined in paragraphs 4.45 to 4.50. From these he will seek to identify the controls on which to place reliance. In general he will ascertain whether suitable controls exist in the order outlined above, that is he will see first whether the completeness controls ensure accuracy of both input and updating. As regards data fields not controlled in this manner, he will enquire into the edit checks and any other programmed procedures. Only then, if important data fields remain uncontrolled, will he normally need to place reliance on the verification of conversion. He will also need to bear in mind, as indicated in paragraph 4.41, that it may not be possible to provide complete assurance as to the accurate input and updating of every data field, particularly as regards transaction data.

4.52 Because of the wide variety of techniques that may be found, it is not practicable to list in the ICQ the various techniques for accuracy of input and updating as is done for completeness. Instead, whenever the accuracy of input and updating is relevant to a control objective, the following questions are asked (the example quoted is in respect of the input and updating of details of goods received in control objective 2):

"1. *Are there adequate controls that the following fields are accurately input and updated (e.g. batch totals, edit checks in programs, reporting of non-matched items):*

   (a) *quantity/value;*
   (b) *inventory/vendor reference fields;*
   (c) *price;*
   (d) *date?*

2. *Are there adequate procedures for:*
   (a) *the agreement of totals, where applicable;*
   (b) *investigation and correction of differences or exceptions?"*

4.53 In addition, where a master file is updated, the following question is asked:

"*Is the method used in the program for the updating of individual accounts appropriate?"*

Computer-generated data

4.54 The circumstances in which the computer may initiate data have been outlined in paragraph 2.14. The computer can be programmed to initiate data under specified conditions in one of the following ways:

   (a) The processing of a transaction may create a specified condition. For example, the processing of a stock issue reduces stock below minimum level and a purchase order is produced. In these cases the condition is normally recognised by a comparison with standing data, for example the minimum stock level. This form of generation of data is likely to be most common where the files are organised as a database.

(b) A condition that triggers the initiation of a transaction may be input. For example, the input of a date will lead to the production of cheques for all suppliers' invoices dated prior to a certain date; the input of a stage of production reached will generate the appropriate charges to work in progress; the input of a requisition code will generate a listing of the components to be issued.

4.55 If data is to be generated by the computer completely and accurately in the circumstances outlined in paragraph 4.54, the following features, which are illustrated in Figure 49, are necessary:

- The signals, such as dates, or stage of production reached, that trigger the generation of data must be input completely and accurately.

- The steps carried out by the program in generating the data must be logically sound. The first step will consist of identifying the data, for

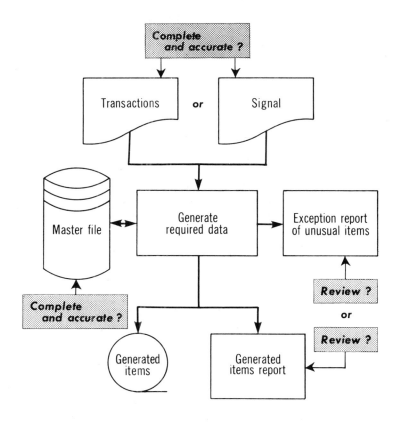

FIG. 49. Computer-generated data (4.55)

179

example, in the case of cheque payments, invoices dated prior to the date signal or, in the case of purchase orders, stock items where the present balance is less than minimum stock level. Further steps will include producing a document, such as a cheque or purchase order, and accumulating the value of transactions generated (purchases, payments) to create a control total.

- The standing data referred to, such as the minimum stock level, or providing the basis of the generated data, such as reorder quantity or a parts explosion, must be reliable. This involves all the controls over the amendment and maintenance of standing data on the file because, unlike manual systems, the standing data normally may not be manually checked on the accounting documents.

- The generated data should be manually reviewed, for example a scrutiny of purchase orders before despatch, or be subject to suitable programmed procedure, for example cheques over a certain amount reported for investigation.

4.56   After the data has been generated by the computer, it will need to be subject to updating controls. These will be similar to those already outlined for input data in paragraphs 4.25 to 4.32 and will be based on the control total accumulated during the generation of the data. In practice updating often takes place at the time the data is generated.

4.57   In control objectives where computer-generated data is relevant, the following questions are asked (the example quoted is in respect of raw materials in control objective 10):

"1. *Are the methods used in the program to generate the data and related control record appropriate (e.g. minor physical count adjustments)?*
  2. *Is there a control over the accuracy of the data generated (e.g. reasonableness check, manual review of generated data)?*
  3. *Are all entries in the materials and supplies inventories file generated by the computer reviewed and approved by a responsible official? (S)*
  4. *Is a total (specify total used) of generated items accumulated by the computer and agreed with a total of items written to/off the materials and supplies inventories file:*
      (a) *manually; or*
      (b) *by the computer and, if so, is adequate evidence of this check printed out?*
  5. *Are there adequate procedures for investigation and correction of differences disclosed by the update reconciliations?"*

Validity of data processed

4.58   Having considered the controls over the input, or generation, and updating of data, it is next appropriate to consider the controls that ensure the validity of the data being processed. It is essential that only valid data is written to master files and printed on reports incorporated in the accounting records. Thus all data should be appropriately authorised or checked.

In many cases the checking procedure will be similar to that used in a non-computer system, as, for example, when goods received notes are checked with the physical goods or shipping documents are checked with goods shipped. Questions relating to these procedures are asked when relevant to a control objective.

4.59 There are, however, the following important features in authorising data in computer systems:

(a) Data is often authorised at the time it is input to the computer rather than at the time the resulting accounting output is produced.

(b) Instead of authorising all data prior to input or after processing, the computer may be programmed to identify and report defined items for manual authorisation, for example excessive overtime. Items passing the programmed procedures are not specifically authorised.

(c) In some cases the ability of the program to test precisely aspects of an item's validity is such that manual authorisation may no longer be required, for example matching hours worked by employees with the employees' master file and rejecting duplicate input.

The significance of these differences is discussed in the following paragraphs.

Timing of authorisation

4.60 The authorisation of data at the time of input, rather than when the resulting accounting output is produced, occurs both with standing data and with transaction data. For example, sales prices will be authorised when they are written to the file, but thereafter the price will not normally be authorised when sales invoices are produced; credit given to customers will be authorised at the time the claim is input and not when the credit note is produced. Where data is authorised at the time of input, it is important to ensure that the authorisation remains effective and that changes cannot be made after authorisation and during the subsequent processing. In some cases the controls for completeness and accuracy of input and updating will indicate the presence of unauthorised data. For example, processed output is sometimes checked in detail with authorised input by one for one checking of standing data amendments, or input is matched with authorised data held on file, such as goods received details matched with a file of purchase orders. In other cases specific procedures will be required. These will normally consist either of authorising the data after control for completeness and accuracy of input and updating has been established, for example by authorising items in batches after batch totals have been established and recorded, or of checking that all items have been authorised after control has been established, for example by checking that all items on serially numbered documents have been authorised. These procedures are illustrated in Figure 50.

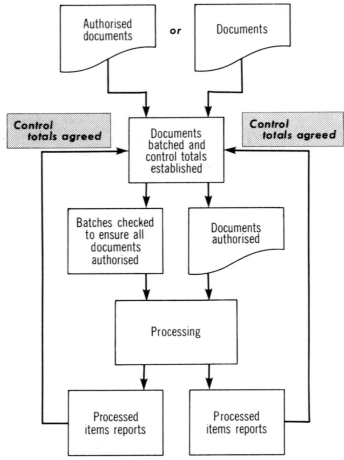

FIG. 50. Timing of authorisation (4.60)

4.61 In control objectives that deal with the input and updating of data there is the following question:

> "*If data is authorised prior to the establishment of the controls for completeness and accuracy of input (e.g. prior to establishment of batch control totals or recording on a sequentially numbered document), are there adequate controls (e.g. checking authorisation after batch control totals are established or sequentially numbered documents raised) that:*
> (a) *no unauthorised alterations are made to authorised data during subsequent processing;*
> (b) *unauthorised data is not added;*
> (c) *authorised items are not omitted from subsequent processing?*"

4.62   Manual authorisation on a selection basis is relied on where the computer is programmed to identify and report defined items for manual authorisation. This will involve the program matching the input with a constant in the program, for example matching hours worked with a standard, and reporting excessive overtime, as illustrated in Figure 51. For this form of authorisation to be effective, the constant must be reasonably fixed, the matching process must be logically sound and the items reported as exceptional must be authorised as acceptable or not.

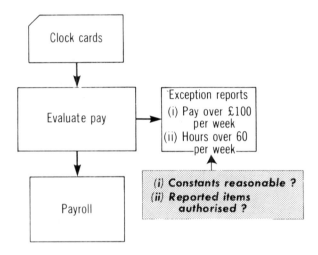

FIG. 51. Selective authorisation (4.62)

Programmed checking of validity

4.63   As an extension to selective manual authorisation, the computer can be programmed to test precisely an item's validity. The computer either accepts or rejects the item. This occurs where the program can match input with the data on a master file, for example matching hours worked by employees with an employees' master file and rejecting duplicate input, or matching with a pipeline file, for example matching suppliers' invoices with a file of purchase orders and goods received details and rejecting invoices where there is no record of order or receipt of goods. In these cases the computer test is so conclusive as to the specified aspects of validity that manual authorisation may be unnecessary. For this form of checking to be effective there must be adequate controls over the data against which the input is matched and the matching process must be

183

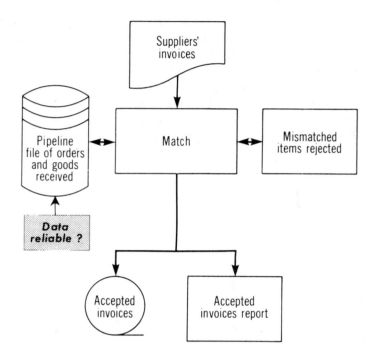

FIG. 52. Programmed checking of validity (4.63)

logically sound. Programmed checking of validity is illustrated in Figure 52.

Calculating, summarising and categorising

4.64 The techniques of calculating, summarising and categorising are described in paragraph 2.13.

Calculating

4.65 Calculating differs from computer-generated data in that it consists of carrying out a calculation on the data input. Controls over the input of the data have already been considered. For computer calculating to be effective the following features, which are illustrated in Figure 53, are necessary:

(a) The standing data referred to, such as prices or rates of pay, must be reliable. This involves all the controls over the amendment and maintenance of standing data on the file because, unlike manual systems, the standing data normally may not be manually checked on the accounting documents.

184

(b) The method used in the program to carry out the calculation must be logically sound.

(c) There should be some check on the accuracy of the calculations. This usually takes the form of a manual review of exceptions, such as excessive wages, produced and reported by the computer, or a manual review of the results of the calculations.

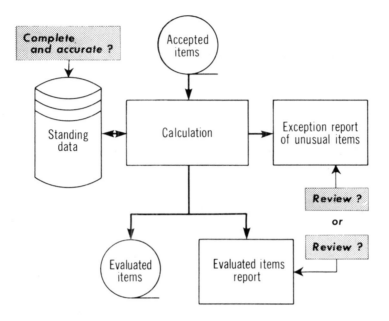

FIG. 53. Calculating (4.65)

4.66   In control objectives where calculating is relevant, questions on the following lines are asked (the example quoted is in respect of the calculation of pay in control objective 6):

> *"List below the standing data fields used in the preparation of payrolls (e.g. rate of pay, deductions, employee number, commission rates) and state on which file these fields are recorded.*

> 1. *In respect of each field listed above, review the answers to the standing data controls section. Are there adequate controls over:*

>> (a) *where applicable, file creation;*
>> (b) *the authorisation of amendments;*

(c) *the completeness of writing amendments to the file;*

(d) *the accuracy of writing amendments to the file;*

(e) *the maintenance of the data on the file?*

2. *As regards the computer calculations of gross amounts due, deductions and net amounts due:*

    (a) *is the method used in the program for the calculation appropriate;*

    (b) *are there adequate controls over the accuracy of the calculation (e.g. an exception report of abnormal pay)?"*

Summarising and categorising

4.67   Summarising and categorising are conveniently considered together. To be effective the following features, which are illustrated in Figure 54, are necessary:

(a) The codes on which summarisation and categorisation are based must be correct and accurately input.

(b) There must be adequate controls over the summarisation. The totals accumulated by the computer will usually be those already discussed in relation to updating, and the controls over completeness of updating outlined in paragraphs 4.25 to 4.32 will also control summarisation.

(c) The basis on which the program carries out categorisation must be sound.

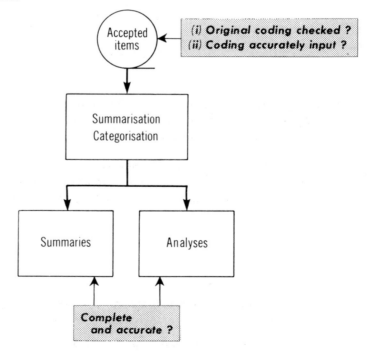

Fig. 54. Summarising and categorising (4.67)

4.68   Summarisation and categorisation questions appear in control objectives which deal with the accurate determination of general ledger entries, for example control objective 13. The relevant questions are as follows:

"1. *Is the coding of transactions for posting to general ledger accounts checked to an appropriate extent?*

2. *Are there adequate controls that the coding of transactions is accurately input (e.g. validity checks in program)?*

3. *Are there adequate controls that computer-produced analyses are complete and accurate (e.g. manual or programmed reconciliations)?*

4. *Is the method used in the program to categorise and summarise computer-produced analyses appropriate?*

5. *Where the computer-produced analyses are further categorised and/or summarised manually, are there adequate controls (e.g. reconciliation of totals) that the manual summaries are complete and accurate?"*

Maintenance of data on files

4.69   Maintenance is the term in common use for the control procedures that ensure that the data stored on master files remains correct until deleted during authorised processing. As regards transaction data the requirements and techniques are similar to those in non-computer systems. However, the maintenance controls over standing data in computer systems normally have no precise equivalent in non-computer systems. This is because it is usually difficult to implement adequate maintenance controls in non-computer systems and standing data is generally checked at the time it is used.

4.70   It used to be held that a major purpose of maintenance controls was to reveal errors arising from corruption of data on the files. Errors arising in this way are now extremely rare and the major reason for maintenance controls is to provide protection against the unauthorised alteration of data on files. This is particularly important in relation to standing data which may remain active on file for considerable periods of time. Experience shows that, despite acceptable input and updating controls, a significant volume of incorrect data can build up on master files in the absence of regular maintenance controls. In addition, maintenance controls provide assurance that the correct generation of the file has been used each time it is updated.

4.71   The most effective maintenance control is the regular reconciliation of an accumulation of items on the file with an independently maintained control account. The entries in the control account may have been derived from original manually-established batch totals. In these cases the auditor may be able to rely on these reconciliations as the principal control for input and updating as well as maintenance. However, it does not matter if the entries into the control account are computer-produced since the purpose of the maintenance control is to ensure that what is on the file as a result of normal processing remains on the file. For the same

187

reason, although less desirable, reliance on programmed reconciliations is acceptable provided the brought forward totals on the current reconciliation report are checked to the carried forward totals on the previous report. This is necessary because a programmed reconciliation will not normally identify that the opening balance is the same as the closing balance when the last reconciliation took place, and unauthorised processing and resulting alterations to control totals may have occurred. These reconciliation procedures are illustrated in Figure 55.

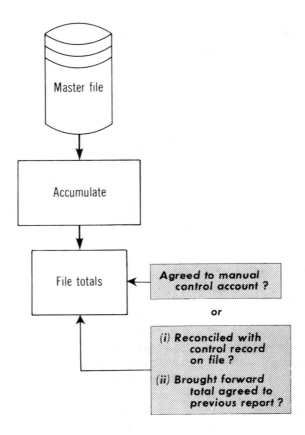

Fɪɢ. 55. Reconciliation of file totals (4.71)

4.72   The frequency of file reconciliation procedures will depend largely on the nature of processing. Where file updating is sequential, it will be normal for reconciliations to be carried out during each processing run because all records are read and can be easily accumulated. Where updating is by direct access methods, particularly in real-time systems, reconciliation procedures are likely to be carried out less frequently, either when the data on the discs is reorganised or periodically using a special program designed for the purpose. This latter method is the one normally used where data is organised on files using database techniques.

Transaction data

4.73 The reconciliation procedures outlined in the preceding paragraphs should be applied to transaction data. It will usually be sufficient for the value balance on the account to be reconciled in this manner. Normally the control account with which the file is reconciled will be in the general ledger and form part of the double-entry book keeping.

4.74 Where the reconciliation procedures are not conclusive, for example carried out by computer without any manual check of brought forward totals, the auditor may be able to rely on data file security controls. If the data files are effectively protected from unauthorised access, the main requirement of maintenance controls is satisfied. Data file security controls are discussed in Chapter 6.

4.75 In the ICQ the questions regarding maintenance of transaction data on files follow the input and updating questions. Thus in control objectives where input and updating of data is relevant, the following questions appear (the example quoted is in respect of the accounts payable file in control objective 5):

"1. *Is an accumulation of the items on the file regularly reconciled with either:*
　　(a) *a manual control account maintained by a user department; or*
　　(b) *a control record on file; and, if so, is adequate evidence of the reconciliation printed out?*

2. *Where the reconciliation is carried out by the computer (1b):*
　　(a) *is the brought forward total checked; or*
　　(b) *if not, are there adequate controls (review the answers to the integrity controls section) to ensure that unauthorised changes cannot be made to data files?*

3. *Are there adequate procedures for investigating differences disclosed by the reconciliations in 1 and 2(a) before any adjustments are made?"*

Standing data

4.76 It is desirable that the more important data fields, such as prices and interest rates, should be subject to the reconciliation procedures outlined above. It may also be desirable to reconcile the number of accounts or

189

records on the file. This is particularly important in the case of accounts payable, because the opening of unauthorised suppliers' accounts and obtaining payment, often through computer-produced cheques, is a known form of fraud in computer systems. For similar reasons the number of employees on payroll files should be regularly reconciled. Specific control accounts outside the double-entry book keeping will need to be maintained for reconciling standing data.

4.77 While it is desirable that the reconciliation procedures should be applied to standing data, it is recognised that many systems are developed without these procedures being applied to most fields of accounting significance and, in these cases, data file security controls and regular cyclical checking will often provide acceptable alternatives.

4.78 The cycle checking would consist of systematically checking the standing data on file with source data. The speed and frequency of checking will depend largely on the importance of the data and the existence of other controls. In circumstances where considerable reliance is placed on this control, it might be appropriate to check all data once a quarter, so that the data is completely checked four times a year.

4.79 It may also be necessary to review the standing data regularly to ensure that it is current. If not, controls relied on may not operate effectively. For example, the failure to maintain realistic credit limits may affect a programmed credit control test. This review of standing data can be carried out by the cycle checking referred to in paragraph 4.78 or the computer may be programmed to report data requiring action, for example prices not amended at time of last general price review.

4.80 The questions relating to the maintenance of standing data are as follows:

"1. *Is the control that the standing data fields of accounting significance remain correctly stored on the file a suitable combination of the following:*
   (a) *adequate controls over security of data files (review answers to the integrity controls section);*
   (b) *regular (e.g. monthly) manual agreement of an independently maintained control total with a print-out of the total of balances on the file by a user department;*
   (c) *regular (e.g. monthly) detailed checking on a cyclical basis of print-outs of items on the file to source data by user departments?*

2. *Is the file regularly examined to identify standing data requiring action (e.g. the provision of exception reports of prices not changed for over twelve months)?*

3. *Are there adequate procedures for:*
   (a) *investigation of differences disclosed by the checking in 1 before any adjustments are made;*
   (b) *investigation and correction of data requiring action in 2?"*

File creation

4.81   When new applications are implemented, the auditor will need to satisfy himself during the audit of the accounting period in which the files were initially created that the opening transaction data and standing data are completely and accurately set up on the new files. This can arise when manual systems are transferred to a computer or when a computer system is changed. Normally the auditor will wish to rely on the relevant controls, as outlined in the following paragraphs.

Transaction data

4.82   The operation of the controls in the new application may be expected to detect errors in the opening transaction data, if such controls are adequate and sufficient time after set-up is available to allow any conversion errors to be disclosed by this means. For example, when a file of accounts receivable balances is set up, the agreement of the total of the balances produced from the new file with the on-going control account will reveal any errors in the total value set up, while the sending of statements to customers and the follow up of queries and unpaid items should identify incorrect allocations.

4.83   In those relatively rare cases where either the controls in the new system are found to be inadequate or insufficient time has elapsed to enable them to be effective, the auditor should consider the need to devise and carry out alternative procedures to satisfy himself that any errors in the opening transaction data that may have occurred on set-up will not result in material error in the financial statements. Often these procedures will take the form of placing reliance on, and testing, the controls over the set-up procedures, for example the detailed checking of output.

4.84   There are no specific questions in the ICQ relating to the set-up of transaction data. This is because normally the controls in the new application, which will already be recorded in the ICQ, will be relied on. Where, instead, the controls over the set-up procedures are relied on, the details can be conveniently recorded in supplementary audit working papers. In this connection, it should be remembered that these procedures are only relevant to the audit of the accounting period during which set-up took place.

Standing data

4.85   Errors in setting up standing data will often not be revealed by the operation of the controls in the new system. This is because, as has already been indicated, when standing data is held on computer files, it is normally checked only at the time it is input and thereafter reliance is placed on the maintenance controls over standing data.

4.86   In these circumstances, the auditor should satisfy himself, during the audit of the accounting period in which the file was initially created, that the opening standing data was completely and accurately set up on the new file. He will often do this by relying on, and testing, the controls over the set-up procedures, for example the detailed checking of output.

4.87 Accordingly, in the standing data controls section, the following detailed question is asked, with a comment that it is only relevant to the audit of the accounting period during which the file was initially created:

"Are there adequate controls that all data fields of accounting significance are completely and accurately set up initially on the file?"

4.88 It should also be noted that the operation of the controls in the new system may detect errors in setting up standing data. For example, exception reports of excess charges might adequately detect material errors in setting up prices.

Disciplines over User Controls

4.89 Disciplines have already been defined as those procedures designed to ensure the continued and proper operation of basic controls and to safeguard assets. It has also been seen how the disciplines will be a combination of supervisory controls, segregation of duties and custodial controls.

4.90 The essential general requirements are that the results of the user controls should be reviewed and approved by a responsible official and that there should be an adequate segregation of duties. In general, the segregation of duties required is that:

- those persons carrying out or checking user controls should be independent of computer operations;

- user controls relating to standing data should be carried out or checked by persons other than those who deal with the related transaction data;

- separate persons should perform or check the basic controls relating to input and updating, and those relating to the maintenance of the control account;

- the reconciliation of control accounts with the subsidiary records should be performed or checked by persons other than those maintaining the control account.

The term *computer operations* includes the functions of system design, programming and computer operating but excludes a data control section within the computer department that is separate from these functions.

4.91 In the ICQ the questions relating to supervisory controls and segregation of duties are placed after the questions relating to the user control concerned. Examples can be seen in the computer questions included in appendix B to Chapter 3.

The Detailed Structure of the ICQ

4.92 So far, a large number of the individual questions asked in the ICQ have been reviewed, but how they are assembled together under the various control objectives has not yet been discussed. The questions relevant to a control objective depend on the nature of the objective and, as each control objective is different, so the questions are different. The reader is best advised to study for himself the computer questions for selected control objectives included in appendix B to Chapter 3. He will find few questions that have not been explained in the previous paragraphs. However, it may be helpful to indicate certain general matters here.

Similar control objectives

4.93 A large number of control objectives are broadly similar in that they are concerned with the processing of the accounting records. These objectives are 1, 2, 5, 10, 12, 21, 30, 31, 35, 37 and 50. Although there are detailed differences between the questions relating to these various control objectives, in general the questions are similar. They deal with the completeness of input and updating, the accuracy of input and updating, computer-generated data and maintenance of data. Likewise the detailed questions for control objectives 13, 22 and 38, which deal with the determination of general ledger entries, are similar.

The standing data controls section

4.94 Whenever standing data is relevant to a control objective, the auditor should assess all aspects of the controls over the standing data. This will include file creation, where appropriate, whether amendments are properly authorised and a consideration of the controls over completeness and accuracy of input and updating and the maintenance of the data on the file. It may also include computer-generated data. It would be unwieldy to ask all the relevant questions relating to standing data each time they apply under the relevant control objective. Accordingly, the questions relating to standing data are asked separately in a standing data controls section. A separate section is filled in for each file holding standing data and the questions are answered for each field of accounting significance. Where satisfactory controls over standing data are relevant to a control objective, there is a question under the control objective asking whether a review of the relevant standing data controls section shows the standing data concerned to be reliable for the purposes of the control objective. There is an example of a question of this type in paragraph 4.66.

Controls relevant to more than one control objective

4.95 Due to the nature of computer processing, individual controls will often be relevant to more than one control objective. This can occur in integrated systems and where computer matching is relied on, as described in the following paragraphs.

Integrated systems

4.96 In integrated systems it is common for two or more master files to be updated from common input. For example, details of goods received may be input to update both accounts payable and materials and supplies inventory. In this case the controls that the details of goods received are completely and accurately input will be important to both control objectives 2 (accounting for goods received) and 10 (materials and supplies inventory). It would be inefficient to record and assess the input controls in detail twice and thus in the second control objective (i.e. 10) there is a question calling for a review of the relevant answers in control objective 2; this is illustrated in Figure 56. It remains necessary in the second control objective, in this case control objective 10, to enquire into any categorisation of the data for the purposes of processing the materials and supplies inventory and the controls over updating the materials and supplies inventory file. Thus, using the example just mentioned, the relevant questions in control objective 10 are:

"1. *Review the answers under control objectives 2, 5, 21 and 31, as applicable. Are there adequate controls that all items are accurately input to the purchases/work in progress/sales applications?*

2. *Is the method used in the program to select and accumulate items relevant to the materials and supplies inventories application appropriate?*

3. *Is a total (specify total used) of selected items accumulated by the computer during the selection run and either:*
   (a) *agreed to the total of items written to/off the materials and supplies inventories file; or*
   (b) *carried through intermediate processing (including summarisation of totals or changes in the totals used) so that it is established that all selected items are updated to the materials and supplies inventories file?*

4. *Is the reconciliation of totals in 3 carried out:*
   (a) *manually; or*
   (b) *by the computer and, if so, is adequate evidence of the check printed out?*

5. *Are there adequate procedures for investigation and correction of differences disclosed by the reconciliation?"*

194

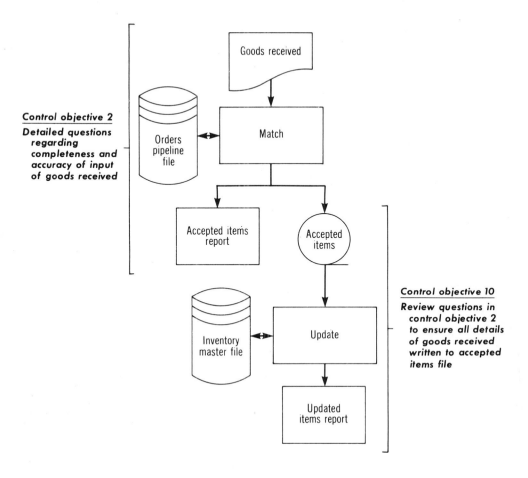

Control objective 2

Detailed questions regarding completeness and accuracy of input of goods received

Control objective 10

Review questions in control objective 2 to ensure all details of goods received written to accepted items file

FIG. 56. Structure of the ICQ – integrated systems (4.96)

Computer matching

4.97   It has been seen how, in many control objectives where input is relevant, computer matching is a likely control technique, for example the matching of despatch notes with customers' orders. However, the controls over both the file to be matched and the matching process will often be important to an earlier control objective. Thus, in the case of goods received, computer matching as an input technique is relevant to control objective 2, but the file of orders and the matching process are relevant to control objective 1 which deals with the ascertainment of open commitments. In order to avoid including the same questions in both control objectives 1 and 2 the questions are set out in full in the earlier objective

195

and, in the later objective, there is a question calling for a review of the answers to the relevant questions in the earlier control objective; this is illustrated in Figure 57.

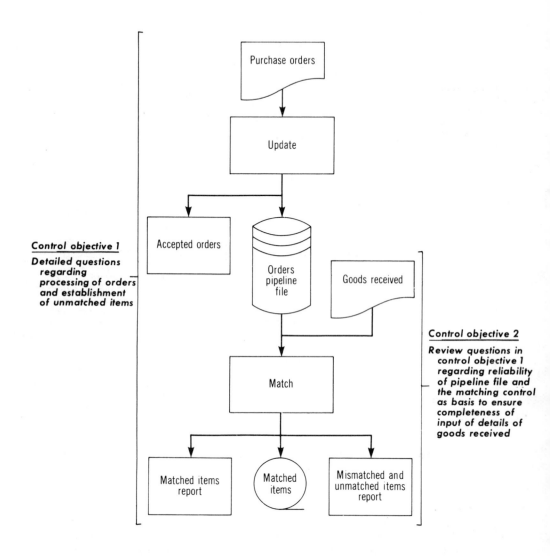

FIG. 57. Structure of the ICQ – computer matching (4.97)

4.98   The matching of purchase orders with goods received may also be relevant to control objective 4 (approval of purchases documentation). Likewise the matching of goods received records with purchase invoices is relevant to control objective 2 (ascertainment of outstanding liabilities), control objective 4 (approval of purchases documentation) and control objective 5 (completeness of input of purchase invoices).

Summary

4.99 User controls and programmed procedures are defined as all those controls and procedures designed to ensure that valid transactions, and only valid transactions, are processed and recorded completely and accurately. The detailed control requirements and techniques, and how they can be evaluated using the ICQ, are conveniently divided between completeness of input and updating, accuracy of input and updating, computer-generated data, validity of data processed, calculating, summarising and categorising, maintenance of data on files and file creation.

4.100 Important considerations regarding these matters can be summarised as follows:

(a) Input and updating. Completeness of input and updating is dealt with separately from accuracy of input and updating. The distinction is made because different techniques are often used to control completeness (i.e. all the transactions) and accuracy (i.e. the data of each transaction). There are various control techniques that may be used and the ICQ is designed to enable the auditor to identify the principal user controls and programmed procedures on which he may wish to place reliance.

(b) Validity of data processed. Checking and authorisation in computer systems introduces new considerations of timing and whether the checking and authorisation is programmed or manual. The different techniques are catered for in the ICQ.

(c) Maintenance of data on files. Maintenance is the term in common use for the control procedures that ensure that the data stored on master files remains correct until deleted during authorised processing. The techniques, particularly as regards standing data, are different to those adopted in non-computer systems, and, as in other areas, the ICQ is designed to assist the auditor identify the most effective control.

(d) File creation. When new applications are implemented, the auditor will need to satisfy himself, during the audit of the accounting period in which the files were initially created, that the opening transaction and standing data was completely and accurately set up on the new files.

5

Evaluation of Controls: Integrity Controls (1)

Introduction

5.01   In this chapter and Chapter 6, the detailed control requirements and techniques relating to integrity controls that may be relevant to the auditor, and how they are evaluated using the ICQ described in Chapter 3, are considered. This chapter is concerned with implementation controls and program security controls, and certain general points regarding the evaluation of integrity controls. Computer operations controls, data file security controls and system software are dealt with in Chapter 6. The discussion in both chapters, as in Chapter 4, is from the point of view of the auditor rather than those concerned in the design of systems of control. As a result, it should not be viewed as a statement of either all, or the best, control techniques that should be used in any particular installation.

Method of Evaluation

Integrity controls section

5.02   Although the integrity controls are relevant to each control objective, it would be unwieldy to ask all the questions that might apply under every control objective. Accordingly, the questions regarding integrity controls are asked separately in the ICQ in the integrity controls section. Under each control objective there is a requirement to ask whether a review of the relevant integrity controls shows them to be adequate for the purposes of the control objective.

5.03   The integrity controls section is arranged in five parts:

- Implementation controls.

- Program security controls.

- Computer operations controls.

- Data file security controls.

- System software.

The first three parts relate to those integrity controls necessary for the effective operation of programmed procedures. The fourth part relates to the maintenance of data on files. The fifth part concerns the adequacy of system software and is relevant to the evaluation of features in the other four parts. For example, a software library system and software label checking will be relevant to program security and computer operations respectively.

Control objectives

5.04 Since the relevant integrity controls are usually similar for all programmed procedures, it is only necessary to ask the questions once in respect of each control objective. Thus, in respect of implementation, program security and computer operations there is for each control objective the following question:

> *"List below the programmed procedures relied upon for the purposes of this control objective.*

> *In respect of the programmed procedures listed above, review the answers to the integrity controls section. Are there adequate controls to ensure that:*
>> (a) *appropriate programmed procedures are implemented in respect of:*
>>> (i) *where applicable, new systems;*
>>> (ii) *program changes;*
>> (b) *unauthorised changes cannot be made to programmed procedures;*
>> (c) *programmed procedures are consistently used?"*

5.05 Likewise, for each control objective where the maintenance of data on files is relevant, and in the standing data controls section as regards the maintenance of standing data on files, there is a question calling for a review, in appropriate circumstances, of the answers to the questions in the integrity controls section dealing with data file security controls. The circumstances in which these questions will be relevant are discussed in paragraphs 6.29 and 6.32, and examples of these questions are given in paragraphs 4.75 and 4.80.

5.06 Even in those cases where he decides not to place reliance thereon, the auditor will normally wish to evaluate the integrity controls from time to time so that he can report to management weaknesses that come to his attention during the evaluation. This approach is particularly desirable in the case of integrity controls, since weaknesses may lead to operational inefficiency and, although computer systems may sometimes start under predominantly user controls, their growth will often involve an increasing dependence on integrity controls.

5.07   In paragraphs 5.12 to 5.64, and in Chapter 6, each of the five parts in the integrity controls section is discussed, together with the considerations to be taken into account in answering the questions. The complete integrity controls section is included with the computer questions in appendix B to Chapter 3. Before discussing the integrity controls section, some general comments regarding the effect of the size and organisation of the computer department on the integrity controls are made in paragraphs 5.08 to 5.11. In both this chapter and Chapter 6, attention is drawn to the possible impact of database systems on control considerations and techniques. At the conclusion of Chapter 6 mention is made of the role of the database administrator in the operation of integrity controls in database systems.

Organisation of the Computer Department

5.08   An important general factor relating to the evaluation of integrity controls will be the structure of the computer department. The organisation of the work and staff in the department will depend largely on the extent of computer processing, the number of staff employed in the department and the control techniques used. In general, the larger the department, the greater will be the opportunity to install a satisfactory system of integrity controls, making use of the software features that are available and providing adequate disciplines over the various controls.

5.09   The organisation chart of a typical large installation is shown in Figure 58. In a department of this size, which might include about two hundred staff, there is not only functional segregation of duties between operations, development and file control but segregations within these functions. For example, system development is distinct from technical support and database administration is separate from the program and data file library. A considerable degree of formal organisation is also possible within functions. Thus, within the operations function, the work of processing, scheduling and job set-up, liaison and data control and preparation is carried out by separately organised and supervised groups. In an installation of this size the auditor should find a comprehensive set of integrity controls, many of which will be software-based, and full disciplines, both as regards segregation of duties and supervision.

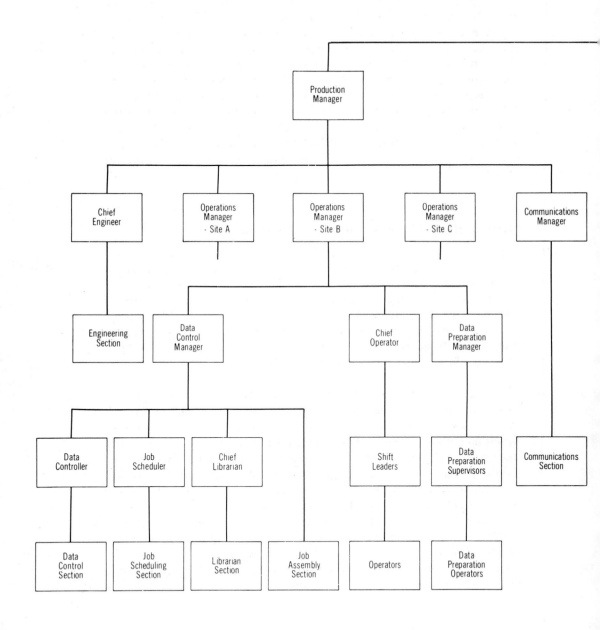

FIG. 58. Organisation chart – large installation (5.09)

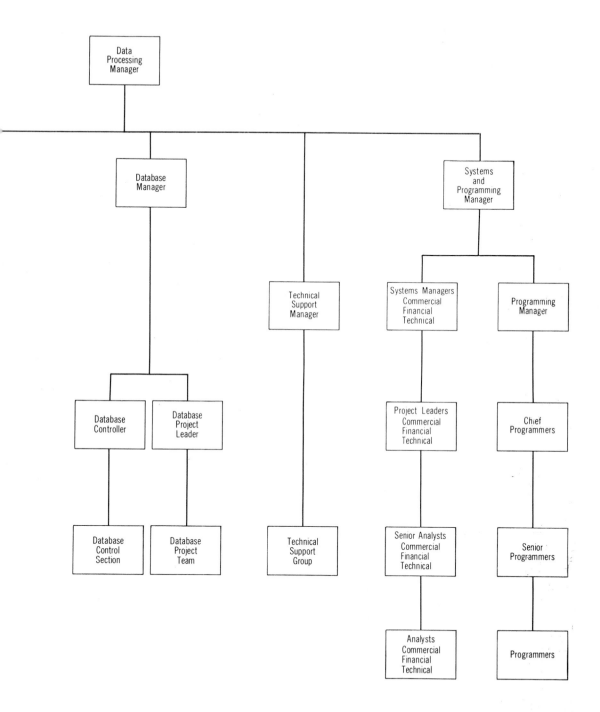

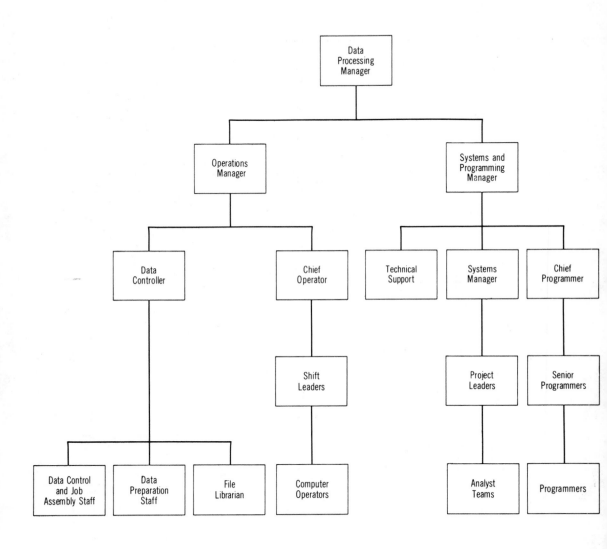

Fɪɢ. 59. Organisation chart – medium-sized installation (5.10)

5.10   The organisation chart of a typical medium-sized installation is shown in Figure 59. A department of this size, which might include about fifty staff, will provide a functional segregation of duties between operations and system development and might, as in the illustration, include a small technical support team. However, the formalisation within functions is less well-developed than in a larger installation. For example, a single manager or supervisor is responsible for operations, data control and the library. Staff in each function are likely to be less restricted in the duties they may carry out. The auditor should find an adequate set of integrity controls, with less reliance on software procedures than in the larger installation. He should also find adequate disciplines, although the supervisory function is likely to be concentrated in the hands of fewer people.

5.11   In the smaller installations, an example of which is shown in Figure 60, which may comprise only about five staff, there is unlikely even to be the broad functional segregation of duties between operations, program maintenance and file control, since the manager will be responsible for all these functions. Likewise, there can be little supervision, since the manager will be undertaking much of the work himself. In very small installations of this type, the auditor is unlikely to be able to place much reliance on the integrity controls because of the absence of disciplines. However, he will usually find that, in these cases, the company has correspondingly strengthened its user controls.

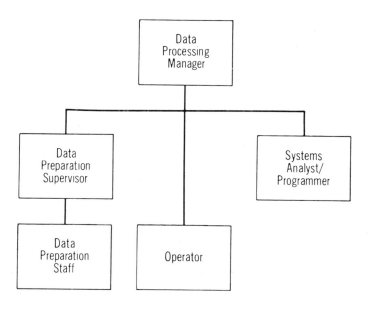

Fig. 60. Organisation chart – small installation (5.11)

Implementation Controls

5.12   Implementation controls are concerned with the suitability of the proposed programmed procedures and their effective implementation in the production programs, both in the case of new systems and subsequent changes to the existing systems. By **production programs** are meant those versions of the application programs which are actually used to process accounting data. They include what are termed the **executable** (i.e. core image) and **source** (for example COBOL) programs. **Application programs** mean the programs unique to the particular accounting application. They do not include the operating system, which is considered under system software. In the ICQ the implementation controls are considered separately for new systems and for program changes.

New systems

5.13   The auditor may frequently not rely on the implementation controls over the introduction of new systems because, in other than the largest and most complex systems, he will decide it is more efficient to test the actual programmed procedures in the programs as at the time the system went operational. However, he will often wish to participate in the implementation procedures in order both to assist in designing the tests he will later wish to carry out, for example audit test data (see paragraph 7.32), and to provide an additional service to clients by bringing any deficiencies to their attention in time for remedial action to be taken. It is thus good practice, even where he does not intend to rely thereon, for the auditor to evaluate implementation controls applicable to the introduction of new systems.

5.14   The controls required for the successful implementation of application programs can be divided between those over system design, program and system testing and cataloguing. The relative importance of these different stages will depend on whether the programs are purpose-built or package programs.

5.15   Purpose-built programs are those designed for a specific company, and may be developed within the computer department or by an outside agency, such as a software house, and tailored to the exact requirements of the user. All stages of implementation are likely to be important although, if the programs were designed by an outside agency, the agency's controls over system design may not be of prime importance to the company.

5.16   Package programs are normally developed by computer manufacturers or software houses for the more common and widely used applications, such as payroll, which tend to be reasonably standardised from one company to another. The user would specify the facilities required of the package by way of parameters (see paragraph 6.07), which would cause the package to carry out processing in the required form. System design and program and system testing should not be a major concern to the client if the package is in common use, although care must be taken to ensure that the package fits into the rest of the system.

5.17 The work undertaken by the company between a study of feasibility and the successful implementation of a computer system is usually significant and can involve a considerable amount of time. During this period the user's requirements are progressively translated from an overall statement of intent to a series of detailed production programs and related instructions in both the computer and user departments. The auditor will need to identify those particular procedures which, if relied on and found to be functioning properly, would enable him to rely on the successful implementation of appropriate programmed procedures. These procedures, which are discussed in the following paragraphs, can be defined as:

- System design and program preparation.
- Program and system testing.
- Cataloguing.

System design and program preparation

5.18 The auditor's major requirement in system design and program preparation is that the programmed procedures are appropriately designed and properly written into the programs. The basis for effective design is the preparation and use of system specifications. These specifications are of two types – outline system descriptions and detailed system descriptions. **Outline system descriptions** should be written in such a way that users can properly understand and agree to the proposed programmed procedures. Likewise, the descriptions should be such as to enable them to form the means for the monitoring of detailed design work by those responsible for system development. In the larger installations monitoring will be carried out by the project supervisor or manager. Further work should not proceed until the outline system descriptions have been properly examined and approved, both in the user and computer departments. In database systems it is desirable that there should be a formal procedure for the new system to be reviewed by those responsible for database administration. This is to help ensure that the new system will not conflict with those already using the same data.

5.19 **Detailed system descriptions** should be written in such a way that the programmed procedures can be understood and be effectively incorporated in the program by the programming staff. In addition, the descriptions should be sufficiently comprehensive and clear to enable supervisors to check the program logic and control the preparation work. It will also be necessary for user departments to understand the details of the programmed procedures so that they can design effective complementary user controls. Detailed programming should not proceed until the detailed system descriptions have been properly examined and approved, in both the user and computer departments.

5.20 The quality of outline and detailed system descriptions is also of major importance when it subsequently becomes necessary to make program changes. It is difficult to make changes effectively unless there is a reliable detailed record of the existing system.

5.21   The following questions regarding system design are asked in the ICQ:

"1. *Are system descriptions and changes thereto prepared as a basis for:*
  (a) *understanding and approval of the programmed procedures by the user departments;*
  (b) *control of system design and programming by the data processing function?*
2. *Are the system descriptions in 1 reviewed and approved by responsible officials: (S)*
  (a) *in the user departments;*
  (b) *in the data processing function?*"

Program and system testing

5.22   Testing should normally be carried out in three distinct stages, program testing, system testing and parallel or pilot running.

Program testing

5.23   Program testing consists of checking the logic of individual programs. The principal method used is desk checking. **Desk checking** comprises checking that the program code is in line with the program specification and consists of analysing the various logical paths in the program. It corresponds to the audit testing technique of program code analysis described in appendix D to Chapter 7. Desk checking should be carried out by a programmer other than the person who designed and wrote the coding.

System testing

5.24   System testing consists of checking that the logic of the various individual programs links together to form a system in line with the requirements of the detailed system description. The principal technique used is **test data.** This technique, when used for audit purposes, is described in appendix B to Chapter 7. When it is used for system testing, there is a need to extend the variety of transactions designed beyond those that are representative of normal transactions. This is because the purpose of the test data is to test exhaustively the logic of the programs in the system as they affect individual transactions. It is thus desirable that the test data is devised by a combined team of programmers and analysts, advised as necessary by the relevant user departments. The results should be carefully scrutinised and the test data should be rerun, and redesigned as necessary, until all logical failures are corrected. Formal procedures are required to decide on any amendments to be made to the programs as a result of problems identified by the system testing and to monitor their successful change. System testing should be performed or checked by persons other than those responsible for the detailed programming.

Parallel or pilot running

5.25   **Parallel running** means operating the new system in parallel with the existing system and checking the results obtained from the dual processing with a view to identifying and investigating differences. There are difficulties in using parallel running for these purposes, for example the cost of double processing and the difficulty of comparison when the results of the new system are not identical to, or are additional to, those of the existing system. For these reasons pilot running is generally favoured. **Pilot running** means progressively introducing the new system while continuing to use the existing system for a lessening portion of the relevant records until the new system is considered fully reliable.

5.26 Parallel or pilot running is the means of testing the complete system in operation including all user procedures. Unlike system testing, the purpose of parallel or pilot running is to test the system's ability to cope with real, rather than test, data and to deal with actual volumes, rather than individual transactions. Accordingly responsibility for parallel or pilot running normally rests with a steering committee, including representatives of the user departments in addition to computer department staff who will provide particular assistance with regard to file creation and training. The new system should not be fully accepted by the relevant user departments, or the existing system be finally dropped, until the full processing cycle has been successfully run, as far as practical, on the new system. It is recognised that some procedures may only apply quarterly or annually and these may have to be simulated. However, opportunity should be provided to process all monthly procedures at least once and this will ensure a repeated test of daily and weekly processing.

5.27 In view of the importance of program and system testing, it is desirable that the roles of the various departments concerned and the criteria for the completion of each stage of testing should be defined. In practice, it would normally be appropriate for computer department officials to decide on the successful conclusion of program and system testing but for the joint user and computer departments' steering committee to decide when the new system was acceptable as a whole, following parallel or pilot running.

5.28 The following questions regarding program and system testing are asked in the ICQ:

"1. *Are the:*
   (a) *methods (e.g. test data; parallel running); and*
   (b) *scope (e.g. volumes tested)*
   of the testing procedures adequate to establish the proper operation of programmed procedures?
2. *Are the testing procedures either performed or checked by persons other than those involved in writing the programs? (D)*"

Cataloguing

5.29 The requirements and procedures in respect of cataloguing new systems are the same as those for cataloguing program changes, and are considered under "Program changes" in paragraphs 5.41 to 5.46.

Program changes

5.30 The auditor will often decide to place reliance on the implementation controls over program changes since, provided these controls are satisfactory, he can limit the number of other tests which he may decide to carry out on the programmed procedures. He may rely on the implementation controls for the rest of the period under audit to ensure that authorised changes were required, effectively designed and properly implemented, and that other changes do not unintentionally affect the operation of programmed procedures.

5.31 The auditor may, however, decide not to rely on the implementation controls over changes on the basis that it is more efficient to increase the level of reperformance which he carries out on the programmed procedures and to spread these tests throughout the period being audited. He may thus satisfy himself that either they continued to function properly or, if changes were made, the new programmed procedures operated satisfactorily. This approach is unlikely to be attractive where the programmed procedures are numerous. Even where he decides not to rely thereon, the auditor may wish to evaluate the implementation controls applicable to program changes in order to bring any deficiencies he notices to the attention of the client.

5.32 A significant amount of work is usually involved in making a change to a program from the time that a request to change is made until the revised program is taken into production. The controls required for the development of program changes are similar to those for new systems. The request for a change must be properly defined to form an adequate basis for its acceptance and the design and testing of the changed program must be carried out to the same high standard as for new systems. There must be suitable approvals of the work done before implementation. Care is also needed to ensure that program changes do not have adverse effects on other systems (as distinct from other programs in the same system). This danger arises where database is used and several systems use the same data. For example, changes involving the deletion or discontinuance of data previously updated to the database should be reviewed carefully in relation to the sub-schemas for other systems. This review is one of the functions of database administration.

5.33 There is a further important practical consideration which arises in the case of program changes and which is not relevant to new systems. There should be a procedure to ensure that all valid requests for changes are accounted for and promptly effected. This is important to the company for operational reasons. It is also important to the auditor because, where he is relying on the controls over changes, it is essential that required changes are made promptly and completely, as well as effectively, since other controls will not necessarily identify an ongoing deficiency which the change was designed to eliminate.

5.34 The auditor, as in the case of new systems, will need to identify those particular procedures which, if found to be working satisfactorily, will enable him to rely on the adequacy of program change procedures. These procedures, which are discussed in the following paragraphs, can be defined as:

- Validity of changes.

- Completeness of changes.

- Testing.

- Cataloguing.

Program change procedures are illustrated in outline in Figure 61.

Validity of changes

5.35 It is important that only valid changes are made. Normally the request to change a program will come to an analyst from a user department or the computer operations staff. The analyst will design the change and pass it to a programmer for coding and the amendment of program documentation. Requests for the changes should be appropriately approved before work on them begins. The seniority of the person responsible for approving the request for a change will often depend on the importance of the change and the strength of other controls. For example, if the request is for a change to the print format of a relatively unimportant report, a lower level of approval would be called for than if the change was to the method of evaluation of inventory. In smaller installations, the most senior persons may need to approve all requests. This is largely a matter of common sense and the precise arrangements to be made will depend on the circumstances. In general it would be expected that a reasonably senior official would authorise all requests for change and, at that time, indicate the level of further supervision and approval required. In order to assist this procedure it is desirable to use standard forms for requests to change programs.

5.36 The following question regarding validity of changes is asked in the ICQ:

"Are all program changes (other than immediate modifications) initiated only on the basis of appropriate written authorisations?"

Completeness of changes

5.37 In order to ensure that all approved requests are processed, and the changes to programs implemented, there will need to be a procedure to account for all changes. This can conveniently take the form of checking the sequence of serially prenumbered documentation or by entering change forms in a register. Outstanding change requests should then be regularly reviewed by a responsible official in the computer department.

211

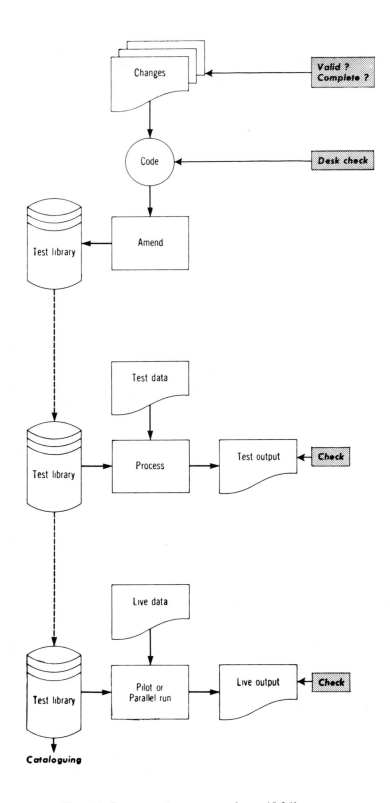

FIG. 61. Program change procedures (5.34)

5.38 The following questions regarding the completeness of changes are asked in the ICQ:

"1. *Are program changes controlled in such a way that it can subsequently be established that they have all been accounted for (e.g. by sequential prenumbering or by entry of change forms in a register)?*
2. *Is a regular review made of modifications not yet implemented to determine reasons for delay?"*

Testing

5.39 The testing procedures for new systems, including program testing, system testing and parallel or pilot running were discussed in paragraphs 5.22 to 5.28 and the same principles apply to the testing of changes. Regard should be had to the quality of the existing documentation, since the design of the change will be based thereon; if the documentation is deficient, there is a chance that the change will be inadequately designed. Likewise, the degree of testing applied will depend on the scope of the change. For example, a change to a print format might only involve desk checking and testing using the print program concerned with a simple data file. Changes affecting calculations, for example new payroll deductions, or special summer bonuses, might also involve system testing, using a comprehensive variety of test data, to test all programs in the system containing the changed program. This would protect against the dangers of unforeseen side effects. Where the changes are major, or affect other suites of programs, it might also be desirable to adopt parallel or pilot running in order to prove the changes against operational volumes of data. The change may also affect user controls and these may require to be tested if the change to user procedures is significant.

5.40 The following questions regarding testing of program changes are asked in the ICQ:

"1. *In order to provide a sound basis for the design and programming of changes:*
   (a) *are systems and programs adequately documented;*
   (b) *are programs written in accordance with suitable programming standards?*
2. *Are the:*
   (a) *methods (e.g. test data); and*
   (b) *scope (e.g. volumes tested)*
   of the testing procedures adequate to establish the proper operation of programmed procedures in:
   (i) *the changed program;*
   (ii) *where applicable, other unchanged programs in the system?*
3. *Are the testing procedures either performed or checked by persons other than those involved in writing the program changes? (D)"*

213

Cataloguing

5.41 **Cataloguing** is defined as the procedures necessary to bring the tested programs into operational use and includes both manual and software procedures. Cataloguing procedures are illustrated in outline in Figure 62.

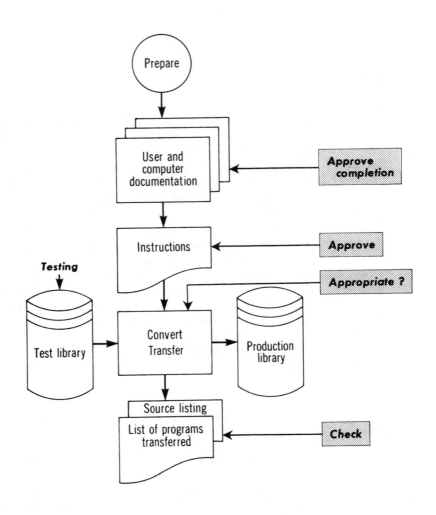

FIG. 62. Cataloguing procedures (5.41)

5.42 The more important manual procedures are those necessary to ensure that testing and documentation are satisfactorily completed before the programs go into production, and that the manual procedures for the new or changed system are ready in both the user and computer departments.

There will need to be a formal manual procedure to instruct the transfer of the new or changed programs, at an appropriate cut-off point, from a test to a production, or operational, status. This procedure will normally comprise a formal decision taken by both computer and user departments, often at a meeting of the steering committee. A procedure of this nature is necessary in order to enable all departments, particularly user departments, to transfer to the new procedures in an orderly manner. The decision to transfer the programs to a production status should thus only be taken on formal evidence of the satisfactory completion of system testing and parallel running, and the completion of the related computer department documentation, for example program documentation, operating instructions and user department procedure manuals.

5.43 The software procedures related to cataloguing include the conversion of the source programs into executable form by the compiler and linkage editor and, where programs are held on-line, the protection of test programs against unauthorised change and transferring the tested programs from a test status on the program library file to a production or operational status. Where programs are changed, the software will often be responsible for deleting previous versions of the program, often copying them onto a back-up file. In some cases both the source and executable versions are transferred from the test to the production library. Controls will be necessary to ensure that the source program is the same as the executable program so that, when changes are made using the source program, no errors are introduced. In less advanced systems, where programs are held off-line, manual controls will be needed to ensure that the previous versions of changed programs are no longer used in processing but are either destroyed or removed to a back-up location.

5.44 Reports produced by the software during cataloguing will include a listing of programs transferred from the test to the production library and a listing of the source version of the new production program. The listings of programs transferred should be checked to ensure that the correct versions of programs have been taken into production. The listings of the source version of new production programs should be checked to ensure that no unauthorised changes have been made subsequent to approval to catalogue and that the source program has been properly converted into executable form.

5.45 The auditor will not normally need to concern himself, in the case of changes, with the software which transfers the programs to the test library, processes the amendments or compiles the amended source program, since errors should be identified through the testing procedures. Likewise, in simple systems, he will not, for similar reasons, need to concern himself with the manual identification and input of the existing source program to which the changes will be made. These matters will, however, be of concern to the client.

215

5.46   The following questions regarding cataloguing are asked in the ICQ:

"1. *Does a responsible official in the user department review, where applicable, and approve: (S)*
   (a) *the instructions for user procedures and controls;*
   (b) *the results and completion of testing;*
   (c) *the date of taking into production of tested programs?*
2. *Does a responsible official in the data processing function review, where applicable, and approve: (S)*
   (a) *the system and program documentation to ensure that it is complete, up-to-date and in accordance with the company's standards;*
   (b) *the instructions for job set-up and computer operations;*
   (c) *the results and completion of testing;*
   (d) *the taking into production of tested programs?*
3. *Are the system software procedures appropriate to ensure that:*
   (a) *tested source programs are properly converted to executable form (e.g. by the compiler and linkage editor);*
   (b) *the correct version of the program is taken into production (e.g. by the checking of generation numbers);*
   (c) *unauthorised changes are not made to tested programs before they are taken into production (e.g. password protection);*
   (d) *all forms of the program (e.g. source, object and executable) are the same?*
4. *Review the answers to the system software section. Are there adequate controls over the implementation and security of system software?*
5. *Is adequate evidence of the system software procedures printed out and reviewed by persons other than those involved in system software or computer operating functions? (D)*
6. *Are there adequate controls over manual procedures relating to cataloguing (e.g. the control of previous versions where programs are held off-line)?*
7. *Are the results of the procedures in 5 and 6 reviewed and approved by a responsible official? (S)*"

Immediate modifications

5.47   Occasionally it may be necessary for amendments to production programs to be made without adhering to the procedures outlined earlier. This might happen, for example, where a processing deadline has to be met or at night, when staff present are at a minimum. In these cases, there will need to be controls to ensure that the proper authorisation, testing and implementation procedures are subsequently followed.

5.48   The following questions regarding immediate modifications are asked in the ICQ:

"1. *Where immediate modifications have to be made to production programs bypassing normal procedures, are there adequate procedures to*

ensure that changes are correctly made and approved (e.g. by retro-
actively applying the standard procedures)?

2. *Are the results of the procedures in 1 reviewed and approved by a*
   responsible official? (S)"

Program Security Controls

5.49   Program security controls are those controls designed to ensure that unauthorised changes cannot be made to the production programs that process accounting data. They do not include the controls over normal program change procedures, which have already been considered under implementation controls. Program security will be of particular concern to the auditor in respect of those programs in which an unauthorised change might benefit the person making the change, for example in systems processing wages and cash payments. The auditor will usually wish, where appropriate, to place reliance on the program security controls, since, provided they are working satisfactorily, he need not spread his tests on the programmed procedures.

5.50   Program security controls will be needed for programs both while in use and while held off-line. **Programs in use** are defined as programs which can be accessed through the system, either by operators processing jobs or through terminals. **Off-line programs** are those held away from the computer, normally in a physical library. A **physical library** is defined as a self-contained area dedicated to the holding of programs and data files when not in use.

Programs in use

5.51   The most likely method of attempting to make an unauthorised change to a program is to submit a job for that purpose. A **job** may be defined as the work to be undertaken by the computer, for example the running of an application program, as instructed by the appropriate user or computer department staff. The job would make changes to the current version of the source program from which an executable program, containing the unauthorised change, would be compiled. It is thus important that all jobs are reviewed. This can be achieved by reviewing a suitable computer report of jobs processed. By comparing this report with the authorised job schedules, any unauthorised accesses of production programs can be identified and investigated. It is also important to control the use of utilities which enable amendments to be made to executable programs. These are dealt with further in paragraphs 5.59 to 5.61.

5.52   In smaller installations, where a computer list of jobs processed is not produced, reliance can be placed on the authorisation of jobs at the time they are set-up and prior to passing them to operators for processing. However, in these cases it will be necessary to ensure that unauthorised changes cannot be made to the jobs after set-up, and that unauthorised jobs are not added. This can often be achieved by the chief operator reporting for investigation any job which is not properly authorised or

217

bears an indication of changed details. Alternatively, all jobs that access and change production programs may be processed at particular times when senior officials are present.

5.53 Where it is not practicable to establish controls of this nature, it may be an acceptable alternative to compare the production programs with independently controlled copies on a regular basis. These copies and the software carrying out the comparison would normally be held either in a permanently supervised physical library or at a remote location. The comparison would often be carried out by the internal audit department who might have custody of the comparison software. In some cases, where the programs are particularly prone to irregular changes, for example in banking applications, a daily comparison of this nature before processing provides a high level of protection.

5.54 The techniques outlined in paragraphs 5.51 to 5.53 are illustrated in Figure 63.

5.55 In smaller installations, the periodic running of test data by responsible officials may be a practical method to ensure that unauthorised changes have not been made.

5.56 Programs should be password-protected so that only authorised personnel can access the programs, either for information or so that amendments can be made. This is particularly important in systems where program maintenance is carried out through terminals. The controls and procedures associated with terminals and passwords, and the appropriate questions in the ICQ, are considered further under data file security controls in paragraphs 6.36 to 6.48.

5.57 In all cases it will be necessary to prevent unauthorised access to production programs during non-production periods i.e. when they are not being used operationally. Specific controls will usually be required for this purpose. These controls might comprise the removal of program files to the library or the presence of an operator during non-production periods.

5.58 The following questions regarding programs in use are asked in the ICQ:

"1. *Is the principal control that unauthorised changes cannot be made to production programs while in use:*
    (a) *manual review of computer-produced report of jobs processed;*
      If yes, answer 2 to 4
    (b) *manual authorisation of jobs before processing;*
      If yes, answer 5 and 6
    (c) *regular comparison of production programs with independently controlled copies;*
      If yes, answer 7 to 10
    (d) *password protection of production programs?*

(Note: ICQ questions relating to password protection are set out in paragraph 6.48.)

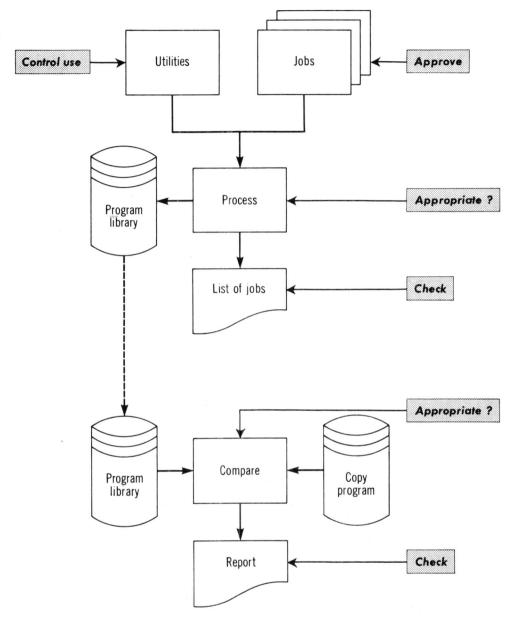

FIG. 63. Program security controls (5.54)

Manual review
2. *Are the system software procedures appropriate to ensure that all production programs accessed are reported?*
3. *Review the answers to the system software section. Are there adequate controls over the implementation and security of system software?*
4. *Are there adequate procedures to review the reports of jobs processed?*

219

Manual authorisation

5. *Are jobs approved by reference to appropriate evidence (e.g. authorised processing schedules)?*
6. *Are there adequate controls that:*
   (a) *no unauthorised changes are made to authorised jobs after authorisation;*
   (b) *unauthorised jobs are not added?*

Program comparisons

7. *Are comparisons made on a surprise basis?*
8. *Are the system software procedures appropriate to achieve a suitable comparison?*
9. *Review the answers to the system software section. Are there adequate controls over the implementation and security of system software?*
10. *Are there adequate procedures for investigation of differences?*

Disciplines

11. *Are the following procedures either performed or checked by persons other than those involved in computer operations, system design and programming: (D)*
    (a) *review of jobs processed; (4)*
    (b) *authorisation of jobs before processing; (5)*
    (c) *investigation of differences arising from program comparisons? (10)*
12. *Are the results of the following procedures reviewed and approved by a responsible official: (S)*
    (a) *review of jobs processed; (4)*
    (b) *authorisation of jobs before processing; (5)*
    (c) *investigation of differences arising from program comparisons? (10)*

Non-production

13. *Are programs adequately protected during periods of non-production (e.g. by removal to the physical library or by the presence of an operator)?"*

Utility programs and physical security

5.59 It is also possible to make changes directly to executable programs using special programs, often called utilities, either provided for that purpose by manufacturers or, in larger installations, written by the system software group. These utilities should be held off-line by a responsible official and should only be issued to manufacturers' engineers or a senior member of the system software group. Their use should, where possible, be restricted to making amendments to the operating system. Use of these utilities can be identified and approved by a review of the system log. It may also be desirable to carry out a regular comparison of executable and source programs, for example by the internal audit department.

5.60 With sufficient technical skill and detailed knowledge of their contents, operators can make changes to production programs. Protection against this possibility is normally provided by a suitable segregation of duties whereby, on the one hand, the operators cannot obtain a detailed knowledge of the program and, on the other hand, those responsible for the development and maintenance of the programs cannot gain unsupervised access to the production program. It is important that this segregation of duties applies at all times, including outside the normal working period.

5.61 The following questions regarding utility programs and segregation of duties are asked in the ICQ:

"1. *Where there are utility programs which can make changes to production programs, is access to and use of these utilities restricted to authorised personnel?*

 2. *Is each use of these utilities identified, reported and reviewed by a responsible official in the data processing function (e.g. as part of the review of system logs)? (S)*

 3. *Are computer operators, job control and other operations personnel responsible for handling and processing production jobs precluded from:* (C)
     (a) *writing or making amendments to production programs and system software;*
     (b) *gaining access to source listings, flowcharts, file layouts and other program documentation?*

 4. *Are system analysts and production program and system software programmers forbidden unsupervised access to the computer room? (C)*

 5. *Do the restrictions in 3 and 4 apply during shifts outside the normal working period (e.g. weekends) and during periods of non-production work (e.g. program testing)?"*

Off-line programs

5.62 Where programs are held off-line, they should be subject to physical library controls whereby they are securely held, only issued on appropriate authority and promptly returned. Back-up copies and program documentation should be protected to avoid unauthorised personnel from obtaining a detailed knowledge of the contents of the programs. Control of back-up copies will also be important if they are used for control purposes, for example comparison with working copies. Back-up copies of programs should be securely held in a library, or outside the installation, and should only be issued to the operations staff on the authority of a responsible official.

5.63 The controls and procedures associated with physical libraries, and the appropriate questions in the ICQ, are considered further under data file security controls in paragraphs 6.49 to 6.57.

Summary

5.64   This chapter has dealt with certain general points regarding the evaluation of integrity controls, and a detailed consideration of implementation controls and program security controls. The other elements of integrity controls, namely computer operations controls, data file security controls and system software are considered in Chapter 6, which also includes a summary relating to integrity controls as a whole.

6

Evaluation of Controls: Integrity Controls (2)

Introduction

6.01   In this chapter the detailed control requirements and techniques relating to computer operations controls, data file security controls and system software, and how they are evaluated using the ICQ described in Chapter 3, are considered. The other elements of integrity controls (implementation controls and program security controls), and certain general points regarding the evaluation of integrity controls, were considered in Chapter 5. The discussion in this chapter, as in Chapters 4 and 5, is from the point of view of the auditor.

Computer Operations Controls

6.02   Computer operations controls are those controls designed to ensure that the programmed procedures are consistently applied during the processing of accounting data. They thus include the controls over all the work relating to the physical assembly in the computer department of the necessary material and its subsequent processing, the controls to ensure that the correct data files are used in processing, and the controls over recovery after a processing failure. These stages of work, and the relevant controls, are considered in the following paragraphs under the headings of job set-up, operations software and computer operating, use of correct data files, and recovery from processing failure. Computer operations controls are illustrated in outline in Figure 64.

6.03   The auditor will usually wish, where appropriate, to place reliance on the computer operations controls, since, provided they are working satisfactorily, he need not spread his tests on the programmed procedures.

Job set-up

6.04   Job set-up is the name normally given to the physical assembly of the material necessary for processing. This material may include the devices holding the relevant programs and data, the job control statements, the run instructions and parameter cards. In more advanced systems there will be less need to assemble devices since the programs will be held on the program library and many data files may be on-line.

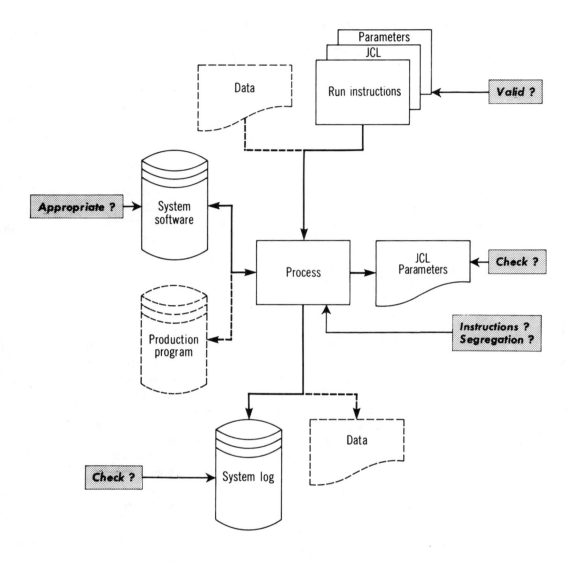

FIG. 64. Computer operations controls (6.02)

6.05   The **job control statements** (which are also often called job control language or, for short, JCL) contain the instructions by which the computer is commanded to execute particular programs using particular files in a particular sequence. They are usually on punched cards but, in more advanced systems, can be held on-line on disc. They are then called into operation by the input of a single card or entry on a terminal.

6.06   The **run instructions** contain the program operating instructions, which give details of the actions to be taken by operators before, during, and at the completion of, the operation of the program, and the current processing instructions, which give details for the suite of programs as a whole, of the programs and files to be used and stationery requirements. These run instructions complement the standard operating instructions which apply to all processing.

6.07   The **parameter cards** include the information that is variable in nature. The most common parameters are dates which are used in, for example, the generation of data such as cheques and the ageing of accounts receivable or inventory balances. Parameters may also be used to indicate whether program steps only used periodically, such as the production of customer statements, should be activated.

6.08   The principal significance of job set-up in relation to computer operations controls is the need to ensure that the job control statements and parameters are properly prepared. The assembly of devices is usually less important from a control point of view since the correctness of the programs and files will be checked before processing commences. However, errors in parameters, such as dates, may not be identified by subsequent controls, particularly as it is usually impracticable to check such resulting accounting output as an aged analysis of accounts receivable. Likewise, the failure to activate periodic routines, either by parameter card or job control statement, may not be revealed. Incorrect entry of job control statements might also lead to programs being run in an incorrect sequence. In addition, it is possible to use job control statements to bypass certain functions in the programs. For these reasons the controls over job set-up are important.

6.09   The normal technique to ensure that valid job control statements and parameters are being used is to maintain approved job set-up instructions and check that the statements and parameters actually used correspond with the instructions.

6.10   The job set-up instructions will have been prepared at the time the system was first developed and will have been updated for changes made since implementation. The preparation and updating of these instructions should be checked by a responsible official before cataloguing of new or changed programs, as indicated in paragraph 5.42.

6.11   Care must be taken to protect the details of the job control statements, and parameters in the job set-up instructions, from unauthorised change. All changes should be authorised and changes to parameters related to accounting data should only be accepted on appropriate user department authority. Details of changes made and the authority therefor should be kept with the instructions. A responsible official should review the instructions from time to time on a surprise basis, and verify that they appear up to date and that any changes are valid.

6.12 Each time the job control statements and parameters are used in processing, the details will be printed by the computer. These details should be checked regularly to the job set-up instructions. This comparison should be carried out or checked by someone other than those responsible for job set-up and computer operations. Where parameters are of particular importance, such as currency or interest rates, it may be desirable for their validity to be specifically checked by the user department concerned.

6.13 The following questions regarding job set-up are asked in the ICQ:

"1. *Are there adequate job set-up instructions (e.g. including details for JCL, parameters and sequence of operations) for:*
   (a) *each application;*
   (b) *system software?*

2. *Are all changes to the instructions initiated only on the basis of appropriate written authorisation?*

3. *Are there adequate controls to ensure that the instructions remain correct and up to date (e.g. periodic independent review of the instructions)?*

4. *Are there adequate controls that the job control statements and parameters used in processing are in accordance with the instructions (e.g. review of computer listing of statements and parameters used)?*

5. *Are the procedures in 4 either performed or checked by persons other than those responsible for job set-up or computer operating? (D)*

6. *Are the results of the procedures in 4 reviewed and approved by a responsible official? (S)"*

Operations software and computer operating

6.14 The procedures which organise and control the activity involved in computer processing will be exercised partly manually and partly by software. In the more advanced systems, the procedures are increasingly carried out by software and the manual functions are then restricted to actions required or requested by the software. The principal control considerations are that the system software used is reliable and that the manual procedures do not, by error or otherwise, interfere with, or affect, normal processing.

6.15 The main system software used is generally known as the operating system. An operating system usually consists of a series of program modules. The principal module is variously known (depending upon the particular computer manufacturer) as the control module, supervisor, monitor, or executive. In its simplest form, the control module is a program, permanently resident in the computer whilst it is in operation, which supervises the running of the application programs. In most operating systems there will also be subsidiary program modules. The control module supervises the operation of the subsidiary program modules, transferring control of the computer to them as and when required. Examples of the more common subsidiary program modules are those used to carry out file handling procedures, to control multiprogramming (where used), to control spooling systems (where used) and to control the manipulation of data.

6.16 In advanced systems, further system software is used which has to interface with the operating system. For example, where remote terminals are used, data communications software is necessary to handle the transmission of data to and from the terminals. In database systems, DBMS is necessary for the processing of data on the database. The facilities of reading and writing included within the DBMS work in conjunction with the file handling module of the operating system.

6.17 The controls over the manual procedures will depend largely on the nature of the system software and the size of the installation. They will normally comprise a combination of procedures designed both to prevent and detect error. The preventive procedures usually include the provision of operating instructions and the establishment, where practicable, of a suitable segregation of duties. The measures to detect error will be based on reviews of operator activity.

6.18 Operator procedures should be based on a framework of standing instructions. These instructions should deal with the operation of the computer and its peripheral equipment, the actions to be taken in the event of machine or program failure and the records to be kept. The standing instructions, when combined with the run instructions, should provide rules for each step that may need to be taken by operators. A responsible official, such as the operations manager, should periodically review the operating instructions and confirm that they remain up to date. Evidence of compliance with operating instructions should be included in the review of processing referred to in paragraph 6.20.

6.19 In the larger installations it is likely that more than one operator will be present during processing and there will thus be opportunities to rotate duties. In addition, the work of operators may be supervised during processing by a chief operator or shift leader. In smaller installations it will be less practicable to provide for a segregation of duties and more emphasis will need to be given to a review of operator actions during processing.

6.20 The review of operator actions will be based on a computer-produced report or, less frequently, a manual report. The system software will usually record on file details of all activity during processing. The details on this file, defined as the **system log**, can be printed out for review. Unusual activity such as hardware malfunction, re-runs and abnormal endings and the resulting operator actions can thus be investigated. However, it should be borne in mind that the information recorded on these logs is voluminous and technical in nature, and a full review is thus often impracticable. Manufacturers' software may be available, or system software may be designed, to analyse the entries as an aid to their investigation.

6.21 Where, as in some smaller installations, the system software does not produce a log in sufficient detail to review unusual activity, or where it is not practicable to review the system log, the review of unusual activity may be based on a fully manual report or a part computer and part manual report. For example, the system software may generate details of time spent on the jobs processed and the operators may enter thereon details of the causes of differences from scheduled times. It would normally only be possible to place reliance on a fully manual log where there was adequate segregation of duties or supervision in the computer room during the processing to which it related.

6.22 The system log should be reviewed by a responsible official or by someone other than those responsible for job set-up or computer operations. Particular attention should be paid to evidence of operators overriding system software checks, for example by overriding retention periods on data files. The person carrying out the review should establish that the report is complete for the period under review and follows on from the previously reviewed system log. This control can be conveniently based on the use of sequentially prenumbered stationery.

6.23 The following questions regarding computer operating are asked in the ICQ:

"Operations software
  1. *Are the system software procedures (e.g. supervisor program) appropriate to ensure that production programs are properly processed?*
  2. *Review the answers to the system software section. Are there adequate controls over the implementation and security of system software?*

Computer operating
  3. *Are there adequate operating instructions for all operator actions?*
  4. *Are all changes to the instructions initiated only on the basis of appropriate written authorisation?*
  5. *Are there adequate controls to ensure that the instructions remain correct and up-to-date (e.g. periodic review by the operations manager)?*
  6. *Is the control that operators comply with operating instructions and do not adversely affect the results of processing a suitable combination of:*

  (a) *supervision in the computer room;*
    If yes, answer 7
  (b) *review of a record of processing?*
    If yes, answer 8 to 13

Supervision
  7. *Is a supervisor present in the computer room at all times, including shifts outside the normal working period?*

Record of processing
  8. *Where the record is computer-produced:*
    (a) *are the system software procedures appropriate to ensure that all unusual situations (e.g. hardware malfunctions, re-runs, abnormal endings) and consequent operator actions are automatically recorded;*

(b) *are there adequate controls over the implementation and sec-*
urity of system software (review the answers to the system
software section)?

9. *Where the record is manually-produced, are there adequate controls*
to ensure that all unusual situations and consequent operator actions
are automatically recorded (e.g. review by the operations supervisor)?

10. *Are there adequate controls to ensure that the records reviewed are*
complete (e.g. recorded on a prenumbered form; recorded on the run
sheet)?

11. *Are all unusual situations and consequent operator actions adequately*
investigated?

12. *Is the investigation in 11 either performed or checked by persons other*
than those involved in computer operations? (D)

13. *Are the results of the procedures in 11 reviewed and approved by a*
responsible official? (S)"

Use of correct data files

6.24 In many cases use of the correct data files will be ensured by the normal
updating and maintenance controls discussed in Chapter 4. However,
particularly as regards those files that contain tables referred to in processing, for example the lists of numbers where sequence checks are used,
specific controls over the use of the correct file will be required.

6.25 Although there will be manual controls over the data files at the time of
issue from the physical library to job set-up, the auditor will usually rely
on the system software to ensure that the correct files are loaded. Each file
held on a device will include a header label containing such information as
the file name and the version number. If a file is so large as to require more
than one device, the header label will also include a sequence number to
identify the part of the file concerned. When the file is loaded for processing, the details on the header label are checked. Additional protection can be achieved in the case of batch systems by the use of retention
periods. When a file is created, the system software adds to the header
label the current date and the number of days for which the data is to be
retained. The system software will not accept the file for processing until
the expiry date of the retention period has been reached. Any operator
override of these controls should be reviewed as indicated in paragraph
6.22.

6.26 The following questions regarding file use are asked in the ICQ:

"1. *Are there adequate procedures to ensure that:*
    (a) *correct files are used (e.g. software check on file-id, internal*
    volume serial number, creation date and generation number);
    (b) *all volumes of a multivolume file are used?*

2. *Where reliance is placed on system software to ensure the use of correct*
files:
    (a) *are the software procedures appropriate (e.g. to distinguish*

229

between different generations of a master file);

(b) *are there adequate controls over the implementation and security of system software (review the answers to the system software section)?*

3. *Is adequate evidence of the system software procedures printed out and reviewed by persons other than those involved in computer operations or system software? (D)*

4. *Are the results of the procedures in 1 and 3 reviewed and approved by a responsible official? (S)"*

Recovery from processing failure

6.27 There should be back-up arrangements so that, in the event of a failure, the recovery process in respect of production programs, system software and data files, does not introduce any erroneous change into the system. The principal techniques that may be employed are discussed in paragraphs 12.13 to 12.15 "Computer Security".

6.28 The following questions regarding recovery from processing failure are asked in the ICQ:

"1. Are there appropriate back-up arrangements over the following so that, in the event of a failure, the recovery process does not introduce an erroneous change into the system:

(a) *production programs;*

(b) *system software;*

(c) *data files?*

2. *Is the action taken during the recovery process reviewed and approved by a responsible official? (S)"*

Data File Security Controls

6.29 Data file security controls are those controls designed to ensure that unauthorised changes cannot be made to data files. The auditor will wish to place reliance on data file security controls where the controls over maintenance of data, discussed in paragraphs 4.69 to 4.80, cannot be relied upon to detect unauthorised changes. The need to place reliance on data file security controls is likely to be greater in the case of standing data than transaction data. This is because it is uncommon for all standing data fields of accounting significance to be subject to regular reconciliation procedures, and any cycle checking of data on files may not be sufficiently frequent to provide timely identification of unauthorised changes.

6.30 Reliance is most likely to be placed on data file security controls in respect of the maintenance of data on files organised as a database since reconciliation procedures will often be carried out less frequently than would be necessary to provide timely identification of unauthorised changes, particularly where the files are on-line to terminals.

6.31   Although the principal reason why the auditor may be concerned with data file security controls is so that no unauthorised changes can be made to the data on files, it should be remembered that there are also important operational reasons why the company should establish suitable controls. These reasons include the need to protect files from being accidentally overwritten or destroyed and against copies of files being taken and the information thereon being used to the company's disadvantage.

6.32   Controls will be required for data files both while in use and while held off-line. **Data files in use** are defined, in a similar manner to programs in use, to include files which can be accessed through the system, either by operators processing jobs or through terminals. Files in use thus include both tapes or discs which have been loaded for a specific processing run but are otherwise stored off-line, as in batch systems, or they may be discs permanently loaded and available for enquiry or updating as in on-line and real-time systems. Files organised as a database would normally be in the latter category. **Off-line data files** are those held in a physical library.

Data files in use

6.33   The particular threat against files in use is that they may be updated in an unauthorised manner. In batch systems, where the files have been loaded for a specific processing run, the problem is limited to controlling the action of operators during the particular run. Files in on-line and real-time systems require, in addition, permanent protection, particularly against access from terminals. Control is required during periods of normal production processing and whilst non-production tasks are being undertaken, such as during maintenance or testing. The control features that protect against unauthorised updating of files are discussed in the following paragraphs under the headings of access by operators, access through terminals and access by production programs.

Access by operators

6.34   The control procedures designed to protect data files from unauthorised access by operators during processing are similar to those already outlined in respect of programs. These procedures, which can usually be carried out at the same time as those for programs, include the review of data files accessed during the processing of jobs, as described in paragraph 5.51, and the controls over computer operating and the use of correct data files discussed in paragraphs 6.14 to 6.22 and 6.24 and 6.25.

6.35   There are utilities which can make direct changes to data files, and their use should be controlled in a similar manner to those used for changing executable programs, outlined in paragraph 5.59. In database systems, it is important to control the use of utilities which may give access to the physical database when it is not under the control of the DBMS, for example when the DBMS is undergoing maintenance. To make a meaningful change in this way it is first necessary to ascertain the physical nature of the database, in particular the relationship between the various data elements contained in the schema. It is therefore important that unauthorised access is not allowed to the schema or its related documentation. The original specification, and subsequent control, of schemas is one of the functions of database administration.

Access through terminals

6.36 The particular concern where input is through terminals, as in on-line and real-time systems, is to protect against the entry of unauthorised input which will subsequently be updated on the data files. The attempt to input this unauthorised data would often be made outside the normal input streams.

6.37 This input of invalid data might be of either transaction data or standing data. Invalid transaction data would normally be a complete transaction either to add to a balance on file, such as a supplier's invoice, or to alter the effect of a transaction already on file, for example a credit note to match a sales invoice on file. Invalid standing data might be of a complete record, such as a fictitious supplier's account, or of a field, such as rate of pay or interest rate. The potential to alter fields is usually increased where files are on-line and records can be displayed at terminals by means of VDUs.

6.38 Unauthorised access to details of the data on file may also be important. The obtaining of information in this way might facilitate subsequent unauthorised input. In addition, the information obtained might reduce the value of a subsequent control. For example, the counting of stock would be less effective if the counter could previously enquire by means of a VDU as to the balance before making the count.

6.39 Where data files are on-line to terminals, there should be a suitable combination of system software and physical security of terminals to protect the files so that only authorised personnel can access the files either to obtain information or to input alterations. These controls, which are discussed in the following paragraphs, are illustrated in outline in Figure 65.

Passwords

6.40 Normally the system software will provide protection by only allowing a terminal to be activated if a valid identification has been input by the potential user and recognised by the program. This identification is normally called a password.

6.41 In simpler systems, the use of the appropriate password may enable the user to obtain, by report or visual display, any record on the file and to input any data. In more complex systems, the password system can be used both to limit users to specified terminals and data and to limit terminals to specific files. Thus, for example, in the case of an accounts receivable file, one password might permit the display or input of name and address data while another password might be needed to display or input credit limits. At the same time, only certain terminals might accept the second password needed to display or input credit limits. Attempted violations should be recorded, printed out and investigated promptly.

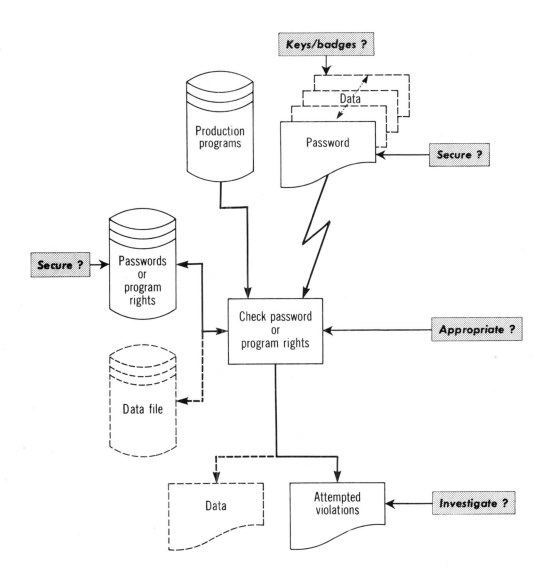

FIG. 65. Data file security controls – on-line files (6.39)

233

6.42 Care should be taken in the design of passwords. If the passwords are logically related, for example by straightforward sequence numbering plus a fixed prefix such as SALES010, SALES020, SALES030, to access the accounts receivable ledger, and each password accesses different data on the file, terminal operators may be able, by trial and error, to obtain access to data fields which should otherwise be inaccessible to them.

6.43 There will need to be suitable controls over the design, maintenance and issue of passwords. Password tables should be controlled, issued and amended by staff independent of computer operations and terminal usage. This activity is often monitored by internal audit.

6.44 Procedures are necessary to ensure that passwords cannot be obtained by unauthorised staff. For this reason details of passwords should not be printed on the terminal at the time they are input. Password tables stored in the computer should be held in unintelligible code form. It is also advisable to change the passwords periodically.

Physical security

6.45 Control can be assisted by restricting physical access to terminals and by requiring the use of an appropriate key or badge to activate the terminal. It is often difficult to restrict physical access unless the terminals are housed in separate rooms under adequate supervision. Care must be taken to ensure that restrictions apply at all relevant times. Sometimes terminal rooms are secure out of office hours but access is relatively easy during the day. Where keys or badges are used, there will need to be a register recording issues to staff so that all keys or badges can be accounted for and so as to ensure that they are only used by authorised staff. Often different keys and badges will allow access to different master files or different fields on master files.

Access by production programs

6.46 In addition to the features outlined above with regard to access by operators or through terminals it is necessary, where database organisation is used, to control the rights of the various production programs to access or modify the data on files. In database systems each application program has an associated sub-schema held on the database library. This defines the logical view of the database for the particular application program, that is, which fields of information the program has access to, and what can be done with each field, for example read only, change, delete, or change and delete.

6.47 Without a sub-schema a program cannot access the database. This restriction is usually of significance in database systems because of the greater amount and variety of data potentially available to application programs. Control of the sub-schemas is thus an important aspect in restricting unauthorised access to data in such systems. The original specification, and subsequent control, of sub-schemas is one of the functions of database administration. Control usually includes the reporting and investigation of attempted unauthorised accesses.

6.48 The following questions regarding password protection and physical access to terminals are asked in the ICQ:

"1. *Where files are software protected, are the system software procedures appropriate to identify and stop unauthorised attempts to access the files?*
   2. *Review the answers to the system software section. Are there adequate controls over the implementation and security of system software?*
   3. *Are there adequate procedures for the investigation of the reports of unauthorised attempts to access data files?*
   4. *Are there adequate controls over the:*
      (a) *issue;*
      (b) *use;*
      (c) *security*
      of passwords?
   5. *Do the restrictions in 4 apply at all times when data files are on-line to terminals (e.g. during testing)?*
   6. *Are there adequate controls over the:*
      (a) *issue;*
      (b) *use;*
      (c) *security*
      of keys and badges that activate terminals?
   7. *Are the following procedures either performed or checked by persons other than those involved in computer operations and terminal use: (D)*
      (a) *investigation of unauthorised attempts to access data files; (3)*
      (b) *issue, use and security of passwords; (4)*
      (c) *issue, use and security of keys and badges? (6)*
   8. *Are the results of the following procedures reviewed and approved by a responsible official: (S)*
      (a) *investigation of unauthorised attempts to access data files; (3)*
      (b) *issue, use and security of passwords; (4)*
      (c) *issue, use and security of keys and badges? (6)*"

Off-line files

6.49 The particular threat against files held off-line is that they may be removed for unauthorised purposes. This can occur where files are not physically protected or can be issued without authority and where files in issue cannot be accounted for. The control features that protect against the unauthorised obtaining of files are discussed below under the headings of physical security and library records.

Physical security

6.50 In order that off-line files may be secure from unauthorised access there should be a lockable storage area, separate from the computer room, preferably supervised by a full-time librarian responsible for the issue, receipt and security of all files. Where the installation is not large enough

235

to warrant a full-time librarian, a member of the control staff should have similar duties. Access to the library should be restricted to staff authorised to obtain and deliver files.

6.51 There will need to be procedures so that files are only issued for authorised processing. This means that processing schedules should be prepared giving details of the files required for processing. Schedules should be prepared for all applications and be approved by a responsible official. Librarians should be instructed only to issue the appropriate files on production of an authorised processing schedule. The specific authority of a responsible official should be necessary for the issue of any file unsupported by a processing schedule.

6.52 Issued files should not be removed from the operations area. Physical control of files in issue will normally be the responsibility of the operations manager or chief operator. Further protection may be afforded by the follow up of files recorded as in issue for an unreasonable length of time.

Library records

6.53 Each removable storage device should be allocated a unique identity number which should be permanently recorded on the device. A record of devices can then be maintained as a means of accounting for and controlling both files issued from the library and those created during processing. The records of devices and files can be maintained either manually or by the system software.

6.54 Where the records are maintained manually, they will normally take the form of a register of devices on which is recorded the name, version number and date created of the file on each device. This information will also be attached to the device itself. Issues of devices should be recorded in the register by the librarian together with the purpose for which they have been issued, as indicated on the processing schedule. Some of these devices will be holding data required for processing, such as master files of standing data. Others will be devices holding data which is no longer required, as, for example, a tape of last month's stores issues. The librarian should ensure that devices holding confidential data which is no longer required are purged before release. The register of devices should be reviewed on a daily basis and any devices outstanding for longer than the requisite period should be followed up.

6.55 In addition to accounting for devices in this manner, it is desirable for the details of files in the library to be independently compared with those created during processing, as indicated on the processing schedule or reported on the system log. This control is particularly important where there is no independent librarian.

6.56 Where the records are maintained by computer, the details of all devices will be input and held on the computer by the system software. The system software will also record, as it processes the files, the name, version number and date created of the file on each device. With this information the system software can produce the processing schedules indicating the devices to be issued. After processing, the computer will produce an updated register of devices, on the basis of which the librarian can check the return of devices issued. The system software will also produce a schedule of files processed. This can be checked by the librarian to ensure that only devices required for processing, as indicated by the processing schedule, have been used.

6.57　The following questions regarding off-line files are asked in the ICQ:

"1. *Are data files securely held when not in use?*

2. *Are data files only issued in accordance with appropriate authorisation?*

3. *Are there adequate records maintained so that data files issued can be accounted for?*

4. *Are there adequate procedures to ensure the prompt return of data files (e.g. by a regular review of the records to determine the reasons why any have not been returned)?*

5. *Are the procedures in 3 and 4 either performed or checked by persons other than those responsible for: (D)*
　　(a) *computer operations;*
　　(b) *system design and programming?*

6. *Are the results of the procedures in 3 and 4 reviewed and approved by a responsible official? (S)*

7. *Where the records in 3 are computer-based, are the system software procedures appropriate to maintain accurate records?*

8. *Review the answers to the system software section. Are there adequate controls over the implementation and security of system software?*

9. *Do the controls in 1 to 3 apply during shifts outside the normal working period (e.g. weekends) and during periods of non-production work (e.g. program testing)?"*

System Software

6.58　At various points in this chapter, and in Chapter 5, reference has been made to system software. System software was defined in Chapter 3 as those programs on whose functioning the auditor may wish to place reliance although they do not process accounting data. System software is relevant to the auditor because it assists in the control both of the programs that process accounting data and of the data files.

6.59　The system software that may be of relevance to the auditor, and which has been referred to earlier in this chapter and in Chapter 5, includes the programs relating to:

(a) Cataloguing (paragraphs 5.43 and 5.44).

(b) Reporting of jobs processed (paragraph 5.51).

(c) Program comparison (paragraph 5.53).

(d) Supervision of application programs (paragraph 6.15).

(e) File handling/DBMS (paragraphs 6.15 and 6.16).

(f) Data communications (paragraph 6.16).

(g) Reporting of operations (paragraph 6.20).

(h) File set-up (paragraph 6.25).

(i) Password protection (paragraphs 6.40 to 6.42).

(j) Library records (paragraph 6.56).

6.60 Having identified those software procedures on which he wishes to place reliance, the auditor will be concerned that they are appropriate, have been properly implemented and are kept secure. The considerations to be taken into account in evaluating the appropriateness of the software procedures have been outlined earlier. In this section the controls over their implementation and security are considered.

Implementation

6.61 The controls required for the successful implementation of system software are substantially similar to those required for the implementation of application programs.

6.62 Where system software is designed by a technical support group within the company, or software supplied from outside is altered, the procedures for system design, outlined in paragraphs 5.18 to 5.20, should be followed. Where system software is supplied from outside by manufacturers or software houses, normally the only work required of the company will be the selection, where appropriate, of options in the software.

6.63 Any changes made by the company to the implemented software will need to be controlled in the manner outlined in paragraphs 5.35 and 5.37. In the case of software, particularly operating systems, supplied by the manufacturers, improvements and modifications will be made from time to time. These modifications will be introduced in the form of new programs received from the manufacturers or by amendments to the existing programs, usually made by the manufacturer's systems engineer.

6.64 When new or amended system software has been loaded, i.e. copied to a disc permanently on-line to the computer, it should be tested to ensure that it performs as intended. Where the software is used with application programs, for example the operating system, tests would normally involve the running of the software with proven application programs so that any anomalies which may occur can be identified as resulting from the system software. This approach will also be important where application programs require modification in order to be compatible with the revised operating system, for example when the company is introducing a database structure for data files, using a DBMS.

6.65 Where the software is unrelated to the running of application programs, for example the software producing the report of operations and file set-up, the proper functioning of the software, and the inclusion of the appropriate options, may be confirmed by a review of the system-generated output.

6.66 The controls over the copying of the tested software onto the installation's library should follow, as appropriate, the procedures for the cataloguing of application programs outlined in paragraphs 5.41 to 5.45.

Security

6.67 Controls, similar to those outlined in paragraphs 5.49 to 5.63, should be used to ensure that unauthorised changes are not made to system software either while in use or when held off-line.

6.68 The questions asked in the ICQ in respect of the implementation and security of system software are similar to those asked in respect of application programs and are included in the integrity controls section of the ICQ in appendix B to Chapter 3.

Database Administration

6.69 The size and complexity of databases often leads to the appointment of specific personnel responsible for all aspects of database administration. These personnel are often collectively called the database administrator (DBA). Their tasks might include the design and maintenance of the schemas and sub-schemas, the maintenance of the DBMS and related software and liaison with users, other computer department staff and outside suppliers. Certain important integrity controls relating to the database may be undertaken by the DBA. These have already been mentioned at the appropriate places in Chapters 5 and 6 and include:

    (a) review of new systems for compatability with the database (paragraph 5.18);

    (b) review of program changes for impact on the database (paragraph 5.32);

    (c) control of schemas and sub-schemas (paragraphs 6.35 and 6.47).

In addition the DBA may have responsibility in relation to maintenance controls over data on the database.

6.70 The DBA may thus combine responsibility for procedures and controls which, in conventional systems, would normally be carried out by separate people. When these procedures and controls are combined to a significant extent in the DBA, it is important, in order to preserve an appropriate segregation of duties, that the DBA is restricted from unsupervised access to the computer room or operation of the computer and cannot initiate transactions.

239

Summary

6.71 Integrity controls are defined as those controls, mainly in the computer department, which are designed to ensure that:

(a) Appropriate programmed procedures are included in the program, both when the system originally becomes operational and when changes are subsequently made. These are defined as implementation controls.

(b) Unauthorised changes cannot be made to operational programmed procedures. These are defined as program security controls.

(c) Programmed procedures are consistently applied. These are defined as computer operations controls.

(d) Unauthorised access cannot be made to data files. These are defined as data file security controls.

6.72 It would be unwieldy to ask all the relevant questions relating to integrity controls under each control objective and, accordingly, the questions regarding integrity controls are asked separately in the ICQ in the integrity controls section. Under each control objective there is a requirement to ask whether a review of the integrity controls shows them to be adequate for the purposes of the control objective.

6.73 Even in those cases where he decides not to place reliance thereon, the auditor will normally wish to evaluate the integrity controls from time to time so that he can report to management weaknesses that come to his attention. This approach is particularly desirable in the case of integrity controls, since weaknesses may lead to deficiencies in operational efficiency and, although computer systems may sometimes start under predominantly user controls, their growth and extension will often cause an increasing dependence on integrity controls.

7

Functional Tests

General Approach

The purpose and scope of functional tests

7.01 The auditor will need to carry out suitable tests to provide evidence that the controls on which he wishes to place reliance have continued to operate properly throughout the period under audit. These tests, which are sometimes called "compliance tests" or "procedural tests", are referred to as **functional tests** in this book.

7.02 The auditor will normally wish to carry out functional tests on all those controls which he identified while completing the ICQ and on which he wishes to place reliance. However, he may decide that, rather than rely on the controls and carry out functional tests, it would be more efficient to extend his validation tests on the financial statements. The nature of these extended validation procedures is described in Chapter 9.

7.03 The auditor will normally carry out his functional tests on the disciplines before those on the basic controls. This is because, unless the disciplines have operated satisfactorily, the auditor is unlikely to be able to place reliance on the proper operation of the basic controls throughout the period under examination. The approach he adopts to the basic controls is thus largely dependent on the results of his tests on the disciplines.

Functional test documentation

7.04 The auditor will need to make a suitable record of the tests carried out in order to justify the conclusions he reaches as to the operation of the controls. A formal programme and record of functional tests should therefore be prepared and should include, as a minimum:

(a) a description of the tests to be performed;

(b) a reference from each functional test to the related question in the ICQ (this assists in ensuring that the tests are complete and emphasises the direct relationship between the tests and the controls);

(c) identification of the levels of test;

(d) an indication of the periods to be tested;

(e) identification of the evidence seen;

(f) identification of any breakdowns or exceptions noted during the performance of the tests, and information as to their disposition;

(g) an indication that the work has been completed, usually the initials of the person completing the work, and the date of its performance.

7.05 In order to assist in assembling a programme and record of functional tests which is appropriate to the system being tested, and to ensure standardisation in the tests carried out, specimen tests can be provided for many of the common control techniques. In each case, the auditor selects the relevant specimen tests and tailors them to fit the precise characteristics of the system. Specimen tests to assist in testing the more common controls are set out in appendix A to this chapter and are referred to where considered helpful in the paragraphs below. An example of the programme and record of functional tests which is used to set out the details of the tests and the work carried out is illustrated in Figure 66.

Programme and Record of Functional Tests

Audit of The A.B.C. Company

Control Objective No 5   Date of Accounts 31/12/78

ICQ Ref.	Details of Test or Reason for omitting Test	Level of Test	Programme Update	Evidence seen Period(s) selected	Exceptions Yes/No	Cleared	Working Paper Ref.	Signature and Date
5·16(a)	Examine the report of missing and duplicate numbers, PLED∅1, for evidence that the items reported	5 reports in latest period	✓	Signed PLED∅1 reports for weeks ending September	Yes – 1 report not signed	✓ See work paper	M/63	J. ST 23/9

FIG. 66. Programme and record of functional tests (7.05)

Types of tests

7.06 Functional testing will normally consist of two distinct steps:

- **Examination of evidence**, i.e. the inspection of records, documents, reconciliation reports and the like, for evidence that a specific discipline or control appears to have been properly carried out, for example the inspection of signatures or initials on a supplier's invoice evidencing that the invoice has been matched with a goods received note.

- **Reperformance**, i.e. the repeating, either in whole or in part, of the same work processes as those performed by the company's employees, for example the actual matching by the auditor of a supplier's invoice with the corresponding goods received note, in order to obtain assurance that the evidence seen on the supplier's invoice actually represents work done. Where the auditor finds errors in the reperformance he carries out, it casts doubts on the reliability of the evidence which he has examined.

7.07   There are some disciplines and basic controls that cannot be tested by examination and reperformance, for example the examination of incoming goods or the physical security of stores. In these circumstances, the controls can be tested by attendance at the relevant location in order to observe and enquire whether the control appears to be operating. When relying on **observation** as a test, the auditor should bear in mind the possibility that the observed control may not be performed when he is not present. He should also make any enquiries he considers necessary to support and amplify his observations; for example, where details of goods received are to be entered on a sequentially numbered document, he should enquire as to the effects of part deliveries, backlog of work and abnormal deliveries on the procedure observed.

The Approach in Computer Systems

The nature of functional tests in a computer system

7.08   As in non-computer systems, the purpose of functional tests is to provide evidence as to whether or not an internal control procedure identified in the ICQ is being operated as planned. However, because of the changes in controls discussed in the previous three chapters, there are often differences in the techniques and extent of functional testing.

7.09   Before deciding to carry out functional tests the auditor should bear in mind that audit efficiency can sometimes be improved by choosing one of the two other approaches which may assist in computer systems. These are:

- The use of computer programs to review and classify large volumes of processed data which may increase the effectiveness of the validation procedures.

- An increase in the level and the spreading of testing of programmed procedures as an alternative to the functional testing of the integrity controls. The auditor may find that he can restrict the increase in tests if there are effective associated user controls, for example the action taken to investigate exception reports and the disciplines over this function. In a similar manner the auditor may be able to increase his tests on the appropriateness of system software and reduce his reliance on other integrity controls.

243

7.10 The techniques for functional testing in computer systems can be further considered under the following headings:

- Disciplines

- User controls

- Integrity controls

- Programmed procedures

Tests of disciplines

7.11 The disciplines over controls in computer systems were defined in paragraphs 3.18 to 3.22 and comprise:

(a) the supervision of the work of persons involved in the operation of basic controls;

(b) the segregation of duties;

(c) custodial controls.

The tests on each of these are considered below.

Supervisory controls

7.12 Tests of the supervisory controls will be largely based on the examination of evidence. The primary evidence examined will be the signature or initials of the person exercising the supervision on the relevant documents or records, for example, in the case of user controls, on a rejection or exception report indicating that all items have been satisfactorily dealt with or, as regards integrity controls, on a program change form indicating that testing has been properly carried out. Particular attention should also be given to other evidence, such as internal memoranda indicating the disposition of unsatisfactory documents or records which have been queried as a result of the supervisory control. Where appropriate, the auditor will also wish to confirm that the material submitted to the supervisor was, prima facie, suitable to enable a satisfactory review to be carried out, for example, in the case of program testing, that details of the test data and the results were submitted to the supervisor. The auditor may also be able to observe the application of the supervisory control to transactions being processed or reports being prepared at the time of his visit.

7.13 Complete reperformance of a supervisory control will often not be possible, partly because the auditor does not have the knowledge and experience of the supervisor concerned, and partly because the nature and extent of the checks carried out by the supervisor may be at his discretion and may not be clearly evidenced. Reperformance is therefore usually limited to the inspection of the supporting documentation that should have been seen, together with evidence of prior checks as required by the company's procedures.

7.14   As a practical matter, it is frequently more efficient to use the same transactions to carry out functional tests of supervisory controls and the related basic controls. The existence of errors in the application of the basic control that were not detected by the supervisor may indicate that the supervisory control is not being applied effectively, and to this extent a test of the basic control can serve the same purpose as a reperformance test of the supervisory control.

Segregation of duties and custodial controls

7.15   The tests of segregation of duties and custodial controls are normally carried out by the examination of signatures and initials on documents and records, and observation and enquiry. It is not usually possible to carry out satisfactory reperformance tests on disciplines of this nature.

7.16   In the case of user controls, the auditor will, for example, review signatures and initials on reconciliation and exception reports to confirm that the persons carrying out the user controls were independent of computer operations, that is to say those responsible for the functions of system design, programming and computer operating. He might, in addition, visit the departments concerned and verify by observation that the independence referred to above was being maintained at the time of his visit.

7.17   As regards integrity controls, the auditor will need to see in relation to physical security that suitable instructions are distributed to all relevant staff. He should visit the appropriate areas and observe that the security measures outlined in the instructions are being maintained. He can also examine evidence that the names of individuals, such as terminal operators, are consistent with instructions. As regards segregation of duties, for example between those involved in system development and maintenance, computer operating and custody of data files, the auditor will wish to examine the computer department organisation charts, written procedures and job descriptions and confirm that they provide for adequate segregation of duties both during and outside the normal working day. He can also visit the data processing department and the computer room and observe that this segregation of duties existed at the time of his visit. In addition, he should, where possible, examine work schedules, time reports, operator logs and similar documentation to confirm that the names of individuals performing duties are consistent with the written procedures.

Tests of user controls

7.18   Functional testing of user controls will normally include both examination of evidence and reperformance. Difficulties in designing and carrying out tests should not be experienced because visible evidence of the operation of the relevant controls, for example the agreement of control totals and the action taken on exception and rejection reports, is normally available. It should be noted that, where large volumes are concerned, complete reperformance may not be practicable. For example, where control is exercised by the reconciliation of the total of a large

245

number of batches with a subsequent total produced by the computer, reperformance of the establishment of the initial total might consist of checking the additions of a sample of batches and tracing the selected batch totals to the control register.

Tests of integrity controls

7.19 The auditor will need to carry out functional tests of the integrity controls that are carried out manually and also to test a sample of system software procedures. He will decide on how many, and which, system software procedures to test in the light of the results of his tests on the other integrity controls, in particular those over the implementation and security of system software.

7.20 Functional testing of those integrity controls that are carried out manually will include examination of evidence, reperformance and observation. Many of the tests will be similar to those for testing user controls, for example the review of computer-produced reports. Other tests will be similar to those carried out in non-computer systems, such as those on the completeness controls over program changes. Certain tests as, for example, those on the testing procedures are unique to testing integrity controls. Examination of evidence is particularly important because, in certain cases, reperformance is not an appropriate technique. This is so, for example, where the auditor is testing the adequacy of documentation, such as system descriptions and operating instructions.

7.21 Various techniques are available to test the appropriateness of system software procedures. Use of these techniques on a regular basis may reduce the degree of reliance that the auditor need place on other integrity controls. The technique selected will depend on the nature of the procedure being tested. For example, in testing the cataloguing procedures the use of audit test data and program code analysis may be suitable in establishing that new or changed programs function properly, thus confirming that they were satisfactorily catalogued. The use of audit test data and program code analysis is considered in greater detail later in this chapter (paragraphs 7.32 to 7.34).

7.22 Computer programs have been developed to assist in, and render more effective, the testing of system software procedures. These include:

    (a) programs which examine the company's production programs and, by comparing them with independently controlled copies, assist in confirming that authorised changes have been properly made or that unauthorised changes have not been made. Examples of such programs which compare the executable and source versions of the client's production programs with independently controlled copies are illustrated in Figures 67 and 68;

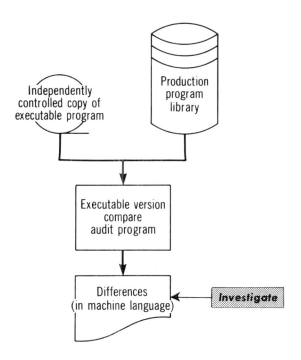

FIG. 67. Audit examination of executable programs (7.22)

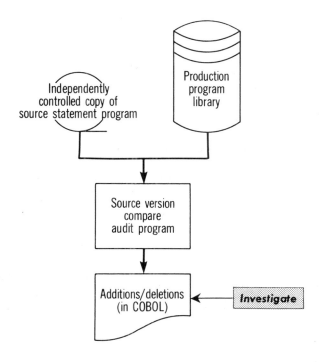

FIG. 68. Audit examination of source statement programs (7.22)

247

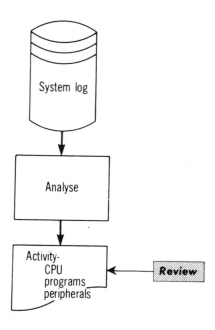

FIG. 69. Audit analysis of system log (7.22)

    (b) programs which will analyse and report defined items on the
system log which the auditor can then compare with the client's
report. An example of such a program is illustrated in Figure 69.

7.23   The system software procedures for password protection can be conveniently tested by the auditor attempting to gain access to a data file or
program from a terminal by using an invalid password. Before using such
a technique the auditor should consider the possible effects, both if the
control should operate properly and if it should fail to operate.

7.24   The auditor may be able to test certain system software procedures while
running his own programs for other audit purposes. Examples include the
reporting of jobs processed and computer operations, job set-up and
library records. He should, however, bear in mind that his presence may
result in controls operating when they might not do so in his absence.

7.25 The auditor will test certain programmed procedures while carrying out the reperformance portion of his functional tests of the implementation controls. These tests, combined with the auditor's functional tests of the remainder of the integrity controls, may serve to satisfy him as to the appropriateness and continued proper operation of the programmed procedures. The auditor may, however, decide to carry out additional tests of programmed procedures. This work will complement the functional tests of integrity controls since it provides further evidence as to whether the integrity controls have continued to operate.

7.26 Tests of programmed procedures are normally carried out by reperformance because it is not possible to test their proper operation by examination of evidence. However, the examination of print-outs, such as lists of missing items, will often provide prima facie evidence that a programmed procedure has continued to operate properly. This examination of evidence will normally be carried out as part of the testing of user controls, for example while testing the investigation of the missing items reported.

7.27 The principal techniques available to test programmed procedures include manual tests, the use of audit test data, program code analysis and simulation using computer audit programs. The choice of technique is often governed by whether there is loss of visible evidence.

Loss of visible evidence

7.28 It is a feature of computer processing that the results of processing may not be printed out in detail. In the absence of such a print-out, the auditor cannot test the operation of programmed procedures by conventional means. There are two ways in which this difficulty can arise. First, totals and analyses may be printed out without supporting details, thus rendering it impossible for the auditor to check the total or analysis. The second situation, although common, is less obvious. Where exception reports and rejection listings are produced, it is often impossible, by reference to the reports or listings, to establish that all items which should have been reported or rejected have been properly treated. These two types of situation are commonly covered by the phrase "loss of audit trail". However, this term is unfortunate in that it implies that the means to check results by conventional tests should be available to auditors and the failure to incorporate this in the system is a matter for criticism. This is not true; what matters is the adequacy of the controls. If the failure to print out constitutes a weakness in control as, for example, if the contents of suspense files were not regularly printed out, the system is deficient and the auditor is correct to draw this to the attention of the company. But if the failure to print out does not represent a weakness, the auditor should normally devise alternative techniques to test the operation of the programmed procedures. For these reasons the term **visible evidence** is used in this book in preference to "audit trail".

Manual tests

7.29 Manual tests can be carried out of programmed procedures where full visible evidence of the programmed procedure is available; for example, where a complete listing of sales invoices is provided, it can be added up to confirm the sales total or, where debtors' statements show all transactions on individual accounts, postings thereto can be checked. Tests will consist of repeating the work that the program carried out and verifying that the results are the same.

7.30 Manual tests can also be carried out where full visible evidence is not provided by the system, but can be created in one of the following ways:

- re-assembling processed data so that it is in the same condition as when the programmed procedure was applied, for example re-assembling batches of sales invoices to test the batch totals posted to the sales ledger control account;

- working on current data before it is sent for processing by the computer, for example testing the additions of batches before they are sent for conversion in order to test the establishment of a total used to control subsequent processing;

- selecting a small number of items from those submitted for processing and processing these in a separate run, for example splitting a batch into two batches, one large and one small, processing the small batch separately and agreeing the resultant computer-produced totals with pre-calculated results;

- simulating a condition which will produce a report if the programmed procedure is working properly, for example altering a batch total to an incorrect figure so that the batch is rejected, or withholding a document so that it is reported as missing (this approach requires careful planning and the agreement of the client);

- requesting a special print-out of items processed, for example a listing of sales invoices included in a sales total produced by the computer.

7.31 Where visible evidence of the operation of a programmed procedure neither exists nor can be created, and the appropriate condition cannot be simulated, it is not possible to carry out manual tests.

Audit test data

7.32 This technique, which is illustrated in Figure 70, consists of devising fictitious data and predicting the results that should be obtained if the programmed procedures operate properly. The data is processed against the client's operational programs and the actual results are checked against the predicted results. This technique is normally used where there is incomplete evidence available of how the procedure operated and

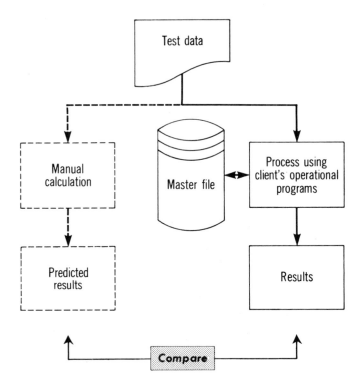

FIG. 70. Audit test data (7.32)

manual tests are either impracticable or inefficient. Audit test data is usually designed to test the operation of several programmed procedures within an application, for example by processing fictitious orders to produce invoices, sales totals and entries in inventory and accounts receivable ledgers. In this case, although it may remain possible to test some of the programmed procedures by manual tests, for example calculations, it will often be more efficient to test them by the use of test data.

7.33   There are important practical considerations when audit test data is used and these are dealt with in appendix B to this chapter. Two illustrations of the use of audit test data are set out in appendix C.

Program code analysis

7.34   Program code analysis comprises the examination by the auditor of source listings of operational programs to determine that the relevant programmed procedures are present and are logically coded. The technical skill required to perform program code analysis is high, as the auditor needs to be familiar with the program language used. The auditor must verify that the coding on the source listing that he is examining is the same

251

as that contained in the operational program which is used for processing. The considerations to be taken into account, and procedures to be followed, when using program code analysis, are discussed in appendix D to this chapter. Program code analysis is illustrated in Figure 71.

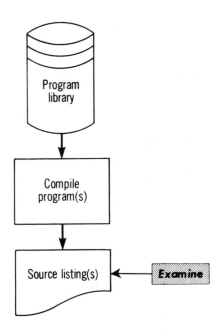

FIG. 71. Program code analysis (7.34)

Use of computer programs

7.35 The auditor usually makes use of his own computer programs to assist in the carrying out of validation procedures. The use of programs in this manner is described in Chapter 9 "Validation Procedures" and Chapter 10 "The Use of Computer Programs". However, the auditor may decide to use his own computer programs to assist in testing programmed procedures. This use of programs is often referred to as **simulation**. There is no fundamental difference between the audit use of computer programs as a validation procedure and as a test of a programmed procedure. The main distinction is that, when used for simulation, the objective of the auditor's program is to check that the company's program is operating correctly by checking and agreeing figures prepared by the company's programs. When used as a validation procedure, the program is also used to provide the auditor with information from the files, over and above that produced by the company, that will be helpful in his audit.

7.36 Examples of the use of a computer audit program as a method of testing programmed procedures include reading a sales invoicing file to verify the production of the sales analysis, reading a file of numbered goods received notes to verify the production of a missing numbers report, and reading a file of stock movements to verify the production of a stock evaluation and analysis report. As the auditor is primarily concerned with those parts of the program that comprise the programmed procedures, it is often unnecessary to duplicate exactly the precise and complete logic of the client's program. The auditor's program may thus be less complicated than that of the client. The use of computer programs for simulation is illustrated in Figure 72.

7.37 One of the practical problems of simulation is that it is often difficult to short-cut the logic of a complex client program. In attempting to do so, the auditor may arrive at different figures from the client and have to spend time correcting his program logic or carrying out a reconciliation. Because of this potential problem it is unlikely that simulation will be an efficient technique where the integrity controls have been tested, and can be relied upon, and only limited reperformance of programmed procedures is required. However, where the integrity controls cannot be completely relied on, simulation of the programmed procedures several times during the year may be a satisfactory alternative. Further, even though the evaluation of the integrity controls indicates them to be

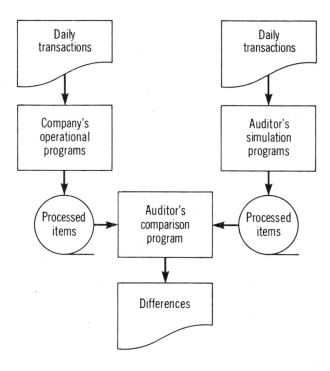

Fig. 72. Use of computer programs for simulation (7.36)

completely satisfactory, the auditor may decide that it is more efficient to simulate programmed procedures several times during the year and reduce the reliance he needs to place on the integrity controls.

7.38 As an extension of his functional tests, the auditor may wish to include checks in his program so that he can indicate to the company what would be the effect of introducing particular procedures; for example, if sales orders had been tested for credit, bad debts of a quantified value might have been avoided. This work goes beyond the normal statutory audit requirements and seeks to identify areas where the company can improve its system. It is therefore in the nature of operational auditing.

Levels of test

7.39 It is not possible to prescribe hard and fast rules for determining levels of test, that is to say the number of times a basic control or discipline should be tested. The level to be selected is, in each case, a matter for judgement by the auditor in the light of all relevant factors. The level depends primarily on the frequency with which the basic control or discipline is exercised; in general, the more frequently it is exercised, the higher the level of test. Thus a higher level of test would be applied to the checking of suppliers' invoices than to a monthly reconciliation of the accounts payable ledger. The levels of reperformance tests will normally be substantially lower than those for examination of evidence. Some guidelines that may be helpful in deciding on levels of test for the various types of control and procedure in computer systems are given below.

Tests of user controls

7.40 It will normally be appropriate to select a level of test that is comparable to that adopted in a non-computer system where the frequency of operation of the control is similar.

Tests of integrity controls

Implementation controls
7.41 As regards new systems, it will normally be appropriate to test that the disciplines were effective in respect of all systems implemented in the period under review. If these tests are satisfactory, it will usually be sufficient to carry out tests on the basic controls as applied to a sample only of the programmed procedures included in such systems. In choosing the sample, regard should be paid to the importance of the system and procedure, the effect if it did not operate properly and, if this happened, the likelihood of it being brought to light by the operation of other controls.

7.42 The level of test applied to program changes should be comparable to that adopted in a non-computer system where the frequency of operation of the control is similar. The procedures will normally be similar for all systems. However, it is desirable to select changes that relate to programmed procedures as distinct from minor changes that only have an operational effect, such as changes to print formats.

Program security, computer operations and data file security controls

7.43 These controls operate at all times and the frequency of their operation is not related to the volume of accounting data processed. The frequency of operation of these controls can be based on the number of programs run. It will often be appropriate to select a level of test comparable to that adopted in a non-computer system where the frequency of operation of the control is similar.

System software

7.44 The nature, extent and timing of tests of the appropriateness of system software are largely a matter of audit judgement. Important factors are the degree of reliance that can be placed on the controls over the implementation and security of system software and the extent to which the results of processing are subject to overall scrutiny or review.

Tests of programmed procedures

7.45 The nature, extent and timing of any additional tests of programmed procedures are also largely a matter of judgement. The following factors should be taken into account:

(a) The degree of reliance that can be placed on the integrity controls. Where reliance on implementation controls is reduced, the auditor should consider increasing the number of different programmed procedures that are tested. Where reliance on program security or computer operations controls is reduced, the auditor should consider increasing the number of times programmed procedures need testing and whether the tests should be spread throughout the period under review.

(b) In selecting programmed procedures to test, the auditor should normally choose those that could have a material effect on the financial statements.

(c) In determining the level of tests, the auditor should consider the nature and size of transactions being processed, and the risk of material error. Systems which deal with payments, cash and accounts receivable are most prone to the possibility of defalcation.

(d) The extent to which the results of processing are subject to overall scrutiny or review. A system which is subject to overall reconciliation of control totals is less susceptible to program error than a system in which transactions are generated by the computer in such a way that the total generated cannot be manually checked.

255

General features

7.46 There are also some general features that the auditor will need to bear in mind when deciding upon his levels of test and these are considered in the following paragraphs.

The reaction to weaknesses in the system of control

7.47 The auditor will be influenced in his selection of levels for test by the weaknesses disclosed in his evaluation of the system. For example, in the absence of a supervisory control, but assuming the existence of an adequate segregation of duties, the auditor might increase his level of tests of the examination of evidence to confirm that the basic controls have continued to operate throughout the period under audit. Conversely, where there are weaknesses relating to the segregation of duties, but adequate supervisory controls, the auditor might increase the level of tests relating to the reperformance of the basic controls in order to obtain assurance as to their proper operation.

The significance of potential errors

7.48 Breakdowns in control will have differing effects depending on the nature of the control. For example, breakdowns in controls over standing data will often be more far-reaching than in the case of individual transactions and a higher level of test of these controls may be appropriate. As a further example, breakdowns in controls over completeness will often be more important than breakdowns in controls over accuracy or validity of individual transactions, because items that should be present, but which have been omitted during processing, will be difficult to identify during validation procedures. As a result controls over completeness generally require a higher level of functional test.

Spreading of tests

7.49 When the auditor proposes to place reliance on controls operating throughout the year, he will need to spread the functional tests of the disciplines. This is necessary in order to obtain assurance as to the continued operation of the underlying basic controls. If the disciplines appear to be operating properly, the reperformance of the basic controls themselves can normally be restricted to one period, usually, though not necessarily, the latest period available at the time of the test.

7.50 It will not normally be necessary to spread functional tests where the controls are of such a nature that their effective performance reveals accumulated errors, including those that may have arisen because of a previous breakdown in the control, for example bank reconciliations.

Complexity of transactions and experience on previous audits

7.51 Where the variety of data processed by the computer is large, or the transactions or calculations are complex, levels of tests should be sufficient to encompass all major variations. Similarly, where experience on previous audits has shown deficiencies in processing, levels of tests may need to be increased over the area concerned.

Summary

7.52 As in non-computer systems, the purpose of functional tests is to provide evidence as to whether or not an internal control procedure identified in the ICQ is being operated as planned. However, because of the changes in controls in computer systems, there are often differences in the techniques and extent of functional testing.

7.53 Before deciding to carry out functional tests the auditor should bear in mind that audit efficiency can sometimes be improved by choosing one of two other approaches which may assist in computer systems. The first alternative is for the auditor to use computer programs to examine large volumes of processed data, which may increase the effectiveness of the validation procedures. The other possibility is to increase the work he carries out on the programmed procedures or system software, thereby reducing his reliance on the integrity controls.

7.54 Tests of user controls and integrity controls carried out manually are similar in nature to those in non-computer systems. Tests of the appropriateness of system software and programmed procedures often require the use of different techniques. These include the use of audit test data, program code analysis and computer programs.

7.55 Adjustments that might be made to the levels of test applicable in non-computer systems are suggested regarding tests on the various types of control and procedure in computer systems.

7: Appendix A
Specimen Tests

1. In this appendix there are examples of the specimen tests that may be used by the auditor in assembling his programme and record of tests.

2. The specimen tests have been prepared for testing user controls, programmed procedures and integrity controls. They have not been designed to test every control but rather to provide a specimen for testing the more common control techniques that are likely to apply in several cases in most applications. As stated in Chapter 7, care is needed to tailor the specimen tests to each particular situation.

3. It is advisable, if using the specimen tests in practice, to provide an index, listing the questions in the ICQ and, where applicable, a cross reference to the typical related tests. Thus, using the questions for control objective 5 (which are included in appendix B to Chapter 3) and the specimen tests included in this appendix, the index would appear as follows:

ICQ Reference	*Specimen Test Number*
5.2	Review results of tests in control objective 2
5.3–5.5	3, 4, 18
5.6–5.10	1, 2, 3, 4, 14
5.11–5.16	1, 3, 4, 13, 18
5.17–5.20	5
5.21–5.27	1, 2, 3, 4, 5, 6, 12, 13, 14, 15, 19
5.28	11
5.29	Review results of tests in control objective 9
5.30–5.33	3, 4, 19
5.34–5.38	2, 8, 9, 19
5.42 & 5.35(b)	Review results of tests of relevant integrity controls

NOTE: 5.39–5.41 relate to non-computer activities and specimen tests are not included in this appendix.

Nature of Control	Specimen Test
User controls 1 *Completeness and accuracy of input* – review of computer-produced reports.	(a) Examine computer reports and see: (i) evidence that reported items or batches (e.g. as outstanding, mismatched or missing) are being dealt with by persons with no incompatible duties (see ICQ); (ii) where appropriate, evidence indicating that the results of the procedures in (i) above have been reviewed and approved by a responsible official. (b) Reperform the clearance of reported items or batches by selecting cleared items or batches and checking that they were properly dealt with.
2 *Completeness and accuracy of input, updating and maintenance* – manual agreement of pre-determined totals.	(a) (i) Examine the register/control account for evidence that the totals/balance are/is being regularly agreed, by persons with no incompatible duties (see ICQ), with the totals printed on the edit/update/maintenance report. (ii) Examine evidence that discrepancies are being dealt with by persons with no incompatible duties (see ICQ). (iii) Where appropriate, examine evidence indicating that the results of the procedures in (i) and (ii) have been reviewed and approved by a responsible official. (b) Reperform the agreement of the totals by: (i) testing agreement of register/control account with the total printed out on the edit/update/maintenance report; (ii) testing the additions of batches and of register/control account. (c) Reperform the clearance of discrepancies by selecting cleared items and checking that they were properly dealt with.

Nature of Control	Specimen Test
3 *Completeness and accuracy of updating* – manual agreement of computer-produced totals.	(a) (i) Examine computer reports or register for evidence that the computer-produced totals are being regularly agreed, by persons with no incompatible duties (see ICQ), with the totals printed out on the update report. (NOTE: take into account summarisation of totals or changes in the totals used). (ii) Examine evidence that differences are investigated and dealt with by persons with no incompatible duties (see ICQ). (iii) Where appropriate, examine evidence indicating that the results of the procedures in (i) and (ii) have been reviewed and approved by a responsible official. (b) Reperform the agreement in (a)(i) above. (c) Where appropriate, reperform the clearance of reconciliation differences by selecting cleared items and checking that they were properly dealt with.
4 *Completeness and accuracy of updating* – manual review of programmed reconcilations.	(a) Examine computer reports and see: (i) that evidence of the reconciliation is examined by persons with no incompatible duties (see ICQ) and suitable action taken on any differences; (ii) where appropriate, evidence indicating that the results of the procedures in (i) above have been reviewed and approved by a responsible official. (b) Where appropriate, reperform the clearance of reconciliation differences by selecting cleared items and checking that they were properly dealt with.
5 *Completeness and accuracy of input and updating* – checking of print-outs.	(a) Test the procedures designed to ensure that all source documents are recorded on an input document.

Nature of Control	Specimen Test
5 *(continued)*	(b) Examine records or files of source documents or retained copies of input documents and verify that there is no undue volume or value of unprocessed items. (c) (i) Examine update reports for evidence that the one for one checking procedures are being carried out. (ii) Reperform the checking by testing items on the update reports with the relevant original documents. (iii) Examine update reports or other evidence that differences are being investigated and corrected by persons with no incompatible duties (see ICQ). (iv) Reperform the clearance of differences by selecting cleared items and checking that they were properly dealt with.
6 *Accuracy of input –* verification of conversion.	(a) Examine evidence that the procedures for verification are being properly carried out. (b) Attend at the conversion department and observe that the fields required to be controlled for accuracy are being verified.
7 *Computer-generated data –* manual review.	(a) Examine computer reports and see: (i) that the data is being manually reviewed by persons with no incompatible duties (see ICQ) and suitable action taken on any items requiring adjustment; (ii) where appropriate, evidence indicating that the results of the procedures in (i) above have been reviewed and approved by a responsible official. (b) Reperform the manual review of items by selecting items and checking by reference to source data that they were properly passed or adjusted.
8 *Maintenance control –* manual control account.	(a) (i) Examine the control account for evidence that it is being regularly agreed to a print-out of total balances on the file by persons with no incompatible duties (see ICQ) and suitable action taken in respect of any differences.

Nature of Control	Specimen Test
8 *(continued)*	(ii) Where appropriate, examine evidence indicating that the results of the procedures in (i) above have been reviewed and approved by a responsible official.
	(b) Reperform the agreement of the control account by:
	(i) testing the make-up of the control account;
	(ii) testing the agreement of the control account.
	(c) Where appropriate, reperform the clearance of differences by selecting cleared differences and checking that they were properly dealt with.
9 *Maintenance control –* computer control record.	(a) Examine reports of computer reconciliations and see:
	(i) that evidence of the reconciliation is examined by persons with no incompatible duties (see ICQ) and suitable action taken on any differences;
	(ii) where appropriate, evidence that the brought forward total appearing on the master file update report is agreed with the carried forward total on the previous report;
	(iii) where appropriate, evidence that the results of the procedures in (i) and (ii) above have been reviewed and approved by a responsible official.
	(b) Where visible evidence of the reconciliation is available, reperform the control in (a)(ii) above by testing the agreement of brought forward and carried forward figures.
	(c) Where appropriate, reperform the clearance of differences by selecting cleared differences and checking that they were properly dealt with.
	(d) Where no evidence of the reconciliation exists, review the results of the tests of integrity controls. Were the results of the tests of data file security controls satisfactory?

Nature of Control	Specimen Test
10 *Maintenance control –* cyclical checking of standing data.	(a) (i) Examine computer reports or source data for evidence that detailed checking is being carried out by persons with no incompatible duties (see ICQ) to the extent and frequency required and suitable action taken in respect of any differences. (ii) Where appropriate, examine evidence indicating that the results of the procedures in (i) above have been reviewed and approved by a responsible official. (b) Reperform control by selecting items from the print-out which have been marked as checked and check them to source data. (c) Where appropriate, reperform the clearance of differences by selecting cleared differences and checking that they were properly dealt with.
11 *Timing of authorisation –* rechecking of authorised data after input controls established.	(a) Examine evidence that authorised data is rechecked by a responsible official after batch totals have been established or sequentially numbered documents raised to ensure that all authorised data is processed. (b) Reperform the rechecking by selecting current batches or serially numbered documents and verify with supporting documentation.
Programmed procedures 12 *Computer matching.*	NOTE: Manual tests only are included. Test the matching process by selecting items to be input and: (a) holding back until reported as missing; (b) altering relevant fields on documents and confirming that they are reported as mismatched.
13 *Computer sequence check.*	Test the sequence check by selecting documents from the current run and: (a) holding back until reported as missing; (b) arranging for documents to be converted twice and seeing that the duplicates are rejected.

Nature of Control	Specimen Test
14 *Computer batch totals.*	Test the computer agreement of batch totals by selecting current batches of documents and: (a) checking the additions and agreeing them to the batch headers; (b) altering the batch headers and checking that the batches are reported or rejected.
15 *Programmed procedures giving rise to rejection or exception reports:* (a) over the *accuracy of input and updating* (e.g. check digit verification, dependency tests); (b) over the *accuracy of calculations* (e.g. reasonableness test on wages giving rise to exception report of abnormal pay); (c) over the *maintenance* of data stored (e.g. dependency tests giving rise to exception report of obsolete stocks; prices which have not moved for a given period).	Test the programmed procedure: (a) where full visible evidence is available, by checking by reference to appropriate data that items are correctly rejected or reported (e.g. where there are listings of both accepted and rejected items; where there is full print-out of the calculated data); or (b) by amending details on selected documents and seeing that these are correctly reported as invalid items or rejected.
16 *Computer-generated data.*	Test the generation of the data by: (a) checking by reference to source data that items were generated at the appropriate time; or (b) obtaining a special print-out of data generated and: (i) confirming by reference to source data that all data has been generated accurately; (ii) seeing that abnormal items are reported on the exception report.
17 *Computer calculating.*	Test the accuracy of calculations by selecting items from computer output and checking the calculations.

Nature of Control	Specimen Test

18 *Computer summarisation.*	Test that all accepted items are included in the total referred to, using one of the following methods:
	
	(a) where transaction listings are available, by verifying that all accepted items are on the listings and checking the additions;
	
	(b) where no transaction listings exist, by:
	
	   (i) requesting a special print-out of transactions and carrying out the tests in (a) above;
	  or
	   (ii) arranging a special run and agreeing pre-calculated results (e.g. splitting a batch into two batches, one large and one small, calculating the results for the small batch and agreeing the results with the update reports).

19 *Computer categorisation and updating.*	Test the accuracy of postings to individual accounts by selecting items from appropriate source data and checking the postings.

Integrity controls
 	
20 *Examination of documentation* (system specifications, job set-up and instructions, operating instructions).
	(a) Examine documentation and confirm that:
	
	   (i) it forms a suitable basis for the controls based thereon (e.g. approval of new programmed procedures, job set-up);
	
	   (ii) it appears to be correct and up to date.
	
	(b) Select extracts from the documentation and confirm with the appropriate user that they are understood and suitable for their purpose.
	
	(c) Where appropriate, select changes to the documentation and see that they have been reviewed by the appropriate persons (see ICQ).

Nature of Control	Specimen Test

21 *Testing* (new systems and program changes).	(a) Examine the results of tests on programmed procedures and confirm that the scope and method of testing was sufficiently comprehensive to test the functioning of the programmed procedures adequately.
	
	(b) In respect of selected programmed procedures, reperform the testing, as appropriate, by:
	
	  (i) examining the predicted results and checking the results with those predicted;
	
	  (ii) obtaining program source listings and checking the inclusion of the appropriate instructions;
	
	  (iii) selecting a period from the parallel running and checking the results to the output from the previous system;
	
	  (iv) selecting a part of the pilot run and checking the results to the system description.

22 *Completeness control –* sequential prenumbering.	(a) Examine records, lists or other documentary evidence indicating that the numerical sequence of prenumbered documents (e.g. program change forms, system log reports) is periodically checked and missing numbers investigated by persons with no incompatible duties (see ICQ).
	
	(b) Where appropriate, examine evidence indicating that the results of the procedures in (a) above have been reviewed and approved by a responsible official.
	
	(c) Reperform control by selecting documents and:
	
	  (i) check numerical sequence;
	
	  (ii) obtain satisfactory explanations for any missing numbers;
	
	  (iii) confirm that the client's procedures for dealing with cancelled or spoiled documents have been followed.

Nature of Control	Specimen Test
23 *Completeness control* – entry in register.	(a) Examine register for evidence that entries therein appear to be up-to-date and are being systematically cleared.
	(b) Where appropriate, examine evidence indicating that the results of the procedures in (a) above have been reviewed and approved by a responsible official.
	(c) Reperform control by testing entries with relevant documentation to establish that the item has either been cleared or is a valid outstanding item.
	(d) Confirm that the client's procedures for dealing with cancelled or spoiled documents have been followed.
24 *Control over outstanding items.*	(a) Examine the client's records of outstanding items and reports, listings, memoranda or other evidence indicating that the records are periodically reviewed, long outstanding items investigated by persons with no incompatible duties (see ICQ) and the results thereof approved by a responsible official.
	(b) Reperform control by reviewing records and obtaining satisfactory explanations for long outstanding items.
25 *Final approval of new systems and program changes.*	(a) Examine documentation for evidence of final approval by responsible officials with no incompatible duties (see ICQ) before cataloguing.
	(b) Examine available evidence of rejections or queries raised by the officials and of checks performed by them in giving final approval.
	(c) Reperform control by selecting a sample of documents examined in (a) above, and:
	(i) seeing that necessary supporting documentation (e.g. results of testing, operating instructions, user procedure manuals) appears to have been properly completed;
	(ii) reperforming any other steps that the responsible officials are supposed to follow.

Nature of Control	Specimen Test
26 *Review of computer-produced reports* (listings from librarian packages, system activity reports, console logs, operating system output).	(a) Examine computer reports and see: (i) evidence that reported items (e.g. jobs processed, operator action) are being dealt with by persons with no incompatible duties (see ICQ); (ii) where appropriate, evidence indicating that the results of the procedures in (i) above have been reviewed and approved by a responsible official. (b) Reperform the clearance of reported items by selecting cleared items and checking that they were properly dealt with.
27 *Validity of program changes.*	(a) Examine a number of requests for changes to operational programs and see that they have been approved by an appropriate official (e.g. the programming manager). (b) Select a number of the requests in (a) above and check to source memoranda and establish that there is an adequate reason for the change.
28 *Physical control of files or programs.*	(a) Visit the computer department and verify that data files/programs not in use are: (i) held with suitable security in the library; and (ii) when issued outside the library, only issued to authorised persons (see ICQ); by persons with no incompatible duties (see ICQ). (b) Examine the record of data files/programs issued from the library and ensure that data files/programs overdue for return are being investigated by persons with no incompatible duties (see ICQ). (c) Reperform control by locating data files/programs held outside the computer room and checking to appropriate records to ensure that: (i) their issue has been properly authorised and recorded; and (ii) they are not overdue for return.

Nature of Control	Specimen Test
System software 29 *Cataloguing.*	Test the cataloguing of new systems and program changes by, as appropriate: (a) obtaining a list of programs held on the library and checking that the new program is held thereon; (b) obtaining program source listings and checking the inclusion of the appropriate instructions; (c) checking the proper cataloguing of jobs run for audit purposes; (d) comparing current executable and/or source programs with previous versions and accounting for differences; (e) devising test data to test new or changed programmed procedures and checking results with those predicted.
30 *Reporting of jobs processed.*	Test the reporting of jobs processed by, as appropriate: (a) comparing with an authorised job schedule and accounting for differences; (b) checking the proper reporting of jobs run for audit purposes; (c) noting details of jobs prior to processing and checking their proper entry on the report.
31 *Program comparison.*	Test the comparison of production programs by comparing current executable or source programs with independently controlled copies and confirming that there are no differences.
32 *Supervision of application programs.*	Test the supervisor program by selecting items and testing that they were properly processed by the application programs, where not adequately covered by other tests on programmed procedures.

Nature of Control	Specimen Test
33 *Reporting of computer operations.*	Test the reporting of computer operations by, as appropriate: (a) comparing entries on the report with those obtained by the auditor (e.g. by using a system log analyser); (b) checking the proper reporting of activity relating to jobs run for audit purposes.
34 *File set-up.*	Test label checking by, as appropriate: (a) noting details of files prior to set-up and checking their proper treatment; (b) selecting invalid files and confirming that they are reported or rejected; (c) checking the proper reporting of files processed by the auditor.
35 *Password protection.*	Test the password protection by inputting invalid passwords and seeing whether they are rejected.
36 *Library records.*	Test the maintenance of library records by, as appropriate: (a) comparing with an authorised job schedule and accounting for differences; (b) checking the proper reporting of programs and files used in jobs run for audit purposes; (c) noting details of programs and files prior to processing and checking their proper entry in the records.

7: Appendix B
The Use of Audit Test Data

The Purpose and Scope of Audit Test Data

1 The principal purpose of audit test data is to test programmed procedures. It may also be useful in testing the effectiveness of such system software as cataloguing. Where information is produced by a program of the company at the year end only, as for example a sales analysis required to calculate a provision for warranties, test data can be used to test the programmed procedures concerned and thus assist validation work.

2 Audit test data consists of fictitious data prepared by the auditor and processed against the company's operational programs. The results are compared with the results calculated manually by the auditor.

3 Audit test data should not be confused with the test data prepared by the company's data processing staff to test the operation of new programs. Such test data is more comprehensive in that it seeks to test every detailed aspect of the programs and often includes unrepresentative data in order to ensure that this will be recognised and treated appropriately by the computer. Audit test data is restricted to testing only particular programmed procedures on which the auditor wishes to rely. In addition, the data is designed to be as representative as possible of the actual data processed by the company. It is thus unusual to include unrepresentative data, as items of this nature would be unlikely to have a material effect on the financial statements.

4 Whenever audit test data is used, it is necessary to establish that the audit test data was run against the programs in current operational use. The procedures required for testing that the correct programs are used are outlined in paragraph 15.

5 Where it has been decided to use audit test data to test particular procedures, it is often practical and efficient to include tests on other procedures that could otherwise still be tested manually. When considering whether to include these extra tests, care must be taken to ensure the test data does not become too complicated and unwieldy.

Volume of Transactions

6 The number of transactions processed should be the minimum required to provide assurance of the correct functioning of the procedures to be tested. However, the variety of data chosen should be sufficient to represent each of the major types of transactions processed. For example, if the object of the test data is to test the correct production of a purchase analysis, it will be necessary to include transactions for each of the major types of purchases, for example inventory items, capital items and expense items.

7 As well as considering variety in terms of types of transactions it may be necessary to consider the size of the individual transactions processed in order to ensure that the programs treat different values in a similar manner. In that event, the volume of data processed must be high enough to enable a representative range of values to be covered.

8 The fewer transactions that are processed, the simpler and cheaper the test data exercise becomes. In addition, it is usually possible to use a transaction to satisfy more than one of the conditions required to be tested. This helps to reduce the number of transactions to be processed. It is helpful to use a matrix to indicate the master file records and transactions which will be used to test the various programmed procedures. In the few cases where a large volume of test transactions is required, or where only the later programs in a processing suite are of interest to the auditor, it may be cost effective to use a **test data generator** to produce the required transactions. Test data generators are software packages which can be used either to construct data to be used in the testing of application programs or to create dummy master files. The user describes the characteristics of the data required. The software then constructs test files containing the generated data and in addition gives the user a listing of the data that has been generated.

Methods of Running Audit Test Data

9 There are two methods of running audit test data which are termed "live" and "dead". Audit test data is classified as **dead** when the data is processed using the company's operational programs, but separately from the company's data, and using copies of master files or dummy files set up for the purpose. Audit test data is classified as **live** where the data is processed at the same time as the company's data, using the actual master files. Usually specific records on the master files will be reserved or created for this purpose. This form of "live" test data is often called an **integrated test facility** (ITF).

10 There are advantages and disadvantages in both "live" and "dead" audit test data. The disadvantages of one method are, in general, the advan-

tages of the other. In practice, the advantages of running "live" usually outweigh the advantages of running "dead".

11 The factors to be taken into account in making the decision whether to run "live" or "dead" are:

- possible processing difficulties;
- ease of achieving the audit objectives;
- complexity of developing the test data;
- confirmation that the correct programs are used;
- availability of computer time.

These factors are discussed in the following paragraphs.

Possible processing difficulties

12 When running "live", processing difficulties seldom arise and the auditor has the added advantage of knowing that the programs are being tested under normal operating conditions. Problems can arise running "dead" because of the need to handle small volumes of data, to create unusual data on master files, for example old data, and to force data through intermediate processing stages. Particular difficulties are usually encountered when trying to simulate a time span in two or three processing runs. When considering running test data in an on-line or real-time system, it may be impracticable to duplicate the company's whole system to run "dead" test data. In such systems, if the company does not possess a set of test files, "live" test data is the only practicable approach.

Ease of achieving the audit objectives

13 Difficulties arise under this heading when running "live" which, in general, do not arise when running "dead". These difficulties are:

- The need to predict and avoid any side effects, for example the inclusion of fictitious inventory lines in a sales catalogue distributed to dealers.

- The testing of totals or analyses. As the test data is included with the actual data, it is not possible to predict what the totals will be. This can often be overcome by creating a dummy branch or department.

- Fictitious information may be included in the company's accounting records at the year end. This is usually acceptable if the value is immaterial. Alternatively, the auditor can insert further fictitious data before the books are closed to reverse the entries made as, for example in the case of sales systems, fictitious credit notes.

- The audit test data may have to remain in the system for a lengthy period to test ageing procedures effectively. In these cases the use of audit test data needs careful planning.

Complexity of developing audit test data

14   It is usually easier to develop data for "live" running because the system is being used in its normal way and it is only necessary to prepare the fictitious data. However, when running "dead", it is necessary to create dummy master files in addition to the test data.

Confirmation that the correct programs are used

15   When running "live", this factor does not arise, since the programs used are the company's actual programs; when running "dead", this assurance does not apply and specific tests are necessary to confirm that the correct programs are used. This can normally be achieved by comparing the name and serial number of the programs used with the system log for the most recent operational run. Where the integrity controls have not been relied on, or where weaknesses or exceptions have been found, it may also be advisable for the auditor to be present during the running of the audit test data.

Availability of computer time

16   This factor does not arise when running "live", but can be important when running "dead", when it may often be difficult to obtain computer time. This is particularly so in on-line and real-time systems.

Procedures for Using Test Data

17   It is advisable to institute formal procedures for the use of audit test data for the following reasons:

(a) the complexity of the technique;
(b) the need for the company to be aware of and to co-operate with the auditor's plans;
(c) the possible side effects on the company;
(d) the different methods of operation;
(e) the need to build up a central pool of experience which can help in identifying suitable cases for using audit test data, designing objectives, preparing data and budgeting costs.

The procedures can easily be standardised and are considered below separately for the first year of use of audit test data, and for second and subsequent years of use.

First year of use

18   Programmed procedures will be identified in the ICQ and the auditor should consider whether the use of audit test data is the most effective method of carrying out tests. The auditor should look at all the programmed procedures in a system and make his decision on the basis of the alternative techniques available and the number of procedures that could be tested using audit test data.

19 A **proposal for the use of audit test data** should be prepared, and then
    approved by the partner responsible for the audit. The proposal should
    state:

- (a) the procedures to be tested by use of audit test data and why this
  is the most effective technique;
- (b) whether the audit test data is to be run "live" or "dead" (if the
  proposal is that the audit test data should be run "live", a statement should be included of how any possible side effects are to be
  overcome. If the proposal is that the audit test data should be run
  "dead", an estimate should be included of the computer time
  expected to be required);
- (c) brief details of the master file records to be created and the volume
  and variety of data to be processed (a matrix showing how the
  individual transactions will test the various programmed procedures should be attached);
- (d) the budgeted costs of running the audit test data in the first year
  and in subsequent years;
- (e) the effect of running the audit test data on existing audit tests;
- (f) any expected practical difficulties, for example verifying the programs used when running "dead".

20 The principle of running audit test data should be agreed with the com-
    pany. It is important for the company to be aware of the auditor's plans,
    particularly where "live" test data is used, so as to be sure that no
    unforeseen side effects take place. It is preferable to confirm any such
    arrangements made with the company in writing, specifying the objec-
    tives, the timing, the method of operation of the test data and any special
    facilities required, for example punching or computer time.

21 The auditor is now in a position to devise and run the test data. He should
    prepare full working papers, including the predicted results and schedules
    of data to be processed. The programme and record of functional tests
    should be amended to take account of the tests carried out by the test
    data. The auditor should give adequate warning for the conversion of the
    test data, where this is required. It is good practice to check the input
    media to avoid processing incorrect data.

22 When the results have been evaluated, a **report** should be prepared for
    those involved in the rest of the audit work. The report should contain:

- (a) any alterations to the proposal;
- (b) any deficiencies found in the programmed procedures tested;
- (c) any difficulties encountered and suggestions for overcoming them;
- (d) any suggestions for adding to the number of programmed procedures to be tested on future occasions;
- (e) confirmation that the audit test data documentation is complete
  and up to date;
- (f) the actual costs of preparing and running the audit test data and the
  reasons for any variances from the budgeted costs.

Second and subsequent years

23   Much of the procedure will be similar in successive years. Instead of devising the audit test data afresh, the auditor will need to make such changes as are necessary to ensure that the data will not be rejected as invalid, for example revising the dates on documents. Care should be taken to ensure that the system has not changed or, if it has, that the audit test data is suitably amended. Proposals and reports should be prepared, but will only need to deal with changes from the previous year. The company should again be informed of the plans to use audit test data.

7: Appendix C

Examples of the Use of Audit Test Data

Example I — Payroll

The system

1 The company has 5,000 employees and maintains its payroll by computer. Starters, leavers and changes in standing data details are processed and checked manually each week. Hours worked are recorded on clock cards and input weekly.

2 In addition to calculating pay, producing the payroll and maintaining employees' earnings records, the computer provides the following reports:

   (a) standing data amendments processed;
   (b) employees for whom no clock cards were submitted;
   (c) employees for whom more than one clock card was submitted (when this situation arises, all clock cards for these employees are rejected);
   (d) clock cards with invalid employee numbers;
   (e) employees for whom total hours worked are in excess of sixty hours;
   (f) employees whose gross rate of pay is in excess of £80.00 per week;
   (g) employees whose gross pay for the week (including overtime) is in excess of £100.00;
   (h) general ledger posting tabulation.

The audit test data

3 The audit objectives to be achieved by running test data together with details of the data to be processed are set out on the matrix on pages 281 and 282.

4   The matrix consists of two parts:

(a) **Summary of data requirements.** The purpose of this summary is to show the number of items needed in the audit test data. As can be seen from the illustration, across the top are shown the details of the master file records required, in this case employees, and listed vertically are the details of the items to be processed, both standing and transaction data. These items are extended to show the master file records affected and enable, in the right hand column, a total to be shown of the data requirements. Thus, in this illustration, the requirement is ten opening master file records, eight standing data amendments and ten clock cards.

(b) **Data processed and procedures tested.** The purpose of this schedule is to show how the items processed test the procedures and thus achieve the objectives of the audit test data. The master file records remain stated across the top, although, as can be seen, the number that remain relevant to the test data reduces as items, such as leavers, are processed. The narrative in the vertical column now changes from items (as in the summary of data requirements) to the procedure being tested by the item. The ICQ reference is included with the details of the procedure to provide easy reference to the other audit documentation. In order to keep the matrix simple, it is often helpful, after each group of tests, to restate the master file records still available for further tests. Examples of this technique can be seen after the tests on the procedures for amendments to standing data and after the tests on the procedures for the completeness and accuracy of the input of clock cards. It will be noted that, when the master file records are restated after the tests on the procedures for the completeness and accuracy of the input of clock cards, those that have no further use are no longer shown.

5   The levels of test suggested are purely for illustration purposes.

Summary of Data Requirements

Test Employees	1	2	3	4	5	6	7	8	9	10	11	12	Total
Opening master file records													
Wages master file	-	-	*	*	*	*	*	*	*	*	*	*	10
Standing data amendments													
Starters		*	*	*									⎫
Leavers													⎪
Pay increase				*	*	*							⎬ 8
Change in tax code							*						⎪
Additional deduction								*					⎭
Previous deduction deleted													
Transaction data													
Clock cards	*	-	*	-	-	*	*	*	*	*	*	*	10

Data Processed and Procedures Tested (1)

Test Data Details	1	2	3	4	5	6	7	8	9	10	11	12	Total
Master file records set up and available for tests	-	-	*	*	*	*	*	*	*	*	*	*	10
Standing payroll data													
Completeness of writing amendments to the master file													
To verify that accepted master file amendments are reported on the amendments listing for checking against copies of authorised input documents (ICQ 6.1(c), SDC 5)													
Starters		*											2
Leavers				*									2
Pay increase					*	*							1
Change in tax code							*						1
Additional deduction								*					1
Previous deduction deleted													
Accuracy of writing amendments to the master file	*												
To verify that all amendments as reported on the amendments listing are written to the correct employee record and included on the print-out of master file details (ICQ 6.1(d), SDC 16)		*	*	-	*	*	*	*	*	*	*		8
Master file records carried forward to transaction tests		*	-	-	*	*	*	*	*	*	*	*	10

Data Processed and Procedures Tested (2)

	Test Data Details												Total
	1	·2	3	4	5	6	7	8	9	10	11	12	
Master file records available for tests ..	*	*	—	—	*	*	*	*	*	*	*	*	10
Payroll preparation													
Completeness of input..													
To verify that the following items are reported as exceptions (ICQ 6.10):													
(a) employees for whom clock cards were not submitted		*							*				2
(b) clock cards having invalid employee numbers			*							*			2
(c) clock cards rejected due to duplicate employee numbers					*					*			2
Accuracy of input													
To verify that clock card hours in excess of 60 hours are reported as exceptions (ICQ 6.17)						*							1
Master file records and transactions available for further tests	*	—	—		—	*	*	*	—	—	*	*	6

Data Processed and Procedures Tested (3)

	Test Data Details								Total
	1	6	7	8	9	10	11	12	
Master file records and transactions available for tests	*	*	*	*			*	*	6
Accuracy of payroll processing									
To verify that the following are reported as exceptions (ICQ 6.21(b)):									
(a) employees whose basic rate of pay exceeds £80.00 per week ..			*						1
(b) employees whose total pre-tax pay exceeds £100.00 per week ..		*	*	*					3
To ensure that gross pay, deductions and net pay are calculated accurately (ICQ 6.21(a)) ..	*	*		*		*	*	*	6
To verify the accumulation of gross pay, deductions and net pay (ICQ 6.21(a)) ..	*	*	*	*		*	*	*	6
To verify that wages are correctly summarised on the nominal ledger posting analysis (ICQ 13.4(b)) ..	*	*	*	*		*	*	*	6
To ensure wages paid and deductions are accurately posted to earnings records (ICQ 7.4) ..	*	*	*	*		*	*	*	6
Master file records and transactions present at the end of processing	*	*	*	*		*	*	*	6

Example II — Purchase Accounting

The system

1 Much of the accounting activity relating to purchases is processed on the computer. Initially purchase requisitions are input through terminals. Requisitions may be rejected for various reasons. Purchase orders are produced for accepted requisitions and the details written to an open orders file. Orders that fail certain reasonableness tests are reported for investigation but are not rejected. This may lead to the processing of purchase order cancellations. Overdue orders are also reported for investigation.

2 Details of goods received are input through the terminals and accepted if they match with the relevant outstanding order. They are deleted from the open order file and used to update the raw materials inventory and an open invoice file.

3 When received, invoices are input and matched with the open invoice file and posted to the accounts payable master file. Details of goods received not matched with invoices within a month are reported for investigation.

4 Cheques are produced by the computer according to rules held in the program.

The audit test data

5 The audit objectives to be achieved by running test data together with details of the data to be processed are set out on the matrix on pages 284 to 287.

6 The matrix is in the same format as that described in the first example. The only new feature is that shown to deal with situations where more than one item relates to a master file record or is necessary for a test. Thus, as can be seen on the "Summary of data requirements", although the auditor has decided that he requires thirty-one purchase requisitions for the various tests related to purchase requisitions, he decides he only needs three inventory file records and five accounts payable records for the relevant tests on the postings to the file. Likewise the thirty-one purchase requisitions can be assembled into six batches for the appropriate test. A further example can be seen in the "Data processed and procedures tested" schedule under the selection of items for payment test.

7 Postings to the general ledger have been ignored. The levels of test suggested are purely for illustration purposes.

Summary of Data Requirements

	Test Purchase Transactions																																	Total
	1	2	3	4	5	6	7	8	9	10	11	12	13	14	15	16	17	18	19	20	21	22	23	24	25	26	27	28	29	30	31	32	33	
Opening master file records																																		
Inventory master file			*			*							*					*			*					*					*			3
Suppliers' master file										*											*						*		*				*	5
Transaction data																																		
Purchase requisitions	*			*	*	*	*	*	*	*	*	*	*	*	*	*	*	*	*	*	*	*	*	*	*	*	*	*	*	*	*			31
Purchase requisition batch headers						*	*	*	*									*											*					6
Purchase order cancellations								*		*	*																							2
Goods received notes												*	*	*	*				*	*	*	*	*	*	*	*	*	*	*	*	*			17
Suppliers' invoices												*	*	*	*							*	*	*	*	*	*	*	*	*	*	*		14

Data Processed and Procedures Tested (1)

	Test Data Details																															Total
	1	2	3	4	5	6	7	8	9	10	11	12	13	14	15	16	17	18	19	20	21	22	23	24	25	26	27	28	29	30	31	
Master file records set up and available for tests – Suppliers' master file																					*								*	*	*	4
Transaction data input Purchase requisitions	*	*	*	*	*	*	*	*	*	*	*	*	*	*	*	*	*	*	*	*	*	*	*	*	*	*	*	*	*	*	*	31
Purchase requisition batch headers	*	*	*	*	*	*																										6
Completeness of input and updating To verify that batches of purchase requisitions are rejected if total disagrees with the total input on the batch header (ICQ 1.12(a))	*	*	*																													3
Accuracy of input and updating To verify that a purchase requisition will not be accepted (and therefore the batch rejected) if (ICQ 1.18(a) and (b)):																																
(a) the stock code number is invalid;				*	*																											2
(b) the supplier number is invalid; or						*	*																									2
(c) the terminal operator does not indicate agreement of supplier's name per the requisition with the name displayed on the screen								*	*																							2
To verify that an accurate purchase order is produced in respect of all requisitions accepted by the computer (ICQ 1.23)										*	*	*	*	*	*	*	*	*	*	*	*	*	*	*	*	*	*	*	*	*	*	22
To verify that an exception report is produced in respect of all orders where the anticipated price is (ICQ 1.18(c) and (d) and 1.23):																																
(a) greater than £10,000;										*	*																					2
(b) greater than standard cost plus 10%; or												*	*																			2
(c) less than standard cost less 10%														*	*																	2
To verify that all order printed are accurately included on the "orders printed" report (ICQ 1.24(a))										*	*	*	*	*	*	*	*	*	*	*	*	*	*	*	*	*	*	*	*	*	*	22
Record of unfulfilled commitments To verify that purchase order cancellations are (ICQ 1.31):																																
(a) reported; and										*	*																					2
(b) deleted from outstanding orders file										*	*																					2
To verify that all orders which have been outstanding for more than 1 month are reported as exceptions (ICQ 1.33)	–	–	–	–	–	–	–	–	–	–	–	–	–	–	*	*	*	–														3
Outstanding orders carried forward for matching with goods received	–	–	–	–	–	–	–	–	–	–	–	–	–	–	*	*	*	*	*	*	*	*	*	*	*	*	*	*	*	*	*	17

285

Data Processed and Procedures Tested (2)

Data Processed and Procedures Tested	Test Data Details																	Total
	12	13	14	15	19	20	21	22	23	24	25	26	27	28	29	30	31	
Outstanding orders brought forward for matching with goods received	*	*	*	*	*	*	*	*	*	*	*	*	*	*	*	*	*	17
Accuracy of input and updating of goods received notes (GRN's)																		
To verify that program edit checks on accuracy of input are operating correctly by ensuring that (ICQ 2.20):																		
(a) error message displayed and input not accepted if part number per GRN not included on the order number previously input		*																1
(b) error message displayed but GRN still accepted when goods received exceed goods ordered		*																1
(c) a printed report is produced in respect of items in (b) above		*																1
To verify that orders matched with GRN's are deleted from the outstanding orders file and written to the outstanding invoices file (ICQ 2.27)	–	*	*	*	*	*	*	*	*	*	*	*	*	*	*	*	*	16
To verify that GRN's not matched with suppliers' invoices within one month are reported (ICQ 2.28)					*	*	*											3
GRN's carried forward for:																		
(a) matching with suppliers' invoices	–	*	*	*	–	–	–	*	*	*	*	*	*	*	*	*	*	13
(b) updating of inventory records	–	*	*	*	*	*	*	*	*	*	*	*	*	*	*	*	*	16
Inventory master file records set up				*								*					*	3
GRN's input during reperformance of goods received processing		*	*	*	*	*	*	*	*	*	*	*	*	***	*	*	*	16
Completeness of input and updating of inventory receipts																		
To verify that all GRN's input are included on the inventory update report. The total per this report is reconciled by the computer with the totals updated to the outstanding invoices file (ICQ 10.16 and 10.21)				*								*					*	3
Accuracy of input and updating of inventory receipts																		
To verify that individual inventory records are accurately updated in respect of goods received (ICQ 10.21)		*	*	*	*	*	*	*	*	*	*	*	*	*	*	*	*	16

Data Processed and Procedures Tested (3)

Test Data Details															Total
	13	14	15	22	23	24	25	26	27	28	29	30	31	32	33	

Suppliers' master file accounts set up and available for testing

  – nil balance

  – negative balance   } 4

  – others

GRNs brought forward for matching with suppliers' invoices   13

Detailed checking of invoices and completeness and accuracy of input

To verify that invoices will be rejected for investigation when they are compared with the outstanding invoices file if a match is not achieved in respect of (ICQ 4.2(b) and (c), 4.4(a) and 4.6):

  (a) purchase order number;   1

  (b) supplier number;   1

  (c) stock number;   1

  (d) quantity received;   1

  (e) price; and   1

  (f) invoice total   1

To verify that invoices are reported as exceptions if the invoice price is (ICQ 4.5):

  (a) more than 5% greater than standard cost   2

  (b) more than 5% less than standard cost   2

Completeness and accuracy of updating

To verify the computer reconciliation of total invoices accepted with the totals updated to the outstanding invoices file and the suppliers' master file (ICQ 5.3)   8

To verify that individual supplier's accounts are accurately updated (ICQ 5.25)   8

Cheque payments – selection of items for payment

To verify that cheques are produced in respect of (ICQ 5.29 and 9.5):

  (a) current balance outstanding when the prompt payment indicator is set; and   1

  (b) balance outstanding at the end of the previous month in respect of all other balances outstanding   1

To verify that cheques are not produced in respect of:

  (a) nil balances; and   1

  (b) negative balances   1

To verify the computer reconciliation of total cheques printed with the amount updated to the suppliers' master file (ICQ 9.7)   2

To verify that payee details are accurately printed on cheques and remittance advices (ICQ 9.8)   2

Maintenance of the accounts payable file

To verify that amounts outstanding on individual suppliers' accounts are accurately reported on the monthly creditors listing until such time as payment is made (ICQ 5.34)   2

Suppliers' master file accounts present at the end of processing   4

7: Appendix D

The Use of Program Code Analysis

The Purpose and Scope of Program Code Analysis

1   The principal purpose of program code analysis is to confirm the existence of programmed procedures in a program or series of programs. The programmed procedures to be confirmed will be those identified in the ICQ. Thus, a major use of program code analysis by the auditor is as a test of programmed procedures. The technique may also be used by the auditor to obtain or confirm an understanding of the programs or parts of programs in the system. In these cases it may not be necessary to carry out all of the steps set out in this appendix.

2   For the technique to be effective, the auditor must either examine the code in object form, which is unlikely to be practicable, or confirm that the code he has examined in source statement form relates to the instructions in the executable programs. He will also need to be satisfied, normally through his tests on the program security controls and computer operations controls, that the code he has examined is that used to process accounting data.

Method of Work

3   Program code analysis consists of four steps, which are discussed in the following paragraphs:

- Identifying the programs to be examined.

- Selecting the form of coding to be examined.

- Analysing the selected coding.

- Confirming that the coding examined is identical to that used to process accounting data.

Identifying the Programs to be Examined

4   It is first necessary to identify the programs or program modules which contain the programmed procedures whose existence it is desired to confirm by program code analysis. This can usually be done by reference

to the company's system documentation. There will normally be a block diagram which sets out the logical sequence of programs within a system. It will then often be necessary to review the detailed specifications of individual programs in order to identify those containing the relevant procedures.

Selecting the Form of Coding to be Examined

5 The auditor will normally decide to examine the source statement program. In order to carry out this examination the auditor will require a knowledge of the source language used. Care is needed in selecting the version of the source statement program for examination. While listings which are held with the program documentation or print-outs of back-up security copies of programs may be easily obtained, they may not be up to date and the auditor, if he uses them, will need to confirm that they are identical to the source statement program from which the current operational program was compiled. It is thus usually preferable to obtain a print-out of the current source statement program. This is conveniently done by arranging to have the program compiled. The auditor can then request compilation options which may be useful in his analysis of the program, such as cross reference listings of data names and verb listings.

Analysing the Selected Coding

6 The need for the auditor to have a working knowledge of the relevant programming language has already been explained. Given this, the auditor can set out to analyse the source coding of the programs concerned. Most programmers recognise that understanding program logic for programs written by someone else is usually difficult. The auditor will find the work easier where the installation adheres to high standards of programming and program documentation. It is important to adopt a planned approach to the review of the coding. Starting from the first program statement and following the coding through line by line to the last statement is unlikely to be an efficient or effective way to proceed.

7 In the following paragraphs a suggested approach to the detailed review of the selected coding is outlined. The approach is based upon three phases of work:

● obtaining an understanding of the files used by the programs being analysed and the data held thereon;

● analysing the logic of the relevant lines of coding;

● ensuring that the relevant lines of coding analysed are not bypassed or distorted by another part of the program or an entirely different program.

These matters are illustrated by reference to terms encountered in COBOL programming, since this is the most commonly used language.

8   Although analysing the selected coding will always require a high degree of skill from the auditor, his job will almost certainly be made easier where the installation employs structured programming techniques. In such cases the logic of programs will be easier to follow because:

     (a) programs developed in this way tend to be better structured;

     (b) less use is made of GO TO statements and, in COBOL, more use made of PERFORM statements;

     (c) IF statements tend to be concentrated into "decision" paragraphs in the programs.

Obtaining an understanding

9   Having obtained the source statement listings relating to the program he wishes to analyse, the auditor should first obtain an understanding of the files, records and data fields used and the manner in which they are used.

10   Obtaining such an understanding will normally involve a study of the source listings and associated program documentation to identify:

- **The data files used**. As a starting point the auditor will normally examine the SELECT clauses to identify all files used in the program and examine the OPEN and CLOSE statements in the procedure division to understand how the files are used in the program. These procedures enable the auditor to identify the function of each file, for example, input file, output file, input and output file.

- **The data records on each relevant file**. The auditor will normally examine the file description (FD) entries for each file. Where more than one data record is defined for a file, the auditor will need to understand the use of each data record in the program and assess its effect on the program steps being examined. Different data records are likely to have different logical paths through parts of the program.

- **The important data fields**. Important fields may be those recorded in file descriptions or working storage fields created by the programs. As well as gaining an understanding of the meaning of the contents of each field, the auditor will need to understand any complexities in respect of field definitions such as RE- DEFINES or RENAMES clauses in COBOL which enable the same data field to be interpreted by programs in different ways.

Where a data dictionary exists, useful information regarding the characteristics of the data may be obtained from the dictionary listing.

11   The auditor should also ascertain whether the program uses switches (either in the program or activated through the job control statements or console) to control program logic at run time. Switches may be used to "turn off" routines in a program which are only required periodically, such as month end procedures. If switches are used, the auditor should understand their use, as they may be important when he carries out his review of the detailed coding.

Analysing the logic

12 The first thing the auditor will wish to do is to identify the paragraph or paragraphs of coding which contain the detailed logic of the programmed procedures, for example the paragraphs in which the matching of despatch notes against sales orders is carried out or the paragraphs in which the program analyses suppliers' invoices. Such identification is not normally difficult and the required paragraphs can normally be identified quickly through the program documentation. Where documentation is poor, identification of the relevant paragraphs may take more time, as it will be necessary to scrutinise the source listing to identify the relevant paragraphs.

13 Having identified the relevant paragraphs of coding, the auditor may proceed to analyse their detailed logic. Most programmed procedures that the auditor wishes to analyse can conveniently be broken down into three elements, which can be called:

- COMPARISON – program statements which will compare data fields with other data fields or constants.

- CALCULATION – program statements which enable data to be manipulated according to normal arithmetic rules.

- WRITING – program statements which print data or output data on magnetic storage devices.

Each element would be made up of a number of program statements.

14 The order of the program elements is variable and a programmed procedure will normally incorporate more than one of the elements set out above. For example, where the program has been written to identify excess stocks based on data fields holding the monthly usage of each stock line for the previous twelve months, the programmed procedure would typically be structured to include the following elements:

(a) total the previous twelve monthly usage fields (CALCULATION);
(b) compare the total in (a) to the current stock balance (COMPARISON);
(c) calculate the value of excess stock by reference to the cost price, where the quantity on hand is greater than (a) (CALCULATION);
(d) total the value of excess stocks (CALCULATION);
(e) compare individual excesses to a constant to identify, high value excess stocks (COMPARISON);
(f) print details of excess stocks (WRITING).

15 The detailed considerations that the auditor must take into account in analysing each element are set out below.

Comparison

16 Comparisons in COBOL programs are normally based upon the IF clause. IF clauses are used to make decisions governing the logical path that data

will follow through the program. To the auditor, they are the most significant parts of the coding in the program he analyses.

17   The auditor should examine the IF clauses in the paragraphs of coding concerned and satisfy himself that:

  (a) the test is a logically valid one to be carried out at that point, for example, where the test is to exclude records not required for further processing, that only logical exclusions are made;

  (b) the correct data fields are used in the test, for example the correct price field is used in evaluating despatch details;

  (c) the definition of each data field used in the test, as set out in the file description or in working storage, is such that the results of the test will be as predicted; this will normally involve examination of the definition of the fields used and consideration, in accordance with the rules of the programming language, of the likely results of the comparison;

  (d) the paths directed for items passing and failing the test are valid. This will normally involve examining the destination of GO TO or PERFORM statements which activate the next logical part of the coding.

Calculation

18   Calculation may involve statements such as ADD, MULTIPLY, SUBTRACT, DIVIDE, and COMPUTE. Again, the auditor can go through distinct stages to satisfy himself that calculations are correctly carried out. These will involve the auditor satisfying himself that:

  (a) the calculation is a logically valid one to be carried out;

  (b) the correct data fields are used in the calculation;

  (c) the definition of each data field used as an operand in the calculation, as defined in the file description or in working storage, is such that the results of the calculation will be as predicted. The auditor should pay particular attention to field sizes and definitions to ensure that they are not likely to be exceeded during a calculation, that they will cope properly with both negative and positive data, and that data containing decimal points or pence is correctly dealt with.

Writing

19   Writing will normally involve outputting records to tapes or discs, or printing data on a printer device. In analysing the coding, the auditor will wish to ensure that:

(a) the correct data fields are moved to the records used for writing data;

(b) the definition of each field to be written, in particular its size, is consistent with the data being moved thereto;

(c) there are no program instructions, which will invalidly suppress the writing of items.

Interrelationship of elements

20   As well as considering the individual elements of comparison, calculation and writing dealt with above, the auditor will also wish to review the order of the elements to ensure that they are logically valid. Where the elements are incorporated into separate programs, the order of these programs should also be examined.

Ensuring that analysed coding is not bypassed

21   Having gone through the steps set out in paragraphs 13 to 20, the auditor will have examined several paragraphs of coding in the relevant program or programs. However, it is possible that the logic examined can be bypassed by coding in either:

- another part of the same program.
- another program in the same system suite.

Another part of the same program

22   The auditor will need to follow the logic of the program backwards and forwards from the paragraphs he has analysed in detail. In so doing he will need first to ensure that the logic of the program provides that all relevant data items, and only those items, are directed to the paragraphs concerned and that the logic of subsequent paragraphs will not invalidate the earlier program steps, for example by failing to direct all relevant items to the writing paragraph. He will also wish to ensure that the logical relationships between paragraphs he has analysed are correct.

23   This part of the auditor's work can be greatly assisted by the use of a software package which can analyse a program and produce a flowchart of the logic. Such flowcharts will normally indicate the paragraphs used in the program, the connecting paths between paragraphs and the comparison tests incorporated into the program. The auditor can use this flowchart to check the logic to and from the paragraphs he has analysed. The auditor will, in effect, be checking the IF, GO TO, and PERFORM statements in the program which are the main statements controlling the program logic. In the absence of a flowcharting package the auditor will normally need to prepare his own logic flowchart.

24   Having established that the logic flow of data through the program is valid, the auditor will next wish to ensure that lines of coding elsewhere in the program do not incorrectly manipulate data fields used in the programmed procedure that he has analysed. To do this it is necessary to examine all lines of coding in the program that use the particular data fields. This examination can be carried out by scrutinising a cross-reference listing of the program. This listing, which may be produced by the flowcharting package or on compilation, will show each data name and verb used in the program, together with the number of each line of coding in which each is used. Having identified the relevant data names, the auditor should check the validity of each line of coding in which they appear. It will be necessary to repeat the process for data names which are redefined versions of fields the auditor is interested in or group fields of which it is a member.

25   Finally, using the cross-reference listing the auditor will need to check the validity of the use of any verbs having the capacity to change data or program logic at run time. An example of such a verb is ALTER. Lines of coding using these verbs should be checked carefully. The programming standards of many installations prohibit the use of such verbs.

Another program in the same system suite

26   The extent to which other programs in the suite need to be examined will depend upon the circumstances in each case. The auditor will be concerned that the completeness and accuracy of data is not distorted by other programs in prior or subsequent processing. Where the auditor determines that the user controls will not detect distortion of data, he will normally adopt the following procedures:

(a) Where the **completeness** of data could be distorted, check the logical flow of data through the relevant prior and subsequent programs. The auditor will direct his attention mainly to the IF, GO TO, PERFORM, and ALTER statements.

(b) Where the **accuracy** of data could be distorted, check the manipulation of the relevant data fields in prior and subsequent programs. The auditor will mainly direct his attention to the ADD, SUBTRACT, MULTIPLY, DIVIDE, COMPUTE and MOVE statements. In advanced systems where a data dictionary exists, reference to the dictionary listing may enable the auditor to identify programs which access the relevant data fields.

Second and subsequent years

27   Once the auditor has analysed the programs in detail, in subsequent years it is normally only necessary to identify changes to those programs and analyse the effects of such changes. Complete re-analysis of the program

295

will only be necessary where the program has been substantially rewritten.

28   The auditor can simplify considerably the task of identifying changes in source statement code from year to year if he is able to use a software package which will compare two versions of a source statement program and identify differences. The auditor would then proceed as follows:

    (a)   in the year in which he analyses the source statement code for the first time the auditor should obtain his own copy of the source statement program;

    (b)   in subsequent years, the auditor uses his source statement compare program to identify changes between the copy taken in (a) and the source statement version for the current operational program;

    (c)   the source statement compare program will highlight, for both old and new versions of the source, the additions, deletions and changes thereto and the auditor's review will be restricted to those changes;

    (d)   the auditor must then consider the effect of the changes on the unchanged parts of the program.

Confirming that the Examined Coding is Identical to that Used to Process Accounting Data

29   After he has examined the relevant coding in the source statement program, the auditor will need to confirm that the examined source statement program is in line with the operational program used to process data.

30   This confirmation can usually be obtained from the tests carried out on the program security controls. In the more advanced installations, when the auditor is most likely to use program code analysis, system software may ensure that the source and executable programs are in line and the auditor can often rely on tests on these procedures. The auditor will need to exercise care where changes can be made directly to executable programs by the use of utilities.

31   The auditor may, as an alternative, be able to make use of software to compare a compiled version of the examined source program with the executable program.

Administrative Procedures

32   It is desirable for the auditor to use administrative procedures on the lines suggested for audit test data in appendix B to this chapter in order to control the use of program code analysis.

8

The Audit Response to Internal Control Weaknesses

The Audit Approach

Identifying weaknesses

8.01　Where the auditor wishes to place reliance on the system of internal control, he will need to identify weaknesses and consider the effect which they may have on his subsequent audit procedures. Weaknesses may arise from the absence of a required control or the failure to exercise a control. The absence of required controls should be identified during completion of the ICQ. The failure to exercise controls should be found during the functional testing. These failures are referred to as **exceptions** and may be either departures or breakdowns.

8.02　A **departure** is defined as an intentional change in a system for a temporary period of time, for example as a result of staff sickness; a **breakdown** is defined as an unintentional change in the system. As soon as it becomes apparent from the carrying out of a functional test that such a departure or breakdown has occurred, enquiries should be made to ascertain whether the departure or breakdown was an isolated incident and has since been corrected and the control re-established. If not, it is not normally necessary to continue the particular functional test because it has served its purpose by indicating a loss of control.

Assessing the effect of weaknesses

8.03　It is an important feature of the audit approach outlined in this book that, as regards each weakness that has been identified, the auditor must make a judgement as to its possible effects, accidental or intentional, on the financial statements and thus as to what changes he should make in his audit work. Depending on its nature a weakness might lead to error in the following manner:

(a) the under- or over-statement of an asset, or liability, in the balance sheet, with a corresponding effect on the profit and loss account; or

(b) the failure to disclose a fraud in respect of which the loss has been written off in the profit and loss account; or

(c) a misclassification of items, as a result of which there could be a failure to disclose an item properly in the balance sheet, profit and loss account or notes to the financial statements.

8.04 The auditor must decide, taking all the relevant factors into account, whether the weakness could lead to a material error appearing in the financial statements. If, in his opinion, material error could not arise, he will not normally make any change to the audit procedures to take account of the weakness. This is because he is not required to refer to the existence of immaterial error in the financial statements on which he is reporting.

8.05 If the auditor decides that material error could occur, he must take appropriate steps to satisfy himself whether or not error has arisen and, if it has, its extent. In order to obtain this satisfaction, he will need to alter or add to the audit procedures which he would otherwise carry out. In those exceptional cases where the effect of a control weakness cannot be ascertained by changes in audit procedures, the auditor will need to consider whether it may be necessary to qualify his audit report.

Assessment of Whether Material Error Could Arise

8.06 Most of the factors that the auditor must take into account in deciding whether a control weakness could lead to material error in the financial statements will relate to the particular circumstances of each weakness. However, there are certain factors that will usually be common to each assessment.

8.07 The common factors are:

(a) whether the assets and liabilities involved are themselves material as regards the financial statements;

(b) whether any related control procedures might identify that material error arose;

(c) the effects of weaknesses in controls over standing data are likely to have greater consequence than those of weaknesses in controls over transaction data;

(d) weaknesses in controls over completeness are likely to have a more serious effect than weaknesses in controls over accuracy or validity of individual transactions;

(e) weaknesses in programmed procedures are more likely to be significant than weaknesses in user controls, particularly if a high volume of data passes through the programmed procedure and/or the results of that programmed procedure are not subject to manual scrutiny or check;

(f) whether a breakdown has been corrected in sufficient time before the end of the financial year, and this is confirmed by appropriate audit tests; it may, however, continue to be necessary to carry out the steps outlined in paragraph 8.16 if the weakness could have provided opportunity for major fraud in the intervening period.

·8.08   Where the auditor has decided that the overall adequacy of implemen-
        tation, program security or computer operations controls is deficient, he
        must review each programmed procedure thereby at risk and decide
        whether material error could arise if the procedure was not operating
        properly.

8.09   Where the auditor's tests of programmed procedures (manual tests, audit
        test data, program code analysis, or use of computer programs) disclose
        that a programmed procedure is not functioning properly, he should first
        ascertain the reason therefor. The cause will usually be that the procedure
        was not properly included in the program (a weakness in implementation
        or program security controls) or the program was not properly used (a
        weakness in computer operations controls). Once the auditor has
        identified the cause, he will need to assess its effect both as regards the
        programmed procedure at fault and other programmed procedures. This
        will usually mean carrying out further tests on the programmed proce-
        dures, or the relevant integrity controls in order to form a view as to the
        extent to which there are weaknesses in such integrity controls. If he
        concludes that the integrity controls are deficient, and that the failure of
        the programmed procedure was not an isolated incident, he will need to
        proceed as in paragraph 8.08.

8.10   Where the auditor has decided that the overall adequacy of standing data
        or data file security controls is deficient, he must review each data field
        thereby at risk, such as rates of pay or sales prices, and decide whether the
        lack of control could lead to material error arising.

8.11   When assessing the effect of breakdowns of controls in computer systems,
        it should be borne in mind that an exception relating to the failure of a
        programmed procedure is unlikely to be an isolated incident, as at best it
        will indicate a breakdown in the integrity controls and at worst a fault in
        the program itself. In the latter case the situation should be immediately
        reported to the client, as the fault will continue until corrected.

Effect on Audit Procedures

8.12   It is not possible to state precisely the effect on audit procedures of
        control weaknesses that could lead to material error. Much will depend
        on the nature and materiality of the assets and liabilities involved and the
        risk of material error arising.

8.13   Where material error could arise, it may be possible to confirm its
        existence or otherwise from an overall review, for example a scrutiny of
        such summary information as totals of processed transactions from
        month to month, comparisons with budgets and previous periods and
        performance indicators, such as gross profit percentages or production
        variances. Where the records of the relevant assets, liabilities or trans-

299

ICQ Ref.	Nature of Weakness and Possible Effect on Financial Statements	Comments of Client
(1)	(2)	(3)
12·28	There are no controls over the depreciation rates used in the calculation of monthly depreciation charges. As a result, the depreciation charge in the P&L account may be misstated, as may be the amounts at which assets are stated in the balance sheet.	K. Morgan – Chief Acct Accepts that controls are missing but considers that material error would be evident in the periodic review of management accounts.

FIG. 73. Record of Control Weaknesses (RCW) (8.18)

actions are held on computer files, it may be possible for the auditor to use his own computer audit programs to assist in confirming whether or not a material error exists. Programs may be used to assess the extent of error in either user controls or programmed procedures.

8.14 As an example in respect of user controls, where continuous stocktaking procedures are found to be in arrears, it may be possible to use a computer audit program to analyse the value of inventory into the periods since it was last counted, for example six months, twelve months, eighteen months, and over eighteen months. This information will show whether a material part of the total inventory has not been counted for an unreasonable period of time.

8.15 As an example in respect of programmed procedures, where an error is discovered in the program for reporting uncleared items on the outstanding despatch notes pipeline file, it may be possible to use a computer audit program to examine the pipeline and prices files to produce a report of evaluated uncleared items analysed by date of entry to the pipeline file. This information will show whether a material volume or value of despatches remains outstanding for an unreasonable period of time.

8.16 If the overall review confirms that material error could be present in an account balance, it will usually be necessary to extend the tests carried out on individual items making up the account balance, or part of the account balance, regarding which doubt has arisen. Where the concern is that material fraud has occurred, for example in respect of the control objectives relating to cash and wages, it may also be necessary to examine more transactions during the period under audit. The nature of these extended validation procedures is discussed further in Chapter 9.

Could Material Error Arise ?		Effect on Nature, Extent and/or Timing of Audit Procedures		Weakness Formally Notified to Client		Weakness Rectified	
Yes/No (4)	Justification (5)	Nature of Amendment Required (6)	Audit Programme Ref. (7)	Method (8)	Date (9)	Date (10)	Audit Programme Revised √ or N/A (11)
Yes	There are no formal procedures that would detect error and depreciation is a material item in the P & L account.	A computer audit program will be used to evaluate and accumulate depreciation charges on all assets.	M/34	Letter	31/10		

Reporting to Client

8.17 The auditor should report formally to the client all control weaknesses that come to his attention and their possible effects. It is also helpful to include, where appropriate, suitable suggestions for overcoming such weaknesses.

Record of Control Weaknesses

8.18 The auditor should record formally the control weaknesses he identifies and the action he takes as a result. This is most conveniently done in a single document. An example of such a document, called a **Record of Control Weaknesses** ("RCW"), is illustrated in Figure 73. Each stage of the auditor's response to a weakness is recorded on the RCW, as explained in the next paragraph.

8.19 When details of the weakness and its possible effect on the financial statements have been recorded (Columns 1 and 2), the weakness should be discussed with the client in case any compensating controls exist which were not apparent to the auditor when the ICQ was completed, and also to ensure that the facts relating to the weakness are correct. The client should be notified at the earliest opportunity so that, where appropriate, he can take corrective action. The client's comments are recorded in Column 3 and, if a compensating control is identified, the ICQ is amended and the RCW marked off accordingly. The auditor's assessment of whether material error could arise and the reason for his decision in this respect are recorded in Columns 4 and 5. Any resulting changes to audit procedures are entered in Columns 6 and 7 and the formal notification to the client recorded in Columns 8 and 9. The subsequent rectification of the weakness and the resulting amendment to the audit procedures are recorded in Columns 10 and 11.

301

Common Weaknesses in Computer Systems

8.20 Weaknesses often occur because of a failure to plan the controls adequately during the early stage of system development. This leads to the development of controls on an ad hoc and unstructured basis. In particular it is common, as indicated in paragraph 4.03, for the need to consider the entire system, both computer and non-computer, as a whole, to be overlooked; the manual controls are often not decided upon until the systems become operational. The need to reconsider existing manual controls when computer processing is introduced may also be overlooked.

8.21 The more common weaknesses include:
   (a) The failure to establish controls over the maintenance of standing data.
   (b) The failure to recognise the need to control reference data.
   (c) Ineffective authorisation procedures, particularly in relation to irregular input, such as adjustments.
   (d) The failure to recognise the importance of supervisory controls.
   (e) The failure to check the accuracy of computer-generated data, for example interest charges, by either reasonableness checks or manual reviews of the generated data.
   (f) Unrealistic settings for the criteria in programmed reasonableness and dependency checks with the result that either too few or too many exceptional items are rejected or reported.
   (g) The failure to establish a proper segregation of duties within the computer department between the functions of system analysts, programmers and computer operators.
   (h) The failure to produce readily digestible reports of computer usage in order that a meaningful review of computer operations can be carried out.
   (i) The absence of control over modifications made to program libraries, particularly as regards ensuring that only properly authorised amendments can be made.
   (j) The failure to safeguard data files against access by unauthorised personnel.
   (k) The failure to ensure that restrictions over the operation of the computer and access to data files are enforced at all times, particularly during evening and weekend shifts.

8.22 The more common breakdowns that are encountered during functional testing include:
   (a) The failure to act promptly on exception reports.
   (b) A build-up of uninvestigated rejections.
   (c) A build-up of suspense items on files.
   (d) Delays in the follow up of outstanding and overdue items, such as the despatch of reminder letters.
   (e) The failure to carry out reconciliation procedures when under time pressure, following delays in processing.
   (f) The low priority often given to cyclical checking of standing data.

(g) Restrictions over the operating of the computer not enforced; in particular, programmers allowed to operate the machine unsupervised to test programs.

(h) A failure to review and approve records of computer usage sufficiently regularly.

(i) Restrictions over access to data files not enforced; in particular, computer operators allowed access to file libraries without first obtaining the required authorisation.

(j) Amendments made to operational program libraries bypassing the normal control procedures and the requirement for authorisation.

Computer Fraud

8.23   Frauds carried out in a computer environment have attracted comment in recent years. In general, these frauds fall into one of three categories:

- **Defalcation**, whereby computer processing is used to assist in the unauthorised obtaining of assets belonging to the company.

- **Misrepresentation**, whereby computer processing is used to assist in the production of financial information which is not derived from authorised transactions.

- **Physical action**, whereby, as a result of breach of security, data or programs are stolen or the computer equipment is attacked.

These are discussed briefly in the following paragraphs.

Defalcation

8.24   There are two main methods by which computer processing can be used to assist in the unauthorised obtaining of assets belonging to the company – fraudulent steps in the program and the processing of unauthorised data.

Fraudulent program steps

8.25   Perhaps surprisingly, there are relatively few published cases of major frauds arising from fraudulent program steps. This is probably mainly because only certain systems, such as payroll production or cash recording in banks, could enable a programmer to include fraudulent steps which would be to his immediate advantage. This may also be partly due to the difficulty of obtaining sufficient knowledge of the system as a whole.

8.26   Fraudulent program steps are best guarded against by a suitable segregation of duties (whereby programmers have no detailed knowledge of the surrounding manual parts of the system and the user controls),

303

adequate testing of new systems and program changes and control over access to programs. Protection can be enhanced by using modular programming techniques whereby no single programmer has knowledge of the full computer system.

Processing unauthorised data

8.27   Defalcation by processing unauthorised data is normally the easiest and thus the most common method of computer fraud. Processing unauthorised data can arise through the input of unauthorised data, manipulation of files, improper use of the printer or suppression of print-outs. It can best be guarded against by an appropriate level and timing of authorisation of all standing data amendments and adjustments, regular maintenance controls over the data on files, strong controls over access to data files in on-line systems and the segregation of duties, where appropriate, between those responsible for approving transaction data and for approving standing data.

Misrepresentation

8.28   Misrepresentation, whereby computer processing is used to assist in the production of financial information which is not derived from authorised transactions, usually involves a significant degree of collusion. Almost certainly material error will arise and therefore the auditor should identify the fraud following the procedures outlined earlier in this chapter. However, frauds of this nature are probably easier to perpetrate in computer systems because of the computer's ability to process large volumes of data without the need to involve numerous staff.

Physical action

8.29   Physical action, whereby, as a result of breach of security, data or programs are stolen or the computer equipment is attacked, is beyond the scope of normal audit work. However, the auditor may be well placed to carry out security reviews and some of the relevant considerations are mentioned in Chapter 12 "Computer Security".

Summary

8.30   It is an important feature of the audit approach herein described that, as regards each weakness, the auditor must decide, taking all the relevant factors into account, whether the weakness could lead to material error appearing in the financial statements. If the auditor decides that material error could occur, he must take the necessary steps to satisfy himself whether or not error has arisen and, if it has, its extent.

9

Validation Procedures

General Approach

Purpose and scope

9.01 **Validation procedures,** which are also called verification procedures or substantive tests, represent the final stage of the audit leading to the expression of an audit opinion. They have as their main objective the substantiation of account balances and other information contained in the balance sheet and profit and loss account and the related notes. In addition, validation procedures complement functional tests, since they provide further evidence as to whether the internal accounting controls have continued to operate.

Relationship with internal control

9.02 Normally the most important factors governing the nature, timing and extent of validation procedures are the materiality of the account balances and the degree of reliance that can be placed on the company's internal controls. Where the internal controls are satisfactory, the validation procedures can be limited and carried out, to an appropriate extent, before the year end. If the controls are unsatisfactory, the validation procedures must be extended and the opportunity for carrying out much of the work before the year end decreases.

Reliance on internal control

9.03 Before deciding upon the nature, timing and extent of his validation procedures, the auditor will usually wish to determine whether he is entitled to place reliance on specific internal controls. He will be able to reach this conclusion only after he has completed his evaluation of the company's internal controls, functionally tested those controls on which he expects to rely and prepared the RCW.

9.04 Even where the auditor has decided not to carry out functional tests, it will still normally be possible to give some recognition to the existence of basic controls, as identified in the ICQ, in determining the nature and extent of validation procedures, provided the results of the validation procedures confirm the operation of such controls.

9.05　In addition to the procedures that form part of the routine internal controls, the auditor should take account of specific procedures carried out at the year end by the company, such as a review of the adequacy of the provision for doubtful accounts, an overall reconciliation of inventory quantities or values, and procedures to ensure the correctness of cut-off.

Extended validation procedures

9.06　Where the auditor cannot, or prefers not to, rely on the internal controls for the purpose of limiting his validation procedures, it will be necessary for him to perform extended validation procedures. These procedures, and their application in computer systems, are dealt with in paragraphs 9.69 to 9.87.

Validation procedures documentation

9.07　The auditor will need to make an appropriate record of the work to be carried out, partly to enable him to ensure that all the planned work takes place and partly to enable a reviewer to see whether the conclusions reached from the validation procedures are justified. A formal audit programme of validation procedures should be prepared and should include as a minimum:

(a) a description of the tests to be performed;

(b) identification of the levels of test;

(c) details of the evidence seen;

(d) details of any errors or exceptions noted during the performance of the work and of their disposition;

(e) an indication that the work has been completed (usually the initials of the person completing the work) and the date when it was carried out.

9.08　The general nature of validation procedures in non-computer systems is similar from company to company. Accordingly it is common for the auditor to develop specimen tests for validation procedures for general use. It is usually necessary to make amendments to these specimen tests when the processing is by computer. This chapter is based on the assumption that the auditor will, in general, be making appropriate alterations to existing tests.

9.09   In order to illustrate the points made in this chapter, a typical section of an
audit programme related to the validation procedures for trade accounts
receivable is set out in appendix A, together with an indication of the
probable changes that would be required for computer systems.
Although the appendix only contains the validation procedures for trade
accounts receivable, the same principles would apply to other sections of
the audit programme where the records are processed by computer. An
example of the format of the programme is illustrated in Figure 74.

Validation Programme

Accounts Receivable

Audit of ... The A.B.C. Company ....   Date of Accounts .. 31/12 ...

Programme	W.P. Ref.	Exceptions Yes/No	Signature and Date
Examine batches of sales invoices for the 3 days before and after the year end and ensure that invoices are included in the correct accounting period. Check that batches were processed in the correct period.	K/17	No.	J.S.T 19/1

FIG. 74. Validation audit programme – accounts receivable (9.09)

Application to computer systems

9.10   When records supporting balance sheet and income and expense
accounts are maintained by computer, the objectives of the validation
procedures and the relationship between the system of internal control
and the validation procedures remain the same. However, because of, first,
the opportunity to make use of computer programs to read the data
held on computer files and, secondly, the distinctive control features in
computer systems, there are often changes in the validation procedures.
In the following paragraphs general matters relating to the nature,
timing and extent of validation procedures, and the impact that computers may have on them, are outlined.

The Nature of Validation Procedures

Types of validation procedures

9.11   Validation procedures may be divided into two main categories:

- Validation tests.
- Other auditing procedures.

Validation tests, as used herein, are direct tests of the items comprising account balances, components thereof, or other financial information for the purpose of substantiating them. **Other auditing procedures**, as used herein, are tests of a more general nature, such as analytical comparisons and reviews, that provide indirect evidence that supports the validity and completeness of the information in the accounts and related notes.

Validation tests

9.12   The nature of the validation tests will vary depending on the account balance being examined, but may include **confirmation, inspection, reperformance** and **vouching**. In order that the effect of computer processing may be more readily seen, these techniques are briefly described in the following paragraphs.

Confirmation

9.13   Confirmation consists of obtaining verification of a fact or condition from a third party. This procedure is generally applied to items comprising an account balance. Confirmations obtained from persons who are independent of the client provide strong support for the existence of the fact or account balance and often serve as the principal validation test related to that account balance, for example confirmation of accounts receivable.

Inspection

9.14   Inspection involves counting and/or examining the physical matter represented by items in the accounts. This procedure is generally performed by management with the auditor participating or observing, although on occasion the auditor performs the count. A typical example of inspection is the physical count of inventory by management while the auditor observes and tests the procedures.

Reperformance

9.15   In many instances an account balance may represent the result of a computation or an accumulation of computations, for example the liability for goods received not invoiced calculated from the total of evaluated goods received notes. The validation of such an account balance often includes reperformance of the computation, either in detail or on an overall basis. Where judgement is the basis of a computation, reperformance of the computation should also include evaluating the reasoning process supporting the judgement in order to determine its propriety. For example, if the client's determination of the provision for doubtful debts, having regard to past experience, is based on a formula related to the age of the receivables, the auditor should evaluate the reasonableness of the formula as well as check the mathematical calculations. The auditor should also perform other procedures regarding the collectibility of accounts receivable in reviewing the adequacy of the provision for doubtful debts, for example a review of cash received after the year end.

Vouching

9.16   Vouching involves the examination of evidence supporting a transaction or item in order to determine its validity. For this purpose, determining validity would normally include ascertaining that there is evidence that the company has performed all the checking of the various supporting documents that its procedures require, examining the supporting documents (on a test basis, where appropriate) and determining whether any aspects of the transaction appear to be unusual, for example a supplier's invoice not addressed to the client.

Reconciliation and account analysis

9.17   **Reconciliation** and **account analysis** are important techniques in implementing validation tests and are briefly described in the following paragraphs.

9.18   Reconciliation consists of identifying the items causing the difference between two amounts, one of which is usually an account balance; common examples include comparing the general ledger balance for accounts receivable with the total of the detailed accounts receivable records by customer, and the book balance for a bank account with the balance shown by the related bank statement. Validation tests should then be performed on the reconciling items to determine whether adjustments are required to the account balance.

9.19   Account analysis involves categorising and summarising the details of an account in a manner that provides an enhanced understanding of the items comprising the balance. There are two principal forms that an account analysis can take. The first is a summary of the activity for the period under examination; the second is an analysis of the composition of the closing balance in which the major items or categories of items are identified. The first type is useful in analysing those accounts, such as property, plant and equipment accounts, where major elements of the account balance at the beginning of the period remain in the account at the end of the period; the second type is useful in analysing those accounts, such as accounts receivable, where there is significant activity and the year end balance consists largely of transactions that occurred during the period covered by the examination. An analysis of accounts receivable can take the form of an ageing of trade accounts receivable (where there are many individual balances) or a detailed listing of employee receivables (where there may be a few balances that are of interest to the auditor). An appropriate account analysis can greatly facilitate the application of validation tests by providing the auditor with a basis for understanding the nature of the items said to comprise the account balance.

Other auditing procedures

9.20 The other auditing procedures that are of relevance when it comes to considering the impact of computer processing on validation procedures are **analyses of fluctuations,** and of **financial trends and ratios.** These are briefly described in the following paragraphs.

Analysis of fluctuations

9.21 Analysis of fluctuations in account balances includes obtaining explanations for unusual changes (or lack of expected change) in recorded amounts as compared to, for example, budgets or amounts of prior years, and evaluating the explanations for reasonableness in relation to other financial information and the auditor's knowledge of the company's affairs. This procedure is normally a necessary supplement to the validation tests and may reveal inappropriate entries in the accounts. For example, additional vouching occasioned by a significant increase in the repairs and maintenance expense accounts might disclose payments that should be included in property, plant and equipment.

Analysis of financial trends and ratios

9.22 Analysis of financial trends and ratios involves reviewing the financial position and performance of the company as expressed by significant performance indicators, such as gross profit percentages, working capital ratios, ratios of receivables, inventories and various expenses to sales, ascertaining whether such indicators have a logical relationship, obtaining reasonable explanations for unusual relationships, and considering whether the findings indicate that changes should be made in the nature, extent or timing of validation tests. For example, increases in inventories in relation to sales or a reduction in gross profit percentages might cause the auditor to extend his tests with respect to the realisability (market value) of inventories. Analysis of financial trends and ratios will usually be performed in conjunction with the analysis of balance sheet and profit and loss account fluctuations due to their close relationship.

Order of work

9.23 The order in which the various validation procedures outlined above are carried out in respect of accounts items is important in relation to the extent of testing. Audit efficiency is normally improved by applying first the appropriate procedures to the item in total, the individual components then being examined to a progressively more detailed degree. In this way, each validation step gives the auditor an increased understanding of, and level of confidence in, the balances under examination. Provided the results of the broader tests are satisfactory, the level of examination in depth can be restricted to an extent which would not be acceptable if the prior understanding had not been obtained. For example, it would normally be appropriate to carry out the reconciliation of the general ledger balance for accounts receivable with the total of the detailed accounts receivable balances and test, by reperformance, the accumulation of the detailed records before carrying out tests on individual items.

9.24   For similar reasons, it will often be desirable to carry out other auditing procedures that are relevant and review appropriate account analyses before carrying out the validation tests in the manner described in paragraph 9.23. For example, before carrying out tests on the value of accounts receivable, it would normally be appropriate to obtain, or prepare, and review analyses of accounts receivable by reference to age and the ratio of accounts receivable to sales. The extent of tests would then be decided on, taking into account the results of these reviews.

The Impact of Computers on the Nature of Validation Procedures

Introduction

9.25   The most important difference in validation procedures, where records supporting account balances are maintained by computer, is the opportunity to read the data by the use of computer programs, as outlined in paragraphs 9.26 to 9.43. Various other differences may also arise which are dealt with in paragraphs 9.44 to 9.52 under the headings "Additional controls on which reliance can be placed", "Improved account analyses" and "Modification of validation tests".

The use of computer programs

9.26   Auditors, confronted with large files of accounting data, quickly found the idea of using computer programs attractive. Using such file interrogation programs offered several major advantages over manual work. First, the work is carried out much faster and more accurately by program. A typical program running on a medium size computer might review and classify around 50,000 accounts in five minutes and with much greater consistency than clerical work. Secondly, as a result, far more data can be reviewed. Invariably in manual auditing a compromise has to be struck between the volume the auditor would like to examine and the volume he can in practice examine. This leads in manual work to the use of sampling techniques of either a formal or informal nature. With a file interrogation program it is often possible to read the whole population in the time it would take an auditor to work out what the sample should be. Thirdly, less paper work is required and generated; it is only necessary to print out the results of the test or the items selected for investigation. Last, and most important, clerical audit time can be devoted to an examination of the items defined by the auditor as significant; in other words, the auditor can concentrate on what matters.

Scope of assistance

9.27 File interrogation programs can be used to assist validation procedures in the following ways, as illustrated in Figure 75:

- The **reperformance** of the company's procedures, for example reperforming the accumulation and ageing of accounts receivable.

- The **selection** of defined items in account balances for the purpose of **confirmation** or **inspection**. The program can also assist in the confirmation work.

- The production of **additional account analyses,** for example an analysis of accounts receivable in relation to credit limits.

These tasks are discussed in the following paragraphs.

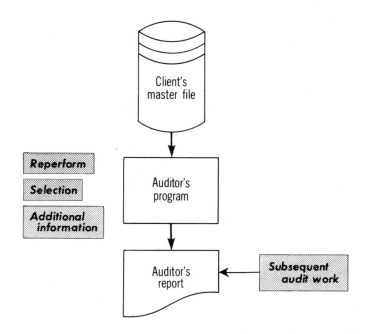

FIG. 75. Use of computer programs – validation procedures (9.27)

Reperformance

9.28   The reperformance of the company's procedures replaces work otherwise carried out manually. However, in most cases, the extent of reperformance will be much higher because all items will be accumulated,
calculated or analysed, whereas, using manual techniques, only a sample
of items would normally be subject to reperformance tests. This
improved testing will usually be most marked in respect of analyses as, for
example, in ageing of accounts receivable and analysing inventories in
relation to usage, which are often difficult to test adequately by manual
means.

Selection

9.29   The selection of items for confirmation or inspection replaces work
otherwise carried out manually. As all items are reviewed in selecting the
sample, the selection methods can be improved. Depending on the nature
of the program, it will be possible to obtain a statistical, systematic or
random sample. The program will also probably be able to divide the
items into strata for selecting the sample, for example debit balances
greater than £1,000, credit balances greater than £500 and a systematic
sample of items between these amounts.

Additional account analyses

9.30   The production of additional information in the form of account analyses
and samples of exceptional items to assist the auditor represents one of
the most significant effects that computers can have on audit procedures.
The review of all data on file and the production of suitable analyses
enables the auditor to identify the areas where problems do, or do not,
exist, as an aid to subsequent validation. For example, by ageing inventories according to his specified criteria, and by comparing balances with
past and forecast usage, the auditor may be able to establish the materiality of old and excessive inventory and decide on the manual investigation that will be necessary.

9.31   File interrogation programs usually enable the auditor to carry out more
effective manual validation procedures than are possible by solely manual means. As illustrated in Figure 76, when programs are used, the
auditor can base his tests on the results of a reading by the computer of all
the data on the files. It must however be remembered that, except in those
cases where the selection or analysis shows the population concerned to
be immaterial, normal manual validation tests will need to be carried out
on the items reported or analysed by the computer program. In particular, the program can only read the data actually on the files and it will
usually be necessary to establish by manual tests that the data is complete.

Procedures for using computer programs

9.32   There will need to be formal procedures, both to prepare the computer
programs and to incorporate the use of the program into the validation
procedures. These latter steps are particularly important in order to

313

Manual tests

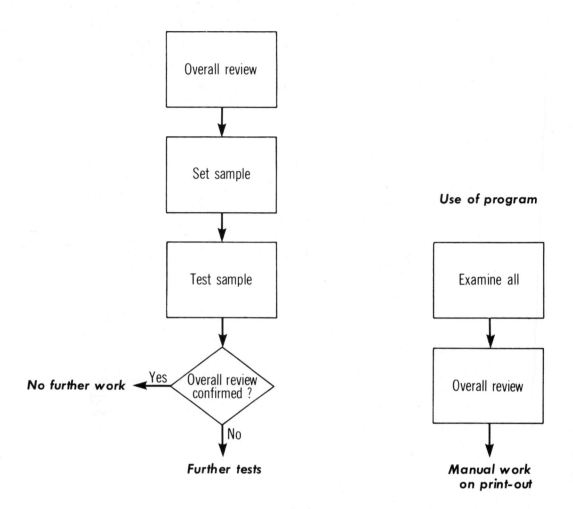

FIG. 76. Influence of computer programs on validation (9.31)

ensure that audit staff understand the relationship of the program to the manual procedures and, on the one hand, avoid unnecessary work and, on the other, understand, and do not overlook, the work required on the information produced by the program.

Preparation of program

9.33   There are various ways in which the auditor can prepare or obtain a suitable program. These, together with the procedures to be followed in preparing, testing and executing a program both in the first and subsequent years of use, are considered in Chapter 10 "The Use of Computer Programs".

9.34 It should not be overlooked that manual work, often of a high quality, will be necessary to interpret the information produced by the computer program and to decide on, and carry out, such subsequent investigation as is needed. The specific work to be done on the results, such as checking to the company's figures, and details of any further tests required, such as manual investigation, should be incorporated in the audit programme.

Examples of uses of computer programs

9.35 The tasks undertaken by file interrogation programs will depend on the audit requirements, the variety of information that is available on the relevant files and the auditor's ability to include his requirements in a program. Certain tasks, when appropriate, are usually included in all uses of programs. These include:

(a) Accumulating the balances or items on the file and reporting separate totals of debits, credits and nil balances and a net total of balances.

(b) Stratifying the balances or items on the file and selecting appropriate samples from all or selected strata for subsequent validation, for example for physical inspection.

(c) Sub-totalling the items making up each balance, comparing the sub-total with the balance and reporting those which disagree.

(d) Identifying, accumulating and reporting transactions dated after the cut-off date for the file.

The nature of the other tasks, which will consist in the main of the production of analyses and report of specified items, will differ according to the application. The more common additional tasks are set out in the following paragraphs under the application concerned. In addition, illustrations of the use of file interrogation programs to assist in the validation of accounts receivable and inventories are set out in appendix B to this chapter.

Accounts payable

9.36 Typical tasks include:

- Matching subsequent period recorded payments against earlier period items and balances and identifying unmatched payments.
- Identifying old invoices or goods received documentation unmatched on the file.
- Identifying unusual transactions, for example large non-stock purchases for particular accounts codes.
- Identifying unusual standing data, for example accounts for inactive suppliers.
- Identifying accounts not reconciled to supplier's statement for a significant length of time.

315

9.37 Typical tasks include:

- Analysing the balances or transactions into age categories. Often a more detailed analysis than that prepared by the company is required. Analysing by transaction type may produce useful information regarding payments on account and unmatched adjustments.
- Identifying balances in excess of credit limits, analysing them into strata by reference to the amount by which the credit limit is exceeded and computing the amount of excess over credit limits.
- Identifying accounts with unusual credit limits or no credit limits.
- Identifying unusual transactions, for example large sales near the year end or transfers between accounts.
- Identifying unmatched transactions, for example payments on account.
- Identifying unusual standing data, for example high discount rates.
- Selecting items for confirmation and printing appropriate confirmation requests. These items can be written to the file and replies can be matched. Information regarding outstanding items and second requests can then be produced.

Inventories

9.38 Typical tasks include:

- Analysing the balances into age categories. This can be done by reference to the date of last receipt or last issue.
- Analysing the balances into categories of number of years' stock held. This can be done by reference to past or forecast issues or other production information. Often this information must first be calculated.
- Identifying balances in excess of maximum stock levels, analysing them into strata by reference to the extent by which the maximum stock level is exceeded and computing the extent of excess over maximum stock levels.
- Identifying items with unusual maximum stock levels or no maximum stock levels.
- Identifying items recorded as obsolete or damaged.
- Identifying items where significant scrap adjustments have been recorded.
- Identifying items with unusual prices, for example by comparing cost and selling prices, by range tests, or comparing current prices with previous prices. Sometimes it is possible to identify items for which the price has not been updated within a given period of time. Balances without prices may also be identified.
- Computing, were appropriate, the amount by which inventory valued at cost price exceeds inventory valued at selling price.
- Analysing the balances into age categories since date last counted.
- Identifying items that existed in the prior year's inventory but do not exist in the current year's inventory.
- Identifying balances with no physical location reference.

Work in progress

9.39 Typical tasks include:

- Analysing the balances into age categories.
- Identifying items where the full value of work done may not be recoverable. This can be achieved by:
  - identifying items whose actual costs exceed authorised or budgeted costs;
  - identifying items whose costs to date exceed fixed selling prices;
  - identifying items whose costs are not rechargeable to customers, such as warranty work;
  - selecting items for comparison of total expected costs to complete with realisable value.
- Identifying balances which include unusual items, for example adjustments.
- Identifying closed work in progress items not invoiced within a reasonable period of time.
- Identifying items which have been open for an unreasonable period of time.

Fixed assets

9.40 Typical tasks include:

- Calculating depreciation and checking the company's figure.
- Identifying fully depreciated assets and calculating what would have been the normal depreciation thereon.
- Identifying unusual depreciation rates.
- Analysing items into age categories since last physically inspected.
- Identifying properties with no title deed reference.

General ledger

9.41 It may be possible to identify items that appear unusual in relation to past periods or budgets.

Loans, mortgages and customers' bank accounts

9.42 These items have certain characteristics similar to accounts receivable. In addition to the relevant tasks mentioned under that heading, typical tasks in relation to these items include:

- Identifying accounts with unusual interest or commission rates; employees' accounts can be particularly scrutinised.
- Identifying accounts with insufficient security.
- Calculating analyses required for statutory purposes, such as Protection of Depositors Act, 1967 and Building Societies Act, 1962.

Specialised businesses

9.43 Similar tasks can be carried out in respect of more specialised businesses. For example, in the case of insurance companies, a variety of tasks can be undertaken in relation to outstanding claims.

317

Additional controls on which reliance can be placed

9.44 Having considered the use of programs, the other factors in computer systems which affect the nature of validation procedures can be considered. The first of these concerns the controls on which reliance can be placed. In computer systems the opportunity often arises to place reliance on controls over procedures which, in non-computer systems, are less formal or less regularly exercised and which the auditor usually finds it more efficient to test as part of his validation procedures. For example, it is likely that the quantity records of items of inventory maintained on computer will be more regularly priced and evaluated than in non-computer systems. As part of this regular stock-valuing process there will be procedures and controls for the amendment and maintenance of prices. The processing of adjustments, such as stocktaking differences, will also be formalised and subject to input and updating controls.

9.45 Similar features will be present in the processing of accounts receivable records and there are likely to be regular formal procedures for processing adjustments and write-offs. The auditor will often find it more efficient to place reliance on the controls over these procedures, to carry out appropriate functional tests, and to reduce his validation tests. This approach has the added advantage that the auditor obtains early warning of weaknesses and exceptions which, if uncorrected, might lead to an increase in his validation work.

Improved account analyses

9.46 The increased amount and variety of data maintained on computer files and the power of computer processing result in the provision by the company of more account analyses, often in the form of exception reports, than is usually the case in non-computer systems. These will include simple analyses of items making up an account balance, for example analyses of inventories, or of accounts receivable by age, as well as more complex analyses making use of data not forming part of the account balance, for example analyses of accounts receivable in relation to credit limits or inventory balances in relation to maximum stock levels. Where information of this nature is available, it can be used by the auditor as an alternative to providing it himself using computer programs. The auditor should enquire into, and use as he thinks appropriate, all relevant computer reports of this nature. Often he can, in this way, obtain a better understanding of the nature of the items that comprise an account balance than is normally possible in non-computer systems.

9.47 When the auditor makes use of analyses and exception reports provided by the company in carrying out his validation procedures, he must satisfy himself that the programmed procedures which relate to their production are functioning properly and that the information produced is complete and accurate. He can do this by testing the procedures as part of his validation procedures or testing the relevant internal controls earlier in the year and relying on and testing the operation of the disciplines for the period until the year end.

Modification of validation tests

9.48   Due to the particular features of computer processing, certain validation procedures either need to be modified or become unnecessary. In addition to the effect on validation procedures of using computer programs (paragraphs 9.26 to 9.43), the additional controls on which reliance can be placed (paragraphs 9.44 and 9.45) and the improved account analyses (paragraphs 9.46 and 9.47), the main changes relate to tests on lists of balances, cut-off tests and reconciliations and are outlined in the following paragraphs.

Lists of balances

9.49   In non-computer systems it is usually necessary to extract balances from ledgers and list them for totalling and agreement with control accounts. The extraction process is often not subject to internal control and thus a substantial level of validation tests may need to be carried out. This checking of balances between ledgers and lists is not necessary in computer systems because the list, where produced, is simply the printing of information held on the files, the balances being accumulated and agreed with the control account or control record. The auditor, however, will still need to check the additions of the list of balances where the file total is not being checked by a file interrogation program.

Cut-off tests

9.50   It is usually easier to carry out more effective cut-off tests in computer systems, particularly in batch systems. The principal requirements are to identify the last processing run for sales, purchases and inventory movements in the period being audited and to confirm by reference to batches of input around that time that data was input in the correct period, and that rejections were properly dealt with. It should be noted that the nominal date of the last processing run may differ from the actual date on which that run occurs as the files may be held open in order to process outstanding transactions. These tests are made even easier where sales or purchases processing are integrated with the related inventory processing. In these cases no cut-off difference between sales and inventory or purchases and inventory, as applicable, is likely to arise, since the updating of accounts receivable or accounts payable and inventories is concurrent. In all cases, it remains necessary to test that the sales and purchases documentation is represented by actual shipments and receipts on the dates recorded on the documents.

Reconciliations

9.51   Reconciliations are usually carried out more regularly in computer systems. The individual balances on computer files such as, for example, accounts receivable files, will usually be reconciled either to an independent control account or to a control record on the file every time the file is updated or reorganised. As a result of these regular reconciliations, the auditor is more likely to carry out functional tests thereon than in a non-computer system and there will usually be less difficulty in investigating any items in reconciliation.

Use of audit test data

9.52 It may sometimes be decided to use audit test data to test the complete and accurate production of analyses and exception reports which the auditor uses during his validation procedures. Where test data is used for this purpose, or as part of the functional testing, it may add to audit efficiency to include additional procedures to assist in validation tests. Examples of this might be the valuation of stocks or the calculation of depreciation. It will usually be appropriate to supplement the use of audit test data in this manner with a scrutiny of actual reports for reasonableness. Although it is possible for the auditor to use test data just to assist in his validation tests, this will seldom be the most efficient approach to the work. The practical matters to be considered when using audit test data are dealt with in appendix B to Chapter 7 "Functional Tests".

The Timing of Validation Procedures

Early validation

9.53 It is often desirable to perform validation procedures as at a date prior to the year end, particularly if the client wishes the audit to be completed shortly after the year end. This may be done in appropriate circumstances without impairing the effectiveness of the audit.

9.54 Validation procedures may be performed on some or all account balances before the year end, if the functional tests provide evidence that reliance can be placed on the relevant controls. In deciding whether early validation is appropriate, the auditor should pay particular attention to disciplines over basic controls relating to custody of assets and, in some circumstances, to segregation of duties because, in their absence, it is unlikely that he will be able to place reliance on continued proper accounting for transactions. On the other hand, early validation may be appropriate in the absence of supervisory controls, since the auditor can examine evidence himself that the basic controls have continued to operate in the intervening period.

9.55 Where, as is normally the case, internal controls, particularly custodial controls and segregation of duties, are better in computer systems than in manual systems, there is usually more scope to perform early validation procedures. This opportunity is usually enhanced by the greater formalisation of procedures in computer systems, for example the matters referred to in paragraphs 9.44 and 9.45.

Examination and review of transactions

9.56 When the auditor decides to carry out his validation procedures on account balances mainly as of the balance sheet date, he may still wish, in the interests of efficiency, to carry out certain validation work prior to the year end. Validation procedures that involve the examination or review of transactions during the year, for example purchases and disposals of fixed assets, can be performed prior to the year end in respect of transactions for part of the year. Transactions for the remainder of the year would then be examined in the course of the validation work carried out as of the balance sheet date.

9.57 Where these examinations and reviews are assisted by a computer program, it is usually relatively easy to run the program regularly throughout the accounting period being audited. This may increase audit effectiveness and give early warning of problem areas.

The Extent of Validation Procedures

General considerations

9.58 The auditor's objective should be to limit his validation procedures as far as possible. The extent to which they can be limited is a matter for the auditor's judgement in the light of a number of different factors. Factors that are normally relevant include:

(a) The degree of reliance that can be placed on the company's internal control.

(b) The materiality of the items in relation to the accounts taken as a whole.

(c) The nature, number and size of the items that comprise the particular account balance.

(d) The extent to which an account balance can be correlated with other accounts and with other information obtained in the course of the audit.

(e) The extent to which exceptions are identified in the course of applying the validation procedures.

The factors that are influenced by computer processing are considered in the following paragraphs.

Reliance on internal control

9.59 When deciding on the extent of validation procedures for computer-based accounting systems, two general factors related to control will often justify a reduction in the levels that would be applied in non-computer systems. These general factors are:

(a) the increased information that can usually be obtained from the other auditing procedures based on improved account analyses produced by the computer; and

(b) the potential in computer systems for improved internal controls over the updating and maintenance of details of account balances and standing data held on computer files.

321

9.60   Where validation procedures are carried out manually on computer-produced data, the factors in paragraph 9.59 should be taken into account. In particular, where tests are carried out on data generated by programmed procedures, for example valuations of inventory or depreciation calculations, considerable reductions in volume can often be made from the levels of test carried out in non-computer systems. This is because the tests are limited to confirming the proper operation of the relevant programs in a particular run. However, it will be necessary to select an adequate variety of items to be tested.

9.61   Where recalculations are carried out by computer programs, all calculations are checked and there is thus no need to decide on a level of test. When deciding on the number of items to be selected by a computer program for subsequent manual verification tests, such as inventory items for counting, or accounts receivable for confirmation, account should be taken of the factors outlined in paragraph 9.59.

The nature, number and size of items comprising the account balance

9.62   The auditor would normally examine a greater proportion of amounts comprising an account balance when judgement is an important consideration. Cash and trade accounts payable, for example, can usually be properly stated without requiring the exercise of judgement. On the other hand, the evaluation of inventories, when substantial amounts of slow-moving items are present, or when the company has partly completed long-term contracts, often involves a considerable element of judgement. This may be an important consideration in deciding whether to use computer programs, whereby not only can all items be reviewed but also useful account analyses can be obtained.

9.63   Some account balances consist of a large number of items with relatively low individual values; other account balances consist of a small number of items with relatively high individual values. The auditor's reaction to these situations is likely to be as follows:

(a)   When a large number of items with relatively low individual values is present, the auditor is likely in non-computer systems always to attempt to place reliance on the results of functional tests of the basic controls and disciplines, on overall statistics as to collectability (receivables) or usage (inventory) and on the results of direct validation tests of a small sample of the items to satisfy himself as to the account balance, rather than to attempt to validate a significant number of the items that comprise the account balance. However, in computer systems the existence of a large number of balances may make the use of computer programs to review and classify the items particularly attractive.

(b)   When an account balance consists of a small number of items with relatively high individual values, the auditor is likely to subject all or a substantial portion of the individual items comprising the account to direct validation tests. The use of computer programs in this situation is unlikely to be advantageous.

Correlation with other accounts and information

9.64   In determining the extent of his validation procedures on a particular account, the auditor should bear in mind:

(a) Information obtained from tests that are performed on related accounts, for example correlating the interest charge with the related debt, after allowing for any variations in the amount outstanding during the period, or the insurance charge with the changes in the insurance prepayment.

(b) Other information that becomes available to him during the course of his audit. For example, a decline in selling prices may indicate the need for extra care in the auditor's review of net realisable value of specific inventories.

9.65   The auditor should be continually aware of the relevance of the information he can obtain in this connection, either from the exception and other reports produced by the client's system or from reports that he obtains, or can obtain, from his own use of computer programs.

Exceptions

9.66   When exceptions (i.e. errors and deviations from established procedures) are found as a result of validation procedures, the auditor should ascertain the reason for each type of exception and consider its effect, both in terms of its implications with respect to the functioning of the client's system of internal control and as regards the account balance under examination and any related account balances. It is important to bear in mind that even a single, seemingly isolated, exception can be an indication of a serious weakness in a control procedure, particularly if the breakdown is in a programmed procedure, or a possibly significant misstatement of an account balance, or both. On the other hand, care is needed to avoid extending validation procedures because of an exception before considering its potential significance.

9.67   In practice it will be necessary to consider, each time an exception is noted, the following points and to amend the validation procedures where appropriate:

(a) What is the likelihood that the exception is isolated?

323

(b) Would a modest increase in the level of tests give any further indication of whether or not the exception is isolated?

(c) What, if any, alternative validation procedures would serve to verify the item under examination?

(d) Does the existence of the exception invalidate the basis on which a decision has been made to perform early validation procedures or to restrict the level of validation procedures, for example where it indicates a previously unidentified control weakness?

(e) Does the exception indicate a possible material mis-statement in the accounts which cannot be confirmed and quantified by alternative or extended validation procedures and therefore gives rise to the possibility of the need for a qualification in the audit report?

9.68   The auditor's initial response to significant exceptions noted during validation should be to inform the company. It will then be necessary for the significant exceptions to be investigated, so as to determine whether the accounts could be materially inaccurate. As it is the company's responsibility to produce accurate accounts, the client should be encouraged to carry out this investigation. If the client is unable to do so, the auditor may need to undertake the necessary work.

Extended validation procedures

General approach

9.69   It has already been indicated that, where the auditor cannot, or prefers not to, rely on the internal controls for the purpose of limiting his validation procedures, it will be necessary for him to perform what are called herein **extended validation procedures**. This term indicates that the auditor's procedures will be modified in either or both of the following ways:

(a) He may alter the procedures, and either go to a greater depth in the procedures already contemplated by, for example, seeking more complete documentary evidence in support of payments made, or perform additional procedures not otherwise contemplated by, for example, confirming accounts payable with suppliers in cases where this would not otherwise have been done.

(b) He may perform more tests of the nature already contemplated by, for example, verifying a greater proportion of the items making up an account balance or, in verifying completeness of recording, by vouching a greater number of items or for a longer period of time.

9.70   Before changing the procedures, the auditor will need to consider carefully the objectives that he wishes to achieve and the most efficient way of achieving them. It will often be helpful to perform other auditing procedures, such as a review of performance indicators, before reaching a decision.

9.71 In some circumstances, only procedures relating to assets and liability accounts will be extended, while in other circumstances transactions in income and expense accounts should also be subject to extended validation procedures. The auditor's satisfaction in respect of the profit and loss account is based primarily upon his satisfaction in respect of balance sheet accounts, correlation of amounts appearing in the profit and loss account with balances appearing on the balance sheet and the performance of other auditing procedures. Where sufficient audit satisfaction has not been achieved through these means, the auditor should identify in what respects satisfaction is lacking and design procedures specifically for the purpose of overcoming that lack of satisfaction. In doing this, he will usually identify through the use of performance indicators which items appearing in the profit and loss account could be materially mis-stated. His extended validation procedures should be designed with these possible mis-statements in mind.

9.72 Extended validation procedures for income and expense accounts will usually take one of two forms:

(a) If the auditor is concerned with the accuracy of amounts appearing for specific income or expense accounts, such as advertising expense, or wages and salaries, he should prepare an analysis of the account in question, or at least of the material items therein, and examine sufficient of the items so identified to assure himself that there is no material mis-statement.

(b) If the auditor is concerned with a particular type of transaction rather than with particular account balances (as might be the case when fraud could arise because of weaknesses in controls over certain types of payments), he should isolate the areas in the income and expense accounts that might be affected by those control weaknesses. For example, the particular weakness may be such that there are adequate controls over payments supported by receiving reports, but not in the case of other payments, in which case the auditor should perform extended validation procedures only with respect to payments that are not supported by receiving reports. In these cases, he should make a sufficient selection of material transactions of the type with which he is concerned from the accounts that might be mis-stated and examine them to the extent necessary to assure himself that no material mis-statement had occurred.

Because the auditor's extended validation procedures in respect of income and expense accounts are designed to overcome problems arising from specific control weaknesses, it is not appropriate for these procedures to include an examination of a selection of all types of transactions affecting a large number of income and expense accounts (sometimes referred to as vouching tests).

Computer systems

9.73 The extended validation procedures explained above are most likely to be adopted in those situations where the auditor cannot rely on the *related* internal controls. However, tĥe auditor may opt to carry out extended validation procedures where he believes it to be more efficient than testing the related controls, although such controls are satisfactory. In practice, most systems of control are a mixture of strengths and weaknesses in user controls and integrity controls and the testing approach adopted will comprise a mixture of functional tests and extended validation procedures.

9.74 Where the auditor either needs or decides to extend his validation procedures, and his work includes any of the following:

(a) reperformance, e.g. checking the ageing of accounts receivable, the valuation of inventories or the accumulation of sales;

(b) scrutiny, for example of rates of pay, interest rates or credit notes to identify unusual, and thus potentially invalid, items;

(c) account analysis, for example, inventory into age categories since data last counted;

the use of file interrogation programs enables large volumes of data on master files, pipeline files or transaction data files to be read and reviewed quickly thus enabling more efficient or effective validation procedures to be carried out than are possible by solely manual means.

9.75 It must of course be remembered that, not only will appropriate manual tests need to be carried out on the items reported and analyses produced in paragraph 9.74(b) and (c), but manual tests may need to be carried out to ensure that the data on the relevant files is complete and accurate.

9.76 A further development of the role of computer programs in extended validation procedures is the use of resident code written by the auditor to review transactions as they are processed through the system by the company's operational programs.

Resident code

Definition and purpose

9.77 **Resident code,** also known as **resident program** or **embedded code,** consists of program steps written by the auditor and inserted into the company's production programs. The auditor's coding may be included within a company's existing operational program. Alternatively, it may be written as a separate program or programs and be processed, at a predetermined point, as part of the company's programs. The principal purpose of the resident code is to review "live" transactions as they are processed, to select items according to criteria specified in the resident code, and to write the selected items to an output file for examination by the auditor. The use of resident code is illustrated in Figure 77.

9.78 Items are normally selected and output on one of the following bases:

- All items passing or failing particular tests specified in the resident code. In this case, the output file is often referred to as a System Control Audit Review File (SCARF).
- A random sample of all items passing through the resident code. In this case, the output file is often referred to as a Sample Audit Review File (SARF).

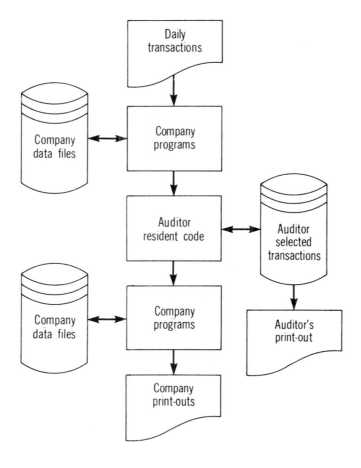

Fɪɢ. 77. Use of computer programs – resident code (9.77)

Uses of resident code

9.79 Within the framework of the audit approach described in this book, the principal reason for which the auditor is likely to use the technique of resident code is to test the validity and/or accuracy of data input to, processed, or output by the company's programs.

9.80 For example, the auditor may design coding to review all purchase invoices submitted to the system and carry out a range of tests thereon. Typical objectives of the resident code might be to:

(a) identify unusually high value invoices;

(b) identify invoices for particular expense accounts;

(c) match purchase invoices against a pipeline file containing details of orders placed and/or goods received;

(d) identify invoices relating to the purchase of fixed assets.

327

9.81   In using resident code in this way, the auditor may, provided the code is secure (see paragraph 9.83), reduce the reliance he would normally place on those user controls and programmed procedures designed to ensure the accuracy and validity of data.

9.82   The use of resident code may also be an appropriate technique for the testing of programmed procedures. For example, the auditor may include resident code to examine despatch notes input, check the calculation of sales invoices, and report high value discounts for agreement to the details on the client's exception report of high value discounts.

Procedures for the use of resident code

9.83   As with the use of file interrogation programs, it will be advisable to establish formal procedures for the use of resident code. The type of procedures that might be adopted are described in Chapter 10. In addition, because of the nature of resident code, it is necessary for the auditor to establish further procedures. These would include:

- The mechanism for turning the auditor's code "on" and "off". A suitable method is the use of run-time parameters which indicate whether the auditor's code is to be activated or not. Internal audit departments often monitor the correct use of the parameters on behalf of the external auditor.

- The treatment of the auditor's output. This may be put into the library to await the next audit visit or the internal audit department may be responsible for printing the output and despatching it to the external auditor.

- The security of the resident code. It has already been stated that resident code may be used where the integrity controls are not relied upon. In this case the auditor therefore needs to adopt alternative procedures to ensure the security of the resident code. A suitable means of doing this would be for the auditor to keep a copy of the relevant programs and periodically carry out a comparison between the retained copies and the operational programs.

Snapshot

9.84   **Snapshot** is a technique which can be considered as an extension of the principle of resident code. It was developed initially as an aid to program development and maintenance. Special coding is incorporated into the application programs when they are written which, when activated, will cause the application programs to record the contents of predetermined parts of main memory at predetermined stages in the processing of a transaction. By this means it is possible to check the actions taken by the program and confirm that the program is operating properly.

9.85   For example, in relation to the accumulation and analysis of the daily sales figure the following information may be reported:

- Prior to accumulation of the invoice – the value of the particular sales invoice and the value held in the accumulator set up to record the daily sales total.

- After accumulation of the invoice – the value held in the accumulator after adding in the sales invoice.

- Prior to analysis of the invoice by nominal ledger code – the values held in the accumulators for sales products.

- After analysis of the invoice – the values held in the accumulators after adding in the sales invoice.

9.86   The special coding is normally activated by an input code entered on the input documents to which it is desired to apply the monitoring procedures.

Interactive enquiry software

9.87   Interactive enquiry programs or languages have been developed for some on-line, real-time and database systems. Where these exist, it will be necessary for the auditor, if he wishes to use and rely on the program in preference to his own computer audit program, to ensure that the program functions correctly and consistently. The auditor will usually obtain this assurance from his tests of the integrity controls.

Summary

9.88   Where records supporting balance sheet and income and expense accounts are maintained by computer, the objectives of the validation procedures and the relationship between the system of internal control and the validation procedures remain the same as in non-computer systems. However, because of the opportunity to make use of file interrogation programs to review the data held on computer files, and the distinctive control features in computer systems, there are often changes in the validation procedures.

9.89   The audit use of computer programs represents the principal change and advance in technique in the audit of computer systems. The two most significant features in using computer programs are that all relevant items are normally reviewed, and that additional information of assistance to the auditor can often be produced. The combination of these two factors usually enables the auditor to carry out more efficient validation procedures than are possible by manual means.

9.90   The distinctive control features in computer systems may also have an effect on validation procedures. The opportunity can arise to place reliance on the controls over procedures which, in non-computer systems, are often less formalised or regular and which the auditor usually finds it more efficient to test in non-computer systems as part of his validation procedures. The increased amount and variety of data maintained on computer files and the power of computer processing result in the provision of more account analyses, often in the form of exception reports, than is usually the case in non-computer systems. In addition, due to the particular features of computer processing, certain validation procedures, which are necessary in non-computer systems, either need to be modified or become unnecessary.

9.91 In carrying out validation procedures in computer systems, there are frequent opportunities to phase many of the procedures into periods prior to the year end.

9.92 When considering the extent of his validation procedures, the auditor can often make considerable reductions from the levels of tests that would be applied in non-computer systems, in particular where validation procedures are carried out on data generated by the computer and the related internal controls can be relied upon. Where a computer audit program is used, all items on the files are reviewed, but the auditor will need to satisfy himself that the data on the files is complete. He must also decide how many items should be selected by the program for subsequent manual tests.

9.93 The use of computer audit programs to review large volumes of processed data may assist extended validation procedures. Alternatively, by means of resident code, the auditor may use a computer audit program to review transactions as they are being processed by the company's programs. The auditor may also be able to make use of interactive enquiry software to review data in advanced systems.

9: Appendix A

Example of a Programme of Validation Procedures

Introduction

1   In this appendix is set out a section of an audit programme relating to the validation of trade accounts receivable. This section of the programme, as is often the case, was designed primarily for use in non-computer systems. However, it was also contemplated that the design would allow amendments to be made so as to alter the tests for use when trade accounts receivable are processed by computer. These alterations can arise either because the auditor is proposing to make use of computer programs or because of the distinctive features of computer systems which cause changes to the manual procedures.

2   As a guide to the identification of those validation procedures which may require to be amended as a result of computer processing, the section of the programme which follows indicates the probable changes that would be required for the two reasons indicated above. These changes are referenced to the paragraphs in the chapter where the change is discussed.

3   Although this appendix deals only with trade accounts receivable, the same principles would apply to validation procedures for other assets and liabilities where the records are processed by computer.

4   In practice the scope of the validation procedures would be greater than the example used in this book in order to recognise that certain validation work might be carried out before the year end and to include the appropriate tests to be carried out in the intervening period and at the year end in these circumstances. Since the principles of early validation are not affected by computer processing, the section of the programme that follows draws no distinction between early and year end validation work.

5   The validation procedures are set out on the left and comments as to the possible changes in computer systems are described on the right, divided between changes arising because of the use of computer programs, and changes arising, even where manual techniques are used, because of the characteristics of computer systems.

Validation Procedures

Performance indicators

1　Identify and review the relevant performance indicators and obtain explanations for any unusual fluctuations or ratios. Note the relevant information, explanations and comments and consider whether they indicate a need to modify validation procedures.

Cut-off

2　(a)　Note on a working paper the client's procedures for ensuring that sales around the validation date are accounted for and matched with cost of sales in the correct period.

　　(b)　Set out below the nature and levels of validation procedures to be applied.

Notes

　　(1)　In most cases the cut-off steps can be carried out in the inventories section of the programme.

　　(2)　Cut-off validation procedures will often include an examination of:

　　　　(i)　records of goods despatched and services performed and related sales invoices for periods before and after the year end;

　　　　(ii)　records of returns and claims from customers and related credit notes for periods before and after the year end;

　　　　(iii)　records of unmatched documents referred to in (i) and (ii) as at the year end;

　　　　(iv)　files of documents referred to in (i) and (ii) unmatched at the date of the visit;

　　　　(v)　sales invoices and credit notes for the period subsequent to the year end to determine whether any significant invoices or credit notes that are applicable to the period under review have been appropriately reflected in the accounts.

Possible amendments in computer systems (numbers in brackets represent the paragraph number in Chapter 9 where the change is discussed)	
Use of computer programs	*Changes to manual tests*
Production of additional analyses (e.g. balances compared with credit limits) as an aid to manual review. (30, 37)	Enquire into and use any improved account analyses as an aid to manual review. (46) Test that any information relied on is complete and accurate. (47)
——	——
——	Consider reducing level. (59)
——	More likely in computer systems with integrated processing. (50)
Investigation, identification and reporting of transactions dated after cut-off date. (35(d))	Tests based on batches of computer input. (50)

3   Determine from the above procedures:

(a) whether receivables for goods despatched and services performed before the year end are properly recorded and that sales are not recorded in the period under review for goods despatched and services performed subsequent to the year end;

(b) whether adjustments to receivables for returns and claims from customers arising before the year end are properly recorded as at the year end.

Total balance of trade accounts receivable

4 (a) Obtain an aged listing of trade accounts receivable by individual customer and compare the total with the balance reflected in the control account(s) in the general ledger.

(b) Reperform (on a test basis where appropriate) the addition of the amounts on the listing, including the analysis columns.

5   Vouch any significant adjustments made by the client in reconciling detailed accounts receivable records with the control account(s) in the general ledger.

Individual balances

6   Compare the balances on individual accounts shown on the listing (step 4) with the detailed accounts receivable records, and vice versa, including a number of accounts in consecutive order irrespective of amount. During this comparison:

(a) determine whether balances have been correctly analysed on the aged listing;

(b) identify and enquire into balances that do not comprise specific items;

(c) enquire into any unusual items (e.g. transfers between accounts).

Possible amendments in computer systems	
Use of computer programs	*Changes to manual tests*
——	——
——	——
——	——
Reperform accumulation and ageing of all amounts including any analysis. (28, 35(a), 37)	Consider reducing level. (59)
——	Less difficulty in investigating any items in reconciliation. (51)
Not necessary. (49)	Not necessary. (49)
Not necessary. (49)	Consider reducing level. (59)
Reperform sub-totalling of all balances. (35(c)) Report disagreements. Identification and reporting of defined items for manual investigation. (37)	Rely on controls and carry out functional tests on matching procedures. (45) Enquire into and use any improved account analyses as an aid to manual review. (46) Test that any information relied on is complete and accurate. (47) Alternatively, rely on controls and carry out functional tests on adjustments. (45)

Validation Procedures

Significant credit balances

7 Enquire into credit balances of significant amount identified on the listing and consider whether they indicate the possible existence of unrecorded sales.

Confirmation

8 (a) Select customers' accounts for confirmation and determine the method of confirmation (positive, negative or combination thereof); obtain statements and check with the detailed accounts receivable records or the list of balances supporting the selected accounts; and send confirmation requests.

   (b) Where replies to positive requests are not received within a reasonable period of time, send second requests.

9 (a) Summarise confirmation coverage and investigate any discrepancies or queries reported by customers.

   (b) Determine that any adjustments required are properly made.

   (c) Consider whether discrepancies or queries indicate weaknesses or irregularities which would cause other audit procedures to be revised.

Alternative to confirmation

10 Where confirmation is not carried out, or where it is not possible to confirm a selected account:

   (a) compare any subsequent remittances credited to these accounts to cash receipts records (and remittance advices if available);

   (b) for items not paid since the year end, examine documentation, such as despatch documents, copies of sales invoices and relevant correspondence, supporting account balances or unpaid items.

Possible amendments in computer systems	
Use of computer programs	*Changes to manual tests*
Identification and reporting of defined items for manual investigation. (35(b))	Enquire into and use any improved account analyses as an aid to manual review. (46) Test that any information relied on is complete and accurate. (47)
Stratification and selection of accounts for confirmation and printing of requests. (35(b), 37)	Consider reducing level. (59)
Matching of replies and production of details regarding outstandings and printing of second requests. (37)	——
Matching of replies and reporting of mismatches. (37)	——
——	——
——	——
——	Consider reducing level. (59)
——	

Doubtful accounts

11 Determine the adequacy of the provision for doubtful accounts at the year end, giving consideration in particular to:

(a) all large balances and particularly old balances (refer to the aged listing – step 6(a));

(b) cash collections subsequent to the year end as shown by the cash receipts records, paying particular attention to partial or round sum receipts;

(c) accounts that appear to be disputed (step 9);

(d) unusual variations in balances (step 1);

(e) any evidence of customers' inability to comply with credit terms, having regard to relevant economic conditions;

(f) security.

Other provisions

12 Consider whether other provisions should be made (e.g. for trade allowances, rebates and claims).

Debts written off

13 Select significant trade accounts receivable that have been written off during the year and review the propriety of and the authority for write-off; examine documentation supporting and authorising the write-off.

Possible amendments in computer systems	
Use of computer programs	*Changes to manual tests*
Production of additional analyses as an aid to manual review. (30, 37) Examples are: (a) balances compared with total value of annual sales; (b) balances on accounts marked as closed; (c) balances for accounts where cash is required when orders are placed; (d) balances on accounts on which dishonoured cheques have been received.	Enquire into and use any improved account analyses as an aid to manual review. (46) Test that any information relied on is complete and accurate. (47)
———	———
Investigation and reporting of items indicated as written off. (29)	Rely on controls and carry out functional tests on write-offs. (45)

9: Appendix B

Examples of the Use of Computer Audit Programs

Introduction

1   In this appendix are given two examples of the use of computer audit programs. The first example concerns an accounts receivable ledger and illustrates the wide variety of information that can be obtained from a file holding relatively little data. The second example relates to an inventories ledger and illustrates the substantial number of objectives that can be included where a wide variety of data is held on the files.

Example I — ACCOUNTS RECEIVABLE LEDGER

Description

2   The items held on the accounts receivable file consist of outstanding invoices, credit notes, unmatched cash and adjustments. Details of cash received, credit notes and credit adjustments are matched against the appropriate invoices and debit adjustments. Cash receipts which have been matched are not written to the file but instead an indicator is set to identify items which have been fully paid and these are then deleted from the file at the end of the month. Cash which cannot be matched and payments on account are written to the file. Credit notes and adjustments are input and held separately on the file until they are deleted as part of the matching of cash receipts. There are approximately 3,000 accounts on the file with a total value of about £2 million.

3   There are two files used in the accounts receivable application, the customer details file and the accounts receivable file. The customer details file holds the names and addresses of customers and is not accessed by the program and has thus not been included in this illustration. The accounts receivable file holds the following records for each customer's account:

(a) Any number of transaction records which hold details of individual transactions.
(b) A trailer record which holds, inter alia, the balance outstanding for that account.

341

File layout

4 The details of the fields in the transaction and trailer records are set out below:

(a) *Transaction record*

FIELD	CHARACTERS	COMMENTS
Account number	5	
Date: Year	2	
Month	2	
Day	2	
Record type indicator	1	Indicators are: 1 = invoice 2 = cash (unmatched) 3 = cash (payment on account) 4 = credit note 5 = adjustment
Transaction value	8	In the case of invoices this field contains the invoice value net of returnable packaging and VAT thereon.
Packing value	8	This field applies to invoices only and contains the value of returnable packaging plus VAT included on the invoice. For transactions other than invoices the field contains zeros.
Transaction reference number	7	
Paid code	1	1 = unpaid 2 = fully paid 3 = partly paid If the transaction is not an invoice or a debit adjustment this field will not be required and accordingly is set to zero.
Status code	1	The field contains a space if the transaction still forms part of the balance outstanding. If the field contains "D" this indicates that the transaction has been matched as part of the cash matching process and that it will be deleted from the file at the end of the month.

37

(b) *Trailer record*

FIELD	CHARACTERS	COMMENTS
Account number	5	
Record type indicator	1	The value of this field is equal to 9 to identify the trailer record.
Fields not used by the program	11	
Date of last payment	6	Format YYMMDD
Balance outstanding	8	££££££ pp
Status code	1	The field is set to equal "D" if the balance outstanding is equal to zero and there has been no movement on the account for two months. This will cause the account to be deleted from the file at the end of the month. In all other cases the field is left blank.
Spare	5	
	37	

Objectives of running the program

5 The objectives included in the program are as follows:

File totals

(a) Check the additions of outstanding balances and establish totals of both debit and credit balances.

(b) Check that the outstanding balance for each customer agrees with the total of the individual outstanding transactions for that customer. Establish a total of any differences.

Cut-off

(c) Establish totals and provide samples of any transactions dated after the year end date to assist in cut-off audit tests.

Provision for bad and doubtful debts

(d) By reference to the record type indicator field, age by record type each of the outstanding transactions into the following categories as an aid in assessing the provision for bad and doubtful debts:

(i) current;

(ii) 1 month old;

(iii) 2 months old;

(iv) 3 months old;

(v) 4–6 months old;

(vi) 7–12 months old;

(vii) over 12 months old.

(NOTE: The company program analyses all items over 3 months old into one category).

(e) As a further aid in assessing the bad and doubtful debts provision, and in addition to the analysis of transactions in (d) above, establish a total and print samples of accounts where, in addition to having invoices outstanding for more than three months, no payments have been received within the last three months.

(f) By reference to the paid code field establish a total and provide samples of invoices which are partly paid to ascertain whether the balance is in dispute and constitutes a doubtful debt. (NOTE: The company can only obtain this information manually at present.)

Provision for credits to customers

(g) Establish a total and provide a sample of the value of returnable packing in the hands of customers as an aid to assess the provision for returnable packing.

Achievement of objectives

6　No particular problems should be encountered in achieving the objectives set out in paragraph 5. Depending on the particular package used it may be necessary to use own coding for the objective in 5(b). This coding would be used to accumulate and store the transaction values for each account for comparison with the balance outstanding field in the trailer record.

Example II — INVENTORIES LEDGER

Description

7　The inventory master file contains the finished goods inventory records. Inventory lines are divided into two types defined as "special lines" and "standard lines". "Special lines" are fast-moving lines which are prone to quick obsolescence, predominantly due to deterioration of the items concerned. "Special lines" held for more than twelve weeks are provided against by the company. "Standard lines" do not deteriorate so quickly. "Standard lines" are provided against by the company on a sliding scale.

8　The file is updated by receipts from suppliers, issues in respect of sales to customers, and adjustments which arise mainly through inventory being scrapped or through the correction of differences discovered during physical stock counts. Inventory is issued on a FIFO basis. There are approximately 6,000 different inventory lines on the file with a value of about £55 million.

9　Inventory is subject to a system of perpetual inventory counting which is designed to ensure that all "standard lines" are counted at least twice a year and "special lines" four times a year. All lines should be counted during the last three months of the financial year.

10 The company's system for pricing is complex. A separate file holds details of cost and selling price histories, and is used by the company to calculate average costs for each stock line monthly. The inventory master file, which is accessed by the program described in this illustration, holds the latest average cost price and the average cost price at the beginning of the financial year. It also holds the latest and opening selling prices. The price histories file is not accessed in this illustration.

11 The company maintains its future sales forecasts on the file in the form of estimated sales for the next twenty-four weeks. These are computed by another application and updated quarterly. Experience has shown the forecasts to be fairly reliable, the average error being only $\pm$ 3.7%. New lines introduced during the quarter will not have a forecast and in these cases the forecast fields are blank.

12 Each inventory line is sold in up to nine variations. Separate forecasts and a separate record of inventory are maintained for each variation.

File layout

13 The details of the fields on the file records are set out below:

(a) *Forecast record*

FIELD	CHARACTERS	COMMENTS
Record type	2	Always 01
Line prefix	4	1001–1999 "special lines" 2000–8000 "standard lines"
Sub-record counter	2	Value may be 0–9 and indicates: (i) number of forecast sub-records following (ii) number of inventory records

Forecast sub-record (can occur up to 9 times indicated by the value of the sub-record counter)

Line suffix – 3 characters

24 week forecast – 3 characters

Future quantity sales forecast in thousands

(maximum)	54	
(maximum)	62	

(b) *Inventory record*

FIELD	CHARACTERS	COMMENTS
(NOTE: Certain fields not used by the program have been omitted)		There may be 0–9 inventory records. There will be 1 inventory record for each forecast sub-record (see above)
Record type	2	Always 02
Line number	7	Line prefix + suffix
Line description	15	
Stock location	6	
Supplier code	6	For generating purchase orders from suppliers' master file
Cost price	6	££££ pp–current average unit cost
Opening cost price	6	££££ pp–average unit cost at commencement of financial year
Selling price	6	££££ pp–current unit price
Opening selling price	6	££££ pp–unit price at commencement of financial year
Inventory quantity	6	Current balance
Opening inventory quantity	6	At commencement of financial year
Maximum stock level	6	
Re-order quantity	6	
Re-order level	6	
Purchases	78	13 fields of 6 characters each recording purchases of stock for each period in the financial year – blank until used
Sales	78	13 fields of 6 characters each recording sales of stock for each period in the financial year – blank until used

FIELD	CHARACTERS	COMMENTS
Weeks since last issue	2	Number of weeks since a sale was last made
Date of last stock count	6	Format DDMMYY. Blank until first count made
Last stock count difference	4	Blank until first count made
Date of next stock count	6	Format DDMMYY
Date of first receipt	6	Format DDMMYY. Date line first stocked – blank until first receipt accepted
Date of last purchase	6	Format DDMMYY
	276	

(c) *File control record*

FIELD	CHARACTERS	COMMENTS
Record type	2	Always 99
Number of inventory records ("special lines")	6	
Number of inventory records ("standard lines")	6	
File total of inventory	10	££££££££ pp – at latest cost value
	24	

Objectives of running the program

14 The objectives included in the program are as follows:

File totals

(a) Check the evaluation of inventory and establish totals of both debit and credit balances.

(b) By reference to the line prefix, analyse total inventory between "special lines" and "standard lines", providing debit and credit totals for each category.

(c) Check the totals established in (a) and (b) above with the file totals on the file control record.

(d) Provide samples of negative stock balances for investigation.

347

Stock pricing

(e) As an aid to the assessment of the reasonableness of current average cost prices, carry out the following comparisons of fields on the file:

> cost price: opening cost price;
> cost price: selling price;
> opening cost price: opening selling price.

Provide totals and print samples of items meeting the following conditions:

(i) current margins significantly more or less than the company's normal margins;
(ii) current margins significantly different to opening margins;
(iii) cost prices in excess of selling prices;
(iv) cost prices showing an abnormally large or small rise during the year;
(v) cost prices which have decreased or not changed during the year.

The comparisons in (i), (ii) and (iv) above will be controlled by parameter cards, the auditor having previously determined what might be regarded as significant or abnormal percentage changes.

Obsolete and slow moving stock

(f) In respect of "special lines", compare the inventory quantity field with the purchases for the thirteen financial periods. Evaluate and analyse inventory over the following categories:

(i) 0–4 weeks old;
(ii) 5–8 weeks old;
(iii) 9–12 weeks old;
(iv) 13–16 weeks old; } The company makes a 100%
(v) over 16 weeks old. } provision against these amounts.

Print samples from categories (iii)–(v).

(g) In respect of "special lines", divide the 24 week forecast field by two to obtain the estimated usage for the next twelve weeks. In respect of items in categories (f)(i)–(iii) above, compare the inventory quantities with the twelve weeks estimated usage and accumulate an evaluated total and print a sample of inventory which it is forecast will not be used within the twelve week period.

(h) In respect of "special lines" introduced in the last quarter and therefore without a valid forecast on file (objective (g) cannot therefore be achieved), compute an average four weeks usage by reference to the date of first receipt field and the issues fields for the three most recent periods. Compare the computed average with the inventory quantity and accumulate an evaluated total of inventory which it is forecast will not be used within twelve weeks. Print a sample of items accumulated.

(i) In respect of "standard lines" other than those introduced in the last quarter, by reference to the weeks since last issued field, analyse the evaluated inventory into the following categories:

    (i) no issues 0–8 weeks;
    (ii) no issues 9–16 weeks;
    (iii) no issues 17–24 weeks;
    (iv) no issues 25–40 weeks;
    (v) no issues 41–56 weeks; } The company makes a 100%
    (vi) no issues over 56 weeks. } provision against these items.

(j) In respect of "standard lines", included in (i)(i)–(iv) above, compare the inventory quantity with the 24 week forecast and analyse inventory into the following categories of estimated future usage of inventory quantities:

    (i) 0–12 weeks;
    (ii) 13–24 weeks;
    (iii) 25–48 weeks;
    (iv) 49–72 weeks; } The company makes the   25%
    (v) 73–96 weeks; } following provisions   50%
    (vi) over 96 weeks. } against these items   100%

Print samples from categories (iii)–(vi).

(k) In respect of "standard lines" covered in (j)(i)–(v) and new "standard lines" (introduced in the last quarter; these have been omitted from (i) and (j)), compute an average four weeks' usage by reference to the issues fields for the thirteen accounting periods and, for stock lines held for less than one year, the date of first receipt field. Compare the computed average with the inventory quantity and analyse evaluated inventory into the following categories of estimated future usage of inventory quantities:

    (i) 0–12 weeks;
    (ii) 13–24 weeks;
    (iii) 25–48 weeks;
    (iv) 49–72 weeks;
    (v) 73–96 weeks;
    (vi) over 96 weeks.

Print samples from categories (iii)–(vi).

(l) Accumulate a total and print a sample of "standard lines" in categories (i)(i)–(iii) and (j)(i)–(iii) where the inventory quantity is in excess of the maximum stock level. Evaluate and accumulate the excess.

Perpetual inventory

(m) By reference to the date of last stock count field establish the total number and value of stock lines which have not been subjected to a physical count in the last quarter. Analyse the totals into the following categories (include items in more than one category if appropriate):

349

(i) new stock lines in the last quarter (identified by reference to the date of first receipt field);

(ii) high value inventory (identified by reference to a parameter specifying the value);

(iii) high value unit cost (identified by reference to a parameter specifying the unit cost value);

(iv) "special lines" (identified by the line prefix);

(v) "standard lines".

In each category the samples printed will be in descending value of inventory held. This will enable the more significant items to be identified for counting.

(n) By reference to the last stock count difference field, establish a total of high value stock count differences. A sample will be printed of high value differences for manual verification that the year end balance was correct.

Management information

15 As well as achieving objectives of direct relevance to the audit it is also possible to achieve certain objectives which are largely operational in nature. Operational objectives enable useful points to be brought to the attention of management. Objectives may be termed operational for two reasons. First, the auditor is unlikely ever to be interested in the information for the purposes of the audit. Secondly, although the information may sometimes be relevant, the auditor is not directly interested in it because other objectives in the program stand in place of those objectives.

16 The operational objectives included in the program were to:

(a) check that all "dead" stock lines were properly cleared from the file by accumulating a total of lines with nil inventory quantity and a date of last purchase more than one year ago;

(b) check that the relationship between maximum stock level, re-order quantity, and re-order level is reasonable by ensuring that re-order quantity plus re-order level does not exceed the maximum stock level;

(c) check the validity of maximum stock levels by comparing the maximum stock level field with the 24 week forecast field. Accumulate a total of items where the maximum stock level is more than twice the 24 week forecast (maximum stock levels are calculated and input manually; they should not exceed twice the 24 week forecast);

(d) provide totals and print samples of items showing an abnormally large or small selling price rise in the year.

17 Unlike the previous example, it is likely that the achievement of the objectives set out above will require a substantial amount of own coding to be incorporated into the basic package. Own coding may be required, inter alia, for the following purposes:

(a) to identify the number of forecast sub-records for each forecast record, based on the value of the sub-record counter;

(b) to match each forecast sub-record with its related inventory record and extract the relevant information from each;

(c) to expand the 24 week forecast field to a six character field;

(d) to manipulate date fields into the format YYMMDD.

10

The Use of Computer Programs

Sources of Programs

Introduction

10.01　There are various sources of programs available to the auditor. He can write a program himself or specify the requirements of a program to be written by someone else. Both these methods result in a "one off" program which can normally only be used on a particular file at one installation. This may be satisfactory for the internal auditor but may prove inefficient for the external auditor who usually wishes to run programs on several applications at different installations. The external auditor is more likely to try and utilise some form of package program. These various sources of programs are discussed in the following paragraphs.

Writing programs

10.02　The design and writing of programs by the auditor is not usually a very practicable approach since the difficulties involved are considerable. In the first place, the necessary technical skill to write programs represents an additional cost. Secondly, even when this training has been achieved, time is required for actually writing the program, and this can be quite expensive even for simple programs. The programs require careful testing before use, and this increases their cost further. Finally, difficulties may well arise because the auditor's program is allocated a relatively low priority in the installation's work schedules for computer time. Accordingly, as far as possible, auditors usually avoid writing "one off" programs.

Specifying programs

10.03　As an alternative to writing a program, the auditor may specify the program and make arrangements for it to be written either by the company or some suitable other source, such as a software house. This has the advantage that the auditor does not need to acquire the technical skill to write the program. It is sometimes argued that there is loss of independence if the auditor obtains help from the company in writing the program. This is not regarded as a problem; it is considered somewhat analogous to requesting schedules from the company in non-computer systems. However, it will be necessary to test the program logic before use, or test the results achieved, in order to be satisfied that the program is properly based on the auditor's specification.

Package programs

10.04   The logic required in most computer programs used by auditors is relatively simple. It is also usually similar from application to application. The auditor wants much the same from an inventories file as an accounts receivable file – accumulate field A; compare field B with field C. Field A may be the stock balance in one case and the customer's balance in the other. Comparing field B with field C may be identifying slow moving inventory items in one case and overdue accounts receivable in the other. Although the difference is very real to the auditor, within the program the logic is similar.

10.05   It is from the two factors – the problems of using the "one off" program, and the broad similarity of logic required as between one program and another – that the idea of the **computer audit package** developed. These packages, which have been developed by the major accounting firms, by software houses, by computer manufacturers and by companies' internal audit or systems departments during the last decade, are general purpose computer programs which can carry out similar tasks on a variety of files at different installations. It is necessary for the auditor to define the configuration on which the program is to be run and the files to be used. In addition, the auditor is left to choose in each case the use he will make of the logic in the program. The auditor's definitions and requirements are input and convert the computer audit package into a specific program to do what the auditor wants in relation to the files concerned.

10.06   An effective computer audit package helps overcome most of the practical problems faced by the auditor in using computer programs. Thus the use of a package enables the auditor to avoid much of the work entailed in writing and testing a program; it also simplifies the work of specification required. The cost to the auditor of using a package is substantially less than that of developing and using a "one off" program. As a result there has been an increasing interest in, and use of, computer audit packages.

Types of programs

10.07   There are several types of programs and packages available to auditors to help them in different areas of their work. The more widely used examples have been mentioned in other parts of this book and may be summarised as follows:

• File interrogation programs – to examine master files, pipeline files, or transaction data files.

• Comparison programs – to compare versions of a program in either source or executable form.

• Flowcharting programs – to chart the logic of source programs and produce verb and data name listings.

• Interactive enquiry programs – to interrogate files in on-line systems.

• Log analysis programs – to analyse a computer's system log.

- Resident code – to examine live transactions as they are processed.
- Test data generators – to create files of test data.

10.08   The file interrogation program, as well as being the first type of computer audit program commonly used by auditors, is still the most widespread. A wide variety of package file interrogation programs have been developed over the years. The different approaches to the use of file interrogation packages and the more important facilities, based on our practical experience, that should be available in them are described in the following paragraphs.

The Computer Audit File Interrogation Package

10.09   Although developed to cope with similar problems, the computer audit file interrogation packages are all different. However, in many cases these differences are more apparent than real. In essence, the packages have been developed in one or the other of two basic ways, which may be termed the "fixed" and "flexible" approaches. Some packages combine the characteristics of both approaches.

The "fixed" approach

10.10   Computer audit packages developed on the "fixed" approach have, as their main design feature, reliability when used by auditors with relatively little technical skill. The capabilities of these packages thus tend to be "fixed" so that the auditor is required to do the minimum in order to activate them. The tasks that they will undertake are often written into the program and cannot be changed. The auditor can do no more than specify which particular tasks are to be included. The computer configurations and file organisations on which they will operate are also often pre-determined and fixed in the program. This may restrict the use of the program to a particular machine or manufacturer. Sometimes different versions of the program are available for different machines or manufacturers. In some cases the programs have their own built-in operating system. This means the program does not require to be linked into the company's operating system. Some "fixed" programs re-format the data on the files being examined to fit pre-determined file descriptions fixed in the program.

10.11   To activate the program the auditor completes a questionnaire which specifies the processing to be carried out. The completed questionnaire is input to the computer and a program is produced to carry out the required tasks. "Fixed" programs may either produce an object program to carry out the tasks or a source program in a high level language, such as COBOL or RPG II. The source program must then be compiled before it can be executed. These latter programs are called program generators, pre-compilers or preprocessors. They introduce some flexibility into the "fixed" program because the source coding can be amended or additional coding inserted without too much difficulty to perform additional tasks.

355

10.12 "Fixed" programs are particularly attractive where the range of configurations, and thus file organisations, is limited. They can be implemented relatively easily but may be limited in the variety of processing they can carry out. This limitation may be offset or eliminated by the provision of a facility for the auditor to include his own coding to carry out additional work. The implementation of a "fixed" approach package is outlined in Figure 78. Completed examples of the type of questionnaire used with a "fixed" package are set out in appendix A.

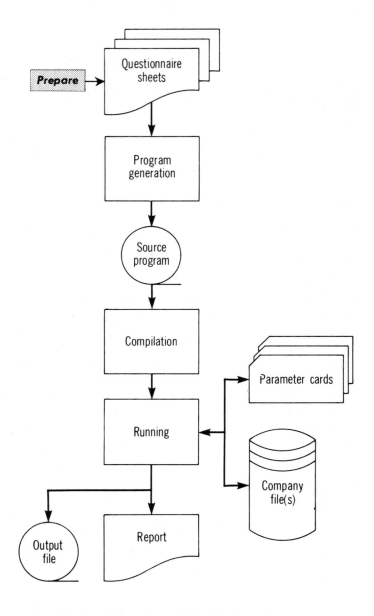

Fig. 78. Implementation of "fixed" approach computer audit package (10.12)

The "flexible" approach

10.13   Computer audit packages developed on the "flexible" approach have, as their main design feature, the flexibility that they can be used in any situation, with little limit on the tasks they can undertake. The implementation of a "flexible" approach package is outlined in Figure 79. They tend to be in the form of skeleton programs, the contents of which must be completed by the auditor for each different application. Such programs normally consist of three parts:

(a) The first part describes the computer environment in which the program is to be run and the files to be accessed. The environment varies considerably from application to application. Therefore, whilst it is possible to include on the coding sheets the standard COBOL clause headings required to be completed, the auditor must make the majority of the detailed entries required to fit the particular installation he is concerned with.

(b) The second part describes the processing required to achieve the audit objectives. Standard coding is normally provided for the more common tasks and the auditor adds to this as necessary,

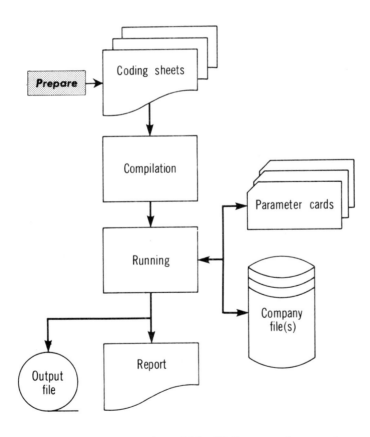

FIG. 79. Implementation of "flexible" approach computer audit package (10.13)

building up a collection of what may be termed modules. The auditor can enter his own coding in this section when the standard coding cannot achieve the required objectives. The extent of "own coding" will depend upon the complexity of the objectives.

(c) The third part contains coding to undertake those tasks which are common to every program, for example reading and printing routines. This coding often requires no amendment by the auditor.

10.14 Programs of this nature can be used relatively easily with a wide variety of configurations and files but may require considerable technical skill to provide the logic to achieve the audit objectives. They are particularly attractive where the range of clients' configurations and file organisations is wide. Completed examples of the type of skeleton program coding sheet used with a "flexible" package are set out in appendix B.

The facilities to be available in a computer audit package

10.15 It is not a purpose of this book to review and analyse the various computer audit packages that are in existence. However, it may be helpful to indicate the more important facilities, based on practical experience, that should be available. The facilities can conveniently be considered separately for the configuration, the files which the program needs and the tasks the program can undertake.

Configuration

10.16 It is helpful if the package can be used on the various different makes of computer that are present in significant numbers in the United Kingdom. This requirement may be less important in other countries. The main problem is to provide for the different methods of data storage and handling that are encountered in practice. This can be a limitation for "fixed" approach packages, although it is reasonably simple to provide separate versions for the main configurations and operating systems.

10.17 Most of the packages are either written in COBOL or generate a COBOL source program. This is a limitation, since it is increasingly important to be able to use the package on the smaller computers. These computers are often only programmed in RPG II. It is therefore necessary to copy the files and examine them on a computer that can process in COBOL, or to produce an RPG II version of the package.

Files

10.18 As regards file structures, most packages can deal satisfactorily with tape and disc fixed length records, but for some packages variable length records and single bit fields can be a problem. Database structures can also cause difficulties. Remedies in use include re-formatting the files using the company's software, writing linkage programs to access the information on the database or running against a back-up copy of the file, where data is held in conventional form. It is also important that the program is capable of accessing data held on more than one file, such as, for example, when stock prices are held on one file and quantities on another file.

Tasks

10.19 It is helpful to assess the logical power of a package in terms of the audit tasks that the auditor may wish to carry out. These are set out in detail for the various accounts items in Chapter 9 but may be considered here in general terms. The variety is, in fact, quite limited. The auditor requires totals and samples of data held on the file, or derived from the data held on the file. He also requires them to be printed out in a convenient manner in order to interpret them. These matters are discussed in the following paragraphs.

Totals

10.20 The totals required may be:

(a) a *single* total of all items on the file, for example all accounts receivable balances;

(b) an *analysis* of all items on the file, for example accounts receivable transactions aged into different categories;

(c) totals of *specified* items on the file, for example accounts receivable whose balances are in excess of their credit limits.

The totals required will usually be of the main value field, for example fixed asset net book value. It may, however, also be of a subsidiary field, for example depreciation for the year, or of a calculated field, for example the notional depreciation charge for the year in respect of fully depreciated assets.

10.21 The requirement for a single total of all items on the file can be satisfied by a simple accumulation facility in the program. The number of simple accumulations will be conditioned by the number of totals of this nature that are required, which is usually relatively few. It will also be necessary to be able to obtain sub-totals based on a reference number on each record, for example departmental totals.

10.22 In order to obtain analyses of all items and totals of specified items, there will need to be a facility to compare. A facility to carry out both single and multiple comparisons is normally required. Single comparisons are required to compare:

(a) any two fields on a record, for example accounts receivable balances in excess of credit limits, or inventory balances where maximum stock level exceeds usage for the year;

(b) any field on the record, with a constant specified by the auditor, for example inventory balances where the stock count date is more than one year old or deposit account balances where the interest rate exceeds a specified percentage;

(c) any field on the record, with a field calculated by the program, for example fixed assets depreciation charge on file with a calculated depreciation charge;

(d) a field calculated by the program, with a constant, for example inventory valued greater than £10,000 where the value has to be calculated from quantity and price.

Multiple comparisons are required to compare any field with more than one other field or constant, for example accounts receivable balances of a certain category *and* size *and* over maximum stock level.

10.23 When one field is compared with another field, it may be desirable to weight one or both fields. This is useful where only large differences are required, for example accounts receivable balances in excess of 150% of their credit limit, or to locate differences between items of data which should have a direct relationship, for example inventory items where the selling price is not equal to 150% of cost price. It will be necessary to be able to compare fields on separate files, for example accounts receivable balances on one file and credit limits on another file.

10.24 From the above it can be seen that the ability to carry out comparisons and accumulate the results into totals is the auditor's principal requirement. To this may be added the need to calculate, both before and after the comparison. Thus, in relation to accounts receivable, it might be necessary for the program to calculate the balance outstanding from the transactions on the record before comparing the calculated balance with the credit limit. Likewise, having carried out the comparison, it might be desirable to calculate the amount, if any, by which the balance exceeded the credit limit. The number of comparisons required will depend on the variety of data on the file and the ingenuity and requirements of the auditor. The number may extend from one to a hundred or more. In "fixed" programs the number of comparisons may be restricted to the maximum permitted by the program. In "flexible" programs as many comparisons as are required can usually be inserted when the program is prepared. Normally the major restriction is the size of the core in which the program must be stored.

10.25 It is likely that the auditor will wish to accumulate all items, satisfying or failing a comparison, select a sample therefrom and print the totals and samples. Unless only a few comparisons are used, this requirement can add materially to the size of the program. Accordingly it is convenient to include the accumulate, sample and print logic once and locate it in a fixed part of the program. It can then be "triggered" whenever necessary from other parts of the program. Experience shows that all the auditor's requirements can be reduced to a simple logic unit which contains the following steps:

(a) Pre-test calculation (as required).

(b) Test for comparison.

(c) Post-test calculation (as required).

(d) Trigger for accumulation, sampling and printing as appropriate.

This logic unit can then be repeated as many times as required.

Samples

10.26   Several packages contain statistical sampling routines. This is advantageous when selecting items for subsequent audit tests, for example inventory balances for physical count, or accounts receivable balances for confirmation routines. In other cases, however, the auditor merely requires a sample as evidence of the items making up a total. In these cases it is useful to have the facility to:

(a) start sampling from a random point on the file;

(b) stratify the sample into any number of levels by value, for example sample debit balances over £2,000 and credit balances over £100;

(c) specify an interval between each item selected, for example every 100th record;

(d) control the maximum number of items to be printed out, for example the first ten in the category.

It is also useful if the whole sample can be written to an output file for sorting and printing or further processing if required. In this way all items in defined categories can be produced if necessary for investigation by the company.

Print-out

10.27   The form of print-out and the presentation of information is of particular significance since the print-out will be used by the auditor and may form an important part of the audit working papers. It is helpful if the totals are printed both as to value and number of records. The percentages that the totals of analyses and specified items represent of the total population can be useful but this facility is less usually provided. It is important that the total value of samples printed out and the percentage that the sample represents of the total in the category are calculated and printed out.   361

10.28   Relevant details of individual items should be printed, together with a reasonably full reason for their selection. Cryptic messages that need decoding are not easily dealt with by the auditor. Individual items should be sorted before printing so that all in the same category are printed together. An example of a suitable print-out of individual items is illustrated in appendix C.

10.29   It is helpful if the auditor can select the order in which totals are printed and specify descriptive details. In this way totals can be grouped under meaningful audit objective headings. An example of part of a print-out provided in this manner is also illustrated in appendix C.

Procedures for Using Computer Programs

Introduction

10.30   It is advisable to establish formal procedures for the use of computer programs. This will help ensure that programs are used only where the costs can be justified, that the right objectives are included and that the costs are budgeted and approved and then controlled against the budget. Examples of suitable procedures are outlined in the following paragraphs. The procedures are set out separately for the first year of use and for second and subsequent years.

First year

Identification

10.31   The need for, or desirability of, using a computer program should be identified during the evaluation of internal control or during pre-validation audit planning. It is helpful to make this identification as early as possible in order that the program can be prepared in sufficient time to assist fully in subsequent audit work.

Specification

10.32   When the need for, or the desirability of, using a computer program has been identified, a specification should be prepared. This specification sets out the objectives of the program, the logic by which they are to be achieved and a detailed budget. The specification, when approved, for example by the partner responsible for computer auditing, can then be the authority to prepare and execute the program on the lines specified. Where the program is to carry out complex processing, and the cost of preparing the specification is likely to be high, it will normally be appropriate to obtain approval to prepare a specification.

Preparation

10.33　The program is next prepared. This work will involve the completion of questionnaires, in the case of program generators, or coding sheets in the case of COBOL-based programs, and the preparation of parameter cards. Parameter cards are input at run time and referred to by the program. They are used to input such data as constants and dates which may change when the program is run on a subsequent occasion.

Compilation

10.34　The questionnaire or coding sheets must be key punched and verified and the program pre-compiled, if relevant, and compiled. At compilation time the auditor will need to exercise control to ensure that all source statements are input to the computer and included in the compilation. This can normally be done by reconciling the number of lines on the compilation listing with the number of statements produced during pre-processing or the number of lines sent for conversion. The compilation of the program will normally give rise to a print-out of diagnostic messages which detail infringements of the programming language rules and which will require to be reviewed by the auditor and corrected where they would affect the correct functioning of the program. Technical assistance may be necessary for this work.

Testing

10.35　In the year in which the program is written, or in any year in which the program is amended, it will usually be necessary to carry out a test run prior to the production run to ensure that the logic of the program is functioning properly. Testing is most conveniently carried out on copies of the relevant company's files. The program may include a test facility to stop processing after reading a certain number of records when a test is made. If this facility is used, the auditor will often be unable to agree the totals produced in the test run with those produced by the company. In these cases, a print-out should be obtained of all items processed, and expected results should be calculated for comparison with the actual results of the run. Where the program is testing for conditions which are not present on the file used for testing, it may be necessary to design specific test data.

Execution

10.36　At execution time the auditor will need to ensure that the correct unamended version of his program is run against the correct data file without unauthorised intervention by the operators.

Control over program

10.37　Normally the program should be run in an "input, compile, load and go" sequence. This means that the program is never catalogued onto the company's program library and the chance of the program being amended between input and running is reduced. The auditor should also scrutinise the JCL for the run to ensure that the correct program is being executed and that the JCL does not include any statements which would adversely affect the running of the program.

363

Control over operation

10.38 The auditor may normally rely upon the integrity controls operated by the company to prevent unauthorised operator intervention during the run. However, where these controls have not been tested, or where exceptions have been found, the auditor should, if possible, attend the run and check all operator intervention. In cases where he cannot attend, it may be necessary to copy the files and run the program at a different installation.

Correct file

10.39 The auditor can normally ensure that the correct file is used in the run by checking a control total, produced by his program, to the company's file control total. He must ensure, however, that the control total will prove that the file is up to date and that no amendment can have been made to the file without the control total being amended. Where checking totals will not ensure this, the auditor should either check the file labels to ensure the correct file is loaded or attend the run at which the file is created and obtain a copy for subsequent processing with his program.

Audit programme

10.40 The audit programme should contain a list of the objectives to be achieved, the information that will be produced and the work to be carried out on the print-outs. It is also necessary to prepare written instructions for the administrative procedures to be followed. These will include the obtaining of the relevant files, the input of the program and parameter cards, the action to be taken on halts and the obtaining of the print-outs.

Completion report

10.41 After the program has been used for the first time, a formal completion report should be prepared. The report should contain a summary of the results obtained by the program, any points of general interest arising from running the program and a comparison between the actual and the budgeted costs.

Storage

10.42 Suitable storage arrangements will be required to hold the program, parameter cards and JCL until the next time they are used. It would not normally be appropriate for this material to be left in the client's program library.

Work plan

10.43 The work in paragraphs 10.32 to 10.42 should be carried out in accordance with a work plan which is similar to an audit programme and is signed off and filed with the program documentation. An example of a work plan is set out in Figure 80. The work will normally be divided

Work Plan

CLIENT ....
APPLICATION ....

SIGNATURE
AND DATE

1   Obtain an up to date copy of the file layout
    from the client

2   Complete the specification and obtain the
    necessary approval

3   Complete the run diagram

4   Complete the environmental worksheets

5   Complete COBOL access coding

6   Complete the worksheets for the REPORTs and
    TASKs

7   Complete any non-standard coding on COBOL
    coding sheets

8   Arrange for completion of the job control
    statements (JCL)

9   Complete keypunching instructions and arrange
    keypunching

10 Complete operating instructions to fit the client's
    system

11 Prepare the program of procedures to be
    followed at run-time

12 Complete the parameter cards

13 Complete the compilation checklist

14 Generate the COBOL or RPG II program

15 Compile the COBOL or RPG II program

16 Test run the program

17 Run the program in accordance with the
    procedures specified in 11 above

18 Review the results of the run to ensure that
    the program has functioned correctly

19 In respect of the work to be carried out on
    the program report prepare, or amend the
    existing, validation procedures and functional tests
    where applicable

20 Prepare running instructions for use in subsequent
    years

21 Prepare completion memorandum

22 File all working papers

FIG. 80. Use of computer audit programs – work plan (10.43)

between audit staff who have been fully trained in the use of the program and audit staff who have been trained to run the program but not to prepare it. The allocation and training of staff is dealt with further in Chapter 13.

Second and subsequent years

10.44 Once the program has been written, it will often be possible to run it in the second and subsequent years without change. However, amendments may be required if there have been any changes in the relevant computer system, master file layouts, JCL or operator instructions. The auditor may also need to amend constants, such as dates and amounts, which will usually involve changes to parameter cards. Where changes are required to the program, audit staff who have been fully trained in the use of the program will probably be required, but otherwise it may often only be necessary to use, in the second and subsequent years, staff who have been trained to run the program but not to prepare it.

Summary

10.45 The form of program most commonly used by the auditor is the file interrogation package. These are general purpose programs which can carry out similar tasks on a variety of files at different installations. Although developed to cope with similar problems, the computer audit packages are all different to a greater or lesser extent.

10.46 The more important facilities, based on practical experience, that should be available in a computer audit package have been indicated in relation to the configuration on which the package will be used, the files to be accessed, the tasks to be undertaken and the format in which the resulting information will be provided.

10.47 It is advisable to establish formal procedures for the use of computer programs. This will help ensure that programs are used only where the costs can be justified, that the right objectives are included, and that the costs are properly controlled. Examples are given of suitable procedures to be followed, and documentation to be prepared.

10: Appendix A

Examples of the Use
of Questionnaires

The package

1   In the package concerned, the user completes the questionnaires which
are key punched and input to an ASSEMBLER program. The questionnaires
are interpreted and analysed by the program and a COBOL program
generated therefrom.

The questionnaires

2   Two types of questionnaire have to be completed:

- *Environment specifications* – to describe the computer, peripheral
  equipment, and input and output files used.

- *Processing specifications* – to describe the comparisons, selections,
  calculations and accumulations to be carried out.

The examples

3   Three completed examples of the questionnaires are included on the
following pages. The purpose of each questionnaire is as follows:

- *Input file specifications* (AG11/12) – to specify the input files being
  used. In the example shown two input files are defined. The layout of
  each file is described on another questionnaire.

- *Selection criteria* (AG30) – to specify the items to be selected by the
  program. In the example shown the program will select items where
  all of the following conditions are satisfied:

    (a) Record type not equal to 0 or 9.
    (b) Stock number not equal to 100, 200 or 300.
    (c) Stock class between 1 and 9.
    (d) Indicator equal to 1.

- *Selection criteria – pre-selection calculations* (AG40) – to specify the
  calculations to be carried out on the items selected by the AG30 and
  how the result is to be treated. In the example shown, the stock items
  selected by the AG30 are valued and the resultant field will be
  printed out on the report under the heading "Inventory Value". A
  total of all items selected will be produced.

INPUT FILE SPECIFICATIONS

PRIMARY *(REQUIRED)*

SECONDARY *(OPTIONAL)*

A	G	1	1
1   4

A	G	1	2
1   4

*DEVICE TYPE

R – Card reader (2540)   D – Disk 2314   F – Disk 3330
S – Card reader (2501)   E – Disk 2311   G – Disk 3340
(T) – Tape

D
5

T
5

RECORD LENGTH

Fixed length records – length of logical record
All other records – length of largest logical record

3	5
6   9

3	5
6   9

BLOCK SIZE

Fixed length records – length of physical block
All other records – length of largest physical block

1	7	5	0
10   13

1	7	5	0
10   13

FILE LABELS

(S) – Standard labels   U – Unlabeled   N – Non-standard labels

S
14

N
14

FORMAT

(F) – Fixed length records   V – Variable length records   U – Undefined record length
                           S – Spanned records

F
15

F
15

DUPLICATES ALLOWED?
(Applies only to a file matching application)

Y – Duplicates exist   (N) – Duplicates do not exist

Y
16

Y
16

Remainder of file specifications applies only to disk files.

ACCESS – SECONDARY FILE ONLY

(Primary file is always accessed sequentially)

(S) – Sequential   R – Random

S
17

17

ORGANIZATION

(S) – Sequential   D – Direct   I – Indexed Sequential

I
18

18

RECORD KEY (Indexed Sequential Only)

Enter input data name

S	T	O	C	K	N	U	M		
19   28

19   28

NOMINAL OR ACTUAL KEY (Random Access Only)

Enter primary input data name or result data name of field containing
the access key

29   38

*For non IBM codes see Appendix. ○Indicates default, if required.

SELECTION CRITERIA

PRE-SELECTIONS FOR CALCULATIONS

AG3Ø   Job # 3

TEST #	IF DATA NAME	IS Relationship	CONSTANT	DATA NAME, VALUE, OR STRING OF VALUES (LOWER LIMIT / UPPER LIMIT)	Conjunction A O	ACTION IF CONDITION IS: TRUE Code	#	FALSE Code	#
Ø1	RECTYP	EQ	S	Ø,9		E		T	Ø2
Ø2	STOCKNUM	EQ	S	1ØØ,2ØØ,3ØØ		E		T	Ø3
Ø3	STKCLASS	NE	S	1,2,3,4,5,6,7,8,9		E		T	Ø4
Ø4	INDICATOR	EQ	X	1		C	Ø1	E	

Test # – Assign a number 01–99 to each test comprised of single or multiple statements.

Data Name – Input file data name being tested.

Relationship– EQ – Equal to   GT – **Greater than**
NE – Not Equal to   GE – Greater than or equal to
LT – Less than   BT – Between range limits
LE – Less than or equal to

Constant – Enter "X" if value is a constant. Enter "S" if value is constant string.

Value – Alpha or numeric constant, string of constants separated by commas (EQ or NE only), or lower and upper limits (BT).

Conjunction – Links condition test in an and/or relation (A=and, O=or). If blank, end of test is assumed.

Actions – Enter actions for true or false result of condition test. If omitted:
True action code: perform all calculations.
False action code: go to next pre-selection test. If last test, exclude record.

Code	Meaning
T	Go to pre-selection test number
C	Perform calculation number
E	Exclude this record

369

SELECTION CRITERIA

PRE-SELECTION CALCULATIONS

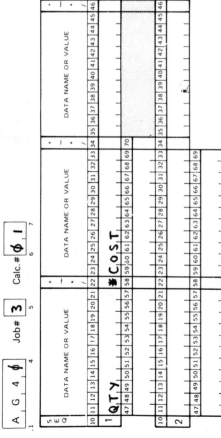

CALCULATIONS

Enter the calculation in algebraic format. Operations enclosed in parentheses ( ) will be performed first. The calculation statement consists of data names and/or numeric values (i.e., "2.5") and operations (+ add, − subtract, * multiply, / divide). A single calculation may contain up to 9 operations on up to 10 data names or numeric constants.

Calc. # — A unique two digit number identifying each calculation.

RESULTS

Result Data Name — Name assigned to the result of calculation.

Size — Size of result field in number of digits.

 # Decimals — Number of decimal positions in the result.

Round — Enter "X" if result should be rounded. If blank, result will be truncated.

Sort — If the result of the calculation is not to be used for sequencing the output report, this parameter should be blank. Indicate sort sequence priority using digits, 1, 2, 3, . . . 9 from major to minor. DO NOT use a priority number previously assigned to an input field for this job. For a descending sort, enter "D". If this is the least significant control field and level totals are not desired, enter "Z".

Print — If the result of the calculation is not printed, no entry is required. If the result is to be printed enter the relative horizontal position using digits 1, 2, . . . 9. Result fields will appear to the right of any printed input fields.

Total — If the result is to be totalled, enter "X" for level totals. If the result column is to be averaged, enter "A".

Column Headings — If the calculation result is to be printed, enter the headings to appear on the report above the result column.

10: Appendix B

Examples of the Use
of Coding Sheets

The package

1 In the package concerned the user completes partly-prepared COBOL coding sheets which are key punched to produce a COBOL source program.

The coding sheets

2 The information required to be completed on the coding sheets will be the same type of information required on the questionnaires in the previous appendix, namely environment coding and processing coding.

The examples

3 Three completed examples of the coding sheets are included on the following pages. The purpose of the first two sheets, as indicated in the explanatory notes to the coding sheets, is to specify the equipment and devices which the program is to use.

4 The purpose of the third coding sheet is to specify the items to be selected by the program and the totals to be accumulated. The totals accumulated may be analysed by the use of parameter cards. The basic block of coding shown may be repeated as many times as required and linked together in any order to create the particular logic required to achieve the audit objectives. Completion of the coding sheet is described in the explanatory notes.

5 In the example shown, the program will select items where the customer's balance is greater than his credit limit. A weighting factor is applied to the credit limit depending on the credit code. The total of differences between the balance and weighted credit limit is accumulated. For individual items selected, the balance, credit limit and credit code will be printed out. The total accumulated will be analysed by credit code and the analysis printed.

PROGRAM ID. __SLED Ø1__

COMPILER __AMERICAN NATIONAL STANDARD__

COMPUTER __ICL 2903__

PREPARED BY __SH__

DATE __5th MAY__

SEQUENCE	A	B		NOTES
Ø Ø 2 Ø Ø Ø	ENVIRONMENT DIVISION.			
Ø 2 Ø		CONFIGURATION SECTION.		
Ø 4 Ø		SOURCE-COMPUTER. ICL 2903.		1
Ø 6 Ø		OBJECT-COMPUTER. ICL 2903		2
Ø 8 Ø		MEMORY 30000 WORDS.		2
1 Ø Ø		SPECIAL-NAMES.		3
1 2 Ø		CHANNEL-1 IS NEW-PAGE.		

1. SOURCE-COMPUTER

   This statement identifies the specific equipment on which the program is to be compiled.

2. OBJECT-COMPUTER

   This statement identifies the specific equipment on which the program is to be run. The MEMORY clause forms part of this statement and no period should be entered between the OBJECT-COMPUTER and MEMORY clauses.

3. SPECIAL-NAMES

   (a) The purpose of this statement is to identify the special-name determined by the manufacturer which, when printing, is used to space to a new page. In the program this name is referred to as NEW-PAGE.

   (b) In addition it is possible that other special-names may be required, e.g. for special currency signs in the print layout. If so, consult the manufacturers' COBOL manual to obtain the correct format of the entry.

PROGRAM ID. SLEDØ1
COMPILER AMERICAN NATIONAL STANDARD
COMPUTER ICL 2963

PREPARED BY 87
DATE 5th MAY

SEQUENCE	A	B	NOTES
ØØ3ØØ		INPUT-OUTPUT SECTION.	
Ø1Ø		FILE-CONTROL.	
Ø2Ø		SELECT C-CARDS	
Ø3Ø		ASSIGN TO CARD-READER 1.	1
Ø5Ø		SELECT P-PRIMARY	
Ø6Ø		ASSIGN TO EDS 1 RESERVE 1.	2
Ø9Ø		SELECT S-SECONDARY	
1Ø0		ASSIGN TO TAPES 1 RESERVE 1.	2
13Ø		SELECT O-OUTFILE	
14Ø		ASSIGN TO TAPES 2 RESERVE 1.	2
17Ø		SELECT R-REPORT	
18Ø		ASSIGN TO PRINTER 1 RESERVE 1.	2

1. The purpose of the FILE-CONTROL paragraph is to identify the devices (i.e. card reader, tape or disk drives and printer) at the installation which will be required for processing input and output.

2. (a) It is emphasised that the assignment specifications will vary from installation to installation. The auditor must, therefore, consult the manufacturer's COBOL manual or the client's programming staff before completing the statements.

(b) All these example entries are part of the assign statement. Each assign statement must terminate with a period. No periods may be used within an assign statement.

PROGRAM ID. **SLED01**
COMPILER AMERICAN NATIONAL STANDARD
COMPUTER **ICL 2903**

PREPARED BY [ ]
DATE **5th MAY**

SEQUENCE / Statement	NOTES
`NOTE THIS-TASK ACCUMULATES THE DIFFERENCE BETWEEN`	1
` X BALANCES ON CUSTOMERS ACCOUNTS AND CREDIT LIMITS`	
` X ON THOSE ACCOUNTS.`	
`101-TASK.`	2
`    IF W-CREDITLIMIT IS GREATER THAN W-BALANCE GO TO 105-TASK.`	3
`    IF W-CREDITCODE IS EQUAL TO 1    GO TO 101-CALC-1.`	2,4
`    IF W-CREDITCODE IS EQUAL TO 2    GO TO 101-CALC-2.`	2,4.5
`    IF W-CREDITCODE IS EQUAL TO 3    GO TO 101-CALC-3.`	2,4.5
`    GO TO 102-TASK.`	6,7
`101-CALC-1. MOVE W-CREDITLIMIT TO W-LIMIT.`	8
`    GO TO 101-ACCUM.`	
`101-CALC-2. MULTIPLY 1.5 BY W-CREDITLIMIT GIVING W-LIMIT.`	
`    GO TO 101-ACCUM.`	
`101-CALC-3. MULTIPLY 2 BY W-CREDITLIMIT GIVING W-LIMIT.`	
`    GO TO 101-ACCUM.`	
`101-ACCUM. SUBTRACT W-LIMIT FROM W-BALANCE GIVING W-EXCESS.`	9
`    MOVE W-EXCESS TO THE-VALUE.`	10
`    MOVE THE-VALUE W-CREDITCODE TO TEST-VALUE.`	2
`    MOVE 101 TO THE-TASK`	
`    PERFORM ADD-AND-SAMPLE.`	
`    IF YES-PRINT-INDICATOR IS EQUAL TO 0 GO TO 101-YES.`	2
`101-REPORT.`	2
`    MOVE W-BALANCE TO R1-ACCBALANCE.`	
`    MOVE W-CREDITLIMIT TO R1-CREDITLIMIT.`	
`    MOVE W-CREDITCODE TO R1-CREDITCODE.`	11
`    PERFORM SAMPLE-REPORT.`	
`101-YES.`	2

374

Notes

1. Enter here a description of this TASK. Do not use full stops. Avoid the use of reserved words (e.g. BY-HYPHENATING-THE-WORDS-TOGETHER).

2. Enter the unique 3 digit reference number. The first character of this is the REPORT number, the second and third being the number of the TASK within the REPORT. Enter the number 5 times, as indicated, in columns 8-10, once, as indicated, in columns 17-19 four times, as indicated, in columns 62-64, and once, as indicated, in columns 73-75.

3. These lines may be used to enter any coding required to carry out calculations before the comparison test.

4. Write any comparison test required. The format of the test will be :-

$$
\text{IF} \left\{ \begin{matrix} \text{identifier-1} \\ \text{literal-1} \end{matrix} \right\} \text{IS} \boxed{\text{NOT}} \begin{bmatrix} \text{GREATER THAN} \\ \text{LESS THAN} \\ \text{EQUAL TO} \end{bmatrix} \left\{ \begin{matrix} \text{identifier-2} \\ \text{identifier-2} \end{matrix} \right\}
$$

$$
\text{identifier-1} \quad \text{IS} \boxed{\text{NOT}} \begin{bmatrix} \text{NUMERIC} \\ \text{ALPHABETIC} \end{bmatrix}
$$

$$
\text{condition-name}
$$

If this test is not required delete this line.

5. If different calculations are to be performed on items passing the different tests, the auditor should code additional paragraphs for each alternative calculation. The names of the additional paragraphs should be in the form NNN-CALC-n where NNN is the TASK number and n is the calculation number. The GO TO statements should then be altered to divert items to the correct calculation. Each of the paragraphs NNN-CALC-n must end with the statement GO TO NNN-ACCUM.

6. Enter the 3 digit reference number of the next TASK in this REPORT if the "FALSE" path is followed. If there are no further TASKS in this REPORT enter "END".

7. If no test is used, delete this line.

8. These lines may be used to enter any coding required to carry out calculations before the TASK total is accumulated.

9. If a field is to be accumulated, delete the 'Ø' and enter the data-name of the field.

10. If the TASK total is to be analysed using SELECT cards, and the analysis is to be based on a field other than that which has been accumulated as the TASK total, delete THE-VALUE and enter the data name of the field here. Any data name entered on this line must be defined in the Environmental Coding as a numeric field.

11. If the auditor requires to print any fields only for samples selected within this TASK, he must enter here the coding necessary to move those fields to the printer. This should be in form :-

MOVE identifier TO R-identifier

where R-identifier is the data-name within R-REPORT as defined in the environmental coding. Fields to be printed for ALL items selected within this REPORT should be moved to the print line in the REPORT section of the Access Coding.

12. Enter the 3 digit reference number of the next TASK in this REPORT, if the "TRUE" path is followed. If there are no further TASKS in this REPORT, enter "END".

10: Appendix C
Example of a Print-out

Contents of the print-out

1   Extracts from a typical print-out produced by an AUDITPAK II program are reproduced overleaf. The print-out relates to the ageing of transactions on an accounts receivable file. The print-out consists of individual items selected and totals of items.

Individual items selected

2   Pages 2 and 3 of the print-out show the individual items printed. Items have been sorted so that all items printed for the same reason are grouped under an appropriate heading. It would have been possible to sort the individual items further, for example, by printing items in ascending or descending value of transaction or account balance or by date of transaction.

Totals of items

3   Pages 5 and 6 of the print-out show the totals accumulated by the program. The totals which, as can be seen, are grouped under the audit objective "To age transactions" are:
   - the total value of transactions (reference 02);
   - an analysis (only part of which is shown) of the total value according to the date of each transaction (references 02–01 to 02–04).

Appropriate descriptions are given to each total.

4   For each of the totals in the analysis the basis of accumulation is shown. This is represented on the print-out by "selection basis". For example, total 02–02 was accumulated by including transactions with dates greater than 770929, that is, after 29th September 1977 and before 29th October 1977. The results in 02–01 confirm that there were no transactions dated after the year end.

5   For each of the totals in the analysis, the basis of printing out individual items supporting the total is shown. The interval between printing of items accumulated and the maximum number to be printed is also shown. Thus, for total 02–02 every 200th item was printed but printing stopped when the print limit of 10 was reached.

6   The figures printed in 02–02 to 02–04 under the headings "Percent" represent the value and count of the totals of the relevant analyses as a percentage of the total value and count, as shown in 02.

377

REPORT DATE * 31-10-77   COOPERS & LYBRAND – AUDITPAK II REPORT   PAGE 2

PROGRAM–IO * AUDITOO1   YEAR END DEBTORS LEDGER   PERIOD ENDED * OCT 1977

REPORT 1   ANALYSIS OF TRANSACTIONS

TASK 02 TOTAL VALUE OF TRANSACTIONS

CUSTOMER NUMBER	DOCUMENT NUMBER	TRANSACTION TYPE	DATE OF TRANSACTION	BILL OF LADING NUMBER	VALUE OF TRANSACTION	ACCOUNT BALANCE
02-03	TRANSACTIONS DATED AFTER 30TH AUG 1977					
P001023	0412177K	R	77 09 26		40.00CR	119.50CR
D002090	0409738E	D	77 09 16	ECO02192	206.27	2281.62
J002281	0404015F	D	77 09 13	72976606	72.00	392.78
G002867	1689463J	F	77 09 23	24822088	0.00	1890.59
H008882	0409049H	O	77 09 01	78389285	41.00	1828.79
B009964	5118896L	F	77 09 28	24125185	424.89	233.33
L011796	1691676C	F	77 09 29	47019940	55.94	29621.84
B015360	1685532C	F	77 09 14	45782959	44.59	469.03
A018385	7000761H	F	77 09 12		36.76CR	873.99
J021499	0393086B	D	77 09 12	47013554	364.05CR	216.20

REPORT DATE * 31-10-77　　COOPERS & LYBRAND - AUDITPAK II REPORT　　PAGE 3

PROGRAM-ID * AUDIT001　　YEAR END DEBTORS LEDGER　　PERIOD ENDED * OCT 1977

REPORT 1

ANALYSIS OF TRANSACTIONS

TASK 02　TOTAL VALUE OF TRANSACTIONS

Q2-04　TRANSACTIONS DATED AFTER 31ST JULY 1977

CUSTOMER NUMBER	DOCUMENT NUMBER	TRANSACTION TYPE	DATE OF TRANSACTION	BILL OF LADING NUMBER	VALUE OF TRANSACTION	ACCOUNT BALANCE
P001023	7000654K	R	77 08 01		11.15CR	236.43CR
C002146	0407554K	D	77 08 27	75388001	35.22	52.13
8002471	1670318H	C	77 08 05	45766358	66.30CR	1800.36
H008882	0402420L	D	77 08 16	78358725	15.26	1774.05
A011038	04033108	R	77 08 26		148.24CR	167.91CR
C013970	0402307K	F	77 08 22	72688679	12.05	1889.68
J016630	0366777L	R	77 08 10		140.00CR	287.13CR
P021563	0007238J	R	77 08 03		12.68CR	25.98CR
A030288	0409794E	T	77 08 11	45992780	21.06	31.58
F049471	0409886C	F	77 08 26	20062642	15011.34CR	7005.07CR
L053553	6284910H	F	77 08 22	15200364	0.00	8383.74
H057808	0388019E	D	77 08 25	78380889	57.29	368.82
A067203	0387457E	D	77 08 23	83308142	25.55	37.65
P087165	6285142G	T	77 08 23	72155659	27.78	29.36
E099621	0402141H	D	77 08 26	78348728	10.00	486.26
J142954	7100460L	R	77 08 04		2583.66CR	1139.24
F193807	0392295K	F	77 08 11	72148845	67.83	301.56
C212361	04085540	R	77 08 30	77631439	31.29	2945.99
J220688	0006535A	F	77 08 22		27.00CR	101.35CR
H238756	U634695H	T	77 08 03		73.17	2137.18

REPORT DATE * 31-10-77   COOPERS & LYBRAND - AUDITPAK II REPORT   PAGE 5

PROGRAM-ID * AUDIT001   YEAR END DEBTORS LEDGER   PERIOD ENDED * OCT 1977

REPORT 1   ANALYSIS OF TRANSACTIONS

TASK NUMBER		TOTAL VALUE IN CURRENCY	PER-CENT	TOTAL COUNTED	PER-CENT
02 TOTAL VALUE OF TRANSACTIONS					
POPULATION	POSITIVE	10,629,037.84		24,178	
	NEGATIVE	2,298,699.39CR		7,465	
	ZERO	0.00		1,225	
	NET TOTAL	8,330,338.45		32,868	
02-01 TRANSACTIONS DATED AFTER YEAR-END					
SELECTION BASIS GT 771029					
INTERVAL 1 NO PRINT LIMIT					
SELECTED	POSITIVE	0.00		0	
	NEGATIVE	0.00		0	
	ZERO	0.00		0	
	NET TOTAL	0.00		0	
PRINTED	POSITIVE	0.00		0	
	NEGATIVE	0.00		0	
	ZERO	0.00		0	
	NET TOTAL	0.00		0	
02-02 TRANSACTIONS DATED AFTER 29TH SEPT 1977					
SELECTION BASIS GT 770929					
INTERVAL 200 PRINT LIMIT 10					
SELECTED	POSITIVE	7,625,633.09	72	11,953	49
	NEGATIVE	997,344.32CR	43	2,588	34
	ZERO	0.00		730	59
	NET TOTAL	6,628,288.77	80	15,271	46
PRINTED	POSITIVE	2,737.11		6	
	NEGATIVE	243.07CR		4	
	ZERO	0.00		0	
	NET TOTAL	2,494.04		10	

AUDIT OBJECTIVE - TO AGE TRANSACTIONS

```
REPORT DATE * 31-10-77          COOPERS & LYBRAND - AUDITPAK II REPORT                    PAGE   6
PROGRAM-IO * AUDIT001           YEAR END DEBTORS LEDGER                    PERIOD ENDED * OCT 1977

  REPORT 1                      ANALYSIS OF TRANSACTIONS

  TASK                                          TOTAL VALUE      PER-        TOTAL      PER-
  NUMBER                                        IN CURRENCY      CENT        COUNTED    CENT

CONTINUED

  02-03    TRANSACTIONS DATED AFTER 30TH AUG 1977

           SELECTION BASIS   GT   770830

           INTERVAL   200   PRINT LIMIT   10

           SELECTED   POSITIVE          1,561,057.89    15          5,085      21
                      NEGATIVE            416,526.91CR  18          1,243      16
                      ZERO                      0.00                  289      23

                      NET TOTAL         1,144,530.98    14          6,617      20

           PRINTED    POSITIVE                844.69                    0
                      NEGATIVE                440.81CR                   3
                      ZERO                      0.00                     1

                      NET TOTAL               403.68                    10

  02-04    TRANSACTIONS DATED AFTER 31ST JULY 1977

           SELECTION BASIS   GT   770731

           INTERVAL   75   PRINT LIMIT   20

           SELECTED   POSITIVE            496,213.16     5          1,708       7
                      NEGATIVE            240,230.42CR   10            625       8
                      ZERO                      0.00                   112       9

                      NET TOTAL           255,982.74      3          2,445       7

           PRINTED    POSITIVE                376.50                    11
                      NEGATIVE             18,000.37CR     1             8
                      ZERO                      0.00                     1

                      NET TOTAL            17,623.87CR                  20
```

11

Service Bureaux

Introduction

11.01 The use of service bureaux to meet the data processing needs of companies is becoming increasingly widespread. There are numerous reasons why companies use a bureau as opposed to an in-house computer. It may be that an economic assessment has indicated lower costs for development and processing or it may be that management feel that computing is best "left to the experts" and they do not wish to involve themselves with specialist staff. Often it is possible to get computing off the ground more quickly with a bureau, perhaps using their application packages. Sometimes it may be a combination of these factors.

11.02 So far as users and the auditor are concerned, the distinguishing feature about processing applications at a bureau is that the processing is done remotely by a separate organisation, whose staff are not employed by the user (i.e. the client) and therefore not under his control. This has an effect on internal control requirements and thus the audit procedures. It also means that the user has to establish a precise working relationship with the bureau. In this chapter, after considering the impact on the auditor, a suggested method by which a user might select a bureau and the considerations in working with a bureau are outlined, since the auditor is often asked to comment on these matters.

General Characteristics

11.03 The characteristics of computer processing, and the examples of computer systems described in Chapter 2, apply equally to service bureaux as to in-house computers. Systems at service bureaux may also be batch, on-line or real-time. The real-time systems usually comprise problem-solving programs which are available to users at remote terminals through time sharing facilities rather than facilities for the processing of accounting data.

Impact on the Auditor

Internal control

11.04 In general, the requirements and techniques of internal control for accounting applications processed at a bureau are similar to those for applications processed on an in-house computer. The main distinction is that, in the case of bureau processing, the user is unlikely to be able to place complete reliance on the integrity controls at the bureau. This is because these controls are not under his supervision. The auditor must take this into account when evaluating programmed procedures and maintenance controls, as indicated in the following paragraphs. These considerations would not, however, arise when the auditor of the user is also the auditor of the bureau. This would be the case, for example, where a service company operated a computer centre for all companies in a group.

Programmed procedures

11.05   Since the user is unlikely to be able to rely fully on the implementation, program security and computer operations controls, he will need to increase reliance on those user controls that can check the proper functioning of programmed procedures.

11.06   In the case of programmed procedures relating to control, such as the identification of missing items, he may be able to rely on the associated user controls on the basis that they would identify either any, or any significant, breakdown in the operation of the program. Where the user decides he requires more positive assurance of the operation of the programmed procedures, he will usually, because of loss of visible evidence, need regularly to verify the operation of the procedure on actual or test data by pre-determining and checking the results of processing the data.

11.07   In the case of programmed procedures relating to accounting, such as the calculation of invoices, although it is less likely that there will be associated user controls to rely on, the user can usually introduce controls to check the computer-produced output on a test basis. Where there is lack of visible evidence, as, for example, in the case of a sales summary, the user will need regularly to pre-determine and check the results of processing actual or test data.

Maintenance controls

11.08   Because he cannot rely on the data file security controls, the user will need to establish a high degree of control over the maintenance of data on master files. As regards transaction data, the user should maintain an independent control account and enquire carefully into discrepancies found on individual balances, such as customers querying statements and differences found during stock checks. As regards standing data, it is highly desirable for the user to maintain independent control accounts over all important data fields. This will require planning when the system is designed. In addition, there should be frequent checking of data on the files with source records held by the user. It will often be necessary specifically to request these special print-outs to be provided by the bureau. It may be possible to arrange for the programs which effect amendments to standing data to identify and report records that have changed since the last print-out.

Receipt of print-outs

11.09   A further feature of bureau processing is that the user cannot control the distribution of printed output. Failure to receive routine print-outs will be obvious but the user will need specific procedures, for example by using a register or arranging for nil returns, to ensure that all non-routine and exception reports are received from the bureau.

Audit procedures

11.10   In general, the audit principles and procedures will be similar to those used when accounting applications are processed on an in-house computer. However, there are some particular points to bear in mind when auditing applications are processed at a bureau and these are summarised in the following paragraphs.

Evaluation of internal control

11.11   Experience shows that, in general, the control techniques used are similar to those in use when processing is in-house. Thus, although there are examples of specific ICQs designed to evaluate the controls in use when processing is at a bureau, the ICQ described in this book is quite adequate for the purpose of the external auditor. Where an internal auditor is required to report on operational controls, he may wish to ask additional specific questions.

11.12   As has been explained, the user, and hence the auditor, is unlikely to be able to place complete reliance on the integrity controls at the bureau. However, the auditor should find compensating controls of the kind outlined in paragraphs 11.06 and 11.07. Where this is the case, he will probably choose to place reliance on these controls. Where such controls do not exist, he should recommend their adoption by the client and he should amend his audit procedures appropriately, perhaps by adopting himself the procedures recommended to the client.

11.13   It may be practicable for the integrity controls at bureaux to be evaluated by a firm acceptable to the auditors of all users who would then place reliance on their evaluation. This approach, which provides a suitable method where many users are sharing the use of a central computer, is often called a **third party review**.

11.14   Firms undertaking such a review will need to make clear in their reports that they are only commenting on the adequacy of integrity controls and that it is the responsibility of the auditors of users to evaluate the user controls and appropriateness of programmed procedures. The auditors of users must understand the scope of the third party review and, before placing reliance on the controls as a whole, will need to be satisfied that the user controls and programmed procedures suitably complement the integrity controls.

Functional tests

11.15   The techniques of functional tests are similar to those used when processing is in-house. The auditor may find that an increase in the extent and the spreading of testing of programmed procedures may be an effective alternative to testing the integrity controls. The use of "live" audit test data is particularly attractive in the case of bureaux, since there is independence from computer operating staff and frequent running of the test data can usually be carried out at little extra cost.

Validation procedures

11.16   Since it may sometimes be difficult to place reliance on programmed procedures, extended validation procedures, in the form of the use of computer programs to examine processed transactions, may be a practical alternative to relying on the internal controls when processing is at a bureau.

11.17   It should be recognised, however, that it may not be convenient for the auditor to run computer programs at the bureau. This may arise because of lack of suitable computer time or because the client's data is held on files with the data of other companies and the bureau takes the view that a security risk may arise. In these cases it will be necessary for the client to arrange for copies of the relevant files of data to be made available to the auditor. The files can then either be examined at the bureau outside operational hours or elsewhere. It should also be noted that running a program at a bureau can be costly because the bureau will usually charge for the time at its normal commercial rates.

11.18   Where the bureau is a computer centre for the various companies in a group, it will often be possible to increase audit efficiency by running file interrogation programs against files containing the records of all companies. If some companies are audited by other firms, the objectives should be agreed beforehand and the relevant print-outs can then be provided to them at an appropriate charge.

Selecting a Bureau

Criteria for selection

11.19   It may be difficult for the management of a company, particularly if they are about to embark upon computer processing for the first time, to know how to begin when selecting a bureau. The objective in the first instance should be to identify not more than six or eight bureaux who appear to meet certain broad criteria which include a good reputation for service as well as for carrying out the type of work envisaged. It is also preferable that they should be within a reasonable distance of the company. The Computing Services Association (CSA) and its published directory is a useful source of reference from which to find a suitable bureau. Alternatively, local trade associations and firms may be able to help. Since communication may be simpler and cheaper, it is desirable that one or more local bureaux should be amongst those chosen for closer consideration.

11.20 Having decided on the initial list of bureaux, the intending user will need to narrow down the final choice. To do so it will be necessary to interview representatives from each bureau so as to form a judgement as to the three or four most likely to be competitive and satisfactory in relation to the following matters:

(a) ownership and financial stability;

(b) reputation and quality of management;

(c) ability to provide the type of service required, for example batch or on-line (the most appropriate method of processing will probably have been indicated by an initial feasibility study);

(d) understanding of the problems of the user's industry and availability of appropriate application packages;

(e) geographical location;

(f) development plans;

(g) broad scale of prices and methods of charging.

Most of these points are self-explanatory. Certainly an intending user will require to be satisfied that, in the event of a significant or prolonged downturn in business, the bureau is likely to be able to ride out the storm. A bureau going out of business can have disastrous consequences for its customers.

11.21 The short-listed bureaux should be invited to submit written proposals based upon a specification of the work to be carried out. This specification would be in writing and give details of applications, volumes of transactions, size of files, method of data capture, processing frequencies, operational deadlines and reporting requirements. Together with the specification there should be a questionnaire prepared by the user to elicit details of:

(a) the organisation and staffing of the bureau;

(b) the nature of the equipment in use and plans for future development as they may affect the user;

(c) proposals for liaison during both the development stages and normal processing;

(d) arrangements that will be made for security and confidentiality of files, reports and programs;

(e) the basis of charging for development work, processing and other services, together with a detailed quotation for the work specified;

387

(f) complete contractual obligations of both parties including any safeguards and guarantees that may be negotiated, for example the method of transporting reports from the bureau to the user and the times by which that work is to be delivered to the user.

Evaluation of proposals

11.22   Bureaux will probably require from two to four weeks to prepare their proposals. During this period, the user should consider all aspects of the selection criteria to be applied, and the relative importance he wishes to attach to each of them. At this stage companies not having extensive experience of data processing would be wise to obtain an independent assessment of tenders and to seek advice on the terms of a contract.

11.23   A careful evaluation of proposals should reveal those bureaux that are most likely to meet the requirements of the specification in an efficient and cost-effective way. Intending users might then visit one or two bureaux, to gain impressions of their general efficiency, and contact existing customers to confirm the performance of the selected bureaux in producing accurate, timely work and in providing good levels of support.

The contract

11.24   After a specific bureau has been selected, it will require the prospective user to sign a contract. Before he does so, the user should understand clearly what he is being asked to pay for in respect of normal and exceptional services, both in terms of development and processing work. He should also discuss and define clearly the liaison function and responsibilities of his own and the bureau staff.

11.25   Other matters that should be defined in the contract will include:

(a) The division of responsibility between bureau and user for all aspects of the work involved, for example who will transport input and output between the bureau and user.

(b) Arrangements for ensuring the safety and confidentiality of the user's data and files, including how many generations of files will be kept and where they will be stored.

(c) Alternative arrangements to be adopted in the event of failure of the bureau's own equipment or services. It is desirable to specify another installation with whom the bureau may have reciprocal processing arrangements in the event of fire or other disaster.

(d) Proprietary rights to software if a bureau-owned application package is not being used. It is normal for application programs written by the user's staff or by the bureau staff on the user's behalf to be owned by the user. Ownership of software is important in the event of the user requiring to have his processing carried out elsewhere for any reason, including termination of contract.

(e) Possible penalties in the event of a default, for example some restitution and course of action should be agreed if the bureau fails to meet processing deadlines. An arbiter should be agreed for the settlement of disputes.

It is advisable for the prospective user's solicitor to examine the contract before it is signed.

Working with a Bureau

11.26   In addition to the formal contract it is important to establish a suitable working relationship with the bureau. The more significant matters, which are dealt with in the following paragraphs, include the arrangements for day-to-day liaison, any systems and programming development work undertaken by the bureau and operational work.

Day-to-day liaison

11.27   Although it is to be expected that the bureau and user will develop an amicable and co-operative relationship, they remain distinct and separate organisations and their dealings with each other require to be formalised. The bureau and the user should each appoint a specific officer through whom all dealings between the bureau and user should be made. It may emphasise the importance of this liaison if the names of the persons responsible for liaison are specified in the contract. It is helpful if the liaison officers are present at all progress meetings, when systems are being developed, and at other meetings when systems are operational.

11.28   All communications with the bureau should be unambiguous and a rule should be established that any oral communications are confirmed in writing as soon as possible. While appearing burdensome, this will ensure that, in the event of a dispute, all relevant facts are available.

Development work

11.29   The user may decide to develop special programs for his work, and this could be undertaken by his own staff or by bureau staff. Alternatively, he may decide that an application package provided by the bureau is suitable. Most application programs will need amendment to meet the user's precise requirements. When the bureau carries out the development work, either on a custom-built basis or using an application package, it will be necessary to agree a development schedule and the frequency of regular progress meetings. Furthermore, in addition to establishing the ownership of the programs as outlined in paragraph 11.25(d), the following matters need to be considered, agreed and, preferably, included in a schedule attached to the contract between the user and the bureau:

(a) The method of charging for each activity, for example whether systems work will be on the basis of a separate fixed price contract or on a time and materials basis.

(b) Whether the bureau responsibility extends to the production of clerical procedures manuals, including all forms of input preparation, and interpretation of reports.

(c) The procedures for specifying, signing off and modifying the systems. After a user department has specified a system, the bureau systems staff will produce a detailed description, often in flowchart form, of how that system will be processed by the computer. It will be the responsibility of the user department to ensure that this detailed description meets its requirements in every way. Only when the user is satisfied, should he sign off that system. Changing user circumstances may require modification to systems that have been operational for a time. Modifications will need to be specified and signed off in the same way as original specifications. It is important to assess the effects of modifications on all aspects of the work being processed. Frequently changes to one program may require changes to be made to other programs of a suite.

(d) The stage at which the systems and programs will be accepted as operational. This should be after the user is satisfied that a period of parallel or pilot running is providing satisfactory results.

(e) How the master files are to be created and checked. If the bureau does this from existing ledgers or records supplied by the user, a print-out should be provided for the user to check the completeness and accuracy of loading the data.

Operational work

11.30 Because the activities of the bureau and the user are usually physically remote from each other, it is necessary to lay down precisely the division of responsibilities for certain operational procedures, of which the more important, in addition to those mentioned in paragraph 11.25 are:

(a) The timing and method of delivery of input data, such as despatch notes, suppliers' invoices and clock cards, to the bureau. In cases where original vouchers leave the user's premises he may wish to consider the use of microfilm or photocopying.

(b) The frequency and scope of processing, and the timing of when the user requires reports based upon input submitted.

(c) The responsibility for exercising controls.

(d) The arrangements for resubmission and reprocessing of rejected items and faulty work. The circumstances under which re-runs are chargeable by the bureau must also be determined in advance.

(e) The processing and charging arrangements for:
  (i) data received late by the bureau;
  (ii) bank and other statutory holidays or week-end working;
  (iii) running of programs.
In this connection it should be noted that the basic methods of charging by bureaux vary from global charges for all work agreed to be carried out during a given period of time to extremely complicated formulae based on the number of transactions processed, lines printed, disc file accesses and various other factors as well as data preparation key-depressions, if applicable. It may therefore be necessary to negotiate special terms for these matters.

(f) The facilities for checking bureau charges for scheduled and extra work. The bureau should be required to furnish sufficient details of the work processed so that the user can understand and check the basis for the charges he is asked to pay.

Summary

11.31 So far as users and their auditors are concerned, the distinguishing feature about processing applications at a bureau is that the processing is done remotely by a separate organisation, whose staff are not employed by the user (i.e. the client) and are therefore not under his control.

11.32 In general, the requirements and techniques of internal control for accounting applications processed at a bureau are similar to those for applications processed on an in-house computer. The main distinction is that, in the case of bureau processing, the user is unlikely to be able to place complete reliance on the integrity controls at the bureau. The auditor must take this into account when evaluating the other controls.

11.33 Likewise, the audit principles and procedures will be similar. However, there are particular points to be borne in mind regarding the evaluation of internal controls, functional tests and validation procedures.

11.34 The user needs to exercise care in both selecting and working with a bureau. Some practical considerations are suggested, since the auditor is often asked to comment on these matters.

12

Computer Security

Introduction

Relevance to the auditor

12.01   It has become recognised in recent years that the security of computer systems is of fundamental importance to the operation of effective and reliable computer procedures. **Security** is usually defined as meaning that the computer facilities are available at all required times, that data is processed completely and accurately and that access to the data in computer systems is restricted to authorised people.

12.02   The complete and accurate processing of data has already been dealt with in this book and access to data has also been dealt with, insofar as it relates to authorised data not being altered. In this chapter we deal with those other aspects of security – protection against disruption of processing, and misappropriation of data or computer facilities – which are of major concern to management. While they are not of primary concern in forming an audit opinion, the auditor will wish to be aware of these matters so that, if appropriate, he can make suitable comments thereon to management. Security reviews can form an important part of the work of internal audit departments, and their reviews in this area often make a major contribution to efficient and reliable processing.

The need for security

12.03   While all systems, computer-based or otherwise, are potentially vulnerable to physical disruption and misappropriation of data and facilities, there are particular difficulties in the computer environment. These difficulties arise from the following factors:

(a) The physical concentration of data processing and storage in one or a small number of locations. As a result the disruption of a relatively small physical unit can have a disproportionately significant effect on the general data processing of the organisation.

(b) The complexity of computer processing. This leads to a concentration, in the hands of a relatively small number of people, of the knowledge of a company's computer systems, and thus of the ability to create and modify them. This increases the opportunity for one or more members of this group, intentionally or otherwise, to be able to influence the procedures carried out by the computer systems, and thereby in some way affect the company adversely.

(c) The development of on-line systems as a common means for the input of data and for making enquiries. This makes it more difficult to identify and control the use of the processing and storage facilities.

(d) The increasing use of computers to carry out processes which could not easily be performed by manual systems. This increases the dependence on the computer and leads to the danger that, should processing be interrupted, it would be difficult to introduce alternative manual processing.

(e) The scale of operation of many computer systems. While providing greater reliability, speed and accuracy, the large scale and interconnected nature of modern systems introduces the risk that a processing failure will have a greater and more widespread effect than a failure in a corresponding manual system.

12.04 It is therefore necessary, as regards each computer installation, to identify and consider the risks of disruption and misappropriation of data and computer facilities, and to decide upon protective security techniques bearing in mind the seriousness of the risks. This process is often called risk management. In the following paragraphs the risks that require consideration are discussed and the techniques for achieving security are outlined. It is not practicable within the scope of this book to provide comprehensive details of the security techniques available. The various techniques that may be used are, however, discussed in general terms. The specific techniques adopted in any particular case will be based on an assessment of the level of trust that is warranted and the degree of security required.

Disruption

The risks

12.05 A disruption occurs whenever the computer system is unable to provide users with the agreed level of service. It is to be expected that, in all but the most reliable of computer installations, some disruption will occur from time to time. The concern of the computer management is to ensure that this disruption is minimised and that recovery can be quick. A computer system consists of a number of complex and interlinked subsystems and failure of any one of these may cause disruption. The major potential causes are described in the following paragraphs.

Accidental disruption

12.06 There is a variety of threats which may arise either individually or in combination and which can have a significant effect if the necessary precautions are not taken. These include:

(a) *Natural calamities.* Both the computer hardware and its environment may be damaged by external forces. The most likely of these is fire. However, the less frequent hazard of flooding, and even catastrophes such as earthquake or the crash of an aircraft should not be ignored in the appropriate circumstances.

(b) *Power supply failure*. This can affect one or more of the computer hardware, the air-conditioning supply, the data preparation equipment or a terminal. Frequently the impact of failure may be different for each piece of equipment. For example, the central system may be able to function for several hours without being affected by the lack of power to its data preparation equipment.

(c) *Hardware malfunction*. It is to be expected that, from time to time, one or more of the components in the computer hardware will malfunction. When this occurs, it may degrade the performance of the system or cause it to fail completely.

(d) *Air-conditioning failure*. Most computer systems are capable of running for some time when deprived of their normal requirements for air-conditioning. However, this is likely to increase the probability of hardware malfunction and extreme temperatures are also likely to cause a degradation of operator performance.

(e) *Software error*. The writing of software, both for operating systems and applications systems, involves many thousands of instructions. No matter how well these systems are tested, they will occasionally fail. The effects of such a failure can vary from minimal to catastrophic.

(f) *Operator error*. While simple operator errors normally have only a minimal impact on the running of the system, it is possible that such errors may, on occasion, have a significant impact. For example, should an operator accidentally remove the disc pack which is supporting a complex communications system, it might take a considerable time to restore the situation.

12.07 While the threats outlined above relate to the direct disruption of processing, they may also cause the loss of information stored by the computer system and this may involve lengthy reconstruction before processing can be restored.

Deliberate disruption

12.08 While deliberate disruption can be effected in different ways, it can, in general, be divided into two basic categories – that involving members of the computer department and that involving outsiders, including the non-computer members of the company's staff.

12.09 The typical computer installation is highly vulnerable to the disgruntled employee. The main threats are:

(a) the physical destruction of the computer or its associated equipment, such as the air-conditioning;

395

(b) the destruction, either physically or logically, of the computerised records;

(c) the modification of programs to cause either the writing of incorrect information or the failure of the operational programs.

12.10 The threats from outsiders are normally physical in nature and involve the destruction of the computer or its associated equipment. However, in on-line systems there is also the risk that programs and files may be attacked by the use of terminals. The levels of threat vary from vandalism and isolated action by a non-computer employee to the more major threats of civil disturbance or riot.

The protective measures

Physical security

12.11 Many of the threats described above, particularly those of a physical nature outlined in paragraphs 12.06(a) to (d) and 12.09(a) and (b), whether accidental or intentional, can be reduced significantly by the proper use of physical techniques. Typically, consideration should be given to:

(a) sound construction of the computer area with secure windows (or no windows in areas of high security), the minimum number of entrances and exits, and the use of fire-resistant materials;

(b) strict control of access to the computer area, using such devices as security badges, security guards and alarm systems;

(c) effective precautions against fire or other natural disruption, including alarm systems, automatic extinguishing systems and frequent inspection of both the computer environment and the fire-fighting equipment;

(d) the provision of an alternative power supply, sufficient to provide power to the computer system, the air-conditioning plant and associated equipment, including, where appropriate, data preparation and terminal equipment;

(e) established and practised procedures to be followed in emergency situations, such as fire, power failure, and physical assault.

System security

12.12 Protection against the threats described above relating to the disruption of programs and files through software and operator error, either accidental or intentional (paragraphs 12.6(e) and (f) and 12.9(b) and (c)), can best be achieved by a combination of the physical security measures outlined above, and the enforcement of proper standards of system development and computer operating. The more important appropriate measures have already been discussed in the consideration of integrity controls in Chapters 5 and 6.

Back-up and recovery

12.13   No matter what precautions are taken, it is certain that, from time to time, some disruptions to processing will occur, and it is prudent to consider what arrangements should be made to provide *back-up* resources to ensure continuity of processing. At its simplest level back-up can consist of an alternative set of clerical procedures which can be brought into use until the processing facility is restored. At a higher level, elements of redundancy can be built into the computer system and its environment. Sometimes this redundancy is provided by standby facilities such as the provision of an alternative power supply as mentioned earlier. More commonly it consists of ensuring that essential services can be provided by applications systems which use, where possible, only a subset of the facilities which are likely to be withdrawn. Thus, in an installation which has, say, six disc drives, no job should require more than four drives, thus allowing for the loss of two drives without disruption to processing.

12.14   To cater for the situation where the computer system is made completely unavailable for use, for example by fire, there should be arrangements for the transfer of urgent work to a *standby* installation, possibly in association with special clerical procedures. Where such expenditure can be justified, it is possible to duplicate computer facilities completely, ideally in a separate location, to ensure continuity of processing.

12.15   When a disruption does occur, it is essential that computer installations have available recovery procedures to ensure that processing can be restarted as quickly as possible. These procedures should include:

    (a) A facility for restarting at an intermediate stage of processing programs terminated before their normal ending or before completing the processing of a transaction. This procedure prevents the whole run having to be reprocessed. The technique used is known as **checkpointing** and involves the recording ("dumping") of the contents of core at various stages during processing. In the event of the program terminating it may be restarted at the previous checkpoint.

    (b) A system of security copying or storing of master files with associated transactions to enable the restoration of any files lost or damaged during the disruption. This procedure should include the keeping of important data in secure or remote locations such as in fire resistant safes.

    (c) Similar procedures to ensure that copies of operating instructions,

397

run instructions, and other essential documentation are available should the originals be lost.

(d) Formal instructions for the restoration of processing or its transfer to other locations.

The use of these procedures should be rehearsed at regular intervals.

12.16   In on-line, real-time and database systems the traditional recovery method of checkpointing, dumping and full reprocessing, described in 12.15 above, is unlikely to be practicable. Dumps need to be taken very frequently and the machine time requirement then tends to become prohibitive. There may also be problems where data has been input from remote terminals, as it may not be possible to reprocess transactions exactly in the order they were originally processed and therefore different results will arise when the recovery process is effected.

12.17   The more commonly used methods of recovery in on-line, real-time and database systems are based on the logging of information as each trans-action is processed. The information logged is the details of the file record being accessed. This information may be the record before or after processing by the transaction and is used in the recovery process in the following manner:

• When logging takes place of the existing contents of each file or database record which is to be accessed by a transaction, before it is processed by that transaction ("before image") – if a failure occurs which affects only the transaction and record being processed the file or database can be restored to its previous correct state by reinstating the "before image" record of the affected record. If a more serious failure occurs, the before image log records are used to overwrite their corres-ponding file or database records to a point before the corruption occurred. This technique is variously known as *backing out, point of failure recovery,* or *roll back.*

• When logging takes place of the contents of the file or database record after it has been processed by a transaction but before the new infor-mation is physically written ("after image") – the file or database is dumped at intervals and, in the event of a processing failure, recovery is achieved by taking the last dump and processing the after image records for transactions since that dump. This technique is normally known as *roll forward.*

12.18   It is one of the functions of the DBMS to monitor the database as processing takes place and to detect any logical damage to the database (for example, incorrect or missing linkages; incorrect record counts). Often the DBMS will automatically put into effect the recovery pro-cedures described above to correct logical damage to the database.

12.19   It is normal for a company to insure computer hardware against most normal risks. However, in the light of threats similar to those outlined above, many companies are taking the concept of insurance much further. The impact of the loss of a computer facility may be much wider than the mere loss of hardware. It is not practicable here to consider this topic in depth and reference should be made to specialist publications. Specific insurance should be considered for the following risks:

    (a) loss of application programs and system software;

    (b) increased cost of operation following a disruption;

    (c) cost of recreating lost data;

    (d) loss of profit to the organisation;

    (e) employee infidelity.

Misappropriation of Data and Computer Facilities

The risks

Data

12.20   There is a variety of ways in which data can be misappropriated in a computer system. These include:

    (a) Files of data can be copied during unauthorised processing.

    (b) Extra copies of print-outs can be obtained.

    (c) Misuse of terminals and other communications equipment. Terminals are frequently less secure physically than the central installation and may be accessible to large numbers of people. Terminals may be left connected to the computer but unattended; logging-in routines showing passwords may be left visible on unattended typewriter terminals or in waste bins. As a result files can be accessed and data displayed or printed at terminals in an unauthorised manner.

    (d) Availability of waste output. User output may become obsolete once an updated print-out is received but may still have considerable value. A mistake by a computer operator, for example the incorrect set-up of the printer, may necessitate the re-running of work and the output, although described as waste, may contain valuable information.

    (e) Output can be examined in an unauthorised manner during handling in the computer department or after it has been passed to users.

12.21   The scale and importance of the misappropriation can range from a situation where a sales clerk who has access, for example, to customer credit files, and gives this information orally to others who can make use of it, to one where complete copies of important files, such as price lists or customer files, are taken, either on magnetic tape or paper, and sold to competitors or a ransom demanded for their return.

12.22   Misuse of data, rather than theft, arises where there is no intention to use the information in a way which could be described as fraud or theft. It can occur when members of staff, who have access to information for certain purposes, use it in other ways, or those who should not have access to the information obtain it. Examples of this misuse could be computer operators learning of the salaries being paid to other employees and discussing them, or casual visitors to an organisation being allowed sight of, and time to examine, sensitive print-outs such as bad debt lists or company profit figures.

Software

12.23   Software, both production programs and system software, developed by a company may be stolen, since it can be valuable to a competitor. In a similar manner to that described above the software may be misappropriated by copying files, obtaining print-outs or accessing systems through terminals. The system and programming documentation is as important in this respect as the software itself. This threat is of particular relevance when staff leave a company's computer department to join competitors or software companies.

Computer time

12.24   Computer staff have been known to sell computer time to outsiders or to use computer time to develop their own programs, either for financial gain or purely from technical interest. This is most relevant in a time-sharing environment where many users have access to the system and in small organisations where little formal control is exercised over the use of the computer facility and the recording thereof.

The protective measures

12.25   Many of the control techniques discussed in Chapters 5 and 6 will be of major importance in protecting data, software and computer facilities from misappropriation. The protective features discussed earlier in this chapter will also be of relevance, particularly those relating to access to the computer area and fidelity guarantees. Further important procedures are outlined in the following paragraphs.

Data file security

12.26 Data file security controls are always of vital importance to protect data from misappropriation. In addition to file library procedures and control over terminals, the following techniques should be considered:

(a) The use of system software which controls access to those files which are currently on the computer system (and in some cases which controls those files stored "off-line") specifying which users may use which files and the purposes for which the user is permitted to have access; for example, the user may be allowed to read data from a file but not to modify or delete records on that file.

(b) The encryption of data on the most sensitive files. This means that all or part of the data stored on the file is in coded form and can only be interpreted by those user programs that have access to a "translation key".

(c) The recording, either on file or in printed form, of all attempts to use files, whether they have been successful or not, together with the available information on the user. This information can be checked at regular intervals to ensure that violations of the security procedures or unusual use of the facilities can be detected.

Computer operations controls

12.27 The controls over computer operating are particularly important in protecting against the dangers of copying programs and data. Records of computer usage should be reviewed with particular reference to re-runs, for which the operating time should be recorded separately. When practical, significant variations between records of usage and CPU meter readings should be identified and investigated. There should be procedures to check that all computer runs are supported by properly authorised job requests.

Physical arrangements

12.28 The computer room and its associated areas, including any terminal areas, should be organised so as to minimise the risk of printed information being seen by passers-by. This could include careful positioning of line printers, the use of transit boxes for print-outs and the screening of terminals.

User department measures

12.29 The control of computer output in user departments is a problem common to many non-computer systems. The techniques for control are thus similar to those used for manual systems:

(a) Control of physical access.

(b) Print-outs, when not in use, should be kept locked away, either in desks or cupboards.

401

(c) Control of copying facilities; if computer print-outs are held in areas where photocopying facilities are available, procedures are required to ensure that unauthorised copies of data are not made.

(d) Obsolete print-outs should be destroyed as confidential waste to ensure that they are not obtained for use by others.

Confidentiality and Privacy

12.30   While the earlier part of this chapter has been concerned with the security of computer systems, it is important to remember the associated, although separate, topic of confidentiality and privacy. There is currently much concern about the keeping of computerised records relating to individuals, the accuracy of the information held in such records and its use. In a number of countries the confidentiality and privacy aspect of computer records has been the subject of legislation, either implemented or planned. Sweden and France have passed such legislation and the United States is following a similar path.

12.31   In the United Kingdom, a number of papers have been published on the subject, perhaps the most notable being the report by the Younger Committee (Report of the Committee on Privacy, dated July 1972, H.M.S.O.) and the White Papers, Computers and Privacy and Computer Safeguards for Privacy (Command 6353 and 6354, dated December 1975). These indicate that the Government has decided to introduce legislation establishing a set of objectives and standards governing the use of computers that handle personal information about individuals in this country, and also establishing a permanent statutory agency to oversee the use of computers in both the public and private sectors; the agency's task would be to ensure that such computers are operated with proper regard for confidentiality and privacy and with the necessary safeguards for the personal information which they contain. To prepare the way for legislation and the setting up of permanent machinery to oversee the use of computers, the Government has set up a Data Protection Committee to advise on the whole subject, after consultation with the appropriate interested parties. The Committee will undoubtedly be strongly influenced by legislation which has been enacted, or is in prospect, in other countries. Management and auditors of all companies which maintain computer records that hold information of a personal nature about employees and members of the public will need to give close attention to the consultation process leading to such legislation and to the impact of the requirements when they become law.

Summary

12.32   Computer security is usually defined as meaning that the computer facilities are available at all required times, that data is processed completely and accurately and that access to the data in computer systems is restricted to authorised people. In this chapter those aspects of computer security which are of particular concern to management have been considered, namely disruption and misappropriation of data on computer files.

12.33   The risks involved should be carefully considered and suitable protective measures determined. This process is often called risk management. The aim of establishing security techniques is to provide and maintain a stable and secure installation. Most security techniques involve some cost and it is thus important that they are directed towards those threats which create a significant risk. It is also important that the benefits and cost of security precautions are carefully considered in each case, as the requirements and remedies may differ.

13

Organisation and Training

Introduction

13.01   In this chapter are outlined some considerations regarding, first, the organisation of computer auditing within a practising firm or internal audit department and, secondly, the training requirements and how these can best be satisfied.

13.02   The comments are based on our practical experience and procedures in a large practice office applying the approach and techniques set out in this book. However, the organisation is similar in our firm's smaller offices in the United Kingdom and in some offices of varying sizes overseas. It is therefore hoped that the suggestions made will be of relevance and practical assistance to organisations of all sizes.

The Organisation of Computer Auditing

Policy

13.03   Specific responsibility will need to be assigned for developing the organisation and techniques for carrying out computer audit work and the related training. In a larger firm this responsibility can be assigned to a specialist committee responsible to the firm's technical committee. In a smaller firm the responsibility is probably more conveniently assigned to an individual responsible directly to the executive committee or the partners as a whole.

13.04   Where there is a specialist committee, it will comprise those partners responsible for computer auditing and, particularly in the early period, partners without responsibility for computer audits, who can comment on proposals from the general audit viewpoint. Where the firm has a consulting division with computer expertise, it is useful for a member of that division to be a member of the committee because of his technical knowledge. In other cases reference can be made to manufacturers when appropriate.

13.05   During the early period of a firm's involvement in computer auditing, the committee or individual will be particularly concerned in developing the firm's techniques and training. Thereafter the monitoring of performance and continuing technical development is likely to predominate.

Client work

13.06　The extent of the skill required to carry out computer audit work successfully will depend primarily on the complexity of the system and the audit techniques used. For example, more skill will be required to evaluate the controls in a complex integrated system, and where computer audit programs are used, than in a simple system, where the controls are largely manually based and where conventional audit techniques are appropriate. Likewise, different levels of skill will be required for the various parts of the audit. For example, the preparation of audit test data and computer audit programs will require more technical skill than the carrying out of manual audit tests.

Computer audit specialists and general audit staff

13.07　In order to carry out computer audit work in the most efficient manner, it is necessary in the training and use of audit staff to recognise the different levels of skill required. It seems best to recognise and train two distinct levels of technical ability although, where computer audit work is extensive, further levels may be advantageously developed. A high level of skill is taught to certain staff to enable them to undertake the more complex computer audit work that may be encountered. These staff are hereafter referred to as **computer audit specialists**. A lower level of skill is taught to the majority of the audit staff, referred to as **general audit staff**, so that they can undertake those aspects of the work which can be effectively taught to large numbers in a short time.

Organisation of computer audit specialists

13.08　Wherever practicable, the computer audit specialists should be organised into a separate group or department, referred to in this chapter as a **computer audit group**. In larger firms there may need to be several groups in different offices. In smaller firms there may be a single group serving several offices. It seems preferable, particularly while experience is being obtained, to restrict the work of such a group to computer auditing. Where there are a number of small offices, it appears better to create a central group of suitable computer audit specialists from the various offices rather than to rely on individuals in each office, who may often only need to spend part of their time on computer auditing.

13.09　The group will be headed by a manager who has himself worked as a computer audit specialist (the **computer audit manager**). He is responsible for planning and reviewing the work of the computer audit specialists on the group. The computer audit manager will report to the partner responsible for the group (the **computer audit partner**). It is advantageous if the partner has also worked as a computer audit specialist.

13.10　In small firms it will not be practicable, or necessary, to have this formal group structure. Where, for example, only one computer audit specialist is needed, it is usually best to train either a manager or a member of staff who is likely to become a manager in the near future. More reliance can be placed on the work of a man in this category and he can supervise the work of general audit staff. He can also form the nucleus of the group that may subsequently be needed if further computer audit work arises.

Selection of staff

13.11 Computer audit specialists are selected in the main from among the general audit staff and given the necessary technical training. However, with the growth in complex systems and the use of techniques such as computer audit programs, there is an increasing opportunity for using technical computer staff as computer audit specialists.

13.12 Selection of computer audit specialists from the general audit staff is not normally restricted to any particular grade or age of staff, although the majority are newly-qualified accountants. Suitability may be based on aptitude tests and/or on proficiency and interest in auditing generally.

13.13 The length of time that staff will normally remain on the computer audit group depends on the policy of the firm. Some firms regard the computer audit group as providing the basis for a career and, in that case, the computer audit specialists serve on the group permanently. This has the advantage of building up a high level of skill on the computer audit group but, on the other hand, may emphasise the separateness of computer auditing, and care is necessary to ensure that the development of the skill of general audit staff is not thereby overlooked. Other firms second staff to the computer audit group for, say, two years. At the conclusion of their secondment they return to the general audit staff. If staff are carefully selected for this work, the firm can gradually build up a significant number of senior staff with computer audit training and experience. However, in these situations, it is less easy to maintain a high level of technical knowledge in the computer audit group.

13.14 The best solution may be a combination of the two approaches, whereby there is a permanent group of specialists, with both audit and computer background, on the computer audit group and a number of selected audit staff on secondment at any time.

13.15 In large firms, where the general audit staff are organised on a group basis with specific clients allocated to each group, it may be possible to train computer audit specialists who are then resident in the groups. This is particularly useful where an audit group serves one or more major clients with numerous computer-based accounting systems. The computer audit specialist's work would continue to be reviewed by the computer audit manager, unless the general audit group manager possessed the necessary skill and experience, perhaps as a result of having previously worked on the computer audit group.

407

Division of work

13.16   Under the arrangements in our firm, the overall responsibility for computer audit work rests with the general audit staff, and it is for them to call
in the computer audit specialist when he is needed to carry out specific
work. In the initial phase, before computer auditing is recognised as being
just one kind of auditing, there may be a tendency for general audit staff to
use computer audit specialists for work which is sufficiently simple to be
undertaken by general audit staff. This would lead to inefficient use of
expensively trained staff and it is thus desirable, particularly in larger
firms, to establish formal rules for division of work.

13.17   Detailed suggestions, based on our practice, for the division of work
between computer audit specialists and general audit staff that may be
found suitable are outlined in the following paragraphs under the headings of the main stages of computer audit work.

Preliminary survey

13.18   The general audit group manager should inform the computer audit
manager as soon as he is aware that a company is planning to install a
computer, change its current machine, use a computer bureau, extend the
use of an existing computer or make substantial amendments to an
existing system. It is important that the computer audit manager is
informed in good time so that any suggestions arising from the evaluation
of controls can be acted upon by the company with the minimum of
inconvenience.

13.19   The computer audit manager will then arrange for a computer audit
specialist to carry out a **preliminary survey**. The purpose of this survey is
to determine the complexity of the accounting systems that are being
developed in order to decide whether the detailed recording of the system
and evaluation of controls should be carried out by computer audit
specialists or general audit staff.

13.20   A brief report will be prepared on completion of the preliminary survey
outlining the main features of the systems and indicating the control
objectives for which computer questions will be required. The report
will include the computer audit specialist's proposal as to whether the
systems should be recorded and evaluated by computer audit specialists or general audit staff and the budgeted costs of the work.

Recording the system and evaluating the controls

13.21   The recording and evaluating of accounting systems may be carried out
by either computer audit specialists or general audit staff, depending on
the complexity of the system. It is important that those members of the
staff who record the system also evaluate the controls.

13.22   Computer audit specialists will normally record the system and evaluate
the controls in respect of more complex computer-based systems and
general audit staff will normally record and evaluate the simpler systems.

It is a major advantage of using the ICQ described in this book that it is easy to distinguish between simple and complex systems. This is achieved by reference to the number of control objectives with computer questions that require to be used for a particular application. As has already been illustrated in paragraphs 3.46 to 3.60, simple systems involve few control objectives with computer questions, while complex systems may require computer questions for many control objectives. Once the initial recording and evaluation have been carried out, general audit staff will normally carry out the annual updating for all systems.

13.23 The computer audit specialist should, during the preliminary survey, be able to identify quickly the scope and complexity of the applications and the control objectives for which the computer questions should be used. This enables the managers and partners concerned to allocate the recording of the system and the evaluation of controls over the relevant applications to computer audit specialists or general audit staff without difficulty. Where the volume of computer audit work is low, it will usually be more efficient to maximise the evaluation work carried out by the computer audit specialist in order to keep him fully employed on computer audit work. Where the volume of work is high, it will usually be more efficient to involve general audit staff to the maximum in evaluation work, thus releasing the time of computer audit specialists for dealing with complex systems.

13.24 At present, in a larger firm, it would probably be appropriate that general audit staff should have responsibility for recording and evaluating payroll, fixed assets, nominal ledger, accounts payable and accounts receivable systems, as defined in the appendix to Chapter 2. All general audit staff would thus require to be trained in the use of computer questions for eight control objectives. Depending on the experience of general audit staff, it will often be desirable for the evaluation work carried out by general audit staff to be reviewed by computer audit managers, as well as by the general audit manager.

13.25 If it is desired, as is often the case, to extend as far as possible their responsibility and work, the evaluation of goods received processing and invoicing systems might next be undertaken by general audit staff. Although this only involves four extra control objectives relating to purchases and sales systems, it is likely to involve six further control objectives relating to stock processing, with the added complexity of understanding and recording integrated systems. Thus, the skill to record and evaluate these systems is often only taught to selected general audit staff. In this way various levels of skill may be taught, appropriate to the requirements of the firm. However, it would be normal to restrict the evaluation of order processing, work in progress, significantly integrated systems and integrity controls to computer audit specialists because of the technical skill that is usually required. Likewise, most systems involving a computer initiating the making of payments to creditors are usually best evaluated by computer audit specialists.

409

Functional tests

13.26   The programme of functional tests should be prepared by those members of the staff who recorded the system and evaluated the controls. Where it is decided to use audit test data or computer programs, the design and implementation work should be carried out by computer audit specialists with assistance from the general audit staff in the setting of objectives and inclusion in the audit programme of the appropriate instructions regarding the running of the test data or program and the audit work to be carried out on the results.

13.27   The responsibility for carrying out functional tests will normally be conditioned by the degree of technical skill required. Computer audit staff will usually carry out the tests on the integrity controls, perform program code analysis and run computer programs and audit test data when for the first time they are used on a particular audit. General audit staff will normally be responsible for carrying out all other functional tests, including, in less complex situations, the running of computer programs and audit test data on second and subsequent occasions. It may also be practicable for general audit staff to carry out the tests on integrity controls where these are not complex.

Validation procedures

13.28   The impact of computer processing on the validation procedures will be identified by the member of the staff who records and evaluates the system. He will make a note of the alterations to be made to the audit programme which was in use before the change to computer processing. The responsibility for making the alterations will depend on the degree of technical skill required. In general, where the alterations relate to validation tests, reconciliations, accounts analyses and other audit procedures that are manually based, the changes will be made by general audit staff. It may be desirable for the revised audit programme to be reviewed by the computer audit manager. Where it is decided to use computer programs or audit test data, the design and implementation work will be carried out by computer audit specialists with assistance from the general audit staff, particularly with regard to the setting of objectives, and the inclusion in the audit programme of appropriate instructions regarding the running of the program or test data and the audit work to be carried out on the results.

13.29   The responsibility for carrying out validation procedures will normally rest with the general audit staff, subject to the need for computer audit specialists, as already indicated, to run computer programs and audit test data.

Functions of computer audit specialists

13.30   The principal functions of computer audit specialists as regards client

- The carrying out of preliminary surveys of new installations and computer-based accounting systems and the making of a recommendation as to whether the detailed recording of the system and evaluation of controls should be carried out by computer audit specialists or general audit staff.

- The evaluation of integrity controls. This work is seldom carried out by general audit staff because of its technical nature. In many cases, for the same reason, computer audit specialists may carry out the functional tests of integrity controls.

- The recording of the system and evaluation of the controls over the more complex computer-based accounting systems.

- The preparation of audit test data and computer programs, and running them in the first year of use. In many cases, for reasons of technical difficulty, computer audit specialists will continue to run them on behalf of general audit staff in subsequent years. Any program code analysis undertaken will be carried out by computer audit specialists.

In addition, computer audit specialists would be available to give any other assistance, such as commenting on the content of management letters, or carrying out a security review as requested by general audit staff or the client. Work carried out by computer audit specialists should be reviewed and approved by computer audit managers and partners.

Functions of general audit staff

13.31 The main functions of general audit staff in this area may be summarised as follows:

- The recording of the system and evaluation of the controls in respect of the simpler computer-based accounting systems.

- The carrying out of the functional and validation tests on the annual audit, except usually for integrity controls and, where computer audit specialists make use of audit test data, computer programs or program code analysis.

In addition, it is the responsibility of the general audit staff to ensure that the computer audit specialists are called in at the appropriate time to carry out preliminary surveys and subsequent work, or where there is doubt whether the most current and effective computer audit techniques are in use.

The role of the manager and partner

13.32 It is an important feature of the audit approach described in this book that managers and partners are involved at each important stage in the audit. In addition to reviewing the results of functional tests and validation procedures, managers and partners are required to participate in planning the work to be done and deciding on the audit response to strengths and weaknesses disclosed by each part of the work.

13.33 The most important decisions requiring manager and partner consideration and approval are:

- Whether the internal controls are to be relied on or extended validation procedures are to be carried out.

- Which control objectives are both relevant and material in relation to the audit.

- Even where controls are satisfactory, whether it will increase audit efficiency to carry out extended validation procedures rather than functional tests. This might be so, for example, in the case of fixed assets where the number of assets held is not numerous.

- The level of functional tests and validation procedures to be carried out.

- The assessment as to whether material error could arise in respect of internal control weaknesses, and the proposed audit response.

The involvement of managers and partners in these decisions helps ensure that, on the one hand, important audit work is not omitted and, on the other hand, time is not wasted on unnecessary procedures.

13.34 The need to involve audit managers and partners at each important stage is of particular importance where the accounting is computer-based. Although such managers and partners will retain full responsibility for the audit as a whole, certain work will often be delegated to computer audit specialists and will be planned and reviewed by the computer audit manager and partner. Procedures are needed to ensure that the audit manager and partner are involved in decisions arising from work undertaken by computer audit specialists.

13.35 The report prepared after the preliminary survey has been carried out, described in paragraph 13.20, provides a convenient basis for the audit manager and partner to plan with the computer audit manager and partner the work required in relation to computer systems. At this stage the following matters should be agreed:

- For which control objectives the computer questions should be used.

- Whether the evaluation is to be carried out by computer audit specialists or general audit staff.

- Whether the implementation controls are to be evaluated with a view to relying thereon for new systems.

- Whether it is likely that proposals will subsequently be made to use such techniques as computer programs, audit test data and program code analysis.

- The budgeted costs of the work to be carried out by computer audit specialists.

13.36   The audit work carried out will be planned, controlled and reviewed either by the audit manager and partner or the computer audit manager and partner, depending on whether the work is done by general audit staff or computer audit specialists. Where work is carried out by computer audit specialists, the detailed budgets should be approved by both the computer audit manager and partner and the audit manager and partner. Where computer programs, audit test data or program code analysis are to be used, proposals will be prepared on the lines indicated earlier in this book. Audit managers and partners should give their approval to these proposals before work commences. Reports of all work carried out by computer audit specialists should be prepared and submitted to the audit manager and partner after approval by the computer audit manager and partner.

Training and development work

Training

13.37   Where the firm undertakes its own training, the computer audit group will normally be responsible, in conjunction with the training department, for developing the computer audit course material for training both computer audit specialists and general audit staff. Computer audit specialists may also present the courses, either alone or in conjunction with training department staff. This approach has the advantage that those teaching have practical experience of the subject. In addition, the development of training material is improved if those responsible have experience of teaching.

Development work

13.38   If a computer audit group is established, this should normally be responsible for developing the firm's computer audit techniques, under the direction of the relevant committee or partner. The amount of this work will depend mainly on the extent to which it is decided to develop documentation specific to the firm as opposed to using published material. Larger firms may wish to design their own documentation so as to integrate this with their existing audit approach and methods. This is likely to apply in particular to the detailed methods of recording the system and evaluating the controls. Specimen functional tests and validation procedures will also need to be designed. Greater technical skill is necessary to design questions for evaluating integrity controls and more use is likely to be made of published material. Considerable technical support is required to develop computer audit software and only the larger firms are likely to find it worth while to allocate resources to projects of this nature.

Control of time

13.39   Experience shows that training and development work can, unless carefully controlled, absorb a disproportionate amount of computer audit

413

specialists' time. It is, therefore, appropriate for the computer audit committee to set budgets for the percentage of time to be allocated to training and development work and for the actual use of time to be monitored against these budgets.

Training

Scope of training

13.40　In all firms involved in computer auditing, there is likely to be a need to train, or provide training for, both general audit staff and computer audit specialists. In this part of the chapter, suggestions as to the training requirements, and how these requirements may be met and from what source, are outlined for both types of staff.

General audit staff

Training requirements

13.41　The training requirements for general audit staff in this area will depend on their role in the computer audit. If their functions are similar to those outlined in paragraph 13.31, the requirement will be a mixture of learning certain techniques and gaining an appreciation of others.

13.42　The techniques that must be learnt are how to record and evaluate simpler systems, how to select and carry out manual functional audit tests and how to select and carry out manual validation procedures.

13.43　In order to carry out these functions satisfactorily, particularly the recording and evaluating of systems, general audit staff require an appreciation of how computers process data and familiarity with examples of typical computer-based accounting systems. In order to carry out functional tests and validation procedures for more complex systems, they need to be able to understand the completed record and evaluation of the system carried out by computer audit specialists. They also need to ensure that their audits are being conducted using the most current and effective methods. This means that they require an appreciation of the more advanced audit techniques that may be used by computer audit specialists such as computer programs, audit test data and program code analysis. This appreciation should include guidance as to the circumstances in which the use of these techniques is likely to be appropriate.

Training courses

13.44　Experience shows that three or four days' training is required to satisfy the requirements outlined above. Traditionally these have been combined in a single course. The outline of a typical course of this type is set out in Figure 81. The advantage of this approach is that all aspects of

Outline of a typical computer audit training course for general audit staff

DAY	HOURS	SUBJECT
1		*Understanding and recording the system*
	1	Computer processing techniques
	2	Examples of computer systems
	1	Flowcharting
	3	Case study – preparing flowcharts for a simple computer-based system.
	7	
2		*Evaluation of control*
	2	Techniques of control
	2	Computer ICQ – description and method of use
	1	Integrity controls
	2	Case study – evaluating the controls in a simple computer-based system.
	7	
3		*Functional audit tests*
	1	Manual tests
	1	Audit test data and other special techniques
	1	Testing integrity controls
	1½	Case study – audit tests for a simple computer-based system.
		Validation procedures
	1	Manual tests
	1½	File interrogation programs – description and procedures for use.
	7	
4	4	Case study – validation procedures, including objectives for using a file interrogation program and reaction to results from the use of the program.
	1	*Planning and reviewing audits*
	2	*General matters*
	7	

FIG. 81. Typical computer audit training course for general audit staff (13.44)

computer auditing can be dealt with at the same time, without the need to reconfirm understanding up to a certain point. The disadvantages are that the course cannot be attended until general audit staff have a good knowledge of the approach to, and techniques for, a non-computer audit, and not all the contents of the course may be required at the same time. If what is taught is not reinforced soon afterwards by practical experience, it is quickly forgotten. In addition, time must be spent on the course dealing with the general audit approach in order to illustrate the complementary nature of the computer audit approach.

13.45 Many of the disadvantages noted above can be overcome by integrating, so far as possible, the manual and computer audit training. Using this approach, there are training courses for each main aspect of the audit, combining the approach and techniques for both computer and non-computer systems. Thus, the training for evaluating the controls would outline the general principles and then deal with their application in both manual and computer systems. The relationship between the manual and computer parts can then be more easily dealt with than in separate courses. Overall, time is saved by not having to outline the general principles on two courses. Perhaps the most important advantage is that staff can be taught the computer audit techniques progressively rather than in one single concentrated course. In this way, the training can be better linked to practical requirements.

13.46 The integrated approach is likely to be particularly attractive in larger firms where most staff are progressively involved in computer audits from the time they join. In smaller firms, where fewer staff are involved in computer audits, the single course approach may be more appropriate.

13.47 It is also useful to provide short appreciation courses for newly-joined or young staff, who will only be working on computer audits in a junior capacity under supervision, and who are not yet ready to attend the main computer audit course. These may consist of a single lecture introduced into a student's course or a special course lasting up to a day. Their purpose is to convey an appreciation of computer audit methods and their relevance to the audit as a whole.

13.48 Where it is decided to extend the functions of the general audit staff in the manner outlined in paragraph 13.25, further training will be required. In these cases it is sensible to restrict attendance at the course to those who will specifically be undertaking the work concerned within the next few months.

13.49 General audit partners and managers will need to attend regular refresher courses in order to keep up to date with the new techniques that become available to assist in the audit of computer systems. Courses of this nature can be quite short; they provide a useful means of communication and discussion between computer audit specialists and general audit staff.

13.50 Larger firms can provide their own training but smaller firms may depend on outside sources. There is no shortage of courses on computer auditing organised by various bodies. Care is needed to ensure that any particular course is relevant and of practical use. The Institute of Chartered Accountants in England and Wales provides suitable training for general audit staff, managers and partners, and details can be obtained from the courses department.

Computer audit specialists

13.51 The training requirements for computer audit specialists will depend on their role in computer audit work and on the complexity of the systems which they have to audit. Because there will be fewer computer audit specialists than general audit staff, it is possible to be more flexible in their training. Computer audit specialists will need:

(a) sufficient computer technical knowledge to evaluate the basic controls and disciplines in the more complex computer-based accounting systems; and

(b) the ability to apply the more advanced audit techniques used by their firm.

These requirements and possible sources of training are discussed in the following paragraphs.

Technical knowledge

13.52 Computer audit specialists are likely to require a knowledge of the control requirements and techniques appropriate to on-line and real-time processing and database organisation. They will probably find it necessary to acquire a general knowledge of input devices, the software which handles the transmission to and processing of data at the mainframe computer, the structure of databases, the role of database management systems and their relationship with the application programs. This general knowledge can then be supplemented by studying any specific features which the auditor will meet at his clients.

13.53 The larger firms may be able to provide training in these matters but it is more likely that the computer audit specialist will attend courses run by the relevant manufacturers. This can be usefully supplemented by the programmed learning courses which are often available. Care will need to be taken to ensure that the courses selected are appropriate to the level of knowledge and the skill required.

More advanced audit techniques

13.54 The computer audit specialist will also require to be trained, as appropriate, in the use of computer programs, audit test data and program code

417

analysis. The computer programs in use may include both those for examining data on files and those to assist in the testing of integrity controls discussed in Chapter 7.

13.55 The use of audit test data can be taught relatively quickly. It is helpful if the theoretical teaching can be consolidated by means of a live case study. To achieve this there must be available a program against which test data can be run with suitable objectives, and a master file with records already set up. Trainees would then design test data which can be run against the program.

13.56 The training required in respect of computer audit programs will depend on the nature of the skill being taught. In larger firms, it will be the firm's own computer audit packages that will be taught and, depending on the complexity of the programs and the amount of technical involvement required of the user, this may take up to several days. In a smaller firm, it may be decided to train staff in available computer audit packages, in which case the scope and length of training will be governed by whoever owns each package. If it is desired to provide computer audit specialists with the ability to do their own coding of programs, they will, if unskilled in programming, also need to attend a suitable programming course. In addition, they will require practical tuition which may involve secondment to a manufacturer for a period of time, unless appropriate training can be obtained within the firm.

13.57 It will also be necessary for computer audit specialists, who wish to carry out program code analysis, to attend courses and obtain practical programming experience, unless they are already competent in programming.

Keeping up to date

13.58 The training outlined earlier for computer audit specialists can only be considered as a basic course; in such a fast-developing area, it is important that they receive such additional specialised knowledge as is necessary to keep up to date. In larger firms it will probably be helpful to hold regular meetings of computer audit specialists, at which technical and audit developments can be discussed, dealing with such matters as operating systems, JCL and database management systems. In smaller firms, computer audit specialists can attend some of the various seminars that are held by computer and accountancy bodies.

13.59 It is helpful to keep in one place reports on the use of computer audit programs and audit test data, and copies of letters commenting on weaknesses in controls in computer systems. In this way computer audit specialists can read of recent experience. The periodicals issued by manufacturers and other relevant bodies can also be helpful as background reading.

Summary

13.60 It is desirable to allocate specific responsibility for the development, organisation and training in respect of computer auditing within a firm. In carrying out the work, at least two levels of skill are necessary. Thus, computer audit specialists might undertake preliminary surveys, evaluate complex systems and integrity controls, and use computer programs, audit test data and program code analysis, while general audit staff might be responsible for the evaluation of simpler systems and for carrying out manual functional tests and validation procedures. Managers and partners should be involved at each important stage in the audit.

13.61 In larger firms, the computer audit specialists would be responsible for development work and the training of computer audit specialists and general audit staff. In smaller firms much of the training may have to be obtained from suitable outside sources. There is no shortage of appropriate courses organised by various bodies.

Conclusion

1 The approach outlined in this book, with its documentation, techniques, division of work between computer specialists and general audit staff and training, is being practised on a widespread basis. Although designed initially for use on predominantly batch systems, it has been refined so as to be applicable successfully to on-line and real-time systems and database organisations.

2 It is certain that the increase in advanced systems will lead to further audit developments. There will need to be a greater awareness by auditors of new techniques and a recognition that the balance of audit effort may change. For example, it is likely that there will be a greater degree of reliance placed by auditors on integrity controls and a development of new techniques to carry out tests thereon. The computer audit specialist will need a greater measure of technical knowledge.

3 However, it is important that these developments should take place within an overall audit framework that seeks to integrate the manual and computer elements of the audit and thus relate the increasingly technical computer elements to a specific audit purpose. Only in this way can the potential benefits of advances in computer technology, and the related audit techniques, be properly realised for the auditor.

4 It is hoped that the suggestions in this book will make a contribution to these developments.

419

Index

Note: References in this index are to chapter and paragraph numbers (for example, 6.34–35). References to appendices are shown by including the appendix letter after the relevant chapter number. For example, paragraphs 7 to 13 of appendix A to Chapter 2 will be shown as 2A.07–13.

426

433